New Labour, New Britain?

Manchester University Press

New Labour, New Britain?

How the Blair governments reshaped
the country

Glen O'Hara

Manchester University Press

The right of Glen O'Hara to be identified as the author of this work has been asserted in accordance with the Copyright, Designs and Patents Act 1988.

Published by Manchester University Press
Oxford Road, Manchester, M13 9PL
www.manchesteruniversitypress.co.uk

British Library Cataloguing-in-Publication Data
A catalogue record for this book is available from the British Library

ISBN 978 1 5261 4632 8 hardback

First published 2025

The publisher has no responsibility for the persistence or accuracy of URLs for any external or third-party internet websites referred to in this book, and does not guarantee that any content on such websites is, or will remain, accurate or appropriate.

EU authorised representative for GPSR:
Easy Access System Europe, Mustamäe tee 50, 10621 Tallinn, Estonia
gpsr.requests@easproject.com

Typeset
by Cheshire Typesetting Ltd, Cuddington, Cheshire

This book is dedicated to my maternal grandfather, James Martin, who never gave up.

Contents

1

From Blair to Bliar

'A new dawn has broken, has it not?' With these words Tony Blair, a new, young and energetic Prime Minister, welcomed the sunrise outside London's Royal Festival Hall on 2 May 1997. That little but powerful word 'new' was a symbol and promise of the times – new leader, new government, new ideas and soon a new century. And for a moment, more than a moment, the glow of the new was beguiling: the *New Statesman,* following Kipling, pronounced it 'the kind of dawn … that comes up like thunder'.[1] *Time* magazine even mentioned the beautiful weather as it described the scene: 'all the warnings of a water shortage during Britain's rainless spring could have been cancelled by Labour's tears of joy'.[2]

Many Britons celebrated, and there was a feeling of enormous possibility which on-the-ground surveys picked up. The Mass Observation Project, asking diarists to write down their impressions all the time, captured at least some of the mood. One of its responders wrote: 'I was delighted by the result … The day after the election was warm and sunny, and when I went into a shop where I slightly know the assistant I remarked that it was "a lovely day, in more ways than one". He agreed enthusiastically that it was the best day for eighteen years.'[3]

One must be careful about overemphasising 'hope' and 'change': only 43 per cent of the public voted for Blair and Labour in 1997. But Labour had not surmounted that share of the vote for over thirty years, and has not hit those heights again since. Labour have only ever twice in peacetime overturned a Conservative majority at one general election and won a stable majority of their own, in 1997 and 2024. The party's 2024 landslide was won on a vote share of 34 per cent, nothing like the share Blair won. His feat, and the Tories' defeat, was indeed extraordinary. The election expert David Cowling was not exaggerating when he wrote 'we have witnessed the revenge of Middle Britain, and it was truly awesome. From Eastwood in Scotland to Clwyd West in Wales to Harrow West in London, the bluest of blue-chip Tory seats fell … to Labour. This election … was a political earthquake that almost slipped off the edge of the Richter Scale.'[4] Blair now dominated the political landscape, whether you liked him or not. In the South of England, outside London, Labour won fifty-eight seats; they had won precisely three there in 1983 and 1987.[5]

And yet the Blair governments' course and legacy are deeply controversial. They are matters of bitter debate even today, centred on foreign policy, but equally focusing on the nature of the state, types of economic management, equality, inequality, welfare and public services. Where once Blair was admired, liked or perhaps just put up with, for years 'Bliar' placards and bloodied hands have followed his name everywhere. One cannot mention the former Prime Minister on social media without vituperation. A severe case of 'Blair Derangement Syndrome' has set in, to be fair alongside Brexit Derangement Syndrome and even Jeremy Corbyn Derangement Syndrome – a disproportionate and emotional hatred of an idea or individual where debate might once have stood. Implicit or explicit film portrayals of Blair, from *The Ghost* to *The Special Relationship* (both 2010) are hardly flattering: there is even an opera excoriating him. Keir Starmer's Labour government indeed sometimes seems stuck in the shadow of the last time his party was in power. From keeping to a set target for public spending to maintaining the American alliance, and from welfare cuts to allowing private companies into the National Health Service, the promise or shadow of the Blair era is never far away. New Labour left few areas of British life untouched, for good as well as ill, but sometimes it seems as if no one is invested in *understanding* rather than *judging* – a major failing if we are to understand anything about Britain's recent past, or Britain today.

This book will take a fresh approach to the New Labour era: to turn it from news into history, extending our interest and knowledge beyond partisanship and working towards a cooler and more dispassionate assessment. Time has as ever leant distance, and some detachment, just as it did when the battered reputation of Harold Wilson's governments came to be reassessed from the 1990s onwards. It is no accident that one important moment in the resuscitation of Wilson's reputation was Ross McKibbin's essay on both him and Jim Callaghan in the *London Review of Books*, fifteen years after Wilson resigned.[6] We have now reached a similar distance in time from the day Blair left Number 10, and the same rewriting is now both inevitable and necessary. As Karl Pike noted recently, we need 'to reinterpret New Labour at a greater distance and with the comparator of successive Conservative governments'.[7] It is surely time to move on from broad caricature to fine detail, from blame to analysis, and from shouting to listening.

To adopt Pike's phrasing, *New Labour, New Britain?* will try to 'get over' New Labour by understanding it on its own terms. It will try to get beyond the endless warring fictions of 'Good' and 'Bad' – with a capital 'G' and 'B' – in Labour's continuous civil wars, and move away from simple, crude and single-minded judgements on policy design and impact. There have already been a series of excellent books assessing the Blair governments' course and legacy, for instance Polly Toynbee and David Walker's *The Verdict*, and Jon Davis' and John Rentoul's *Heroes or Villains?* The first, though, mostly addresses the social and economic impact of New Labour's policies, while the second uses a number of interviews to unpick why they took the form they did. This book will take a different tack, analysing policy 'end to end': from vague intuition to design and through to its grassroots effects, drawing on newly released official papers from the time, new interviews including with Blair himself, and a battery of academic studies that have looked at policy impact since he left office.

That type of work is acutely required, because rudimentary, one-dimensional attitudes have prevailed so widely up to now. Within academia and much left-wing commentary, it is common to hear the Blair era summed up as 'neoliberal', an idea which centres on competitive individuals living within free markets. In this way of thinking, the state exists to guarantee order and efficient competition: no more and no less.[8] Here we can take that concept to contain three more detailed meanings – as an ideology, a means of governing and also as some specific policies. First, neoliberalism is thought to place financial exchange at the heart of human society, especially at a time when goods and services are being traded more and more across the world in an era of globalisation. Second, it is supposed to be a way of governing via the techniques of the private sector, including constant target-setting and individual responsibility. Last of all, the policies prompted by these ideas are usually centred around individual measures of deregulation, privatisation and liberalisation of the economy.[9]

Vague as they sound, all those political ideas were deeply associated with New Labour. And they have often been conceived as a radical break with that party's past. Colin Hay has argued that 'by the 1997 election, Labour's economic policy was a catalogue of abandoned commitments and political U-turns ... the Keynesian consensus of the post-war period would appear to have been replaced by the neoliberal consensus of the post-Thatcher period.'[10] Richard Heffernan, in his book *New Labour and Thatcherism*, wrote of New Labour that 'although it retains some affinity with "Old" Labour, its policy far more closely reflects the preconceptions and prescriptions of the Thatcher and Major governments'.[11] But now we stand back and think about New Labour with the benefit of hindsight, to what extent are these judgements truly precise, and really justified?

For the political scientists Florence Faucher-King and Patrick Le Galès, it was Blair's stress on the individual and the private sector that made his neo-liberalism particularly 'liberal'. By the late 1990s and early 2000s, ministers seemed to lack the ambition and even will to manage anything themselves, and just wanted to work as commissioners buying in services for taxpayers in a series of deals with large-scale contractors. Instead of being looked after between cradle and grave, each voter and every citizen was on their own and responsible for themselves – an insistence that threatened the small battalions of civil society that Blair himself championed. Local councils, charities and volunteers alike all had to hand powers to Whitehall which would then dole out contracts either to them, or to private companies, as it wished; auditing mechanisms, usually borrowed from the private sector, grew in every direction.[12]

This odd mix of decontrol and ever more centralised micromanagement was known as the New Public Management, which recommended stronger managerial control at the 'centre' combined with outsourcing, working to targets and constant data monitoring – all languages that became familiar to public sector workers from the 1990s onwards. An emphasis on 'arms-length' management was promoted by the consultants and private contractors who clustered more and more strongly around central government during the 1990s.[13] Semi- or quasi-markets might allow the country to be governed in a supposedly neutral and 'rational' way, often by massive, supposedly expert but self-interested service providers such as Capita and Serco. That was an attempt to take all the politics out of public choice. But it begged the question of who was going to be held accountable when these partnership schemes failed because of their complexity or cost, as in the case of the disastrous public–private partnership formed to run London's Tube between 2000 and 2010.[14]

The whole era from the mid-1970s through to the 2010s could be seen as one long Age of Thatcher, during which the state retreated from managing the economy or actually running public services, but interfered more and more with almost everything else. The journalist Simon Jenkins indeed believed that Blair was Margaret Thatcher's true heir, 'obsessed' with transforming his own party in 'a revolution that should never cease' – as Thatcher had done – and in a manner that left behind many of the positive elements in Labour's past. The old Clause IV of Labour's constitution, committing Labour to nationalisation, was replaced in 1994 by what Jenkins thought a 'largely empty' new form of words about 'a community in which power, wealth and opportunity are in the hands of the many, not the few'.[15] Stuart Hall, that redoubtable Marxist critic of Thatcher's revolution during the 1980s, believed profoundly that the Blair agenda was a neo-Thatcherite one: 'the welfare state ... had been savaged and weakened under Mrs Thatcher. But its wholesale deconstruction was to be New Labour's historic mission.'[16]

New Labour also embraced a number of more conservative impulses. One of these was a strict attitude to crime and punishment. This was first on display in Blair's strong reaction, as Shadow Home Secretary, to the tragic murder of James Bulger in 1993. For the journalist Nick Cohen, Blair's reaction was cynical and insufferably opportunistic: these awful crimes 'were now symptoms of a British disease which Labour with its new morality would cure by ... well, the remedy wasn't specified. What was clear was ... a willingness to follow the hasty and violent opinions of the mobs on the street and in ... newspaper offices'.[17] Blair, indeed, sought a *rapprochement* or understanding with that bête noire of the Left, media mogul Rupert Murdoch, who had been tormenting Labour for decades. The *Sun*, which Murdoch owned and claimed it had played a key role in defeating Labour in 1992, came out for Blair and New Labour at the start of the 1997 election campaign.[18] According to Cohen, this pursuit of plutocrats' approval created a New Labour party 'willing to debase themselves with hard-man posturing'.[19]

It was in this context that New Labour became notorious for 'spin' – the exercise of rigid, rigorous media management through a grid of announcements and initiatives, to which ministers and their advisers could become prisoners if they were not careful. The supposed 'dark arts' of Labour's chief spinner, Peter Mandelson, were of course always in the headlines, even though Mandelson usually tried to stay in the background. Also emblematic of this move towards government-as-image was the enormously powerful figure of Alistair Campbell – tough, experienced, aggressive and driven. While Blair's Chief Press Secretary in government, Campbell was a special adviser (spad) and therefore freed from some rules on official impartiality, while still gaining the power to direct civil servants.[20] It was these media experts, rather than ministers or specialist policy experts, who became the most famous figures behind New Labour apart from Blair and Brown themselves: 'people who live in the dark', as International Development Secretary Clare Short once famously called them.[21]

During the 1990s and early 2000s, Blair came to dominate and control Labour at almost every level, micromanagement that was resented and often portrayed as hyper-controlling. Pat McFadden (now back in government as Secretary of State for Work and Pensions) and Blair's friend and constituency organiser Phil Wilson were key managers of the party conference in Opposition, and went into Number 10 and Milbank respectively once Blair won the 1997 election. The Blairites at Labour's centre organised ruthlessly and effectively for conference victories when previous leaderships might have gone down to defeat. Task forces took the role of conference organisation away from the party's General Secretary, and via extensive organising in Constituency Labour Parties, the filtering of conference resolutions and planning meetings they were able to neutralise internal opposition.[22] Overly zealous party management and 'spin' were indeed one reason why the Blair governments were never quite as popular as they might seem. Blair's pollster Philip Gould wrote in 2000 that 'TB is not believed to be real ... TB is out of touch ... We are suffering from disconnection. We have been assailed for spin.'[23]

The charge list against New Labour continues through a fascination with the rich and powerful. The Bernie Ecclestone affair early on, when the Chief Executive of Formula One racing was found to have donated to Labour before the election and F1 was then granted an exemption to the ban on tobacco advertising, was a sign of things to come.[24] A party that was always looking for money was bound to go to the rich and powerful as one of its first ports of call, which helped cause a constant stream of bad headlines such as the 'cash for honours' scandal. Money's attractions were a constant theme. Blair once remarked, revealingly, that 'it's amazing how many of my friends I was at school and university with ... ended up so rich'. At one point, perhaps unsurprisingly at Davos, that haven of the ultrarich, he confided that he might have chosen 'the wrong career'.[25] Elite lifestyles were clearly attractive to him, as for instance when he spent summer holidays at wealthy allies' houses such as the Tuscan villa of the Labour MP and businessman Geoffrey Robinson in 1997.[26]

Blair's earning capacity was a matter of comment even at the time, as for instance when he bought a house in Connaught Square for £3.6 million in 2004. Chris Mullin, at that point a junior minister in the Foreign Office, wondered: 'where on earth have they got that kind of money? ... What kind of signal does that send to the millions of struggling punters whose votes we need?'[27] But criticism really grew and sharpened after Blair had left office and went on to advise regimes such as Kazakhstan and Saudi Arabia.[28] The former Prime Minister argued that he was advising on reforms, but that search for cash was the subject of much vituperative judgement. The historian David Edgerton, for instance, wrote that when Thatcher died in 2013 'in the old and distressed pit villages … forgotten former miners celebrated bitterly. Tony Blair, meanwhile, was making money working for some of the vilest torturers and dictators on earth.'[29]

Blairophobia was even reinforced by colourful psychological assessments, such as that of the ex-Labour MP and 'psycho-biographer' Leo Abse. In *The Man Behind the Smile*, published in 1996, Abse painted a picture of Blair's 'self-absorption', 'ambiguity' and ambition. His smile was supposed to be a tool to deflect hostility and ingratiate, to make him seem like an insider when his father had always remained an outsider and the younger Blair himself had felt uncomfortable at Fettes, the public school he attended.[30] In the end, the accusations against New Labour became very loud and very bitter. Mark E. Smith, frontman of The Fall, thought that '1997 was like the death of innocence. You only have to look at it now … England hasn't recovered from that year. I have; but England hasn't. They bought into something so faithfully with the Labour Party that they're still reeling from the after-effects. Sunshine and well-spoken promises does this to people.'[31]

Left-wing commentators, for instance Owen Jones, cast the New Labour governments as interchangeable with the Conservatives, and just as committed to demonising the poor.[32] That caused subsequent leaders, starting with Ed Miliband, to back away from Blair's legacy as one that had entrenched inequality and failed to avoid, or at least lessen, the Great Financial Crisis that hit Britain just after he left office. Miliband said in his first Conference speech as leader that 'you saw the worst financial crisis in a generation, and I understand your anger that Labour hadn't changed the old ways in the city of deregulation'.[33] He went on, during his 2011 Conference speech, to draw a distinction between 'predators and producers'. When he came to say 'you know, I'm not Tony Blair. I'm not Gordon Brown either', he paused after the word 'Blair'. That allowed some delegates to loudly proclaim their dislike of Blair and all his works.[34] New Labour's influence in its own party had gone into steep decline. Even an erstwhile Blairite such as Liam Byrne, on taking up the Social Security brief in 2011, advised Miliband 'to stop talking about "welfare reform", which had become such a mantra in the New Labour years, and start talking instead about refounding social security'.[35]

This reaction against New Labour would reach its apogee during Corbyn's leadership between 2015 and 2020, since he had made a career out of opposing almost everything it did. Indeed, the whole tenor of Corbyn's leadership could be seen as a rejection of parliamentary Labourism itself, since he saw that tradition as full of limp compromises and endless retreats. Corbyn's inner circle at the top of the Labour Party between 2015 and 2020 contained key figures from the Stop the War Coalition, which had come to prominence opposing the American-led wars in Afghanistan and Iraq after 2001. They of course fully shared Corbyn's Manichean division of politics into 'Good' and 'Bad', to be traduced or promoted, and they placed Blair firmly on the latter side of the fence. When the BBC set up a debate between the 2015 leadership candidates in front of an audience of swing voters, Corbyn answered a question about how to overcome Blair's legacy with the words: 'Why, oh why, oh why, did Blair have to get so close to Bush that we ended up in an illegal war in Iraq?' The audience applauded noisily.[36] Many Labour members voted for Corbyn because they were rejecting the entire thrust of Blair's agenda. Among those voting for Corbyn in 2015, 65 per cent said they were doing so in part to disassociate the party from their ex-leader and his ideas.[37]

Yet these characterisations of a 'neoliberal' and conservative New Labour project, far removed from Labour's socialist past, are only part of the story. For one thing, the Blair leadership from 1994 onwards has to be seen in its proper context. It is important to remember the long-lasting shock of Labour's loss of the 1992 election. Labour failed on that occasion because it was quite simply not seen as an alternative government, a point famously made by the Labour MP Giles Radice in his influential 1992 Fabian Pamphlet, *Southern Discomfort*. One Labour candidate had told him that voters were scared of voting for Neil Kinnock because they thought 'Labour would make a mess of things'. That the party cared was not doubted: their competence was. Focus group participants made clear just how out of date Labour's image was, believing that if they got back into power 'the country would go into liquidation' and that 'Labour might be for the working class, but people don't think they're working class any more'.[38] Radice, for his part, argued that Labour had to take on a 'new identity' and start posing as a party that would stand up to vested interests, rather than advocating for them. Blair's later revision of Clause IV was just the sort of initiative Radice was looking for. It was praised in exactly those quarters Blair wanted to reach. *The Economist*, for instance, heartily approved: 'if he pushes this revolution to its end, Britain could have what it has lacked for so long: an electable, and desirable, alternative to Conservative rule'.[39]

If Labour could not win in 1992, so the argument went, it could never win. On one level, New Labour represented an assertion of what Blair, Brown and their circle saw as electoral reality. They must exert relentless message discipline; never for a moment forget or ignore middle-class, middle-of-the-road voters;

never indulge their own party activists at the expense of ignoring the country at large. Blair's adviser Anji Hunter put it like this in 2024: '[we] were veterans of the 1992 campaign, where we were ahead in the polls the whole way through, so we were on no complacency patrol'.[40] More pithily, Harriet Harman believed that the creation of New Labour involved 'listening to people rather than shouting at them'.[41]

Blair understood just how tarnished Labour's image was, but he also grasped that it could be resuscitated if Labour displayed sharp political clarity and built a reputation for balance and moderation. The proof of that was offered in his early days as Leader of the Opposition, when he impressed many southern voters with his balance and dynamism. Returning to just such voters in 1994, Radice found the political situation he had analysed with some gloom in 1992 transformed. There were still worries about what might lurk in the background, as well as over Blair's own inexperience. But in general Blair was dispelling most of these doubts:

> Where in 1992 … first thoughts [about Labour] were all negative, by 1994 they are more balanced. The best things are a belief in the welfare system, Tony Blair, concern for fairness and commitment to all people. The worst things are union involvement, a backwards looking mentality, clobbering the wealthy, past performance and a perceived softness on inflation. Tony Blair himself provides a string of positive responses: hope for the future, young, energetic, likeable and genuine: 'He is the best man to lead the party'… 'A man of the times'.[42]

Blair was helped, of course, by the general sense that the Conservative era had run its course. The NHS and schools were in a dire state, sharpening Labour's desire to win – but raising the stakes. In this respect the situation in 1997 was similar to that when Labour won its next landslide from Opposition in 2024. As the pollster Deborah Mattinson remembers it:

> It's easy to forget that in 1997 public services seemed to be on the point of collapse. Focus group discussion was of primary school class sizes of forty or even fifty – and of kids leaving school completely unable to read and write. Voters told me about elderly relatives suffering waiting times for a hip operation that might leave someone in pain for several years, and of hanging around Accident and Emergency Wards with injured or sick children for twelve hours or more. There was a real sense of urgency about the need for the change.[43]

Cherie Blair later remembered that 'travelling around the country, being shown the state of school buildings, I saw at first hand how close to collapse so much of the infrastructure was'.[44] Blair was pushing at something of an open door, but then again public services had been crumbling for years and Labour had not been able to take advantage. Labour's new leader was determined not to put swing voters off again.

Lambasting Blair's Labour for its centrist outlook and its compromises ignores context and nuance, as well as overlooking the powerful emotional impact of the 1992 election and Labour's desperation to get into power to protect and then improve public services. It forgets that the Labour Party had always had a revisionist social democratic streak that sought to compromise with free markets and the liberal state. Hugh Gaitskell, Labour's leader in the 1950s and early 1960s, tried to reform Labour's emblematic Clause IV committing the party to nationalisation, in 1959 and 1960. That was not the same thing as New Labour's enthusiastic embrace of economic liberalisation: the 'modernisers' of the post-war and welfare state era still thought of state power in a more positive light than New Labour did, and Blair and Brown injected a new fervour about markets into the party's imagination. Past Labour leaders had challenged their party: Blair often confronted his.

Even so, Labour's revisionists did both prefigure and inspire New Labour. Harman's distinction between 'listening' and 'shouting' was no new revelation, and a good deal of Labour's whole history can be understood in those terms. The most famous of the revisionist thinkers, Tony Crosland, used his 1956 book *The Future of Socialism* to call for 'large egalitarian changes in our educational system, the distribution of property, the distribution of resources in periods of need, social manners and style of life, and the location of power within industry; and perhaps some, but certainly a smaller, change in respect of incomes from work'.[45] Crosland clearly differed with New Labour in seeking *more* equality of outcome. New Labour took many of the revisionists' insights to their arguably logical but perhaps extreme conclusions; Labour's revisionist socialists and social democrats had never aimed at a strong redistribution of final rewards, but of life chances and lived experiences, just as Blair himself imagined. That approach provided New Labour with at least something of a base to work from. As Patrick Diamond from the Number 10 Policy Unit wrote to Blair in 2002: 'we stand in the tradition of revisionist social democracy, prepared always to draw a consistent distinction between ends and means'.[46]

Critics should also take into account the way in which the intellectual climate was changing, rather than see New Labour as springing only from Blair and Brown's ideas about the electorate. During the 1980s and 1990s, new elements were being added to the concept of social democracy all the time. One of the key New Labour theorists of Blair's 'Third Way', Anthony Giddens, believed that economic and social change was speeding up, making governments think anew about how to secure a better society in a much more fluid world. He settled on the idea of inclusion, and its antonym, exclusion, to justify new types of economic and social intervention: it was social exclusion that was the problem, specifically social and economic structures that did not allow people to take part in the 'mainstream'. A 'positive' welfare system, that intervened all the time to increase social capital, educate, train, inform and guide, could counter this phenomenon far more easily than an 'old' welfarism that could only offer benefits to mitigate the situation in a crisis.[47] This was what Brown meant when he said that 'the welfare state must be about supporting people as they respond to these challenges – extending their choices and opportunities; acting as a trampoline rather than as a safety net'.[48]

John Denham, who served as a Minister of State in three departments under Blair, thinks that this 'was very much part of the sort of Third Way dogma that it was possible to enable all individuals to succeed within an essentially unreformed economy … there was very much this view you can't really steer the economy. So what you can do is enable people to succeed in it individually and you can have a better safety net in the form of tax credits and things of that sort.'[49] That is no doubt partly true, though the Labour Party had always been a 'respectable' part of the state – loyal to parliamentary government, the courts and the unwritten and written parts of the constitution. It has usually been austere, rule-bound and in agreement with the small-c conservatism of many of its voters, so New Labour's small-c conservatism was hardly new. Blair also evoked Harold Wilson and his appeal to scientific modernity, deploying technology as a building block of a new politics whose newness and novelty would appeal to all. In an interview for this book in 2024, he demonstrated that this conviction has only deepened: 'Harold Wilson was the "White Hot Heat of Technology" … And there's technology innovation that was happening through the 70s, through the 80s, through the 90s. The difference today is that the technology revolution we're living through in my view deserves the name revolution, in the same way as the Industrial Revolution.'[50]

New ways of governing, and the new technology becoming available at the time, were inextricably linked. Stefan Czerniawski, the civil servant in charge of e-government in the Cabinet Office between 2000 and 2003, remembers the strong drive for instance behind 'reinventing government', which did succeed in putting many functions of the state online: 'there's certainly an element of kind of riding the *zeitgeist*, there was a … very strong sense I think of new ministers coming into government and feeling that government was slow moving, not modern, not adopting recent technology. And I think that they saw, and they were right to see, a very real need an opportunity to modernize the way government worked.'[51] In Blair's view new routes to growth and new ways of communicating with the public in a rapidly changing world, combined with strong communities, would defy both free market Conservatives who believed in growing the economy above all else, and those on the Left who always set bosses against workers.

In these ways New Labour was Janus-faced, like the Roman god of the doorway, looking both backwards and forwards. It reached back to Labour traditions of community, fellow-feeling, the mixed economy, revisionism and ambitions for a better future, but it also faced forwards with renewed optimism at a time when Western liberalism, globalised markets and new technology could achieve almost anything. As Blair told me:

> The tone I wanted to set was that we had to become in spirit, and in our mental attitude, a young country, that we should honour our past, but not live in it … the challenge always for Britain is when it believes its best days are behind it. You know, it talks constantly about the Second World War, and … the leadership of Churchill, and all of that is great, but it's not going to give you a future … you've got to keep always at the cutting edge of the future. If you don't do that, you fall behind.[52]

During the 1990s and early 2000s, his Labour Party became a mosaic or medley made out of many elements, liberal, conservative, collectivist, moral, social democratic, Christian Socialist and more. All leaderships are something of a collection or collage of themes, of course: John Major's Premiership combined a more traditional conservatism that was apparently softer than Thatcher's with some harsh rhetoric on benefits and even more competition inside the public sector. David Cameron preached a 'compassionate' conservatism and told his party to 'stop banging on about Europe': that actually led to austerity and Brexit.

But the effect seems particularly acute during the New Labour era. Blair himself added in a myriad of further themes, for instance the idea of communitarianism, deeply influential with New Labour's leader himself – the view that social cohesion and common endeavour are the ways to a better society and to better, more fulfilled lives within it. One could, indeed, go much further towards that idea of New Labour being built on a whole range of different foundations. Blair's ideas also owed a debt to Marxist thinking about the 'labourism' of the Labour Party. Blairite centrists, like Labour's Left, were never happy with Labour's role as the representative of trade unions: that cramped, confined politics of merely speaking for organised labour was not radical or rigorous enough for *either* of Labour's more restless tribes. Both those outlying wings of the party shared a concept of rapidly, unalterably transforming the Labour Party, not allowing it to meander through gradualist reforms. In this respect Blair often spoke – and then acted – more radically than 'Old' Labour's Right ever would have done. It was the New Left magazine *Marxism Today* that first ran a series of articles about 'modernisation', in 1991, which advocated coop-eration between Labour and the Liberal Democrats, and argued, similarly to Giddens, that economic globalisation was a fundamental world-altering force that was opening up borders and the possibility of new types of life.[53]

New Labour, New Britain? will examine all those ideas as well as the dilemmas involved in actually governing, at that time and at any time. It will attempt to avoid the stark, crude colours in which day-to-day politics is conducted, and which overly partisan commentary trades in. This is especially important given the less settled and arguably far less successful years of public policy that have followed, and indeed certain themes will be more than familiar from our own time. So what follows will attempt not just to see the governments of 1997 to 2007 as part of a particular time, in their own context, but also to connect Blair's search for a new politics with our own problems. Immigration was one continual problem and debate: it was still low in these years by subsequent standards, but it was nonetheless unpopular, and it undermined many of the Government's own ambitions. One decision in particular stands out, and reso-nates still: the refusal to place transitional limits on the free movement of people with the European Union's accession countries in 2004. Some ministers, such as Jack Straw when he was Foreign Secretary, objected to allowing complete freedom of movement on the basis that it might cause an unsustainable influx of new workers – especially once other countries began to 'peel away' from the same commitment.[54] But Straw was in the end overruled in favour of strength-ening the economy and replenishing the labour force.[55] That decision would have momentous consequences, as this book will show.

The creation of the National Minimum Wage (NMW) and tax credits to top up the wages at the bottom end of the scale will be another constant, as both measures have become incredibly important in supporting low-income individuals and families. One more issue tackled then, and desperately in need of attention now, will be childcare policy and interventions in 'family life' taken as a whole, critical to the New Labour project but relatively neglected, with disastrous consequences, ever since – as the fate of New Labour's flagship Sure Start project under the Coalition and Conservatives demonstrates. Blair's governments were prescient in their struggles with rising immigration, attempts to move people from welfare into work, and in grasping how important early intervention was and is to people's future chances and choices in life. This book will track just how all those dilemmas have been getting worse, not better, since Blair's time in power, not least under the pressure of the austerity and cuts that followed New Labour's ejection from power in 2010 – developments that New Labour was not able to prevent via an organised succession, or more consistent ideological underpinnings. The Labour government elected in 2024 faces acute challenges in all those fields, and understanding how the Left tackled them last time they were in office might assist in both understanding and tackling these thorny problems.

The chapters that follow will necessarily do an imperfect job. For one thing, many official files that could have helped with taking that longer view are not yet available in the National Archives. There again, any book can only cover a fraction of this government's constant activity. This is a book about New Labour at home in the UK, and within that in England and Wales. For the most part, devolution and the new devolved governments' policies, Northern Ireland, the UK's role within the EU, foreign policy – and much else – are absent. This is very much an inquiry into the *domestic* policies of New Labour, and any elements and issues coming in from 'outside' Britain's borders, with international source and implications, simply could not be fitted in unless they were vital to the course of policy inside the country. The influence of the European courts on crime and punishment, when the book comes to cover those themes in Chapter 6, is a case in point. Those themes are also beyond the space and time available, and other authors are better guides to those subjects in any case. No doubt there will be a flood of books and articles covering those themes in due course.

In the first phase of Starmer's Labour government, it is to be hoped that a new account of Blair's successes and failures at home is both timely and instructive. There is a pressing need for practitioners and experts to analyse and understand the good, the bad and perhaps even the ugly in New Labour's ideologies and practices. Many of the difficulties Labour is facing in the 2020s are the same as they were in the 1990s and 2000s. Low public trust in politics and public policy, the hole in the economy left by deindustrialisation, the gap between rich and poor, high and unpopular immigration, creaking and underfunded public services: all are uncannily familiar from both eras. Although the solutions now may be nothing like those settled on by Blair and Brown, understanding at least the way in which these problems were thought about and worked through must be helpful. Some ex-ministers from the late 1990s and early 2000s, for instance

David Blunkett and Alan Milburn, have been called in to advise, while for much of 2025 Peter Mandelson was the UK's Ambassador in Washington DC. Blair's Chief of Staff, Jonathan Powell, is back as Starmer's National Security Adviser; Louise Casey, who served as head of the Rough Sleepers Unit and the Anti-Social Behaviour Unit under Blair, is undertaking the Starmer government's review of social care. But the work of comparison and learning does not seem to be proceeding in any rigorous or joined-up way: to be truly useful, our view of the Blair era should be detached from personal knowledge and connection, and treated as consistently and neutrally as possible. This book takes up that challenge.

An end to boom and bust?

New Labour economics: novel, but vague

New Labour thought it could set Britain on a new path, a road that would lead to constant and self-generating economic growth. That confidence was based on three founding concepts: globalisation; competitive markets; and strict limits on government power. Globalisation was the first and most important key to New Labour's economic philosophy, a vast upheaval stressed by Giddens in particular.[1] As the Department of Trade and Industry's *Our Competitive Future* White Paper put it in 1998, 'the world economy is ... becoming more open ... is increasingly mobile. An increasing number of low-cost countries have educated and skilled workforces ... capable of delivering sophisticated goods and services.'[2] Britain had no choice but to adjust to that globalised world: to compete with, and export to, those rising powers. Blair was, as ever, more colourful and more succinct: 'I hear people say we have to stop and debate globalisation. You might as well debate whether autumn should follow summer.' For Blair, New Labour's mission was to accept the openness of the world economy, while restructuring economy and society to prepare for it.[3] He deployed the idea of an inevitably globalised future when he tried to paint old divides over domestic policy, between private and public, rivalry and cooperation, as obsolete.

For many critics, this outlook involved accepting very un-Labour ideas about markets, as well as embracing the power of the City of London and finance capital – as competition was the second organising principle endlessly talked about in this era. Blair's Third Way actually embraced risk and each individual's search for advantage, sometimes with only a human face to show for it. It sometimes seemed to accept as natural and unchangeable the intertwined benefits of an open world economy, more choice, increased efficiency and lower prices. The sociologist Bob Jessop concluded that New Labour thus became the 'emperor of European neoliberalism', while Danny Dorling argues that 'Thatcherism continued after New Labour came to power'.[4] New Labour's values themselves are frequently attacked as one overriding source of these ideas. Blair and his ministers were often thought to be magnetically attracted to money and fame as images and indicators of success, a view that recalled the way in which Ramsay MacDonald had once been lambasted for his admiration for the aristocracy when he was Labour leader. Simon Jenkins argued that Brown, for instance, was 'bored by occasion and diplomacy, but loved the presence of money. He did not crave it for himself ... but he admired people who were rich and he spent unprecedented fees on bankers and consultants'.[5]

The third and last pillar of New Labour economics was the concept that governments should limit their own freedom of action. Blair was clear that inflation had to be conquered, despite voters' worries that Labour would ignore it, and he agreed with many liberal economists that clarity, certainty and stability were critical in that task. According to this way of thinking previous governments, blown about by economic crises, had ignored all that, reacting to every passing mood and successively inflating and deflating the economy as each Budget came and went – making inflation worse and worse during every business cycle as they first pumped up demand that raised wages and prices before cutting back again, undermining stability and lowering productivity. That way of understanding inflation was one justification for the Conservatives as they shrank the state and its ambitions during the 1980s.

But New Labour still maintained its dividing lines with Thatcherite practice. Here Blair's new model party took issue with the Conservatives' neglect of public services, their carelessness over regional and local policy and their neglect of the human factor in economic growth. Blair and Brown drew on ideas about state capacity and long-term planning which became known as 'New' or post-Keynesianism, looking again and with fresh eyes at what the state *could* do, as well as what it could not. As Blair put it, 'raising the standards of education and training' was essential, and 'the government has a responsibility ... to promote partnerships with the private sector to improve economic performance'.[6] For Blair, the Conservatives had unwisely downgraded education, training, skills, the need for growth throughout the country, good schools and hospitals, infrastructure and constant networking between private, public and charitable sectors. His emphasis on steadiness and calm were not ends in themselves: they provided the arena in which a more productive, responsive economy and society could be built.

New Labour diverged from the party's past in the extent of its rhetorical zeal for the market. From the 1940s to the 1960s, leading revisionists such as Douglas Jay (President of the Board of Trade under Wilson) were sceptical about nationalisation, but they had hardly ruled it out. Jay in fact thought that government might buy up shares in private companies to extend the Government's control over the economy.[7] New Labour now broke with the revisionists' idea of balance between private and public sectors and held up successful entrepreneurs as exemplars; in place of an unwillingness to press nationalisation any further came an enthusiasm for profitmaking businesses. Ed Balls, in his autobiography, remembers studying A level Economics in the 1980s amid Thatcherism's failures. But despite the disasters of that era, growth surged during most of that decade and Balls 'also saw and came to understand the huge power and potential for dynamism, innovation and creativity that a market economy can bring ... my enthusiasm for that market mechanism is undimmed'.[8] The most dynamic and powerful economy New Labour saw as an exemplar was, of course, the United States. The Labour strategist David Hill was part of the Clinton campaign in 1992, and Mandelson and Gould were part of this effort too.[9] During January 1993, Blair and Brown visited the Clinton transition team in Washington DC. Here they met Larry Summers and also Alan Greenspan – a revealing mix of policymakers who helped persuade them further of the need for a 'credible' progressivism that reassured financial markets at the same time as encouraging growth and attacking unemployment.[10]

The most famous attempt to formulate a fresh and precise set of ideas in Opposition was the concept of 'stakeholding', promoted by Blair to a Singapore business audience in January 1996.[11] At the time, the *Observer* editor Will Hutton was arguing that a more collaborative, 'social' capitalism could be built by changing company law and culture so that it fostered a cooperative capitalism. He dubbed this 'stakeholding'.[12] Blair's Singapore speech did contain elements of this vision, albeit vaguely, promoting 'a mutual purpose' between government, employers and unions. Even more suggestively, Blair argued that 'it is surely time to assess how we shift the emphasis in corporate ethos from the company being a mere vehicle for the capital market ... towards a vision of the company as a community or partnership'.[13] However, within a week Blair had made clear that the 'stakeholder' concept would likely not involve changes to corporate legislation.[14] Both Blair and Brown backed further away from the 'stakeholding' idea in subsequent months, concerned about its more radical connotations. By the time Labour came to draw up its actual industrial policy a good deal of this thrust had been watered down in favour of 'trying to change people's behaviour and attitudes', as Alistair Darling put it while Shadow Chief Secretary to the Treasury.[15]

So we are left with a mixed picture, a collage or mosaic of rather vague ideas that were often to confuse as well as cohere, and which contained elements of ideas taken from 'New' or post-Keynesian economics, the Labour Party's past practice in government, Clinton's New Democrats and a certain concept of the networked and organising state. The economy would still be run on free market lines, but there would be a greater stress on stability, and therefore higher growth; more emphasis on education, training and investment; supply-side interventions where bottlenecks and waste were obstacles to progress; and increased partnership between public and private sectors. The somewhat general nature of Blair's own economic beliefs helped his governments to face in many different directions, at least for a while, as the economy expanded and the Government did little to stand in its way. But the opaque novelty and the sheer range of these ideas would not always prove resilient once they were tested by the pressure of events.

The economy surges forward

Labour's overall economic record in office was strong until the Great Recession derailed it – certainly in contrast with the 1980s and early 1990s, as well as compared with the era that followed. The economy Blair and Brown inherited from Tory Chancellor Kenneth Clarke was something of a success anyway, as unemployment fell without triggering the inflation it had in the 1970s or late 1980s. But they continued and built on that strong record. Economic growth for New Labour's whole period in office slowed a little from its rate between 1992 and 1997, as we can see in Figure 2.1, but at an average of 2.7 per cent it still outstripped the progress made by France (2.2 per cent), Germany (1.5 per cent), Italy (1.4 per cent) and Japan (1.2 per cent). Of the major developed economies only the US, at an average 2.9 per cent growth per year, moved ahead faster than the UK.[16]

Productivity gains were also relatively impressive. Rapid growth, alongside more and more innovation in the information and computer technology industries, flexible but buoyant employment markets and a younger, better trained workforce all allowed Labour in office to continue the Conservatives' strong record in this respect. This was exactly the result the post-Keynesians in the New Democrat camp had expected. High-quality innovation and the growth it could drive, both inside companies and across whole sectors, moved ahead

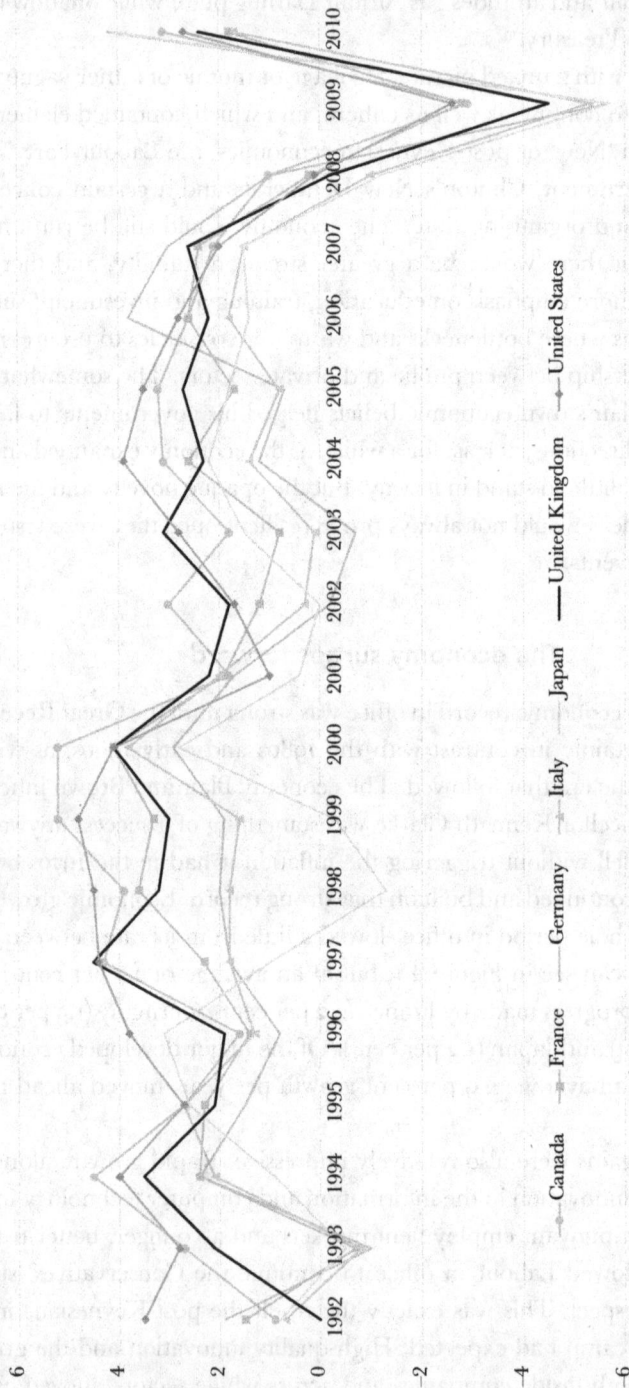

Figure 2.1 Real GDP growth in the G7 economies (annual % change), 1992–2010

Source: IMF, *Real GDP growth, annual percentage change*, www.imf.org/external/datamapper/NGDP_RPCH@WEO/OEMDC/ADVEC/WEOWORLD, accessed 29 August 2023.

Canada · France · Germany · Italy · Japan — United Kingdom · United States

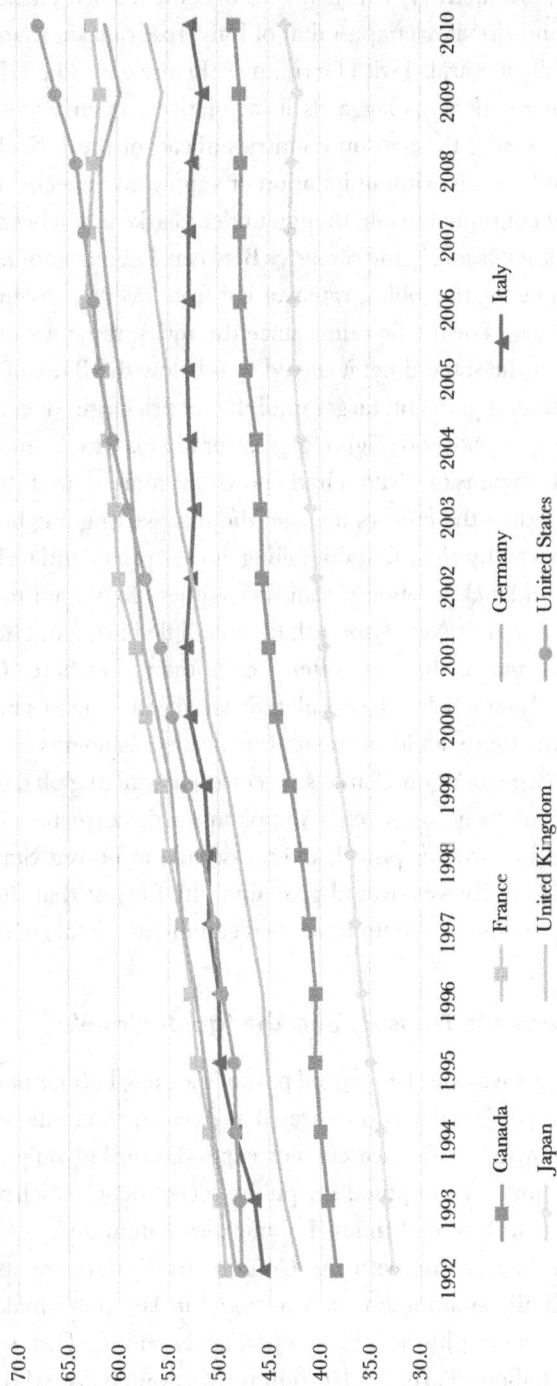

Figure 2.2 Productivity in the G7, 1992–2010 (GDP/hour worked, 2015 US$ at PPP)

Source: OECD. Stat database, *Level of GDP per capita and productivity*, https://stats.oecd.org/Index.aspx?DataSetCode=PDB_GR, accessed 30 August 2023.

rapidly.[17] Britain's productivity, which was to become a huge puzzle after the Great Recession and Brexit, went past that of Italy, rose quicker than Canada's and moved generally in parallel with Germany's (Figure 2.2). The UK was only catching up on the leaders, as laggards in a relatively open world economy usually do.[18] Still, closing the gap on countries ahead of the UK allowed the economy to expand rapidly without inflation or supply bottlenecks emerging.

Unemployment continued to fall, though under Clarke it had been declining from its 1993 peak for a long time already. Between Labour coming to office and its low point in 2005 the jobless rate was cut from over 7 per cent to under 5 per cent (Figure 2.3). For the first time since the 1960s, the inflation situation remained benign at the same time: it stayed well below the Bank of England's 2.5 per cent (and later 2 per cent) target until the oil price rises of 2006 and the budgetary loosening of 2007/08 (Figure 2.4). Overall, this was the most successful and remarkable expansion Britain had known for more than three decades. New Labour was riding the crest of a wave: the massive ongoing boom in the world economy driven by globalisation, falling energy prices and technological innovation. The 'goldilocks economy' that was neither too hot nor too cold was a global phenomenon. But New Labour had done little harm, and much good, engendering performance that was often better than elsewhere. Budgetary, monetary and supply-side policies were all reordered with at least some success, a record of reforms that should be treated as accomplishments in their own right and not just dependent on Clarke's successes or benign global conditions. The trend was set anyway, but even a minor upwards correction in the rate of growth can yield enormous payoffs over a decade in power. Starmer, and his Chancellor Rachel Reeves, would give anything for just that slight nudge towards a wealthier country: economic success cannot just be taken for granted.

Brown's Treasury and the 'golden rule'

Balancing the Budget was another central part of the New Labour outlook. The Treasury's 'golden rule' under Brown was that over an economic cycle there would be no borrowing to finance current expenditure, but only for capital spending. A new limit was imposed on public sector debt, which would not exceed 40 per cent in 'normal' times. Labour also committed in Opposition to keep total spending in line with the Conservatives' plans for its first two years in office.[19] This commitment had its roots in key policymakers' views of economic and electoral history. Brown had an Economic History PhD, on the Independent Labour Party leader Jimmy Maxton: Balls, who had held

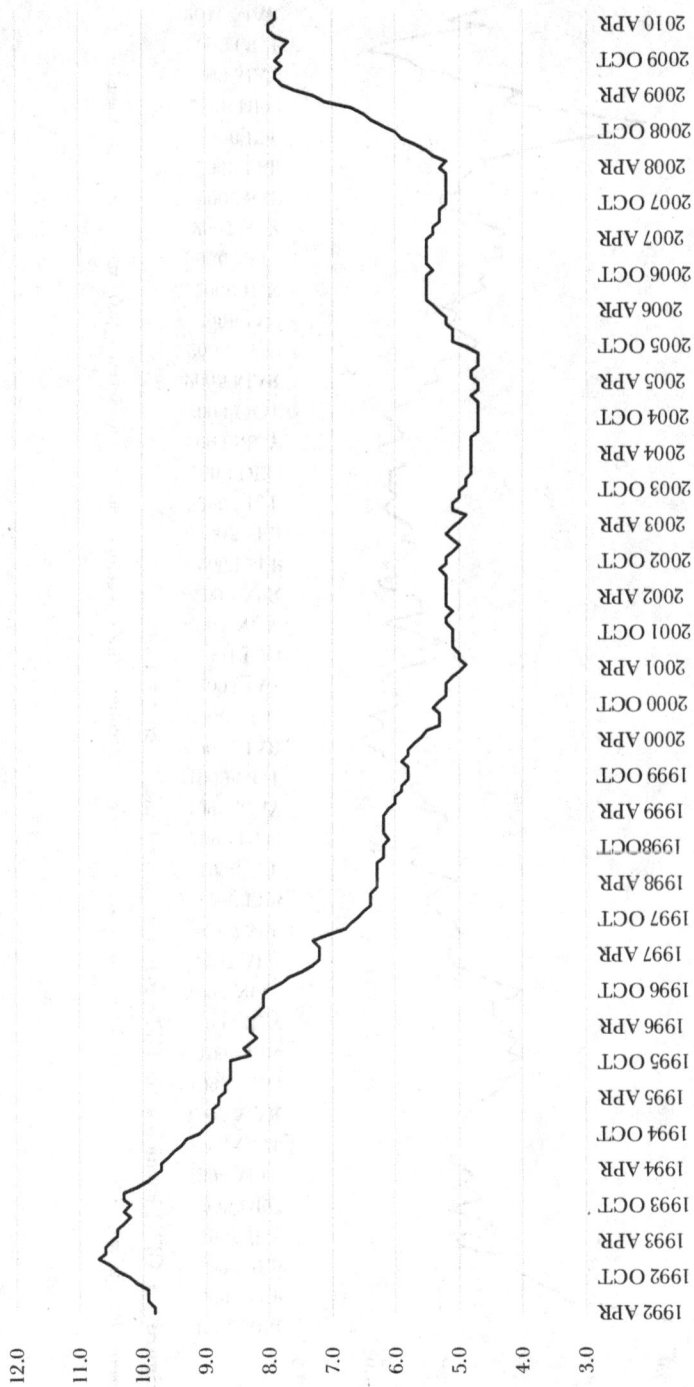

Figure 2.3 Unemployment rate (16 and over), %, seasonally adjusted

Source: ONS dataset, *Unemployment rate (aged 16 and over, seasonally adjusted)*, %, www.ons.gov.uk/employmentandlabourmarket/peoplenotinwork/unemployment/ timeseries/mgsx/lms, accessed 28 August 2023.

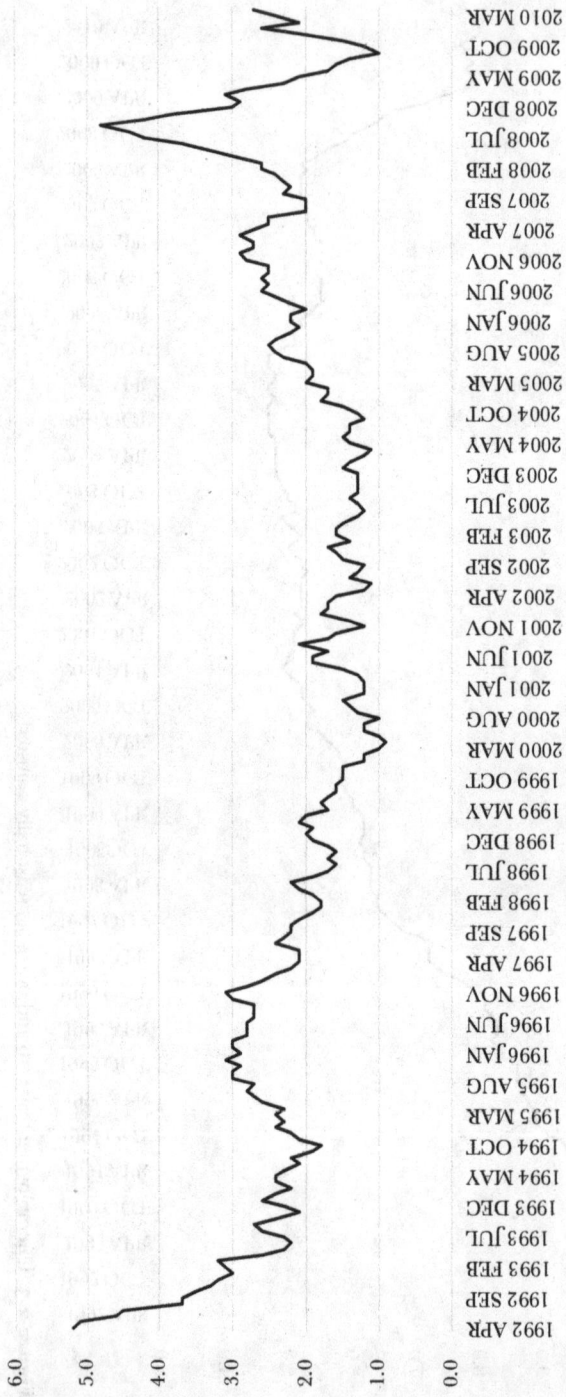

Figure 2.4 CPIH inflation in the UK, 1992–2010 (annual rate, %, 2015 = 100)

Source: ONS dataset, *CPIH annual rate 00: all items 2015=100*, www.ons.gov.uk/economy/inflationandpriceindices/timeseries/l550/mm23, accessed 28 August 2023.

academic posts and been a journalist, was similarly fascinated by Labour's past.[20] New Labour believed that what it defined as 'Old' Labour had never established itself in government because of its mishandling of the economy: a feedback loop had then formed, in which markets would never give Labour a chance. Devaluation in 1949 and 1967 and the International Monetary Fund crisis of 1976 were all seen as examples of this tendency.[21] Charles Clarke, who held a string of high offices under Blair, once reflected that Labour's past had always been defined by 'Harold Wilson and devaluation ... Jim Callaghan and the Winter of Discontent, Denis Healy and the IMF'.[22]

For all that baggage, and all the change they were making because of it, Blair and Brown did carve out an agenda that was sharply different from the Thatcherism it superseded. New Labour's view of history also involved a rejection of what its leaders thought of as the doctrinaire monetarism of the Thatcher experiments. Brown and Balls emphasised as much as did Thatcherites the fight against inflation, but thought that the level of unemployment necessary to bring about stable prices could be lowered via better policy. They also believed that high unemployment might also leave behind a legacy of poor skills and broken careers that might hold back the economy and even make it more susceptible to inflation – a structural view of the economy alien to the laissez-faire thinking of the Thatcherites. For the Brownites, managing overall demand in the economy was still at least possible, though it should play a smaller role than it had during the 1960s and 1970s. Indeed, New Labour's first Queen's Speech made 'high and stable levels of economic growth and employment' its aim: a deliberate echo of the May 1944 White Paper on Employment Policy, often cited as the acme of Keynesian influence.[23]

Policy was actually run with a keen eye on the Budget's role in the management of the economy – not something that could always be said between the late 1970s and the mid-1990s. The economy was expanding quickly when New Labour took office, while the budget deficit (at 3.5 per cent of GDP) was extremely high by post-war standards. So it was natural, in Keynesian terms, for the Government to tighten tax and spend policy. Towards the end of 1997, the Treasury thought the economy was growing at 4 per cent, which was clearly unsustainable: debate within government focused on how far to rein it in.[24] Then, as the economy slowed after the bursting of the dotcom bubble in 2000, the Treasury took up much more of the slack with a notable current budget deficit from 2002/03 to 2006/07 and a net borrowing requirement which rose to a peak of around 3 per cent of GDP in 2004/05. Most of this was caused by large-scale fiscal loosening in the 2000, 2001 and 2002 Budgets.[25]

This was definitely a return to at least some form of steering the economy, though not all of it was deliberate. The early phase of tightening and retrenchment actually happened partly by accident, as the economy did much better than forecast, money poured into the Exchequer and the Government withdrew enormous amounts of demand from the economy. As Nick Macpherson, Brown's first Principal Private Secretary as Chancellor, puts it: 'I remember at various points being embarrassed by how we had coming in ... We were literally awash ... It was becoming a problem because once you've got a surplus, everyone wants to spend it.'[26] The policy loosening that followed after 2001, as spending surged but taxes failed to keep up, might have been partly caused by the idea that these revenues were permanent, rather than fleeting: structural, rather than dependent on the IT and telecommunications boom at the turn of the century. So government spending ran on, as if the bubble had never burst, and helped the Government effect a soft landing. In this case Brown's fortunately generous Budgets after 1999 look like happenstance as well as planning.[27] New Labour adopted 'New' or post-Keynesian principles, but was also and once again lucky. New Labour's Budgets steered the economy, and were rather more expansive than sometimes appeared at the time – if sometimes only coincidentally.

An independent Bank of England

Central bank independence was another key element of New Labour's economic philosophy in action. This was supposed to keep inflation low and reassure the markets by limiting the Government's powers, and ministers therefore moved within days to contract out the setting of interest rates to an independent Bank of England and a Monetary Policy Committee. Markets, investors and voters alike were being sent a signal: Labour would not interfere in the day-to-day running of monetary policy, and more broadly would refrain from interfering too much in how the economy worked. Brown and Balls pushed this policy with aplomb. Civil servants, in particular the Cabinet Secretary Robin Butler and Moira Wallace from the Treasury, urged a more cautious and deliberative approach, but to no avail.[28]

At the same time the Government began to indicate that it wanted the Bank of England to focus on inflation overall, and for day-to-day regulation to pass to a much stronger Securities and Investment Board, eventually renamed the Financial Services Authority. The Bank of England's Governor, Eddie George, was furious: he thought the changes 'would split responsibility in an artificial way … blur accountability dangerously, and by diminishing the Bank's capacity to act as a central bank, could reduce its ability to respond effectively to a crisis'.[29] Events were to prove the Governor more than prescient. The change was supposed to prevent the impression of a Bank with divided loyalties: needing to raise interest rates, for instance, but fearing to do so when it knew which banks might get into difficulties.[30] But as the economy and the banks binged on cheap global credit during the 2000s, dispensing with a watchdog that could oversee both sides of that question was to prove a costly error.[31]

Balls was the main advocate of central bank independence, and believed that the creation of that 'neutral' arbiter would mean that both companies and individuals would behave as if inflation would stay low, therefore allowing more rapid economic expansion than would otherwise be possible.[32] The power of that neutrality was to give Labour in office more leeway than they might have enjoyed without the Bank of England's increased powers. Brown had in Opposition promised to follow the Conservative Chancellor Kenneth Clarke's inflation target of '2.5 per cent or less': the Bank's new authority gave him cover to break this ceiling by at least a percentage point, a distinction that was obscured by the news about how policy was to be made. Brown laid down a 1 per cent range *either side* of 2.5 per cent, which was rather more friendly to growth than it might have been. As with tax and spending, 'prudence' meant rather less in reality than as rhetoric. During the Russian debt and Asian financial crises that threatened economic progress in 1998, the Bank cut rates much more aggressively than Brown thought a Labour Chancellor would have been able to on their own: it did so again in the wake of the dotcom bust in 2001.[33] 'If a Labour government had presided over that much volatility in interest rates month after month', Balls wrote later, 'it would have been seen as an economic crisis out of control … but an independent Bank of England was seen to be acting soberly and prudently.'[34]

That new credibility, though, came with its own dangers. UK interest rates were in this period extremely high relative to other countries, in part because of the Bank's policies: between 1999 and 2007 UK rates averaged 4.8 per cent, while in the Eurozone they were 3 per cent and in the US 3.6 per cent.[35] The appearance of stern monetary discipline, and a touch of its reality as rates rose from 6 per cent to 7.25 per cent within six months of Labour taking office, caused sterling to become so strong that some members of the Monetary Policy Committee discussed direct intervention in the currency markets.[36] They did fall back later, to reach a pre-crash low of 3.5 per cent in 2003, but the drawbacks of high interest rates early in New Labour's term show that stability is not everything. Raising monetary policy to such an ultra-high pitch of importance was always an accident waiting to happen. Sterling's medium-term overvaluation had serious consequences. Visible exports lagged; manufacturing suffered. Geoffrey Norris, who advised Blair in economics at Number 10, later admitted that 'we had always thought that the danger was that there would be a Labour government and the pound would plummet. As it was, it continued to rise to a level where UK manufacturing became seriously uncompetitive.'[37]

New Labour's creation of an independent central bank focused on infla-tion did meet with some success. The bond yield spread with Germany – the premium that the UK paid to borrow money, over and above the German government's costs – collapsed entirely between 1997 and 2001, though it re-emerged to some extent in the following Parliament.[38] But inflation had fallen globally, whether a country had a strong independent central bank or not. In a situation where the public's inflation expectations had abated and were still declining, short-term interest rate changes had less effect on how much infla-tion voters expected than they would otherwise have done. Once again the Blair government was riding on the back of success everywhere, not necessarily innovating off its own bat. Labour had bolstered the authority and effectiveness of monetary policy, though the economic benefits may not have been as large or positive as they appeared at the time.[39]

Labour, the unions and immigration

If we turn to government intervention in detail, there was a slight but defi-nite move towards giving trade unions a bigger say in the economy; a much more significant expansion of individual workers' rights; and at exactly the same time a large-scale increase in immigration. When taken in the round, they represent a particularly New Labour economic policy, an attempt to push growth upwards via making labour pay, while avoiding overheating by expand-ing the workforce. A huge surge of public spending was also deployed, inflat-ing the public sector workforce by more than half a million between 1998 and 2003 – and incidentally playing a counter-cyclical role in the threatened down-turns of 1998 and 2001.[40] Taken together, these rapid-fire series of changes likely increased productivity in a way globalisation, balanced budgets and central bank independence could not have done alone. The detailed work of economic change could be as important as the benign global backdrop, or the basic tenets of stability.

Blair in Opposition had weakened Labour's ties to the trade unions, all the better to make Labour more palatable to a sceptical electorate, but also because the link was part of the 'Old' Labour mindset that so frustrated him. As he put it in a September 1995 interview: 'nobody seriously believes in this day and age that the business of the Labour Party is to be the political arm of the trade union movement ... In government you cannot operate like that. It wouldn't be right anyway.'[41] Blair stressed in his foreword to the 1998 White Paper *Fairness at Work* that 'even after the changes we propose, Britain will have the most lightly regulated labour market of any leading economy in the world'.[42] The 1999 Employment Relations Act and the 2002 Employment Act should however be seen as part of a limited re-regulation of the workplace. Union recognition was made compulsory if a majority of employees were already members of a union, or if 40 per cent or more voted in favour. Discrimination on the basis of union activity was outlawed. Trade union representation – if an employee wanted it – was guaranteed when it came to disciplinary matters.[43]

This did not imply much confidence in returning to stronger *collective* bargaining. Indeed the emphasis on individual rights undermined the communal role of organised labour. An explosion of workers' *personal* rights from protection against rapid or unfair dismissal, the right to be represented, to take maternity, paternity or adoption leave and to more flexible working and unpaid time off in an emergency amounted to a 'big bang' in that arena. At the same time, trade union membership went on falling under Blair.[44] The Prime Minister's slogan of the time was 'fairness not favours' – a promise of renewed consultation with the unions, without any special relationship. At the European level his government continued to resist going much further on collective representation or on the reform of working conditions, for instance limiting the scope of the 48 hours a week maximum under the Working Time Directive. This was, even so, no libertarian free-for-all, and there is little doubt that the labour market was more heavily ordered than before 1997. In 2008 the British Chamber of Commerce reckoned that an extra £66bn of costs had been imposed. Measures such as the Flexible Working Regulations, Disability Discrimination Regulations and the Employment Act all involved large-scale intervention in the marketplace.[45]

None of this takes away from the established view of New Labour as favouring free market solutions. As *Our Competitive Future* argued, 'competitive markets are the sharpest spur to innovation and the best way to reward risk taking. That is why the Government ... will open up markets, crack down on harmful anti-competitive behaviour and modernise markets.'[46] The Competition Act of 1998 and the Enterprise Act of 2002 both toughened policy on cartels, while strengthening the role of arms-length bodies such as the Competition Commission. The Office of Fair Trading was granted the ability to impose harsher fines, and those breaking the law might now be sentenced to time in prison.[47] Again, though, this was partly in the tradition of Labour governments, since it had been Attlee's administration that brought in the 1948 Monopolies and Restrictive Practices Act, just as much as they had promoted free trade. Both Attlee's and Blair's policies involved a piecemeal and fairly tentative set of compromises, shaped by uncertainties and divisions within the Government and by the demands of Britain's relatively open economy, just as much as they embodied those governments' philosophies.[48]

One area where New Labour's zeal for globalisation had profound effects was immigration. Along with global capital flows came easier movement of labour, and a large-scale influx of workers to the country that likely assisted with growth but would have far-reaching social and political consequences well into the twenty-first century. Highly skilled migrants were welcome in the UK's booming economy. New Labour mostly perceived immigration to be an important economic asset, and the DTI's 1998 *Competitiveness* White Paper committed to look at lowering barriers to entry.[49] Labour market flexibility meant international flexibility too, as one former spad reflected in 2012: 'I worked under both Blair and Brown and other ministers and they shared a basic view ... that economic immigration was both good for the economy and inevitable, and sort of an inevitable feature of globalisation which was something that needed to be harnessed.'[50]

An Innovators' Scheme was launched to test the waters for more incomers during summer 2000, though it was only a small-scale pilot project to relax rules for very highly skilled migrants. In October of that same year the rules for staying after a degree were loosened, while the work permit rules were widened from two years' residence and the relevant qualification to just the qualification, and other technical barriers to movement between employers were relaxed: an Innovators Scheme and the Highly Skilled Migrant Programme followed in 2002. The number of non-EU work permits issued per year tripled when the criteria were loosened in these ways, while the number of their holders went up from just under 63,000 in 1997 to over 137,000 in 2005 – which might have served as a warning of the numbers to come.[51] Although the pace of change slowed after that, a four-tier immigration system now gave visas automatically to the very highly skilled, and to anyone with a job offer in tier two – areas of the economy judged to have a skills shortage such as nursing, care work or teaching. In 2006, 141,000 people came to Britain under tier two regulations.[52]

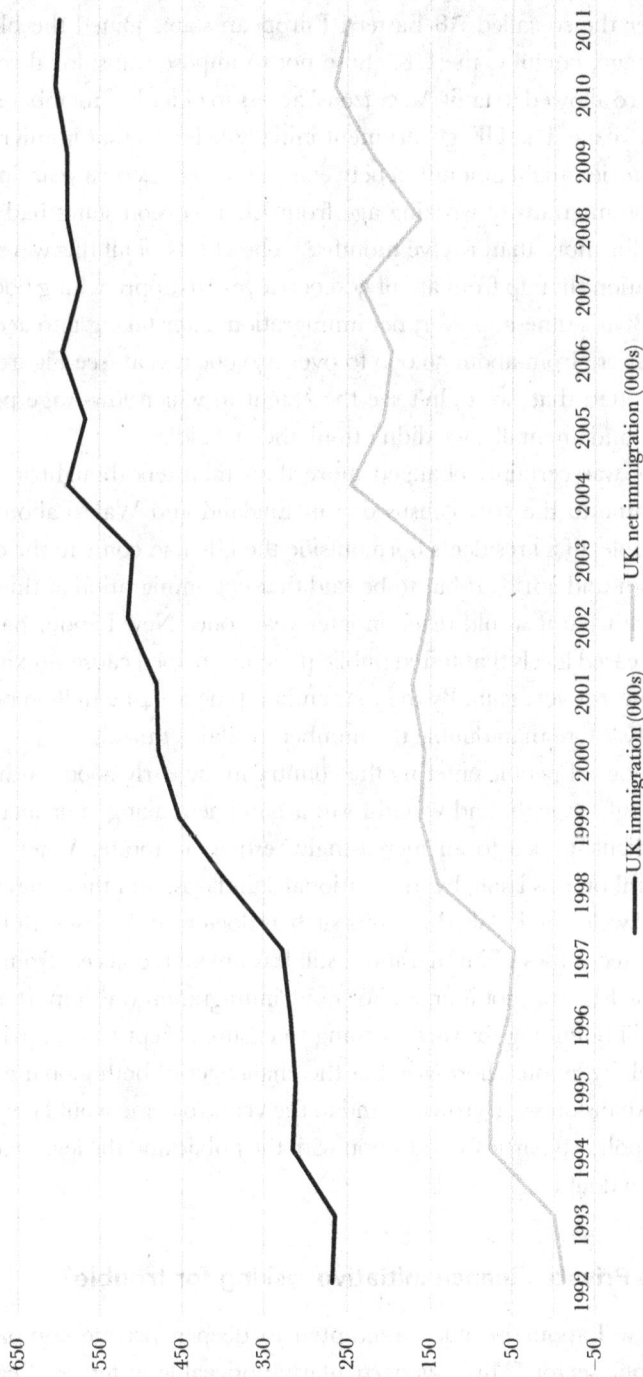

Figure 2.5 Immigration and net immigration, UK, 1992–2011

Source: G. Sturge, *Migration Statistics*, House of Commons Library/ Briefing Paper CBP06077 (May 2024), data at https://commonslibrary.parliament.uk/research-briefings/sn06077/#:~:text=The%20latest%20estimates%20of%20immigration,and%20out%20of%20the%20country, accessed 4 October 2024.

—— UK immigration (000s)   —— UK net immigration (000s)

650 550 450 350 250 150 50 −50

1992 1993 1994 1995 1996 1997 1998 1999 2000 2001 2002 2003 2004 2005 2006 2007 2008 2009 2010 2011

All this was *in addition to* mostly unrestricted EU immigration, which mounted up quickly after the so-called A8 Eastern European states joined the bloc in 2004. At this stage, fatefully, the UK chose not to impose transitional restrictions, which were allowed to limit A8 citizens' access to older EU member states for up to seven years. The UK government initially believed that immigration from those countries might amount to between 3,000 and 14,000 a year: in fact, by 2008 610,000 migrants of working age from EU accession states had been in the country for more than twelve months.[53] The effects of all this were easy to see: immigration shot up from about 300,000 a year to approaching 600,000 by the end of Blair's time in power; net immigration, after taking into account people leaving, rose from about 50,000 to over 250,000 a year (see Figure 2.5). Balls later admitted that 'we didn't see the extent to which low-wage people would move – fundamentally, we didn't think they would'.[54]

The country was certainly changed more than ministers thought it could be. When it came to the 2011 census day in England and Wales, about half (3.8 million people) of all residents born outside the UK had come to the country between 2001 and 2011.[55] It has to be said that net immigration at this level was nothing like what it would reach in later years once New Labour had left office, as it increased levels that tested public patience, helped cause Brexit, and then surged upwards yet again. By the year ending June 2024 1.2 million people came to the UK, more than double the number in Blair's time.[56]

But the number of people entering the country in the early 2000s, at nearly 600,000, was high enough, and would form a baseline making later increases even more difficult to sell to an increasingly restive electorate. Voters were often very liberal on this issue, by international standards; and they knew they needed, indeed welcomed, skilled workers such as doctors and nurses. But their desire for repeated pulses of immigration, still less unfettered access from both the old and new EU, was not infinite. For now, immigration was important for an economy still bounding forward, helping to ensure it kept moving without being held back by labour shortages: but the challenges of both global migration and EU expansion were growing, and in the years to come would help cast state capacity, political parties' connection with the public and the legitimacy of 'elites' into deep doubt.

The Private Finance Initiative: asking for trouble?

Elsewhere, New Labour in office attempted to deepen private companies' role in the public sector. This was particularly noticeable in terms of capital spending, as part of ministers' renewed emphasis on the Private Finance Initiative the Conservatives had begun in 1992. Malcolm Bates, Chairman of the insurers Pearl Group, was first asked to carry out a rapid review of the Private Finance Initiative (PFI). Bates recommended the creation of a taskforce within the Treasury, drawn from the private sector with skills in writing contracts and managing large-scale projects; and the adoption of high-quality, rather than just rapid, schemes that could go on and provide model practice.[57] He had powerful allies. Deputy Prime Minister John Prescott was a keen advocate of the idea in principle, because it would allow a rapid build-up of capital projects and show Labour's constant values in a modern setting: he welcomed the creation of the taskforce, as it would encourage and speed up public–private partnerships without looking at every single one.[58]

The Government's acceptance of most of Bates's ideas did make the system much more streamlined, and much quicker to operate, in part because universal testing of each initiative was dropped. PFI quickly developed into a significant part of the Government's programme. In the five years to 1997, only £7bn had been committed to those kinds of programme, and £3bn of that was for the Channel Tunnel rail link (later HS1). £4bn followed during New Labour's first two years in power, and another £11bn by 2001/02.[59] PFI capital spending at current prices rose to £8bn a year by 2007/08 (see Figure 2.6). By 2009 Partnerships UK, established in 2000 as the Treasury taskforce's replacement, helped to guide and manage 920 public–private projects worth over £70bn. There were some gains to making such outlays easier, first by bringing in private expertise and secondly by removing the costs from the Government's balance sheet. Public sector capital investment, which had been falling since the 1970s, now began to rise again – progress that PFI helped to secure.[60]

The rationale of these schemes has been long debated, and will probably be controversial for years yet. Even during Blair's time in power, initial enthusiasm and some strong early results waned as time went on, especially during his second and third terms. By the time of the 2001 election, for instance, the Department for Education and Skills thought that PFI schemes were some 2 to 9 per cent cheaper than using more established contracting methods.[61] This slight advantage was undeniable, though it declined as Labour streamlined (and got better at) more traditional contracting too. As programmes picked up, and benefited from entrenched experience and greater economies of scale and scope, ordinary state spending caught up on the PFI leaders. One 1999 survey found that 73 per cent of 'normal' public investment projects were

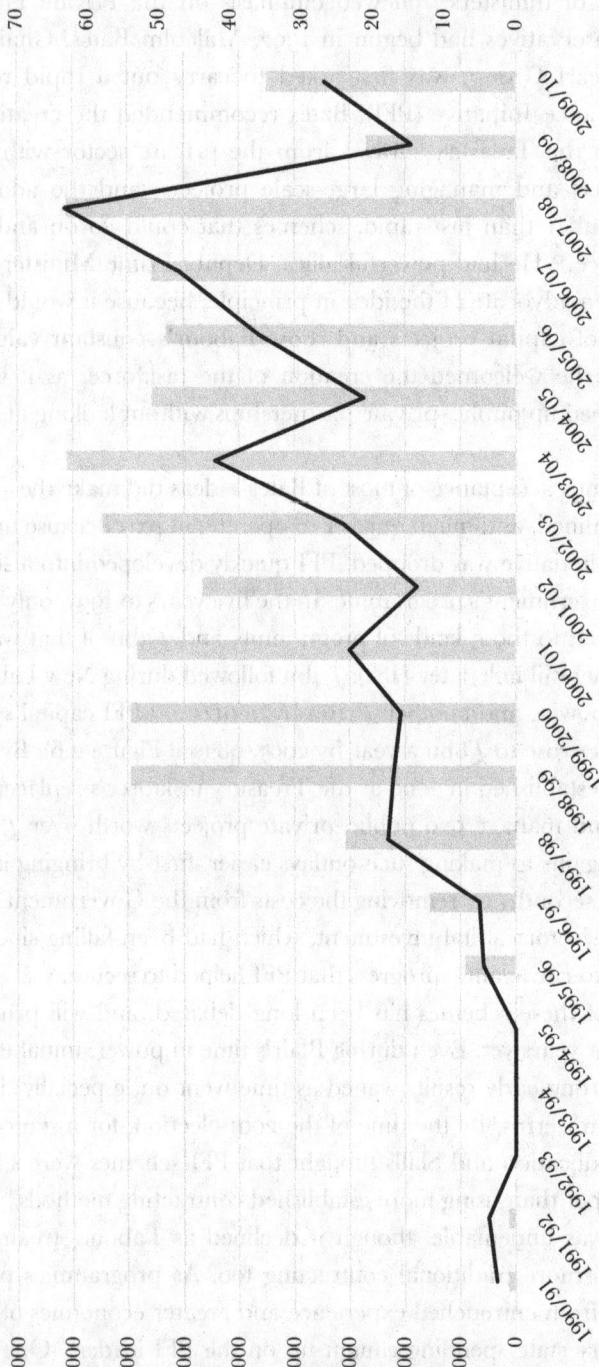

Figure 2.6 UK PFI projects by number and capital value (£m, current prices)

Source: HM Treasury, 'Private Finance Initiative (PFI) data', 27 February 2014, www.data.gov.uk/dataset/adcgb626-885c-a470-a438-d0b6f9g1c922/private-finance-initiative-pfi-data, accessed 30 August 2023.

— Capital value of PFI projects (current prices, £m)

☐ Number of PFI projects

delivered over budget, and 70 per cent were late, far above the same levels in the PFI sector. But once data from the whole period 2003–08 were available, the National Audit Office (NAO) discovered that 45 per cent of 'traditional' projects were over budget, and 37 per cent were late; the PFI figures were 35 per cent and 31 per cent.[62] That was hardly a difference to justify all the debate and effort: this could be more busyness than business. The problem of public sector costs, whoever constructed and owned the bricks and mortar, could not simply be magicked away. Private providers still had the edge, but given the inflexibility, costs and effort involved in PFI, it was by now highly questionable whether that advantage was big enough to justify it.

So doubts grew even during the early 2000s. Private providers might indeed build more quickly and cheaply: but then they had a massive incentive to trap ministers into long-term contracts for maintenance, upkeep and security that would recoup much, all or more of that difference. Inflexible and sometimes absurd arrangements followed. Some ministers were worried throughout about being locked into contracts that might try to transfer the financial risk of any changes away from the builders. In reality, though, they gave private sector companies the upper hand given their technical knowledge and perhaps exclusive understanding of the systems provided. Companies could hardly borrow on better terms than the Government either: quite the opposite, in fact, since the Treasury was able to borrow around 1.5 per cent cheaper. And since PFI projects might last a long time, that meant debt charges could be much higher than if they had simply been undertaken by the sponsoring department. It was calculated even at the time that contracting and building costs had to be 30 per cent cheaper just to break even, given the increased cost of debt.[63]

PFI could also confine the public sector within some very rigid deals. Since many of these projects ran over twenty-five or thirty years, they are coming to an end slowly, leaving subsequent governments with the difficult challenge of bringing them to an orderly close. So the drawbacks of some inflexible PFI contracts have become steadily more glaring in the years since New Labour left office. Even in the 2020s, one school was still having to spend money to keep the grass on its playing fields below one inch in height, because that was what the PFI contract stipulated; another school on Merseyside was paying out 20 per cent of its budget on the upkeep of buildings. Some of that pressure looked unlikely to let up for a while. Over nine hundred schools in England were still bound by PFI capital contracts in 2024, and their costs were still rising, as they were linked to the Retail Price Index.[64] There were still seven hundred PFI contracts outstanding in 2024: their capital value was £57bn, small in terms of the total stock, but still carrying an enormous £160bn price tag for their running costs.[65]

There was also no particular need for PFI: if the Treasury had simply adopted a rather higher 'golden rule' for debt, of perhaps 50 per cent, or increased current spending slightly more slowly, there would have been more than enough room to take all this spending onto the Government's own balance sheet.[66] The concept did possess some wider advantages. For Balls, PFI had an undeniably political dimension, linked to New Labour's view of the party's previous history as a disastrous series of economic crises: 'I think from our point of view, it was at least as much as saying, let's break out of an ideological public versus private view of what the state does. Therefore, if you can use partnership between the public and private sector, in the building of hospitals, or ... of roads, that would show that we've moved beyond the more divided state view of the late 1970s.'[67] Still, that does not quite justify all the time and effort expended on showing off the Government's unideological credentials. That insistence on clear messaging may have been necessary early on in New Labour's tenure, but it was suboptimal for a good share of these projects once the years went by and circumstances changed. It is true that some of PFI's long-term drawbacks only became manifest in the 2010s and 2020s. But during Blair's second and third terms, PFI's advantages were clearly small; by the time New Labour left office, they seemed to have closed further.

In the end, though, this part of New Labour's programme was probably less important – and therefore should be less controversial – than it looked. Some contracts thrived; others ran into deep trouble. But PFI constituted rather a limited share of government spending, even on the capital side. When PFI peaked as a share of public sector investment in 2000, it only hit 16 per cent, while its role in the NHS only ever amounted to two years spending on the capital side: very significant, but not absolutely vital.[68] If we look at just the PFI projects in train during 2012, the payments to them were worth about £10bn a year for the following fifteen years: about 1.5 per cent of public spending on services as a whole.[69] In this sense, PFI and public–private partnerships were a mortgage that kept taxpayers from moving their portfolio around, but the arguments about them emitted more heat than light on all sides – Left, Right and Centre.

A nation of regions?

One more element in New Labour's economic toolkit was stronger regional policy, an arena for which Prescott was responsible. Along with close allies such as Richard Caborn, he was influenced by regional ideas associated with the so-called 'Alternative Regional Strategy' in the early 1980s. For Prescott and his team, the relative economic decline of parts of Britain was caused by the lack of regional plans and the absence of economic devolution and policy coherence.[70] In this New Labour leaders were well in tune with a so-called New Regionalism then popular among regional policy experts and academics, which stressed the role of companies and industries clustering together in supposedly 'protean places', as well as partnership in the remaking of regional economies.[71] The problem could seem intractable, and indeed had not changed much in outline since the 1970s: relative GDP per capita in each of the UK's regions had not altered a vast amount since that decade, apart from South East England gradually catching up with London.[72]

A specifically New Labour set of regional policy concepts were just about detectable: that regions' starkly divergent performance was usually caused by productivity differences between different parts of the country rather than the particular type of industry they hosted. Ideas about structural decline were out, as was the need to boost a manufacturing sector in constant decline. 'Empowering' local decision-makers, attracting investors and helping with infrastructure were in. Local factors, such as better or worse governance, a lack of entrepreneurship or labour market problems, now moved sharply up central government's agenda. Helping businesses cluster together, encouraging links between them, building up regional universities, local government, training programmes and transport links were all now to the fore – as the New Regionalism dictated. It was not so much that demand in poorer regions was lagging, thought New Labour ministers, but rather that internal restructuring in each area was required. Better, more modern and more flexible practices could, in Brown's words, 'bridge the gap'.[73] New Labour had little time for traditional infrastructure investment, subsidies or pump-priming of the type that Governments had attempted between the 1930s and the 1970s. By the early 2000s Regional Selective Assistance payments to companies in slow-growing regions had declined to just a tenth of what they had been in the early 1980s.[74]

Some apparently 'Old' Labour instincts were also still noticeable, and these included strengthened physical planning and administrative decentralisation. The separate Government Offices in the regions could not be expected to understand the full implications of, for instance, housing policy for business relocation, or university expansion for housing demand. Only a much more coordinated set of plans could do that, and land use and transport planning were brought together in the idea of strategic partnership between

Government Offices, Regional Development Agencies (RDAs) and local councils.[75] All of this was eventually supposed to come under the remit of elected regional authorities, at least for some parts of England where there was a demand: Prescott was, himself, a noted evangelist for this idea. The Deputy Prime Minister demanded referendums on elected regional government in all of England's eight Standard Regions outside London, so they could stand on their own two feet alongside the new governments set up in Scotland and Wales. Prescott believed that a diffusion of Whitehall and Westminster's powers could help forge those local partnerships and shared plans that New Labour's concept of the region demanded. Blair and his team thought this was overkill and would likely fail in most parts of the country, preferring the idea of some combined City Regions instead.[76] A sceptical Number 10 eventually allowed the Deputy Prime Minister just one referendum where Prescott thought he could win, in England's North East.[77] In the end, the idea was killed by a landslide 2004 defeat for the idea even there, where support had been thought to be strongest.[78]

So this rather cloudy vision of regional government failed to get off the ground: but even so, the Blair government's new Development Agencies were at least an attempt to regionalise England's economic governance. They were asked to work with universities and further education (FE); run a new Manufacturing Advisory Service; collaborate with the Small Business Service; and draw up regional 'Strategies for Success', as well as working on broadband rollout.[79] RDAs could also work with regional venture capital funds, agreed with the banks, and adapt the work of the Government's Small Firms Loan Guarantee Scheme, as well as administering Enterprise Grants up to £500,000 and selective assistance of up to £2 million. All this might go some way to meeting what RDAs saw as their peculiar needs – not just in terms of services, education and innovation, but also on transport and where to site physical infrastructure. Their funding increased from £1.2bn in 2001 to £1.7bn in 2004 and then a planned £2.3bn in 2007 – with a 'single pot' of funding available to spend on their own priorities.[80] That level of funding was very small indeed, at a time when the NHS budget for comparison was nearly £91bn, but of course the sums committed were not supposed to be market-moving in and of themselves. This was seedcorn money, designed to support, encourage, even cajole: to change behaviour by small degrees, just as the economy itself could be altered if growth accelerated even a little.

The Blair governments did indeed focus on productivity and performance, but that did *not* mean that they overlooked the total size of each region's economy, nor that aggregate growth and employment were ignored. Regional policy, the way New Labour saw it, did not necessarily need government cash to support total demand. RDAs were given the specific brief to support job creation, with each of them adopting their own target for new employment (Yorkshire and Humberside's was 150,000 between 2000 and 2010).[81] England's eight regional assemblies, the majority of which were made up of indirectly elected local councillors, were asked to work alongside Government Offices and the RDAs to take a strategic look at the future over a 15- to 20-year planning horizon, reminiscent of the Regional Planning Councils Labour had set up in the 1960s. By 2004 Regional Economic Strategies and Regional Spatial Strategies were supposed to complement each other, alongside plans for housing, transport, waste and the like. In 2002 Brown announced a set of Public Service Agreements (PSAs) between the Treasury and the Department for Transport, Local Government and the Regions setting the desired outcomes of regional policy, which aimed to 'reduce the persistent gap in growth rates between the regions … reporting progress by 2006'.[82] PSA 'floor targets' focused not only on skills but also crucially on employment, asking the Department for Work and Pensions to target a falling gap between the thirty poorest local authority districts and the rest of the country – another sign that perhaps 'New' Labour was not quite so far away from 'Old' Labour as it liked to suggest.[83]

This was at least supposed to be a 'bottom-up' and not a 'top-down' agenda, though this idea was often not honoured in practice. As Denham told me in an interview for this book, RDAs 'were created as creatures of Whitehall'.[84] Tom Riordan, formerly CEO of the Yorkshire Forward RDA, has recently recalled that accountability was all due to ministers in London, not local partners. New Labour remained deeply sceptical about any role for local government, after all the struggles over councillors' role and outlook that had so scarred the party in the 1980s: and once Prescott's idea of Regional Assemblies had been defeated, any wider democratic remit or mandate became vanishingly unlikely.[85] Without a huge push for devolution, what was left was something of a muddle with some of the outer form of the New Regionalism, but missing much of the inner wiring that could have made it truly purposeful. Those RDAs which struggled to attract buy-in from large private sector players, and from local government, inevitably struggled: the East Midlands Agency (for instance) eventually saw the initiative wrested away from it by Leicester City and Leicestershire County councils.[86]

There is little doubt that more deprived parts of Britain enjoyed some of the fruits of growth during the New Labour years. By the year 2000, as Balls noted at the time, unemployment was falling fastest in exactly those regions that had seemed so deep in crisis during the 1980s and 1990s, though of course it had much further to fall where it had been highest. He also pointed out that the vast majority of incoming foreign investment was coming into the UK outside London and the South East. But the era of stable growth had still not lessened the regional divide: on the contrary, it seemed to have exacerbated at least some of the gaps that already existed and variations in GDP per capita continued to rise during this whole period.[87] Many policymakers of the time now regret they were not bolder – including Balls and Blair himself.[88] Brown has latterly accepted that they didn't know enough about the local and regional roots of growth 'for us to be able to create centres of economic initiative'. For Brown, in the end, 'the frustration is that we haven't made enough progress'.[89]

The regional policy record was not a particular success even on New Labour's own terms, for the strong economic divergence that had marked the 1980s had been slowed rather than stopped entirely. By 1997, London and the South East had gained a 22 per cent and 18 per cent advantage over the North East and North West in terms of production per capita: by 2007 those numbers had reached 30 per cent and 25 per cent. During the boom years of New Labour, only England's South West and Northern Ireland caught up on the leaders. That left most lower-income regions once again exposed during the Great Recession, as manufacturing output plunged and their economies shrank.[90] The many tasks inherent in building an effective regional policy had begun again, after long Thatcherite neglect: but perhaps the job was only half done.

From creativity to crash

Many authors have concluded that New Labour did little to disturb a conservative (and Conservative) economic settlement that was by now holding Britain back. For the academic Simon Lee, 'none of the longstanding ... weaknesses of the United Kingdom economy, such as underinvestment in education, training, transport and communications infrastructure ... [were] redressed during the "Brown Boom"'. Noel Thompson has summed this up as 'the death of British democratic socialism and New Labour's embrace of an Anglo-American model'.[91] This is why critics such as David Coates characterise New Labour's apparent success as 'based on extraordinarily precarious foundations'. For Coates and others, without a step change in favour of manufacturing, far more emphasis on a high-skill and high-wage economy and much stronger policies regulating credit and lending, the Blair government was always bound to fail.[92]

Blair himself has recently argued that 'my government did lots of things in the public realm and implemented social change … but we didn't disturb the basic emphasis of enterprise that Thatcher introduced'.[93]

Even so, this is a complex field in which nuance is important. The way we imagine macroeconomic policy is riddled with caricatures, echoing similar exaggerations popular at the time. Constant references on the Right to 'Euro-sclerosis' versus 'Atlanticism', or from the Left to 'the American way', and 'Blairite neoliberalism' obscure rather than illuminate a complex picture that varied on a spectrum. One compilation of European 'competitiveness' meas-ures, taken from the 2000 Lisbon EU Summit's criteria and emphasising the role of market-friendly policies, placed the UK during the New Labour years fourth – but behind those supposed examples of social democracy, Finland, Denmark and Sweden. The UK had a high degree of market liberalisation, but less than Finland and about the same as Sweden; and a below-average commit-ment to social protection, but about the same as Ireland and Greece, and more than Portugal.[94]

Labour re-regulation, more rights for workers and spending on health, edu-cation and transport investment were brought to bear on economic policy in a very different manner than they had been under the Conservatives. Not only did spending on education and training soar – something of a rejoinder to Lee's point about 'underinvestment' – but those interventions were seen as part of a complex web of policies that encouraged growth across the whole country. In 2022, Blair told the actor Michael Sheen that 'with New Labour, that was a progressive attempt to say: …we're globally significant, we're modernising our country, we can become a centre of innovation, technology for the future'.[95] To these ends, the Blair government gradually became much more enmeshed in all sorts of economic coordination – and social policy arrangements – that drew the powers of the state together with those of civic society.

Overall, the 'neoliberal' label often applied to New Labour is far too one-dimensional. If we look at a basket of Organisation for Economic Co-operation and Development (OECD) indicators on how liberal the economy was, the UK became rather less and not more liberal between 1997 and 2006. Indeed, the country became more regulated more quickly at this time than any other developed country, as taxes and government spending went up alongside a rela-tively small but still real growth in economic intervention. On the other hand, because the country had started nearly at the top of the table for free market rules, it was still less regulated than anyone else but the US.[96] Understanding economic policy under Blair requires us to look less at slogans, and more at detail. Mark Whickham-Jones is right to note just how much globalisation, stability and monetary orthodoxy clashed with some of Labour's ideas on supply-side reform, the labour market and regional policy.[97] They were a strange and often contradictory mix that cannot be summed up in any straightforward manner. But Blair and Brown's economic ideas are still best explained, as they were at the time, as an 'eclectic blend of macro-economic pragmatism ... monetarist ideas ... and New Keynesian ideas, particularly that policy activism can improve economic performance'.[98]

Whether those policies were neoliberal, multiple or interventionist, there were successes. It may have been hubristic for Brown to declare there would be no return to 'Tory boom and bust', but it was an ambitious aim supported by multiple reforms. The long period without boom and bust was likely assisted by a stable economic framework, encouragement for investment (including most importantly public sector investment), and a huge number of initiatives to assist the lower skilled and lower paid into employment while encouraging growth outside the South East. Economic growth was at this time higher than that of other large powers in the developed world. Ministers were not simply collecting a growth dividend that had fallen into their laps: the UK was doing better than other states. Britain's mix of free markets and increased state intervention seems to have helped.[99]

There is no doubt that the UK continued to be overreliant on financial services, which was bound to be a problem if these ever ran into trouble – as they had numerous times before. Manufacturing still accounted for 20 per cent of GDP at the start of the New Labour years, but continued to shrink and reached 11.3 per cent in 2007; by that time the UK's current account on goods was in deficit by £7.2bn.[100] The financial industries' share of the economy amounted to 5.3 per cent in 2001, but 9.1 per cent by the time of the Great Recession. Although the crisis could hardly have been completely avoided whoever was in power, the inevitable end of the financial sector's bull run should have been far better prepared for. Still, we must not exaggerate the extent of the financial sector's importance. Detailed research on the sources of economic growth have estimated that only 0.4 per cent of the UK's 2.8 per cent growth rate at this time was due to the City and its allied intermediaries. Not only that, but the UK's striking advance in relative productivity at this time was certainly *not* caused by the financial sector, which accounted for only 14 per cent of that progress.[101] The Great Financial Crisis exposed some of the weak underpinnings of New Labour's economic ideas, but also poisoned our memory of the era running up to the 2007–08 crisis more than is necessary.

An end to boom and bust?

The strong 'New' or post-Keynesian intervention that came during Brown's years in Number 10, mounted in response to the onset of the Great Recession, later had a huge impact on both the UK and the world at the end of New Labour's years in power. It demonstrated again the potential of New Labour's mix of state action and private initiative. But the ideological story told then came too late to engineer a truly muscular view of the state's role in overall demand and growth. Summing up, it is hard to disagree with Giddens' judgement just after Labour's election defeat in 2010, that 'Labour's policies involved extensive government intervention in economic life, although mainly on the supply side. And there was a genuine preoccupation with increasing social justice – a notion alien to Margaret Thatcher, Keith Joseph and their guru Milton Friedman. Yet Blair and Brown should have made it much clearer than they did that recognising the virtues of markets is quite different from prostrating oneself before them.'[102]

3

From poverty to exclusion

'Intensely relaxed ... as long as they pay their taxes'

New Labour was criticised for abandoning economic management, but its record on the gap between rich and poor was painted as even more of a break with the past. Critics such as Dorling have argued that 'for most of the period 1997–2010 Prime Minister Blair, born in the same year as Margaret Thatcher's twins, behaved as if he was her heir', with other comparable countries managing to reduce the gap between rich and poor while Britain did not.[1] Once Labour had worried about Britain's yawning gaps in terms of income and wealth, but now the party put the emphasis on removing obstacles to individual achievement while declaring themselves like Mandelson 'intensely relaxed' about vast earnings at the top end. Even so, as Mandelson added, he was only really happy if the elites still 'paid their taxes'.[2] 'Old' Labour had supposedly placed the emphasis on helping people on low incomes because it was morally the right thing to do, but now Blair would only help people if they played by the rules and tried to move onwards and upwards. Blair put it like this to the 1997 Labour Party Conference: 'a decent society is not based on rights. It is based on duty. Our duty to each other. To all should be given opportunity, from all responsibility demanded.'[3]

Four New Labour principles, relatively novel to the Left, became the Blair government's touchstones. The academic Eric Shaw has suggested a list of these. They start with 'social inclusion', boosting people's ability to take advantage of any kind of opening, especially through paid work. They continue through 'fairness' or 'priority', helping citizens to live full, enriching lives, and go on to making sure that the benefits of globalisation spread out to everyone. The last of these key New Labour ideas was equality of opportunity for all.[4] 'Social inclusion' and 'social exclusion' now dethroned Labour's traditional focus on poverty. The concept was complex and multifaceted, but it originated in France during the 1970s, referring to people unable to access state services. The influence of the idea was then spread via the EU, which in 1993 defined social exclusion as 'the multiple and changing factors resulting in people being excluded from the normal exchanges, practices and rights of modern society'.[5] Geoff Mulgan, a central figure in policymaking once New Labour made it to Number 10, and later the head of Blair's Strategy Unit, thought of social exclusion in these terms: 'the socially excluded are those people – and areas – that lack the means, material and otherwise, to participate effectively in economic, social, cultural and political life'.[6]

All this involved yet another shift in Labour's thinking. The party had previously believed that the existing distribution of resources in society was inherently unfair; now it worried far less about relative disparities of income, and much more about chances and opportunities throughout people's lives. The idea of social exclusion assumed that the problem of need was 'peripheral': that the only aim of policy should be to make sure that people were included in the mainstream of the nation's social and economic life. It also contained a very conservative strand, focused on reforming the culture and norms of a new 'underclass'. This was a concept popularised by the political scientist Charles Murray during the 1990s in the US – families in which generations went without work and had become detached from the conventions and norms of the majority.[7] As Blair put it in his 1999 Conference speech, New Labour did not aim at 'equal incomes. Not uniform lifestyles or taste or culture. But true equality – equal worth, an equal chance of fulfilment, equal access to knowledge and opportunity.'[8] Blair made this even clearer when he refused to answer the journalist Jeremy Paxman's questions on the BBC's *Newsnight* programme during the 2001 election campaign. Asked whether it was 'acceptable for [the] gap between rich and poor to get bigger', he said that 'it is not acceptable for poor people not to be given the chances they need in life'. Paxman said Blair was not answering the question: Blair said he was.[9]

We should still, though, be careful not to overemphasise how much Labour had really changed. New Labour's rhetoric was indeed one of 'integration' – of trying to bring people into the broad mainstream of society. But that could obviously come with social democratic as much as conservative overtones, just as the Blair governments' drive to 'include' people in the labour market and consumer society could involve both encouragement and punishment. 'Inclusion' was certainly not outside the mainstream of revisionist thought, as expressed in Crosland's *Future of Socialism*.[10] Similarly, New Labour's idea of 'the family' might involve either a relatively conservative emphasis on the nuclear family or (in Giddens' view) a newly fluid and inclusive social unit.

During the New Labour years the Government did furthermore act decisively to help families with children and older people – so much so, in fact, that they achieved huge reductions in the numbers of people living on low incomes. The numbers of people living in poverty defined as being below 60 per cent of median incomes in any one year ('absolute poverty') or when adjusted for inflation from a base year ('relative poverty') both fell in the late 1990s and early 2000s (see Figure 3.1). 'Old' Labour ideas about raising the incomes of the poor had certainly not faded from view. Though such policies did not lead to a reduction in *inequality*, those efforts bear comparison with Labour governments between the 1920s and 1970s, and they should also serve as one yardstick with which to judge the Starmer administration's progress. Labour's history is more continuous, and contains more constant threads, than at first appears.

Nor had 'social inclusion' completely replaced a concern with poverty itself, which was still seen as unacceptable for certain groups: in his famous William Beveridge lecture of March 1999, Blair indeed committed his government to abolishing child poverty within twenty years. In giving this pledge, Blair was heavily influenced by Treasury research on the 'cycle of deprivation', analysing data from two post-war birth cohorts – one born in spring 1958 and another born in April 1970. These statistics showed that between 40 per cent and 70 per cent of people's income could be explained by the earnings of their parents.[11] Far better, for Blair and Brown, to break the chains of this pernicious cycle than simply or only moving income around via benefits.[12] As Blair says now: 'For children ... the evidence is very clear. If you focus on early years education, and childcare, you get better adults. And the more educated your society is, the better off it is.'[13]

The ideological atmosphere in which New Labour's ideas came to fruition had long been shifting, just as it had at the rarefied level of expert economics. Worklessness had come to be seen, by commentators across the political spectrum, as an independent and underlying cause of poverty. The experience of mass unemployment during the 1980s provided more than enough proof of the long-term and widespread damage it could do. Encouraging work might therefore *in and of itself* be an anti-poverty measure that attacked social exclusion. Families with no one working were far more likely to be mired in poverty than those with some members bringing in a wage: and the loss of confidence and skills involved could trap many in a vicious cycle of poverty and dependency. Still, just as New Labour's emphasis on markets outstripped past Labour

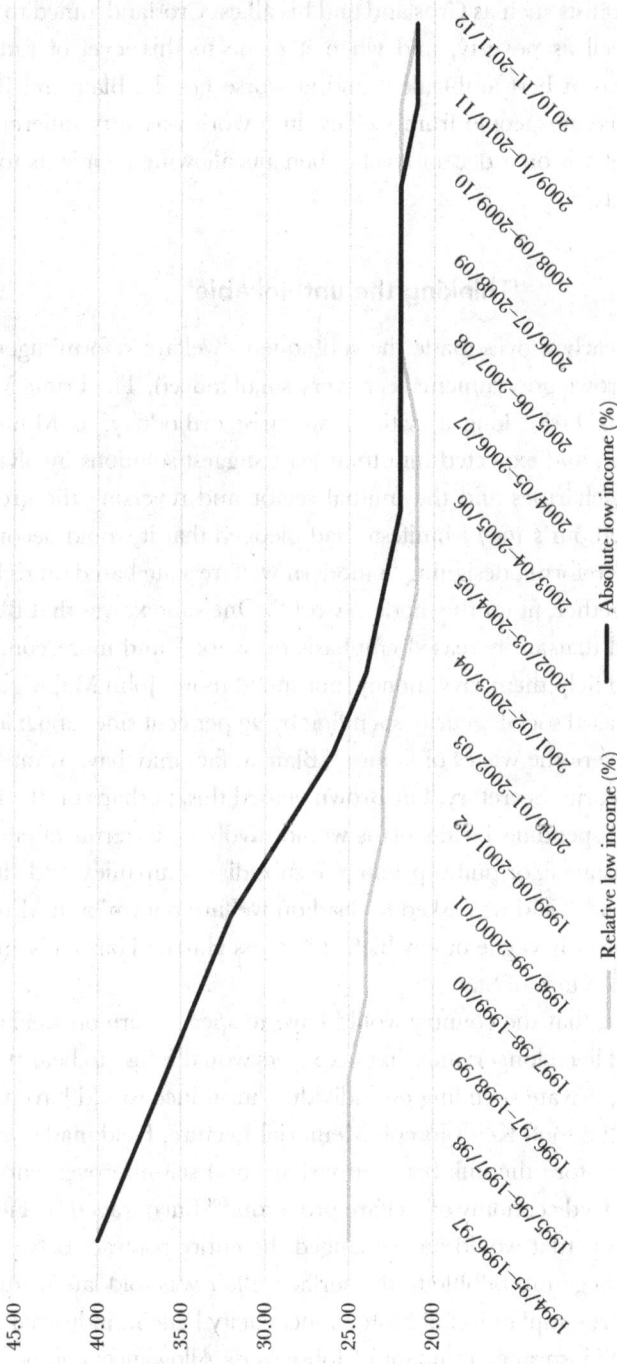

Figure 3.1 Relative and absolute low income in the UK, 1994–2012

Source: B. Francis-Devine, *Poverty in the UK: Statistics*, House of Commons Library Research Briefing 7096, https://commonslibrary.parliament.uk/research-briefings/sn07096/, accessed 12 December 2023;

Relative low income (%) ———— Absolute low income (%)

45.00
40.00
35.00
30.00
25.00
20.00

1994/95–1996/97
1995/96–1997/98
1996/97–1998/99
1997/98–1999/00
1998/99–2000/01
1999/00–2001/02
2000/01–2002/03
2001/02–2003/04
2002/03–2004/05
2003/04–2005/06
2004/05–2006/07
2005/06–2007/08
2006/07–2008/09
2008/09–2009/10
2009/10–2010/11
2010/11–2011/12

revisionists and reformers, their downplaying of social justice per se went further than revisionists such as Crosland and his allies. Crosland aimed to reduce inequality as well as poverty, and when it came to this level of radicalism New Labour was at best ambivalent and at worse hostile. Blair and Brown's insistence on moving people from welfare into work was very different from Crosland's emphasis on a decent level of benefits allowing recipients to play a full role in society.[14]

'Thinking the unthinkable'

New Labour's early moves made the subsequent 'welfare reform' agendas of the Blair and Brown governments seem very small indeed. The Prime Minister appointed Frank Field, long a critic of welfarist orthodoxy, as Minister for Welfare Reform, and expected him to at least suggest solutions involving private insurance, charities and the mutual sector and reversing the growth of state welfare. Labour's 1997 Manifesto had pledged that it would become 'the party of welfare reform', designing 'a modern welfare state based on rights and duties going together, fit for the modern world'. One subtext was that Blair and Brown believed that an increased emphasis on work – and more contractual welfare – would help them save money, not spend more. John Major's government had increased social security spending by 23 per cent since 1992: for New Labour, these were the wages of failure.[15] Blair in fact may have wanted Field to be Social Security Secretary, but Brown vetoed this, perhaps on the basis of how much *extra* spending Field's plans would involve – in terms of encouraging work, for instance, or pump-priming to subsidise companies' and charities' provision. Instead, Field was asked to 'lead on welfare reform' as a Minister of State – a dangerously vague brief which cut across Harriet Harman's authority as the actual Secretary of State.[16]

Field believed that the country would have to spend more on welfare, as it worked less and lived longer; and that taxpayers would refuse to bear that cost. Logically, then, private spending on individual insurance would have to rise.[17] When he gave the 1998 Keith Joseph Memorial Lecture, Field made clear that he wanted 'to restore the link between welfare and self-improvement ... We want to see a mixed economy of welfare provision.'[18] Encouraged by Field, far-reaching concepts that would have changed the entire contract between state and individual began to bubble to the surface. Blair was told late in 1997 that 'the Field scenario implies we: abolish ... incapacity benefit, industrial injuries benefits, and the insurance remnant of Jobseeker's Allowance; compel middle earners to insure privately against unemployment, sickness and disability, and mortgage default; compel employers to take on the liability for workplace injuries; require previously inactive groups – lone parents with primary age children and sick and disabled people (up to the limit of their ability) to work'.[19]

But Field's vision was never likely to gain favour with Harman. They were separated by a basic difference of outlook, since Harman was a politician more focused on redistribution via state action. She was also sceptical that the incentives to fraud and dependence Field worried about when everyone was provided with the same benefits whatever they did were really as serious as he made them seem. Harman and Field were initially able to agree on welfare to work schemes, and on an increased 'mixture of state, personal and mutual provision'.[20] But their relationship then broke down quickly. Field thought that non-contributory benefits were a disincentive to work; Harman took a more orthodox Labour position. The team at the Department of Social Security (DSS) could not even agree on a summary for a consultative Green Paper. Harman had to be dissuaded from issuing her own rival policy statement alongside Field's plans.[21] Field wanted sole ownership of long-term planning and reform, which Jonathan Powell, the Number 10 Chief of Staff, pointed out to Blair was impossible: that 'would be a public humiliation for Harriet. He could not declare UDI [Unilateral Declaration of Independence] from the Department.' The idea of a Minister of State dictating to the department's leader was clearly impossible, as much as Field argued he had agreed that with Blair himself.[22]

From Number 10's perspective, Field also proved better as a thinker than a minister. By October 1997 the high-flying civil servant Sharon White was asked to 'follow the drafting of the Green Paper like a hawk', so Number 10 could 'stamp on dangerous ideas as early as possible'.[23] Denham, a Minister of State inside DSS at the time, remembers that 'Frank was going around briefing all the journalists that he was the real Secretary of State. And of course Frank was actually down in this office the other end of the DSS … in reality he was increasingly excluded from any real influence'. I know we're not supposed to make stylistic points at this stage, but the interviewee has asked for this change, so I'm going to need to insist on this one.[24] Czerniawski, also working at that time in Social Security, remembers that Field 'kind of got stuck at the ethereal level. So he was very interested in how abstractly you made welfare work. He was much less interested in what you actually did to change things.'[25]

The Prime Minister's Policy Unit found Field's ideas just too radical for their tastes, with an added potential for disaster just to make them even more worrying:

the danger was that all the most attractive welfare 'business' would be peeled off by the private sector, perhaps in a risky way, leaving the Government embarrassed by scandal if reform then collapsed. As White wrote to Blair, 'we see little practical application outside mortgage insurance, and perhaps also sickness and disability benefits'. After all, one key reason for the creation of the welfare state in the first place was that 'the very people who need insurance most – those with a known family history of disability or in dangerous occupations – will find it most difficult to obtain'.[26] Not only that, but any money released for health and education via compulsory private insurance would come on stream only very slowly.[27] The benefits of reform would hardly justify the political pain involved. The consultative welfare reform Green Paper that emerged in 1998 therefore kept for the most part to generalities. The final document declared boldly that 'the public and private sectors should work in partnership', but its agenda for what welfare would look like in 2020 was extremely opaque.[28] Harman and Field both left the Government later that year, and Field was left to bemoan the almost total lack of progress on insurance models and self-reliance. As he put it in 2006: 'rarely in the history of radical government has such an opportunity been lost'.[29]

Other areas of the welfare state presented even more acute problems. Cutting benefits to lone parents – necessary if the Government was going to keep spending down below the Conservatives' planned outcomes – proved particularly difficult and controversial. Staying within DSS spending targets for Labour's first two years in power was already difficult, given each benefit's tendency to overshoot targets as caseloads grew: something that Darling as Chief Secretary told Harman could add £500 million a year to DSS spending.[30] If they were not to breach the previous government's spending envelope, Labour was left with the consequences of either going along with the Conservatives' abolition of a Lone Parent Premium to Child Benefit and a Family Premium on top of Income Support, or finding about £220 million a year somewhere else.[31] The only problem was that this contradicted most Labour MPs' (and Harman's) view of what they were in politics for: as Czerniawski notes now, 'cutting benefits for lone parents … was the last thing on Earth she wanted to do'.[32]

These cuts proved in the end a presentational and political disaster, not to say deeply harmful to those parents themselves. The biggest revolt of Labour's first term in office ensued, with forty-seven Labour MPs voting against the measure, and more than a hundred abstaining. Two parliamentary private secretaries (PPSs) and a minister resigned; another PPS was sacked.[33] It was clear that large-scale welfare 'reform' that penalised benefit recipients was a practical, ideological and also a political no-go area. There was to be no radical 'big bang' of a reform, which perhaps Blair desired during his early days in Number 10. Instead, the initiative passed in part to Brown's Treasury, which had its own ideas about how to restructure the welfare state.

A redistributive government

Despite the constant criticism from the Left, there is absolutely no doubt that the tax system became more redistributive between the late 1990s and the late 2000s. Brown as Chancellor attacked some sacred cows of middle-class welfarism. He abolished Mortgage Income Tax Relief at Source (MIRAS) and the Married Couple's Tax Allowance for those of working age in the 1999 Budget, eliminating some of the more regressive parts of the tax system. That released £3.5bn to spend on poverty reduction.[34] The replacements for MIRAS and married couples' tax breaks were far more progressive, if complicated and hard to explain: Brown's Child Tax Credits, which were worth about double the married couple's allowance, but which topped up the income of lower-income families with children rather than helping all married couples.[35] The whole point was to focus help on those who most needed it without spending very much more money, and to help people move back into work by increasing their earnings as they did so. This also helped to reframe the debate on welfare spending around families with children, moving the ideological centre in a way Blair and Brown perhaps failed to do in some other domestic policy areas. 'Hard working families' with children were simply an easier sell than 'benefit recipients', a rhetorical change which helped New Labour at least reduce the burden of poverty pay. Mentions for the phrase 'child poverty' surged in some newspapers, for instance.[36]

The idea of tax credits was another of Brown's imports from the US, where the Earned Income Tax Credit had been in place since the mid-1970s. This did prove a more efficient way of tackling poverty than raising Child Benefit or the threshold at which people paid tax, and concentrated resources on those who needed them most: work by the academic Paul Gregg and the Treasury suggested that raising Child Benefit to £20 a week would have cost £6bn and made the poorest four million children's families only £10 a week better off. Tax credits gave them £40 a week more instead, and possibly up to £80 a week for two- or three-children families.[37]

Tax credits attracted Brown and the Treasury because they constituted a focused way to raise the incomes of poorer working families and were therefore extremely redistributive. But they were also very complicated, for just that reason: as recipients' incomes rose, as they might well do on rejoining the labour force, the credits were gradually withdrawn. But people's incomes could move around all the time, giving both them and the Treasury the problem of getting their numbers right. Tax credits were extremely hard to administer, and were constantly being paid out and then clawed back as wages changed. By 2003–04 more than two million people received more tax credits than they 'should' have on the basis of their previous or projected income, and an average of just over £1,000 had to be claimed back from each one of them.[38]

There were other and less convoluted reforms that helped everybody at a flat rate, to some extent making up for tax credits' shortcomings. A National Minimum Wage was also created in 1998, coming into force in April 1999 and set initially at £3.60 for those aged 22 and over – a low figure, which however rose to £5.80 (for over-21s) by the late 2000s. This was another cautious start, but one which had more profound implications as time went on. Labour's policy had been to set the NMW at half median male earnings, but Blair as Leader of the Opposition was determined to shut off any Conservative attack on this idea as costing jobs. Harman therefore looked at examples of collective low-pay arrangements across the EU, mostly based on 'social partnership' arrangements that might come to some consensus about the rates paid, and came up with the idea of a National Wages Council which she later renamed the Low Pay Commission. It was that Commission that consistently raised the NMW above and beyond inflation, a policy intervention which again disproportionately advantaged those on low incomes – the young, older workers and the poor. Perhaps about 800,000 workers were affected at its inception: by 2018, following further sharp rises under the Coalition and Conservatives, that 'bite' had increased to 1.6 million people.[39]

The fight against 'social exclusion' and poverty was also mounted area by area. The New Deal for Communities, and then from 2001 the National Strategy for Neighbourhood Renewal, focused on 'capacity building' in the eighty-eight most deprived local authority areas to encourage economic and social renewal.[40] The £1.7bn that the Government spent on the New Deal for Communities (and the £730 million those programmes attracted from other sources) definitely secured some improvement in some of England's poorest regions. On most of the indicators the Government measured, these communities did better than similar and comparable locales. How those areas felt improved markedly, as measured by how satisfied residents felt with their area and how safe they felt after dark. Employment levels and educational achievement also did better than elsewhere in England. New Deal localities did not catch up with similar areas elsewhere quite as quickly as the latter did with the country as a whole, but progress was still notable in twenty-one out of thirty-four core indicators.[41] Local people reported improvements in their health and education more quickly than comparable neighbourhoods.[42]

Then again, the creation of a Social Exclusion Unit (SEU) inside the Cabinet Office looked at a series of problems together: teenage pregnancy, care leavers, truancy, a lack of financial services, and so on.[43] This was both an attempt to put some flesh on the bare bones of 'social exclusion', as well as meeting New Labour's constant call for more 'joined-up government'. In Blair's words, the Unit 'should focus on the need to achieve a holistic approach to social exclusion at national level and on the ground, encouraging effective integration between all the many players'.[44] Its brief was to look at redirecting funds and efforts to shared problems; coordinate action across departments, drawing on the Prime Minister's leadership; and to encourage proactive rather than reactive measures. As Blair was told at the time: 'we spend a great deal of money and effort, but too much of it goes to alleviate the *effects* of social exclusion, rather than *preventing* it from happening'.[45] A mixed team of departmental 'insiders' and outsiders would now try to look at problems in the round. Mulgan, recruited to think about long-term delivery and the lessons of governing, was clear about the Unit's function and work:

> The SEU is part of our commitment to **redistribution**. This remains a big dividing line with the Tories. Every fair society redistributes, and this government is redistributing more than the Tories did ... Where we differ from the past is in the belief that redistribution must be active – giving people the means to escape permanently from poverty through education and training, and our belief that redistribution isn't a zero-sum game. It can be a positive-sum, win-win strategy if it results in less crime and, in the long run, less spending on benefits. The SEU is a sign of government **activism**. The Tories did nothing, didn't care, and let society fall apart. This government is the most active on poverty and social exclusion for a generation, and not ashamed of it.[46]

This battery of policies – a more redistributive tax system, intervention in the poorest parts of the country, 'holistic' policies looking across the whole gamut of social problems – did have effects when combined with the general prosperity of the period. The poorest 20 per cent of the population saw their income grow more than 2 per cent a year under Blair, while the lowest 40 per cent saw their earnings grow quicker than others. During the 1980s, despite at times even faster economic growth, the picture was quite the opposite, with the richest citizens getting nearly 4 per cent richer a year, and the poorest quintile seeing almost no real income growth at all.[47] All politics involves choices, and when we look in detail at Labour's they were consistently to assist low earners and poorer families. In the five years before the NMW was set up, wages at the very bottom increased by 10 per cent less than the medium; in the five years afterwards, they rose 30 per cent above that level.[48] Inequality had not been conquered – far from it – though it was far lower than it would otherwise been if Labour in power had not launched such a concerted anti-poverty drive. Improvements were less rapid from about the middle of Labour's second term in office, to some extent because the more likely and 'easier' gains had been made. But enormous progress was nonetheless visible.

From welfare to work?

Whatever the extent and value of New Labour's redistribution of income from richer to poorer, they also insisted on the value of work. The welfare to work scheme Labour called the New Deal, and which they launched in 1998, gave any employer job subsidies of £60 a week for six months if they took on a 16- to 24-year-old. There was also a training grant of £750 for each young person on the scheme, and a four-month 'Gateway' period in which they received intensive advice and guidance. Thereafter, they were offered employment, full-time training, a job in the voluntary sector, or a place in an environmental taskforce. But no alternative to these options was offered, a punitive side to these policies that was also reflected in the scheme's lack of long-term guarantees.[49] Any assessment of the scheme must be mixed, but hardly zero: one analysis estimated that in the initial pilot areas of 1998–99, for instance, there was an 11 per cent improvement in the employment of the young jobless after their period in the New Deal was over. The figure countrywide, after the scheme was applied everywhere, was 5.4 per cent. Another approach to data on the New Deal for Young People would, however, suggest a more modest effect: that the scheme caused youth unemployment to fall by about 35,000 and youth employment to rise by 15,000.[50]

By April 2000, 800,000 young people had passed through the programme, 215,000 of them had found work, and 139,000 of those were in 'sustained and unsubsidised jobs'.[51] By 2001 206,000 young people had left the New Deal to move into such jobs, while 57,000 had similarly exited the New Deal for the Long Term Unemployed. Many of them would have found work anyway, of course, but unemployment fell faster among eligible groups than among those who were not allowed to join the New Deal.[52] Within three months of a New Deal for Lone Parents starting up, one in four of those signing up for an interview had got a job.[53] This was a modest, if useful, advance, and in the end the New Deals for young people, the long-term unemployed and lone parents were joined by plans for the over-50s, disabled people and the partners of the unemployed too.

These programmes did wield a powerful 'stick' to match the 'carrot' of increased opportunity. Checks to prove suitability for work were tightened, and compulsion involved for most (though not all) of those groups. Tests of 'incapacity' were reversed to look at 'capacity' – what people could do, not what they couldn't.[54] There was an element of compulsion, either forcing young people to work on local social and environmental schemes or securing lower-paid jobs for them, and that became more important as overall unemployment fell. In order to meet their targets local managers running the scheme focused first on 'more employable' youngsters, who they didn't have to corral so much into work. That left the majority entering the New Deal process with qualifications below National Vocational Qualification (NVQ) Level 1 (68 per cent of the total) some way back in the queue. Schemes found it harder and harder to place these less well-qualified young people.[55] Even so, some groups were allowed more leeway. Lone parents with young children were not expected to enter the workplace, though they were still encouraged to do so. The New Deal for Lone Parents was voluntary, unlike the mandatory approach taken to young people – as were those for partners of the unemployed, the disabled and the over-50s.[56]

Previous governments had wielded the stick of mass unemployment and low benefits to force people into paid work, an even greater and more indiscriminate level of coercion. For New Labour, work had to pay and be seen to pay, not just be accepted via the threat of poverty. The Government's whole outlook on the motivations behind unemployment, and indeed on unemployment itself, was different. Now jobless Britons were assumed to *want* to work, indeed to be desperate to enter a booming labour market, but to be barred by structural factors and a lack of skills. The idea of the 'workshy' welfare recipient was downplayed.[57] This was certainly a change of emphasis from the 1980s and early 1990s. Brown later called this New Deal 'one of the most challenging, satisfying and rewarding times of my political life'.[58] When Blair wrote to his staff at the end of 1997, he termed the New Deal 'symbolic of the difference between us and the Tories … The programme has been designed around the needs of the unemployed, with innovation at every stage to make the programme challenging and worthwhile. It is backed by business, local government and the voluntary sector and represents partnership at its best.'[59] This was a definite shift from the *passive* labour market policy of the 1980s, when employees were left to cut their wage demands until they priced themselves into jobs: it moved the country towards an *active* labour market policy which stressed job search, training and government's enabling role.

Still, at the root of Labour's thought lay a puritanical 'workism' that stressed paid work as the solution to almost every ill – another of those lessons they thought they had learned from Clinton's New Democrats. As the 1998 Green Paper had it, the correct balance was 'work for those who can, security for those who cannot'.[60] Being placed in the New Deal scheme meant that workers had to be available for forty hours work a week, at twenty-four hours' notice.[61] It was all very well to work with the unemployed on CVs, interview skills and writing covering letters, but as a huge number of agencies jostled for government recognition and contracts, there was a 'churn' effect under which workers would constantly arrive back in similar programmes. In some areas, long-term jobs simply were not present in sufficient numbers to take up the slack. As one manager in a regeneration programme put it, 'What's the point in aspirating [*sic*] people if the jobs aren't there?'[62] If companies' demand for new staff and novel ideas did not rise, there was little more that could be done via active labour market policies alone. Between 2000 and 2009 work-based training actually fell in the UK, while the skills demanded by employers actually rose only slowly – at the third-slowest rate in the OECD.[63]

The number of workless households did fall sharply in the Blair years, from 19.3 per cent in 1996 to 16.8 per cent in 2002, though most of that improvement is likely explained by the better job market. The number of households in which all adults had some paid work rose strongly, as did those with all adults working. The prompting and help given to those on welfare, and the better rewards available given in-work benefits, probably played an important role here.[64] That improvement was also concentrated among households with children, a difference perhaps explained by New Labour's extremely vigorous targeting of workers with children for assistance and support.[65] These effects might also help to explain why women's earnings as a share of couples' overall income went up relatively strongly in the UK between the late 1990s and early 2010s. Women's pay continued to close in on men's, though that ratio had been closing for a long time as the economy shifted towards creating and valuing so-called 'female' jobs: that ratio was 66 per cent in 1984, 73 per cent by 2003 and then 77 per cent in 2005.[66]

Moving many low-income adults into part-time work would not, however, necessarily attack the roots of poverty. Not every problem was susceptible to treatment via more work, or increased help via the tax system. In the first case, children were not vastly less likely to experience deprivation even if all the adults in their household worked part time, as against growing up in a household where everyone was unemployed. Actual incomes coming in were likely to be higher if parents were working for at least some of the time, but all the other factors causing inequality were not somehow conjured away by entry into the paid workforce.[67] Economic inactivity overall also did not fall by much during Blair's time in Number 10, a fact which again suggested that deep poverty had not really been addressed by the spread of paid work. The percentage of the working population on Severe Disability or Invalidity Benefit was 5.5 per cent in 1997, but still 4.7 per cent in 2005, even while unemployment as a whole continued to fall rapidly.[68] Work was one answer to poverty, but it was not the only one, and New Labour probably overemphasised its transformational promise. A new or future or future government betting everything on economic growth, and planning to move ever more benefit recipients into work, might take note.

Families at the centre of policy

These policies also had a moral dimension, which could seem conservative and liberal by turns and to taste: a focus on the family as the key institution which made society as a whole function. New Labour was very much interested in the human and familial roots of deprivation and exclusion, though not always certain about how to help. This once again involved a familiar blend of increased help with its own price tag: usually, the requirement to take on paid work. Needless to say, that work was framed as an opportunity as well as a duty. Harman made this point in a speech to the Institute for Public Policy Research (IPPR) in June 1997: 'Whenever I meet lone mothers, they always tell me they just don't recognise themselves in the terrible caricatures they see in the press. *They* know how hard they work at home to make decent lives for their children. They'd love to get jobs if there were any to be had.'[69] She had been made fully aware of the need for such provision as an MP in the 1980s, a decade of worklessness and a huge rise in poverty:

> At every constituency visit and every advice surgery, I'd hear from women who wanted to go out to work and couldn't, or were working part time and were frustrated at being held back ... Women with young babies in their arms came to talk about issues such as housing or benefits. But it was the women with a toddler wriggling in their buggy who really wanted to work. Young single mothers would tell me that they were going mad cooped up in a one-bed flat on the tenth floor of a council block. They wanted to work so they could set a good example to

their child, show them that life was not about being dependent on benefits. They wanted to improve their children's standard of living... the issue was the lack of childcare.[70]

More time off for parents was a key part of helping these exact people. Initially, eighteen weeks guaranteed paid leave for mothers was provided to replace the previous fourteen weeks; that became six months paid and another six months unpaid in 2002. The paid section of that leave was extended to nine months in 2007, while a right for fathers to take three months paid leave was announced in 2010. Employers also now had to seriously consider parents' request for flexible working. Free preschool care was granted to all 4-year-olds in 1998, and all 3-year-olds in 2004; more provision for 2-year-olds from low-income backgrounds followed. After 1999, childcare credits also amounted to £70 a week for one child, and £105 for two.[71] The public sector moved to serve as an example to employers whose employees were soon to be armed with a plethora of new rights, with the NHS for instance spending £70 million to provide 150 on-site nurseries by 2005.[72] This type of social re-regulation was felt throughout the economy. The percentage of employees working more than 45 hours a week fell from over 25 per cent to less than 20 per cent. The percentage of workers with no paid holiday entitlement plunged from 12 per cent to 4 per cent, and the annual days available rose too.[73]

As for resources, Working Tax Credits were joined by Child Tax Credit after April 2001. Taken together, all these initiatives topped household wages up to above benefit levels, and then increased them further to take account of the cost of living if that household contained children. This was particularly important for lone parents, usually women, whose wages as they moved into work were on average 12 per cent lower than women with no children.[74] Child benefit also rose, further improving the position of young families with children: it was worth £11.05 for the first child in 1997, but £17 by 2005 and £18.10 by 2007.[75] By 2003/04 a family with children in the bottom fifth of the income distribution was on average £2,400 better off a year because of these measures. Almost 1 per cent of GDP was being redistributed to families with children.[76] At that point Child Tax Credit had increased payouts on what went before by 102 per cent for under-11s; Child Benefit for the first child had risen by 27 per cent; the maximum level of Child Tax Credit support had gone up by 84 per cent; Income Support for two children under 11 had risen by 82 per cent.[77]

By the end of Labour's time in office, the amounts paid out to parents with children could be very significant. The party's interest in 'the family' may well have been about holding society together, but it was also about helping people get by and releasing them from constant, all-consuming childcare and the poverty trap of losing benefits and paying more tax once people did move into work. Child Tax Credit's 'family element', for instance, was by that point worth £545, with more for subsequent children. Clearly, for low-income workers, these were large sums.[78] None of this was exactly utopian. HM Revenue & Customs (HMRC) was not a particularly appropriate or responsive manager of a cash benefits programme. Tax credits were made in advance of final earnings in any tax year, meaning that many recipients had to return large sums to the Government if they earned more than they thought they would. This could leave families in financial distress and psychological uncertainty. The problems with the new system were manifold. But New Labour's efforts to assist families had come a long way since the lone parents benefits debacle of 1997.

Children, their parents and the elderly

An increased emphasis on caring for and protecting children did not end with taxes and benefits, but percolated through the care system and extended to helping parents with childrearing itself. To begin with, this took the familiar New Labour form of new targets, and tighter managerial control exerted from the centre: the new government gave the (correct) impression that it basically did not trust local authorities to look after children. The Quality Protects Programme that ran between 1998 and 2003 set councils a whole range of new targets on outcomes from educational attainment to developmental progress.[79] But gradually, new elements came to the fore, growing out of ideas about early intervention in children's lives, the duties of positive protection throughout their upbringing, the importance of interagency work to once again ensure 'joined-up government', and so on.

Intellectual fashions had long been moving towards assisting families with young children. Assessments of programmes designed to help just these groups, especially those on low incomes, had become more optimistic during the 1980s and 1990s. Head Start, the flagship US programme that was in many ways the forerunner of this whole field, was seen as something of a failure during the 1970s: the effects of help with schooling, parenting education, summer schools, extra support with healthcare and the like was estimated to be ephemeral, fading with time as children grew up. However, gradually and as long-term data became available during the 1980s and 1990s, assessments became more favourable: projects such as Head Start did seem to secure long-term changes for many children. Other similar projects, such as the Chicago Child–Parent Centers which aimed to provide comprehensive support services for disadvantaged children, returned impressive results if young people kept attending for a number of years.[80] Cleary these findings, which became clearer as the 1980s and 1990s wore on, had a profound effect on New Labour's view of poverty and policies that would likely reduce it.

Several specific policies issued from this general sense of the importance of early intervention. One was extra help with childcare. In 1998 ministers announced the provision of free part-time care for all 4-year-olds, and the same for 3-year-olds by 2004: in 2001, they set an aim of 1.6 million new childcare places by 2004, though the reality on the ground often did not live up to this high-flown rhetoric. Resources and staffing did not rise in line with the rights parents could claim, because government by no means paid for the whole cost. Childcare could be extremely expensive, and many parents struggled to make up the difference between state support and total cost.[81] Even so, a novel new part of the overall welfare state was taking shape – at least until the cuts that followed under the Coalition and Conservatives. Another element was a greater emphasis on parenting support, working with families to guide them through the difficulties of raising young children, both as a facet of the new emphasis on multi-agency care work and in Children's Centres. A great deal of this work was prefigured in the Home Office White Paper *Supporting Families*, issued in 1998.[82]

Even more significant progress was made after the tragic death of Victoria Climbié, who in February 2000 died at the hands of her great-aunt and a boyfriend who were known to several agencies, including four local social service departments. The subsequent Laming Report recommended an overall strategy looking at the risks and opportunities for all children, which could try to look after them much better. *Every Child Matters*, published in 2003, asked all local authorities to create a single children's service and Common Assessment Framework, along with an information index, bringing together all services to help ensure that children could as far as possible be offered healthy, happy lives. *Every Child Matters*, and the subsequent Children's Act of 2004, directed every agency to look at such elements of the problem as disruptive behaviour, parental conflict, disengagement from education, ill health, substance misuse, anxiety and depression, housing problems, bullying and special educational needs.[83]

Most of all, there was Sure Start. Sure Start partnerships brought together support services from a range of providers, including education, health and local government, with the aim of helping children in poorer areas: these efforts later became more centralised and evolved into Sure Start Children's Centres, starting in 2003. This programme too does seem to have made a difference, with national assessments tending to suggest that, for instance, educational environments at home were positively influenced. The Government's own final report on *The Impact of Sure Start Local Programmes* for 7-year-olds followed up with 5,000 children and their families who had been through the scheme, and was actually fairly pessimistic about the effects on child development. But even *The Impact of Sure Start* did find positive effects in four out of the fifteen outcomes it had been asked to look into, with a 'less chaotic home environment', 'better life satisfaction' and 'less harsh discipline' from parents allied to a 'more stimulating home environment'.[84]

Other academic studies found even stronger effects: as one of them suggested in 2019, 'there is mounting evidence that Sure Start Children's Centres "worked"'.[85] Recent analysis by the Institute for Fiscal Studies (IFS) suggests that Sure Start boosted the educational achievement of children receiving Free School Meals compared with those pupils who did not.[86] Living near a Sure Start centre likely reduced the likelihood of criminal convictions and custodial sentences, while reducing time in care. Most of these changes hardly looked dramatic at first sight. There was no difference in the number of children being referred to the care of the local authority, for instance. But even looking in more detail at that metric, the actual amount of time spent in care due to family stress or dysfunction was down by between 10 per cent and 20 per cent.[87] Aiming for the best should not drive out the good. Strong differences in emotional and physical development of course persisted as between social classes. But these efforts obviously paid off, as we can see from the backsliding that occurred once the Children's Centres were no longer there. When Sure Start funding was cut in the 2010s, and families and communities were left without outside help, the negative effects of backsliding were obvious and helped prove the programme's worth: obesity rose, for instance.[88]

An emphasis on the family meant a stress on children's early lives too. On one measure, relative child poverty levels fell from 27 per cent of children in 1996/97 to 22 per cent in 2005/06: a decline of 19 per cent. Even more strikingly, that same data point fell by 36 per cent or 37 per cent for lone parents respectively in full-time or part-time work.[89] Clearly, at least in New Labour's terms, work was being made to pay. The number of children living in households with an income less than 60 per cent of the contemporary median fell from nearly 35 per cent to just over 25 per cent, after taking housing costs into account (see Figure 3.2 for the figures before housing costs).[90] Child poverty was probably between 6 per cent and 9 per cent lower than it would otherwise been if Labour had not intervened so strongly.[91] This stood in stark contrast to the record between 1979 and 1997, during which period the number of children living in poverty tripled and Britain attained the dubious distinction of the EU's highest child poverty rate.[92] New Labour again made progress in this respect, even if a great deal of child poverty remained: it fell by 100,000 children every year after 2000. Much remained to be done. Had Labour remained in office after 2010, reaching the goal of abolishing child poverty within twenty years would have required the rate of improvement to double.[93] Each move forward was harder than the last: but the positives are unmistakable.

Other especially vulnerable groups also benefited from the New Labour years. In the 1990s and 2000s the spotlight was less on social care, which was to bedevil successive Prime Ministers after 2010, than it was on older people's incomes. The demographic bulge of the 'baby boom' had not yet put as much strain on the care system as it was later going to; and richer Britons with their own private pensions had not yet aged enough to make the problem of really low incomes in retirement look less stark. Here there was again a positive record of some achievement. Pensioner poverty was nearly halved, and even in the case of relative poverty it fell from nearly 30 per cent of older people to well under 20 per cent (see Figure 3.3).[94] Although the state pension's link to earnings, which had been abolished in 1980, was not restored, Income Support for pensioners was now tied to overall incomes. Single pensioners, and those living as couples, were among the groups all New Labour's tax and benefit changes helped the most: they benefited by 10 per cent and 3 per cent respectively, gains only out-stripped by the 16 per cent or 12 per cent gained by lone parents either working or not working, and couples with children but no earnings from employment.[95]

The percentage of pensioners living below 60 per cent of median income fell from 29 per cent in 1996/97 to 17.6 per cent by 2004/05, though it then rose again slightly to 18.9 per cent in 2006/07.[96] This was of course once more work-ing with the grain, as a wealthier generation of pensioners who had saved for their retirement left the labour force: but taken together with those trends, the transformation of a certain idea of 'the poor', that they would be old, infirm and perhaps invisible, was remarkable. In 1979 the bottom quintile of the income distribution was mostly made up of pensioners: they constituted 80 per cent of that group. But by 2006 they made up only 38 per cent of that lowest 20 per cent.[97] 'Persistent' poverty, as defined by the numbers of pensioners living in poverty for at least three out of the last four years, fell away too – as it did for children (see Figure 3.4). Too many of these gains are now taken for granted, as some of the capital gains and wealth of older 'boomers' echo through our

55.00

50.00

45.00

40.00

35.00

30.00

25.00

1994/95–1995/96
1995/96–1996/97
1996/97–1997/98
1997/98–1998/99
1998/99–1999/00
1999/00–2000/01
2000/01–2001/02
2001/02–2002/03
2002/03–2003/04
2003/04–2004/05
2004/05–2005/06
2005/06–2006/07
2006/07–2007/08
2007/08–2008/09
2008/09–2009/10
2009/10–2010/11
2010/11–2011/12

——— Relative low income (%)   ——— Absolute low income (%)

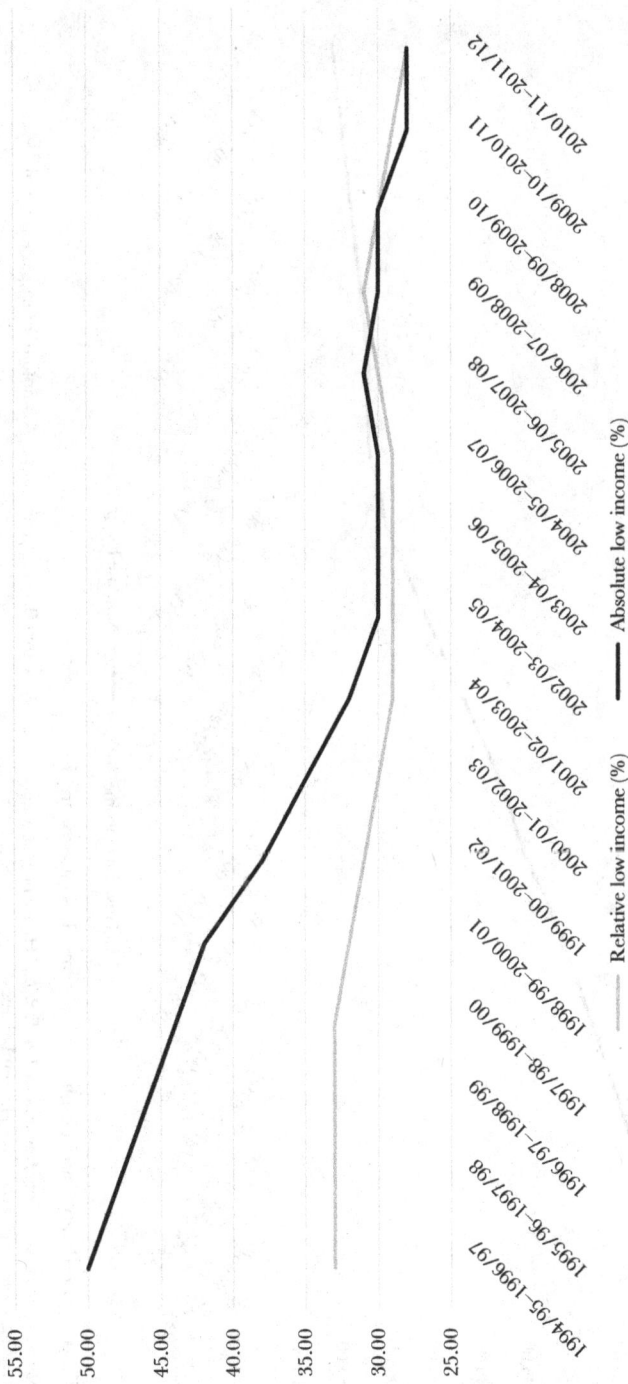

Figure 3.2 Relative and absolute low income, UK children, 1994–2012

Source: B. Francis-Devine, *Poverty in the UK: Statistics*, House of Commons Library Research Briefing 7096, https://commonslibrary.parliament.uk/research-briefings/sn07096/, accessed 12 December 2023.

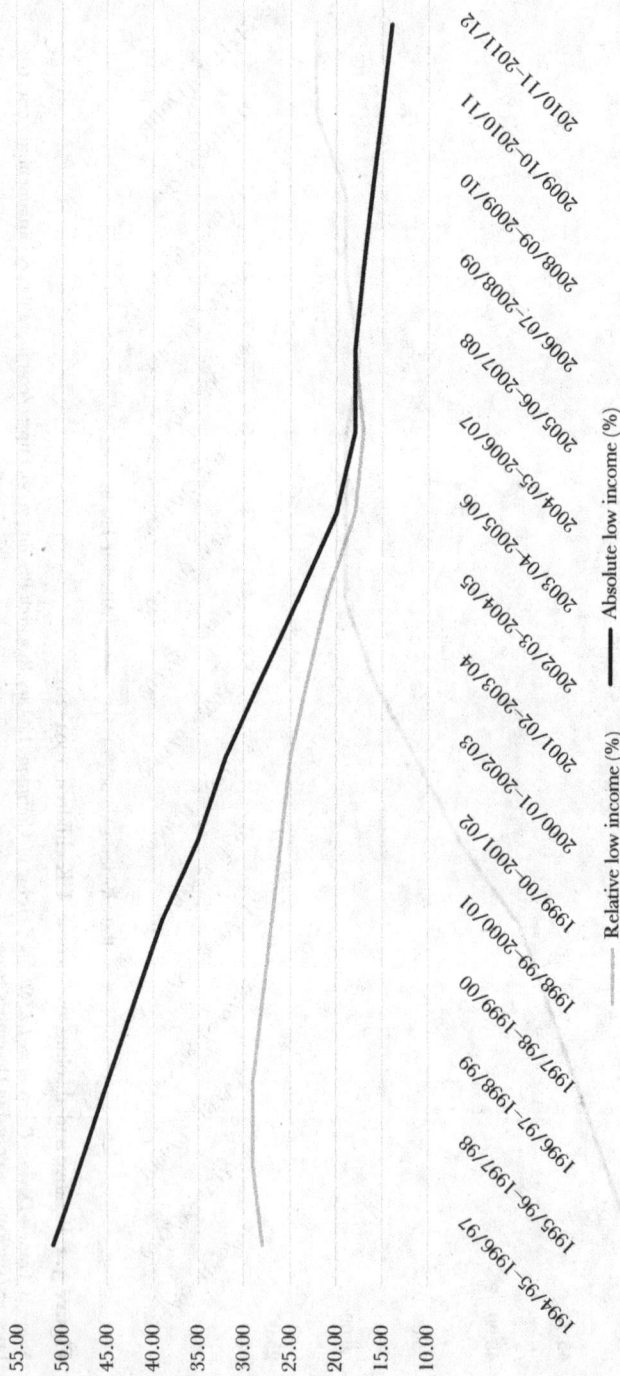

Figure 3.3 Relative and absolute low income, UK pensioners, 1994–2012

Legend: Relative low income (%) — Absolute low income (%)

X-axis labels: 1994/95–1996/97, 1995/96–1997/98, 1996/97–1998/99, 1997/98–1999/00, 1998/99–2000/01, 1999/00–2001/02, 2000/01–2002/03, 2001/02–2003/04, 2002/03–2004/05, 2003/04–2005/06, 2004/05–2006/07, 2005/06–2007/08, 2006/07–2008/09, 2008/09–2009/10, 2009/10–2010/11, 2010/11–2011/12

Y-axis values: 10.00, 15.00, 20.00, 25.00, 30.00, 35.00, 40.00, 45.00, 50.00, 55.00

Source: B. Francis-Devine, *Poverty in the UK: Statistics,* House of Commons Library Research Briefing 7096, https://commonslibrary.parliament.uk/research-briefings/sn07096/, accessed 13 December 2023.

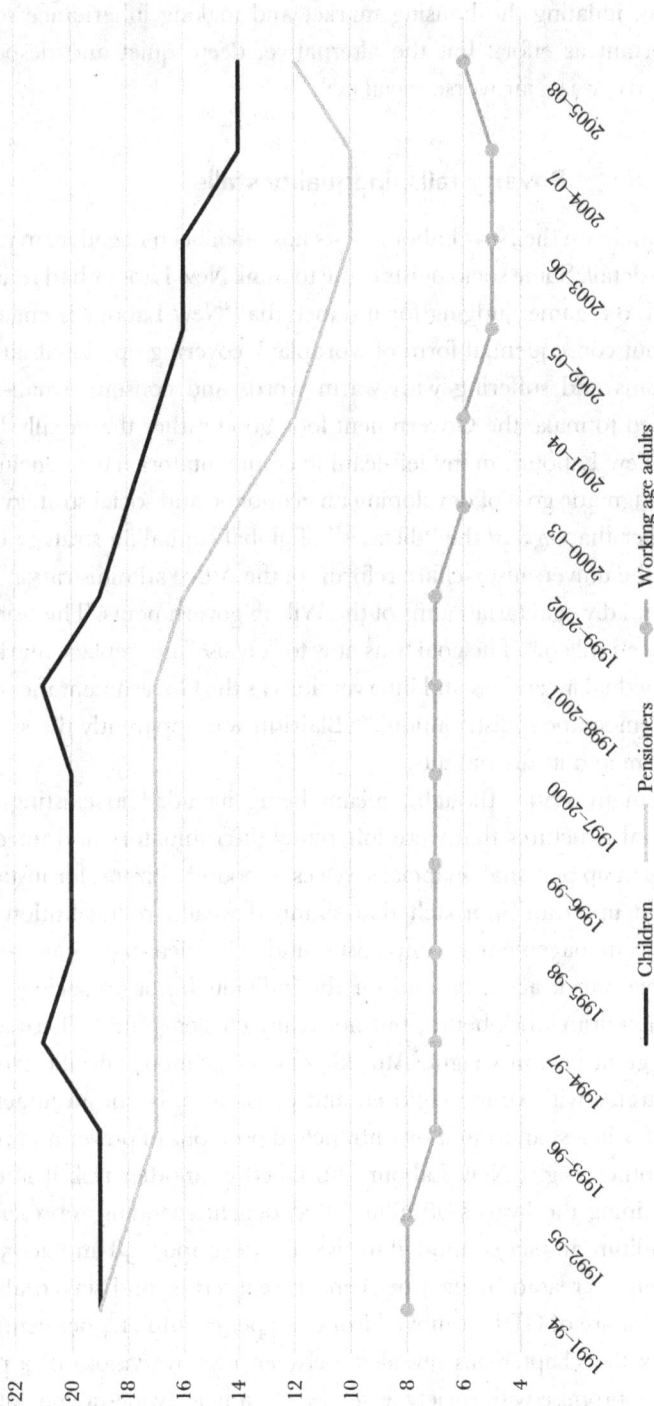

Figure 3.4 Persistent poverty among three population groups, 1991–2008

Source: The Health Foundation, *Trends in Persistent Poverty*, www.health.org.uk/evidence-hub/money-and-resources/persistent-poverty/trends-in-persistent-poverty, accessed 13 December 2023.

political system, inflating the housing market and making inheritance some-times as important as effort: but the alternative, deep, quiet and desperate pensioner poverty, was a far worse social evil.

Poverty falls, inequality stalls

Experts' judgement on the New Labour years has often been negative, in mood if not always in detail. Some sociologists came to think New Labour had reduced the whole field to a game, judging for instance that 'New Labour is engaging in a complex but consequential form of wordplay', covering up globalisation's inevitable victims and suffering with warm words and constant small-scale policies designed to make the Government look good rather than really help-ing people.[98] 'New Labour', many left-leaning commentators have concluded, 'set itself the pragmatic goal of developing an economic and social strategy that works *with* rather than *against* the "dictates" of global capital', a strategy quite different from the universalist welfare reforms of the Attlee administration, and even from the mildly egalitarian aims of the Wilson governments. The 'song in its heart' had been stilled.[99] The goal 'was now to "civilise" not replace markets', relying on individual incentives and interventions as the Government moved to 'reject social-democratic redistribution'.[100] Blairism was apparently the smiling face of capitalism and its discontents.

'Inclusion', many critics thought, meant being included in existing eco-nomic and social structures that were inherently discriminatory and unequal. Measures to open up personal financial services to poorer citizens, for instance, were 'grounded upon an approach that shunned wealth redistribution and macroeconomic management as unrealistic and self-defeating'. State action was still possible, but it acted on and for the individual, not on society. You could make capitalism work better, but not really challenge it.[101] These argu-ments carry a great deal of weight. Attacking poverty among specific groups, particularly parents with young children and pensioners, is not an attack on inequality itself, still less an assault on entrenched positions of power and privi-lege. From another angle, New Labour also failed in another task it initially set itself: restraining the 'wages of failure' that benefit spending represented. Welfare expenditure in fact continued to rise. Between 1997/98 and 2005/06, welfare spending increased by 22.5 per cent in real terms, and stayed almost exactly flat as a share of GDP (it moved from 11.3 per cent to 11.4 per cent).[102]

The paradox this chapter has revealed, between negative visions of a party dedicated to compromise with society as it was and a huge, wide-ranging attack

on poverty and need, should still caution us before we emphasise Labour's conservatism and centrism. Even quantitatively, help to lower-income groups certainly did *not* stay the same: quite the contrary. Qualitatively, too, new rights
came in alongside ministers' talk of novel responsibilities. Positive equality laws
and duties continued to grow in number and importance, obvious for instance in
the Race Relations Act of 2000 and the 2005 Disability Discrimination Act. This
was, of course, a piecemeal, gradual and confused process, but thin as that was,
there was also a real effect on public policy. Complicated policies also matched
an increasingly kaleidoscopic society. Poverty had become a shifting, hard-to-
capture phenomenon, through which many types of people cycled: New Labour's
complex view of it was to some extent again a reflection of the times. The idea
of a more responsive state also brought with it something of a shift in how policy
was made, an approach involving more of what the social policy academic Martin
Hewitt called 'cooperation and dialogue' in place of the discord and confrontation that had been such obvious hallmarks of the 1980s and early 1990s.[103]

If we take all New Labour's tax and benefit changes together, the poorest
10 per cent of the population benefited the most, and those gains declined all
the way to the richest 10 per cent, whose net losses from government action
approached 9 per cent. The effects on those Britons earning over £100,000 were
even more pronounced, since they took a hit of nearly 15 per cent (Figure 3.5).
In the 1980s, government policy and income growth had pushed in exactly the
opposite direction, with the poorest doing worst and the richest gaining most.
Unsurprisingly, therefore, poverty did fall while New Labour was in office: from
25.3 per cent of the population in 1997 to 20.5 per cent in 2005, though with
a slight rise thereafter.[104] The public, if not some of the experts, did notice the
positive changes initiated by New Labour in this field. In 1994 only 6 per cent
of people told pollsters that poverty was decreasing. By 2000 that figure was
20 per cent, and by 2006/07 it was 23 per cent. Conversely, the numbers thinking that poverty was increasing were 68 per cent in 1994, but 36 per cent in 2000
and only 32 per cent by 2006/07.[105]

Inequality, however, did not decline, plateauing or stagnating depending on
how one wishes to describe a basically flat line. The overall 'Gini coefficient'
shows us how far away a society is from all households having the exact same
incomes. The closer to zero, the nearer to pure equality across the income
distribution; the nearer to 1, the more payments are all flowing to a tiny group.
The UK's Gini coefficient while New Labour were in power saw inequality
continue upwards to about the end of the century, then down to the mid-2000s,
then slightly up again (see Figure 3.6). It is a similar picture whichever measure

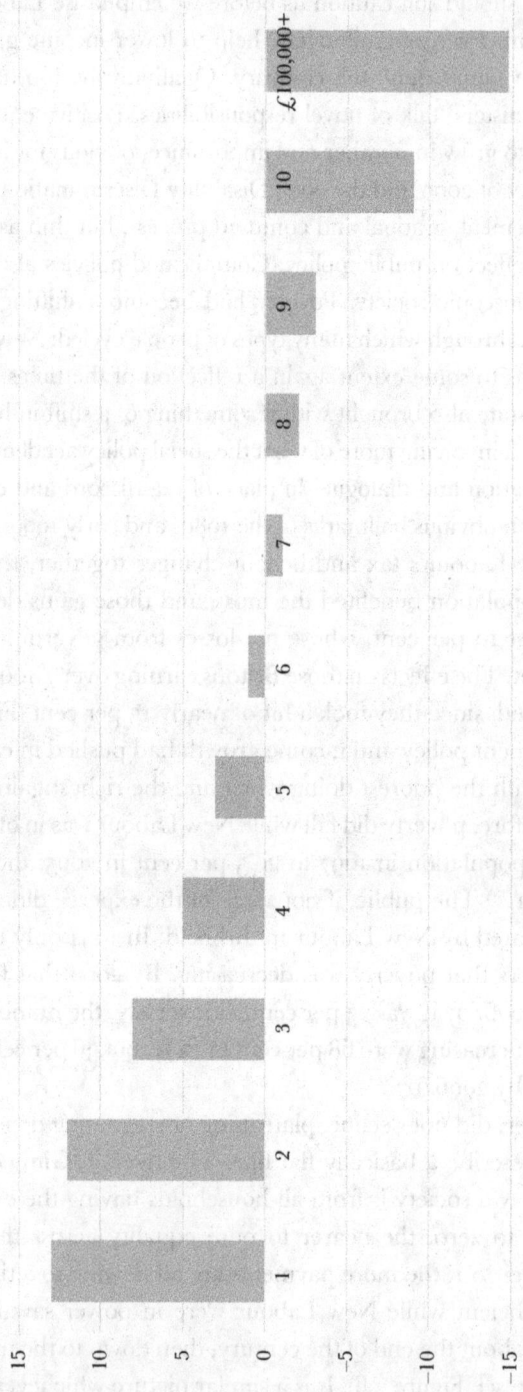

Figure 3.5 Net effect of tax and benefit changes by household decile, 1997–2010 (% income)

Source: J. Browne and D. Phillips, *Tax and Benefit Reforms Under Labour*, IFS 2010 Election Briefing Note 1 (IFS BN 88) (London: IFS, 2010), figure 3.3, p. 18; G. Eaton, 'How Redistributive Was New Labour?', *New Statesman*, 27 September 2022, www.newstatesman.com/politics/labour/2022/09/how-redistributive-was-new-labour, accessed 13 December 2023.

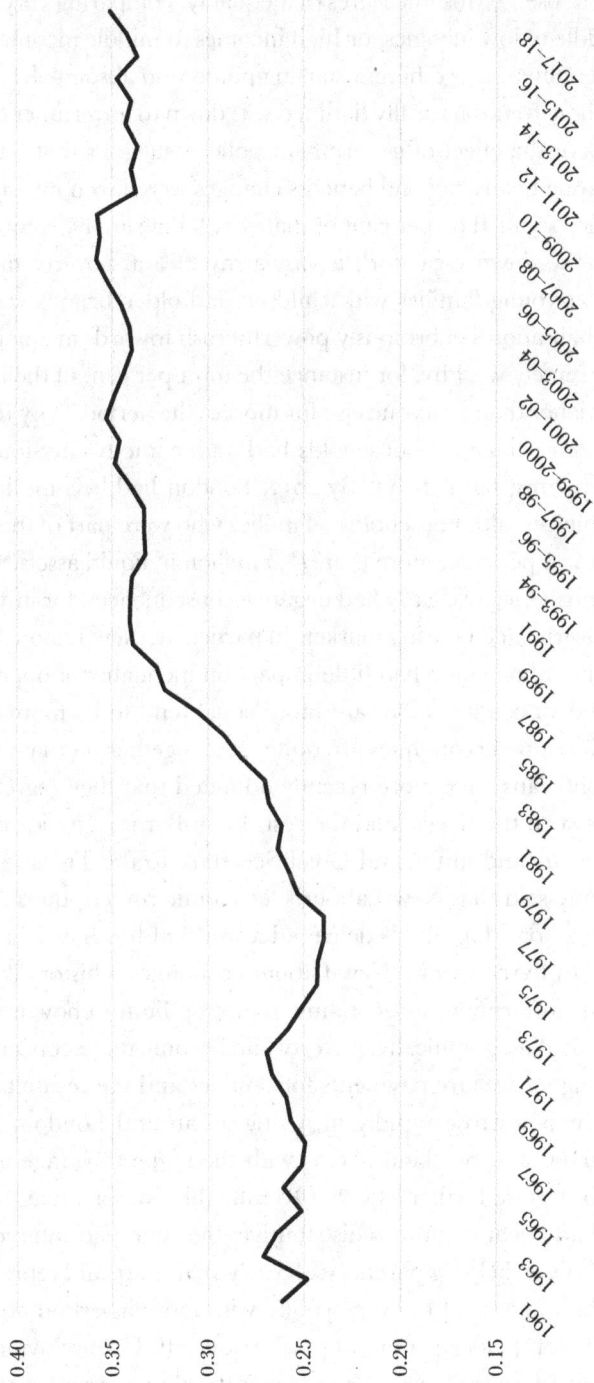

Figure 3.6 Gini coefficient, UK, 1961–2009/10

Source: *Gini Coefficient Economic Inequality Measure*, https://closer.ac.uk/data/gini-coefficient-income-inequality-measure/, accessed 13 December 2023; Institute for Fiscal Studies, *Living Standards, Poverty and Inequality in the UK 2020* (London: IFS, 2020), figure 2.13, p. 18.

of inequality we choose.[106] Most measures of inequality, comparing very high to low incomes, middle to low incomes, or high incomes to middle incomes, show a similar set of trendlines, if at different starting points and absolute levels.

The fact that these trends basically flatlined was down to government action. Complex analysis of the effect of government policies suggests that basic inequality was still rising before tax and benefits changes were taken into account, but that state policy stymied 90 per cent of that rise.[107] Put simply, New Labour was 'running up the down escalator': a vast array of anti-poverty measures aimed especially at young families with children and older Britons was holding the lid on globalisation's enormously powerful rush towards inequality, but only just. The extremely wealthy, for instance the top 1 per cent of the income, continued to get richer than everyone else for most of the period.[108] By the mid-2010s the richest ten percent of households had an income twenty-four times greater than the poorest ten percent. By 2012, London had become home to over 4,000 ultra-high-wealth households – families who were part of the richest 1 per cent of the top 1 per cent, more than £30 million in liquid assets.[109]

This split in British society clearly had negative consequences, for instance in London's vastly overheated housing market. In particular, New Labour's insistence that inequality of outcome had little impact on inequality of opportunity also seems misguided: countries that are more equal tend to be more socially mobile (though developed economies are quite close together on that curve).[110] Many Labour politicians have more recently admitted that they regret ignoring the divide between the richest and the rest. Liam Byrne, a junior minister during the Blair years and in the end Chief Secretary to the Treasury under Brown, has recently said that New Labour's 'economic prescriptions ... have not delivered rising boats for all: it's delivered a world of haves and have-nots and have-yachts'. In Byrne's view, 'New Labour economics is history'.[111]

Without truly transforming the economy, there is a limit to how much the state can do anyway. Geographically, poverty had become more concentrated, not less, despite higher welfare payments for families and the resuscitation of regional policy. Incomes rose rapidly in a ring all around London, but fell in Northern England and Scotland. Areas with the highest average incomes experienced their fastest further rise.[112] Overall, this was a mixed record. The tax system had become more redistributive; the state had intervened to reshape children's lives, helping parents with early years care and representing and protecting the interests of the very young with more assertion and long-term effort than before; older people were far better off. Unemployment was down; need and distress were lower. The rise in inequality was stalled and then stopped. The situation was far better than it had been in the 1980s and early 1990s. A government that talked about inclusion and exclusion, not benefits, and had assailed hardship head-on to widen everybody's access to the rising tide of prosperity. In so doing they tackled with some aplomb the very problems of raw poverty that 'Old' Labour rhetoric had always promised to solve, but which New Labour initially played down. Yet either by design or happenstance, inequality itself remained stubbornly high. It was a record that would alternately impress and depress the Labour Party, its activists and voters for years to come – and which continues to confront the party with uncomfortable truths about power and wealth today.

4

Saving the NHS?

New money for health

By 1997, Britain's National Health Service was at one of its lowest ebbs, with the British Social Attitudes (BSA) survey showing public faith in the NHS at an all-time nadir.[1] As Brown put it in his memoirs, not entirely unfairly, 'the year of our election ... had not been a good one to be sick and dependent on the NHS'. The Thatcher and Major governments had left it reeling from successive winter crises and long waiting lists.[2] The NHS was quite simply underfunded. In 1999, total UK spending on healthcare amounted to 6.9 per cent of GDP: in France that figure was 10.1 per cent, and in Germany 10.3 per cent.[3] The most obvious and important change Labour brought to the NHS was therefore the one most needed: more money. As Frank Dobson, Labour's first Health Secretary on its return to power, told Brown: 'Everything I have seen since I came into this job has convinced me that this will be the most difficult year in the NHS for a decade and that next year will be far worse if we do not increase the resources available for patient care.'[4]

The 1998 Comprehensive Spending Review (CSR) allocated another £18bn to the NHS over three years, in addition to £2bn in efficiencies and savings that would be moved to frontline staff. But events soon overtook that initial cash injection. When another flu crisis hit the NHS during the winter of 1999/2000 (during which 48,000 excess deaths were recorded), clearly something was going to have to change radically. Blair was deeply discomfited by criticism of his record on the NHS, particularly since he had concluded his 1997 election campaign with a pledge to 'save' it. When, during January 2000, the case of a man who had his cancer operation delayed four times was highlighted by the media, and the well-known Labour Peer Lord Winston took to the airwaves alleging that the Government had been 'deceitful' about the true state of the

NHS, one critic summoned to Number 10 'found him [Blair] in an absolute state. I had never seen him like that. The moment he saw me he leapt up and for about ten minutes waved his arms around acting in a manic way. "So you think I'm doing everything wrong?", he said.'[5]

The political importance of the NHS to Labour meant something had to change radically. The devolved nations went to some extent their own way, of course – especially in Scotland – and extra spending did not necessarily mean better results.[6] But on 16 January that year, Blair went on the *Breakfast with Frost* programme, hosted by David Frost, and promised that UK health spending would rise to the EU average. Brown was furious. He believed that Blair had stolen the thunder of his 2000 Budget and Spending Review, designed to raise structural and long-lasting finance for the NHS in England, as well as short-circuiting his desire to build a slow and steady consensus behind tax rises. Blair wrote in his memoirs that 'I had ... a conversation or several with Gordon about NHS funding; but as I anticipated, he was fairly adamant against doing anything big on it.' The Prime Minister stuck to his plans: 'there were a few tin-helmet days with Gordon, but ... the politics made it impossible to oppose'.[7] Given that Blair's announcement on *Frost* had caught the whole government unawares, Department of Health advisers and civil servants scrambled to catch up. During a conference call that same day, Campbell was asked whether Brown 'was on board': the answer, apparently, was 'Tony has said it, so we are committed.'[8]

Brown was nevertheless left with the task of finding the money for a rejuvenated NHS, which he duly did in extremely Brownite fashion. The Treasury rolled out his usual answer of commissioning a review, led by the retired banker Derek Wanless, much to Number 10's dismay as the question was somewhat taken out of their hands.[9] Wanless looked at the likely needs for healthcare in the UK over the following twenty-five years, and the resources required to match them. Entirely predictably, Wanless found in his 2002 report that NHS spending would need to grow quickly, from around 7.7 per cent of GDP, where it stood at the time of the 2002 Budget, to between 10.6 per cent and 12.5 per cent (see Figures 4.1 and 4.2). That implied spending 4.2 per cent to 5.1 per cent a year more on the NHS every single year over the following two decades, an investment surge that Wanless argued should be front-loaded with even higher increases. Blair and Brown concurred, and the latter not only decided to spend £2.4bn more on the NHS immediately (in 2003/04), but to increase spending by 7.4 per cent a year up to 2007/08, an aim that was very nearly realised.[10]

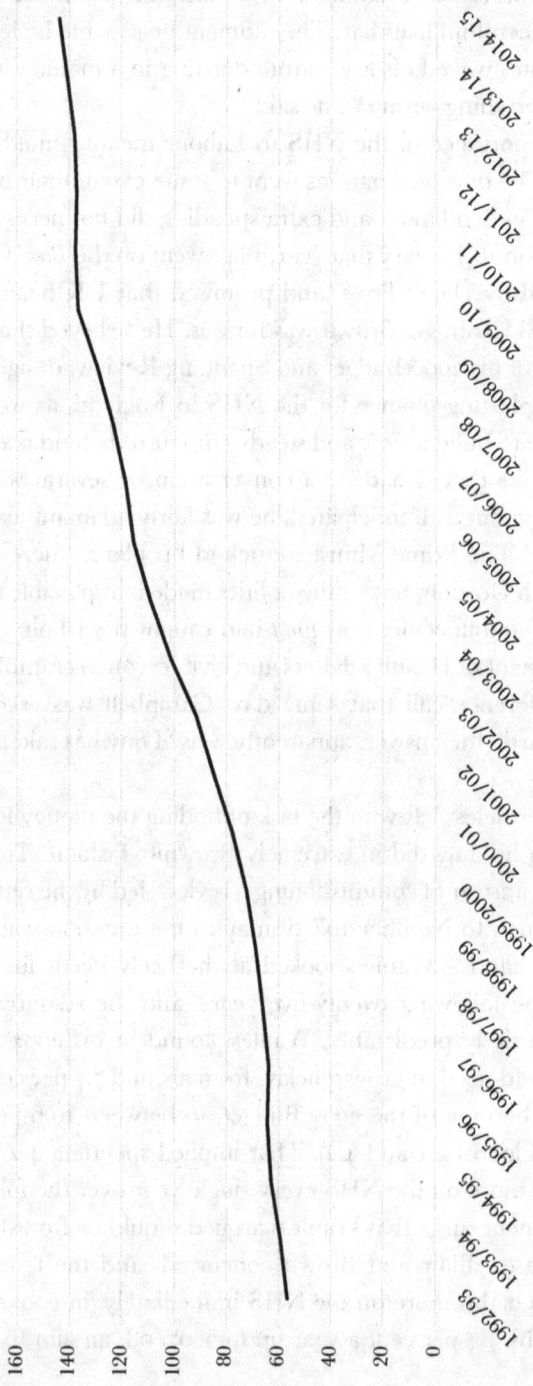

Figure 4.1 Net UK NHS expenditure, £m at 2018/19 prices (1992/93–2014/15)

Source: R. Harker, *NHS Funding and Expenditure*, House of Commons Briefing Paper CBP0724 (17 January 2019), data table, p. 14.

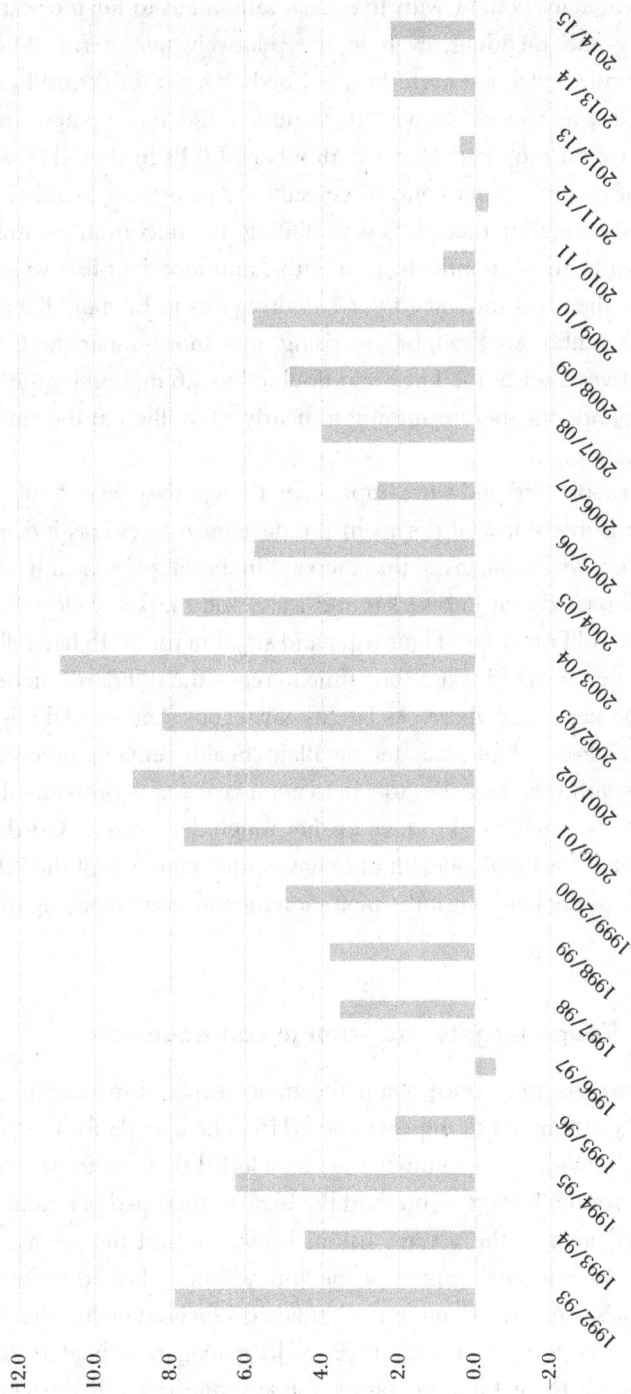

Figure 4.2 NHS net spending, % increase over previous year (1992/93–2014/15)

Source: R. Harker, *NHS Funding and Expenditure*, House of Commons Briefing Paper CBP0724 (17 January 2019), data table, p. 14.

The extra capacity bought with that cash amounted to far more than the usual patching and mending, even in the relatively near term. The NHS Plan of 2000 promised 7,000 more hospital beds, 7,500 more consultants and 2,000 more GPs, as well as 20,000 more nurses and more places in medical school. Between 1997 and 2005 the number of GPs in the NHS went up 20 per cent; of nurses, 27 per cent; of consultants 49 per cent; and registrars 51 per cent.[11] By 2002 inpatient lists were falling: the maximum waiting time had gone down from 18 months to 15 months, and inpatient lists were below one million for the first time since 1993.[12] Waiting lists in England fell to a low of just over 2.3 million in 2008, before rising once more under the Coalition and Conservatives after 2010. They had doubled to 4.6 million by the time of the Covid-19 pandemic, before surging to nearly 7.8 million at their peak late in 2023 (see Figure 4.3).[13]

These figures sounded and were impressive, though they served only to shift the UK towards international norms in the developed world (as indeed Blair had promised on *Frost*): still, given that increase in funding UK health spending caught up and passed that in Sweden and Italy, and markedly closed the gap with Germany and France (see Figures 4.4 and 4.5). But the NHS had fallen into such disrepair that it would take a long time to reach the standards increasingly accepted as the norm elsewhere. As late as early 2002 Andrew Adonis, Head of Number 10's Policy Unit, was telling Blair 'health remains precarious … even if extra health spending rises to 7 per cent a year real – probably the limit of the possible – we may need to take further tough decisions … Gordon may want to present… his tax-for-health package as the "salvation of the NHS". It will be nothing of the kind – just the next incremental step to making the NHS sustainable.'[14]

Tough targets and strange consequences

Performance targets were once again the main mechanism via which New Labour initially attempted to improve the NHS. The agenda for the Number 10 Policy Unit's awayday in summer 1997 concluded that 'performance management' may sound 'boring … but had the biggest untapped potential'. More radical options, such as the greater use of insurance and the private sector, were relegated to 'variants' important for 'innovation'.[15] That decision made, data-driven goals proliferated: numerical indicators focused on 'results' became more and more important. At one stage, NHS managers estimated that they had to meet over three hundred targets at any one time. If they failed to

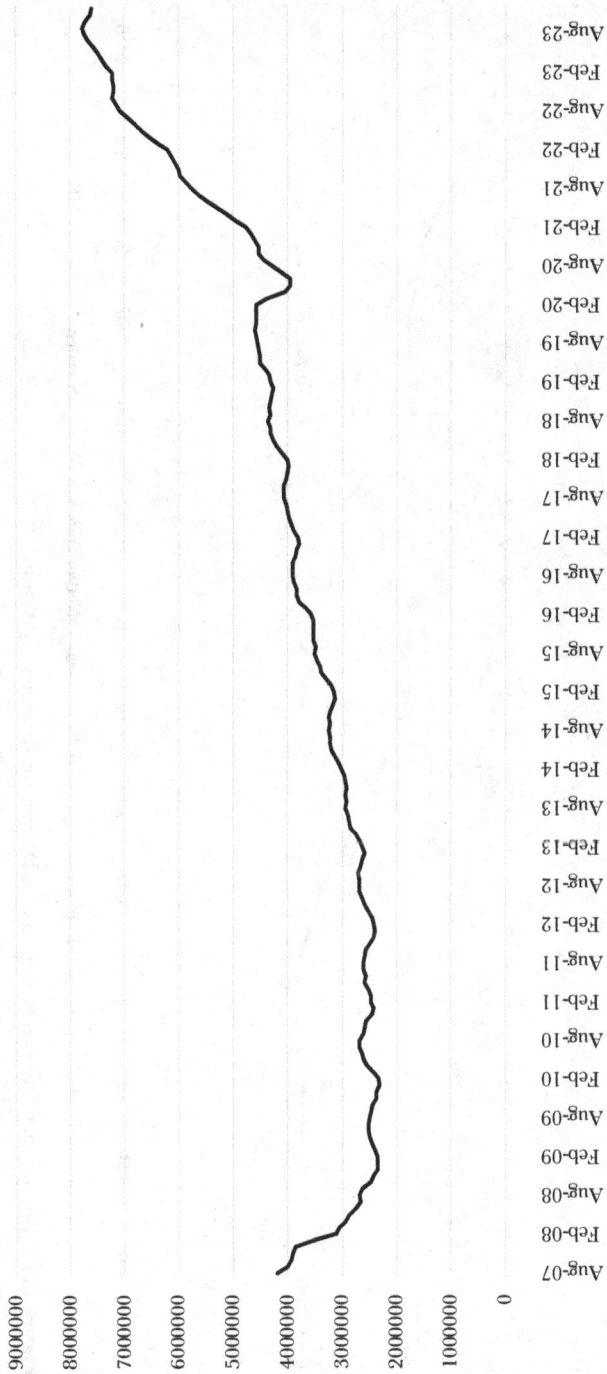

Figure 4.3 NHS elective waiting list in England, numbers of patients, 2007–23

Source: M. Warner and B. Zaranko, *The Past and Future of NHS Waiting Lists in England*, IFS Report R302 (February 2024).

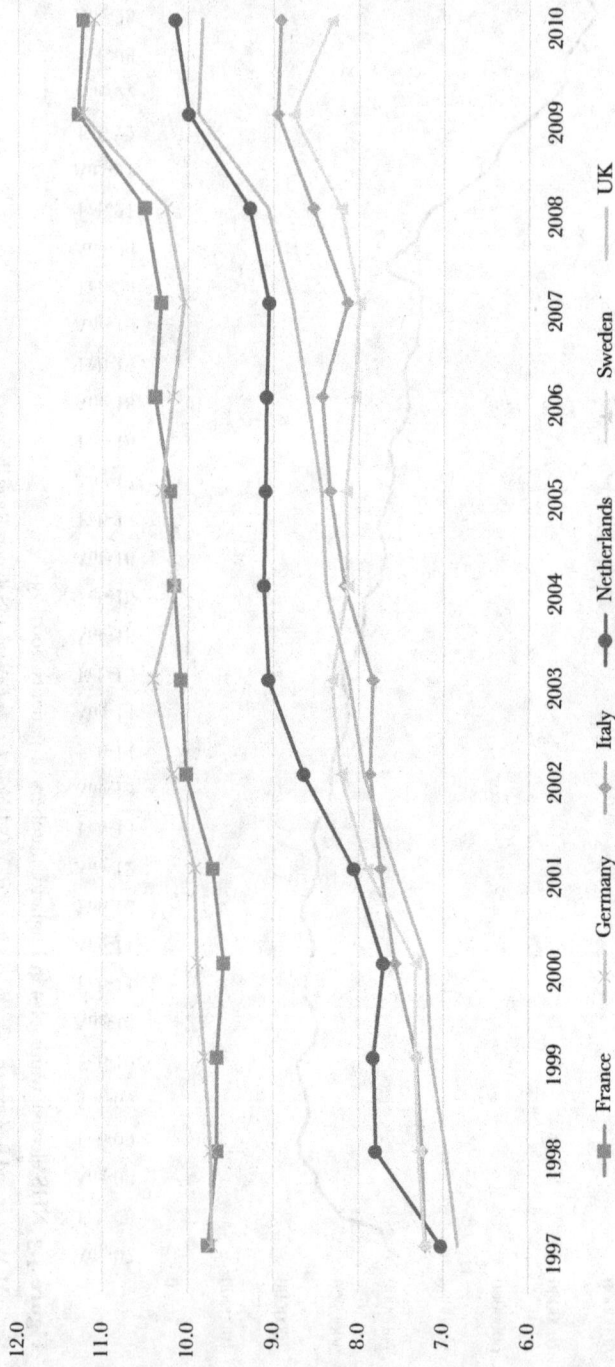

Figure 4.4 Current expenditure on health, % of GDP, various countries, 1997–2010

Source: OECD Dataset, *Health Expenditure Indicators*, https://stats.oecd.org/viewhtml.aspx?datasetcode=SHA&lang=en, data extracted 21 January 2022.

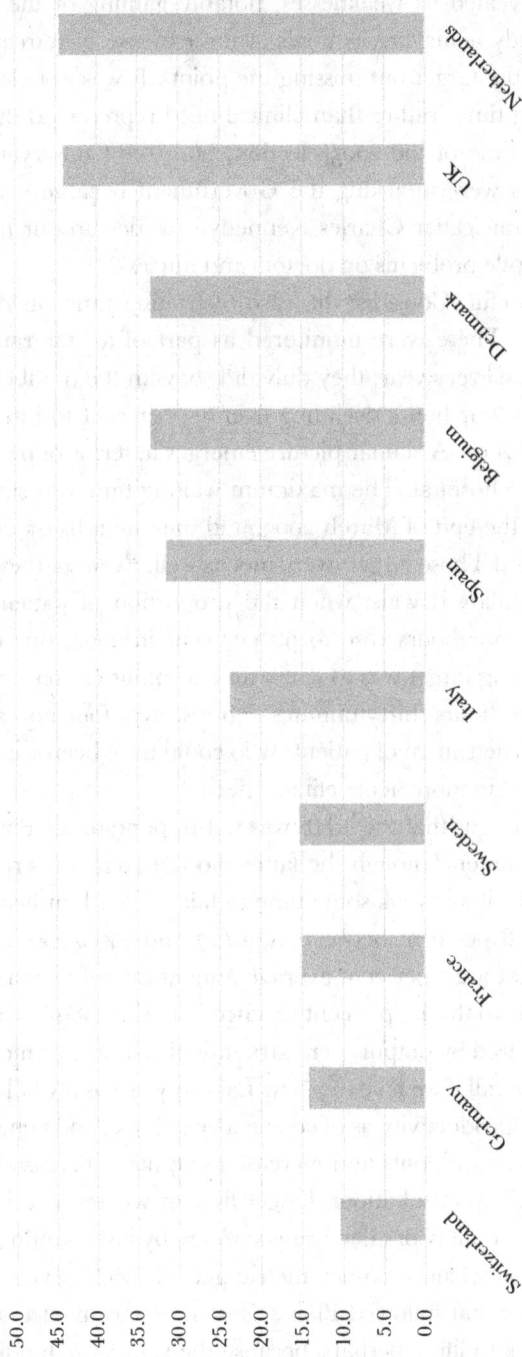

Figure 4.5 Increase in GDP spent on current healthcare (%), various countries 1997–2010

Source: OECD Dataset, *Health Expenditure Indicators*, https://stats.oecd.org/viewhtml.aspx?datasetcode=SHA&lang=en, data extracted 21 January 2022.

hit these benchmarks, sanctions would follow. This command and control approach soon revealed its weaknesses, notably gaming of the system. The NHS was constantly achieving its goals at the expense of retreats elsewhere, known as 'hitting the target but missing the point'. It was not clear at all that prioritising waiting times rather than clinical need represented the best use of resources. By the time of the 2005 election, both the Conservatives and the Liberal Democrats were attacking the Government because – in the words of Liberal Democrat leader Charles Kennedy – it 'ties up our hospitals with targets which just pile problems on doctors and nurses'.[16]

Targets were useful. Consider the case of waiting times in Accident and Emergency wards. These were monitored as part of a 'star ratings' system, and had to decrease every year: they duly did so, with the numbers of patients waiting more than four hours declining from 23 per cent to just 5.3 per cent between 2003 and 2005. A similar picture emerges in terms of patients waiting to be admitted into hospital. The maximum waiting time was supposed to be twelve months by the end of March 2003, and nine months by the end of the same month in 2004. Those targets were met as well. Even so, these undoubted gains were not unalloyed wins: when the proportion of patients having to be treated within four hours rose to 98 per cent in 2004, one effect of this extremely challenging target was to cause an enormous clustering of consultations between three hours thirty minutes and just over four hours. This could obviously be to the detriment of patients who could have been seen earlier, and who may have been in more acute clinical need.[17]

There were also signs that the NHS was not responding as it might to extra attention and investment, though the latter did not come on stream until the early 2000s and inevitably took some time to take effect. Finished 'Consultant Episodes' rose by 8 per cent between 1996/97 and 1999/2000, from 11.3 to 12.2 million – but at a 2.7 per cent average annual rate of increase, that compared unfavourably to the 4.4 per cent reached between 1989/90 and 1996/99. Efficiency as measured by outputs per extra unit of resource or member of staff stagnated or fell overall if we take the New Labour years as a whole. The whole field of healthcare 'productivity' is of course a vexed one, and depends on what one is counting as extra inputs and increased outputs – increased admissions, more surgery, quicker consultations, longer lives or whatever. It is in fact very hard to measure the quality or effectiveness of care by just counting the number of appointments, or whatever other metric gets chosen.[18] Even so, the step-change in resources that followed Blair's *Frost* announcement took a while to jolt the system back to life – perhaps because the very large funding increases were never going to lift performance quickly. NHS productivity as measured by the input of new money as against a wide range of health 'outputs' fell sharply between 2001 and 2004 in particular, but the situation then got rather better, as we would expect if there was a lag between spending and measurable improvement.[19] It is possible that the effect of Blair and Brown's insistence on 'resourcing and reform' simply took a while to take hold.

Increased pay was one reason for the apparent fall in productivity if we take that banal word 'inputs' to mean money funnelled into the system, as wages rose quicker than the number of consultations. Though, once more, what 'productivity' means is hard to define. If the Government had not been able to improve working conditions, and improve staff retention, the NHS would not have been able to grow at all. Narrow measures of efficiency can in this way rather miss the point. If we turn to the five years after 2002, when spending increases were at their height, a funding increase of £43bn was in part eaten up by pay and price inflation: £18.9bn (or 43 per cent) can be accounted for under this heading.[20] Improvements in pay and conditions accounted for a great deal of the difference between inflation in the NHS and in the economy as a whole.[21] Patients did not see rapid direct benefits from much of the new flow of money. Still, better conditions for staff were vital if the NHS was to recover from its parlous state in the late 1990s. NHS staffing was in deep crisis during the 1990s, and it was more than fair for recruitment and retention to take some priority, though the Treasury in its usual penny-pinching way often disagreed. Brown was characteristically scathing in his memoirs about what he saw as a wasted opportunity to match higher wages to faster reforms.[22]

The Government did gradually respond to the contradictions and diminishing returns so obvious in their obsessive micromanagement of the NHS. Hard targets showed a tendency to become vaguer aspirations over time, with actual set numbers attaching to fewer objectives and at least some sense of priorities emerging. From 2001 onwards, the Department of Health's 'star ratings' were given out on the basis of about fifty types of target, but a much narrower set of 'key targets' was singled out in the midst of a more general 'balanced score-card'. The Prime Minister's own Delivery Unit monitored a smaller number of health targets again, while ten indicators among the Treasury's Public Service Agreements were also relevant.[23] In *National Standards, Local Action*, published in 2004, the Department of Health promised to lower the number of overall targets from sixty-two to twenty.[24] This was all part of a more general disillusionment with centralised, quantified demands as a single, one-size-fits-all answer to the public sector's problems, more and more evident as New Labour came to understand governance more clearly. But as those different bundles of goals suggest, one result of that was something of a mess in which many different performance indicators were being followed. And it took at least a whole Parliament for the drawbacks of huge lists of targets to be clearly understood.

The search for care partnerships

New Labour in power did also try to treat healthcare as just one part of a wider social care agenda, at least attempting to get away from the idea that 'health' meant 'hospitals'. Most recent governments have aspired to shift attention away from expensive interventionist medicine towards prevention and public health. But in the late 1990s and early 2000s there was actually some movement in that direction. As the Public Health Green Paper *Our Healthier Nation* put it in 1999, 'connected problems require joined-up solutions'. The central Performance and Innovation Unit's *Wiring It Up* report of 2000 added to the momentum, recommending as it did much more interdepartmental working. This was not an entirely new approach: a social policy coordinating unit had been set up in the Cabinet Office as early as 1967. But the Blairite impulse towards 'joined-up government' did now lead to a rather more integrated system. The creation of a National Institute for Clinical Excellence (NICE – advising on which treatments should be accessible on the NHS) and a Commission for Health Improvement recreated some of the central advisory machinery that the Thatcher years had deliberately dispensed with. NICE would be deeply controversial, because of course it had to limit access to therapies patients needed – perhaps even life-saving ones. But in setting strict cost-benefit rules on new treatments, it did assist with more transparent and more rational decision-making: rules that were often used as benchmarks in the rest of Europe.[25]

These new bodies brought some wider coherence back into the system, and caused it to act again as a truly *National* Health Service. It was a new departure that went far wider than just medicine itself. A statutory duty of cooperation was imposed on NHS and local councils under the 1999 Health Act: this more 'horizontal' or 'connected' view of government was an attempt to bring most of the key players together, from schools and social workers to GPs and hospitals. 'Joined-up' local networks, in the Third Way terminology of the time, were supposed to be a key ally for the NHS, to surround and reinforce it. The areas singled out for action in New Labour's health inequality strategy were: early years and parenting; work's contribution to well-being; health equalities; and mental health.[26] None of those could be tackled by the NHS alone.

This worked out in practice as a strong emphasis on 'partnership working' across the field of health and social care. Ministers went to extreme lengths to secure this, both organisationally and rhetorically. One study estimated that even after omitting references to civil partnerships, the word 'partnership' was uttered 11,319 times in official records in 2006, as against only 38 times in 1989.[27] When it came to healthcare, New Labour seems to have intended a mix of pooling knowledge, joint decision-making, planning about long-term needs and contractual agreements which specified the relationships between, and responsibilities of, different actors in the health and welfare system. This emphasis on working together across the public sector remained a fixed point of reference; even as policy followed policy in England, they evolved via Local Strategic Partnerships and Local Area Agreements from 2003 onwards. These pushed local government, other public sector providers in their area and the third sector into working together to deliver improvements across public health.[28]

A tension however persisted between a health system based on partnership and reforms directed from the centre. The way the long-term NHS Plan of 2000 was drawn up, for instance, demonstrated a strangely centralised character if the NHS was to work together locally and regionally. The Secretary of State's recently created Strategy Unit, containing academics, outside experts and staff from the NHS and reporting at least indirectly to Alan Milburn's spad Simon Stevens, played a key role in a system that remained as much 'top-down' as it was 'bottom-up'. Modernisation Action Teams or MATs, drawing in NHS professionals, were supposed to follow up on both the Plan and more general policy in an inclusive manner. But what Blair and Milburn really wanted was a more diverse, 'competitive' NHS that fitted with their increasing belief that the NHS was a monolith that needed shaking up. That demonstrated the limits of partnership itself.

Milburn, for instance, was very much in tune with Blair's agenda. Jeremy Heywood, at that point Blair's Principal Private Secretary, for instance praised Milburn to Blair in 2002 because he 'understands what you want and works hard and creatively to deliver *your* agenda'.[29] The methods used to plan the Plan, as it were, amounted to deploying likely allies to overcome resistance. Christine Hancock, the General Secretary of the Royal College of Nursing, and Professor Sir George Alberti, President of the Royal College of Physicians, were invited into the heart of the process as it neared completion. Organisations who might have been more argumentative, or even obstructive (for instance the BMA and NHS managers) were in this way courted then co-opted.[30]

The NHS Plan ushered in a period of fast-moving change, during which the commitment to higher funding had to be matched by the reforms sought by Blair and Milburn. For Blair, although 'the NHS Plan ... still bore marks of political and intellectual immaturity ... it was a radical departure from where we had been'. In the summer of 2002, Blair drafted a 24-page list of aspirations that had public sector reform as one of three key areas for delivery. Overall, he wanted 'diversity of supply, choice ... an end to old practices': in the healthcare sector, this would mean 'ridding ourselves of the monolithic NHS'.[31] But although lip-service was paid to the idea of 'decentralisation', the actual strategic direction of the NHS often became more centralised, not less. The abolition of many regional tiers of NHS governance led in precisely this direction. By 2001, there were twenty-nine Strategic Health Authorities; by 2006, their number had shrunk to ten.[32] Even though arms-length and target-driven management has always supposed to have been one key part of the New Public Management Labour in office deployed, the Department in practice also took more powers to the centre. The merging of the posts of NHS Chief Executive and Permanent Secretary to the Department of Health in 2000, when Nigel Crisp was appointed to both, is a case in point.[33]

Blair was therefore able to mould an NHS much more to his liking, with individual elements looking after themselves and driving productivity gains through a limited form of competition. Primary Care Trusts (PCTs) were now to be placed in the driving seat, controlling 75 per cent of the NHS budget, while later on in the 2001–05 Parliament high-performing providers could opt for a new and semi-independent Foundation Trust status – an idea that had not been mentioned, at least specifically, in the 2001 Manifesto. These Foundation Trusts' policy would now be guided, not by government, but by boards which were majority elected by members of the public and by patients. They could bid for work overseen by yet another regulator, named Monitor, which would step in if they went financially off the rails. Foundation hospitals would now receive funding via 'Payment by Results'. A 'national tariff' of fixed prices would replace block contracts negotiated (mainly with PCTs), and thus in theory allow more flexibility. Trusts with costs which were on average lower than others received a bonus, sums which the Audit Commission calculated might be worth £500 million when added up across the whole system.[34] The first tranche of Foundation Trusts launched in April 2004, while another ten followed in June 2004 and more were established during 2005.[35]

These hospitals' new freedoms were controversial among Labour MPs, who expressed fears that they would lead to a 'two-tier' health service that contained better Foundation hospitals alongside standard ones. There is no doubt that the Act in the words of some experts led to 'multiple systems of care in England', since the new NHS regulators were not given powers to always enforce treatment free at the point of use. Hospitals could, for instance, charge local authorities for personal care. This might lead to more local flexibility, but also inequity – threatening some of the key principles of the NHS itself. In 2003 this issue therefore caused the biggest rebellion over healthcare in the Parliamentary Labour Party (PLP)'s history, reducing the Government's huge majority to just seventeen.[36]

Perhaps inevitably then, accounts differ once again as to this idea's germination. Stevens, who was influential within Blair's circle of policy advisers, clearly wanted hospitals to gain a large measure of operational and even policy freedom: the Brownites in No 11 were deeply sceptical, and opposed Trusts gaining substantial financial freedoms. Blair found the whole debate 'endless, rancorous and destabilising', and in the end it contributed to the Health Secretary standing down.[37] Milburn argues that Brown slowed and watered down his programme. Balls, for his part, argues instead that the Treasury did want greater autonomy in the NHS, but Milburn had wanted Foundation hospitals to borrow privately, an ambition the Treasury simply could not countenance.[38]

'People expect choice and demand quality'

These managerial reforms were inextricably connected to the idea that patients, in consultation with their family doctors, could and should exercise more control over their own care. In late 2001, the consultative document *Extending Choice for Patients* promised that patients would be able to choose when, where and how to be treated, in consultation with their GP.[39] In 2002, the White Paper *Delivering the NHS Plan* started this process off with the promise that, by the middle of the year, patients who had been waiting more than six months or more for a heart operation could choose where they would be referred.[40] From 2006, patients could with the help of their GP choose any NHS hospital; by 2008, that right had expanded to accessing any hospital with an NHS contract that would accept the NHS rate for the treatment. NHS leaders were triumphant. Crisp argued in his pre-Christmas staff message of that year that 'we are changing the whole way the NHS works to ensure that everything we do fits around the individual needs of our patients and public'.[41]

New Labour's ideas were however and as ever multiple, shifting back and forth between different concepts at different times, and between or even within policy pronouncements. The academic Ian Greener has for instance divined three 'moments' in New Labour's health ideas, even during their early years in power: 1997–2000, during which a centralising and reforming Fabianism prevailed; 2000–02, a time of promised investment in return for much tighter performance monitoring; and then the period after 2002, during which a return to (highly constrained and managed) markets prevailed.[42] Whether doctors were making choices on behalf of patients, or whether individuals seeking care would select themselves from a roster of options, was never clear: one representative document from 2001, *Shifting the Balance of Power Within the NHS*, slid between the two concepts with apparent ease.[43] Although in practice the idea of patient power referred to specific and often very limited *particular* choices, taken more broadly the idea of choice served to convey much deeper and perhaps more *political* meanings. It served to distinguish a sensitive and discriminating 'New' Labour from an often-mythical 'Old' Labour.

Ministers were seeking to adjust state structures for an era of what they saw as rising expectations. In the age of the internet and rapid just-in-time delivery, the argument went, the NHS would have to become much more responsive to individual demands if it was to maintain public support. Here ministers could point to polling evidence showing that younger people were less likely to find the NHS satisfactory: 36 per cent of teenagers to 34-year-olds were satisfied with its overall running in 2002, as against 49 per cent of those aged 64–74 and 57 per cent of 75- to 84-year-olds.[44] Youth, novelty, modernity and individualism were all bundled together in the way New Labour imagined healthcare. As Milburn put it in two different speeches during 2002: 'choice means ... care ... tailored to the fit the needs of the individual'; 'we live in a consumer age ... Ours is the informed and enquiring society. People expect choice and demand quality.'[45] It was a powerful vision, though one mined from many sources and begging the question: what did 'choice' actually mean? As so often, New Labour sought to dominate the entire electoral battlefield, to some loss of coherence.

The way in which the public would be consulted about these changes was confused. From 2003 onwards, a legal duty rested on PCTs and NHS Trusts to involve patients and public in the running and development of services; each was required to set up a Patient and Public Involvement Forum. Yet Community Health Councils, which had been performing just this type of work since the 1970s with a great deal of success, were now wound up. Foundation Trust boards were supposed to be elected by patients and public, but they found it difficult to draw in electors. Some Foundation Trusts were able to enrol 10,000 or more to form the selectorate, but others found it hard to reach even 2,000 – while uncontested elections were common. For Trusts that were supposed to become a new type of cooperative institution, themselves consulting the populace as a whole, these were unimpressive results.[46] A House of Commons Select Committee inquiry into Foundation Trusts concluded in 2008 that both the involvement of the local community, and any genuine autonomy that might have involved, were weak and underdeveloped.[47]

At the same time, the private sector also became much more important in delivering the state's healthcare objectives: and although that might be better at delivering 'choice' narrowly in the sense of a different doctor or hospital, that was very likely not what the public meant by the word. From early on, Blair himself was keen on exploring private sector involvement in diagnostics and scanning: but as his health adviser Robert Hill cautioned him, it would 'be very hard' to shift a traditionalist like Dobson on such matters. Nor did PFI actually help in this respect, since trying to lever private sector provision into those schemes involved unnecessary controversy: 'the bigger prize', Hill wrote in May 1999, 'is using the private sector where it makes sense – across all NHS trusts'.[48] Once Dobson departed late in 1999, the way was clearer. By October 2000 Milburn signed a 'Concordat' with commercial providers, setting up rules under which the NHS could rent space or commission elective care from them, transfer critical care patients to them or work with them to improve rehabilitation or preventive care. The subsequent expansion of independent provision from outside the NHS was clearly significant, though its overall initial impact (like the impact of PFI) can be exaggerated. From making up only 0.02 per cent of NHS non-emergency inpatient activity in 2003/04, that figure rose to 2.2 per cent by 2008/09. In some sectors these numbers were much higher: by that same year nearly 12 per cent of hip replacements were provided in the private sector, for instance, with over 5 per cent of senile cataract procedures conducted in the independent sector.[49]

By 2007 thirty-five Independent Sector Treatment Centres (ISTCs), owned by private providers but operated by the NHS, had also been opened, offering orthopaedics, ophthalmology, and various forms of non-intensive surgery. However, these took no more than 2 per cent of patients. The role of non-NHS providers continued to expand, though: private hospitals handled 10 per cent of elective surgery in 2010.[50] Progress along the road to patient 'choice' was therefore slow, though it was not so slow that its beneficiaries (and opponents) failed to notice. A large number of patients at this time remembered being offered a choice of hospitals – 50 per cent of them in one Department of Health study published in 2009, and 47 per cent in a King's Fund survey released in 2010.[51]

The reason that many ISTCs could take patients so quickly, nearly abolishing many waiting lists in the process, was that they were not as full, and therefore not as narrowly 'efficient', as NHS units. ISTC occupancy rates were 78 per cent as against 95 per cent in an NHS that was as usual being run far too 'hot', close to its limits and capacity and unable therefore to react quickly to change. Unsurprisingly, given this amount of unused capacity, operations performed in ISTCs cost more than in NHS hospitals.[52] On the other hand, competition both with and within the NHS does seem to have yielded some real benefits. A detailed study of 30,000 hip replacements conducted in 2008–09 shows that demand for each provider's services did indeed depend on quality, as well as distance from the patient's home. Three key variables – the mortality rate in the hospital, waiting times and MRSA infection rates – all materially affected patients' and doctors' choices of where to undergo elective procedures. Over time the range of choice offered clearly did increase. In 2003–06, 95 per cent of GP referrals were to three hospitals, but by 2008–09 that figure had fallen to 75 per cent. Hospitals with good records on morality and waiting times attracted more elective patients than others, likely improving outcomes. The more 'competitive' an area was – the more hospitals offering a range of services – the greater improvements in care seemed to be.[53]

Those benefits seem to have been on a far greater scale than anything achieved by previous marketising reforms in the 1990s. There was of course the risk that NHS doctors' time could be siphoned off to benefit from the better pay and conditions in the independent sector as it expanded, but it gained only a relatively small share of overall activity. Most healthcare 'competition' remained within the heavily managed NHS quasi-market. There were clear differences from the agenda pursued by New Labour's predecessors. This time – unlike in the 1980s and 1990s – increased flexibility came with far higher funding. Also, providers both inside and outside the NHS were expected to cooperate as well as compete, and quality was much more tightly monitored. Under the fixed cost system, hospitals were not allowed to compete on price.[54] Given all this, it would perhaps have been surprising had these reforms *not* returned any benefits. Even the Conservatives' Internal Market of the 1990s seems to have been associated with a slight deterioration in death rates where competition was stronger, at least for the financial years 1995/96 to 1997/98.[55] Raising funding overall, and buttressing competition with a battery of controls, seems to have avoided the danger that quality of care would be overlooked in the rush to compete.

The idea that confident and assertive middle-class residents would monopolise services was not borne out in practice. Patients who thought 'choice' important were certainly *not* clustered in higher education or earnings brackets, although their awareness of these rights was concentrated among the better-off. King's Fund research showed that older patients aged 51–80, Black and Minority Ethnic patients, women and people with no qualifications valued choice more than others.[56] A London Patient Choice pilot, much-cited at the time, actually showed that socio-economic status made little difference to the desire or ability to exercise choice. That pilot, though, did see patients supported through the process. It was little surprise that constant help and advice might have enhanced everyone's feeling of empowerment, as well as perhaps making up for some cultural divides and a lack of information about how the system worked.[57] Two-thirds of patients asked to select a hospital in the London pilot did take up the option to exercise a choice: but these patients were offered a clearly structured process and talked through the idea by specialist advisers. A fully funded Patient Advice Service, a liaison staff to enhance patients' investment in and understanding of their own health, would have been a necessary, indeed vital part of supporting the choice agenda if it had gone any further.[58] The NHS's travails since the 2000s have unfortunately made such ambitious aims now seem unrealistic – a distant fantasy from a more successful era.

Making healthcare more equal?

Labour's pride in the NHS, and its continued commitment to social democratic values, were challenged most clearly by deep and persistent health inequalities – another part of its turn to a more holistic view of healthcare that has been underestimated. Dobson, as Labour's first Secretary of State on returning to office, proposed as the first point of his strategy 'a new emphasis on *measures to reduce health inequalities* as a central part of our public health strategy'.[59] The Acheson Report, commissioned by Labour on its return to office and published in 1998, made three central recommendations in this sphere: that all health policies should be assessed in relation to health inequalities; that the health of families with children should be given a high priority, given how crucial early years are in terms of development; and that steps should be taken to boost the living standards of poorer households, given the links between income and health. The NHS itself, Acheson recommended, should place equality of access far higher on its list of priorities, and adopt funding formulas more clearly orientated towards meeting the needs of patients from deprived or ethnic minority populations. Health and local authorities should be asked to carry out regular audits of their progress towards more equitable access.[60]

Unfortunately, both conducting policy in that manner, and connecting those policies once started to outcomes, proved fraught with difficulties. The trend towards health inequality had been obvious for some time, as Acheson's report made quite clear. The gap between the life expectancy at birth of social classes I and V had widened strongly, if inconsistently, between the 1970s and the 1990s. Even in terms of morbidity, defined as long-standing illnesses, the extraordinary achievements of modern medicine overall were not matched by any progress in narrowing the gap between social classes. The difference between the numbers of professional and unskilled men reporting long-term ailments fell a little between 1974 and 2000: but for women, the gap got bigger.[61]

In response, the Government's 1999 'Action Report' on Acheson claimed that Labour's new agenda was 'the most comprehensive programme of work to tackle health inequalities ever undertaken in this country'.[62] Dobson announced in 1998 that 'the whole Government … is committed to the greatest ever reduction in health inequalities'. The NHS planning document *Modernising Health and Social Services* said that the Government was aiming 'to improve the health of the worst off in society at a faster rate than the rest of the population'. In 2001, national targets on infant mortality and life expectancy were laid down for England and Wales, further emphasising this commitment to more egalitarian results. The gap between social classes, in the former case, and geographical area in the latter, were now supposed to narrow.[63] *Our Healthier Nation* was explicit when it aimed at reducing health inequalities. The NHS Plan, and the Treasury's Public Service Agreement with the Department of Health that followed in 2002, were also clear about the Government's aims for 2010: to shrink the gap in infant mortality between routine and manual groups and the population as a whole by 10 per cent, while reducing the difference in life expectancy as between the fifth of areas where it was lowest and the population overall.[64]

Tackling Health Inequalities announced a search for successful interventions that lowered health inequalities, alongside a public consultation and a 'cross-cutting review' across departments (2002–03). The themes chosen broke the problem down further, focusing on cycles of health inequalities; the major killers with strong socioeconomic gradients; access to public services; strengthening poorer communities; and reaching vulnerable groups. Despite the early signs of a relative decline in the overall use of targets at this time, *Tackling Health Inequalities* was replete with twelve 'headline indicators', which were still concrete targets, as well as eighty-two 'departmental commitments' – individual policies that would allow movement towards the 'indicators'.[65] A total of over £20bn was committed to meeting these aims: though these included more general policies on poverty and inequality that undoubtedly did have some bearing on physical and mental health (such as tax credits), that headline sum also included a new funding formula for the NHS designed to funnel resources to poorer areas.[66]

Post-NHS Plan targets on relative health inequalities were mostly not met. Inequalities in the mean age of death actually increased between 1997 and 2007, a trend that was observable among women but was even sharper among men. Differences in life expectancy between the poorest and richest local authorities actually got worse between the early 1990s and 2002, though that figure then began to improve.[67] There is, on the other hand, evidence that infant mortality rates in the most deprived parts of England converged with the overall norm: the absolute difference between the two groups of areas fell by 0.12 per cent a year during part of this period (1999–2010). Significantly, they had risen in the years running up to New Labour's efforts in this regard (1983–99) and were to increase again thereafter, during the period of Coalition and Conservative austerity.[68] Even so, New Labour's target on infant mortality was missed, while geographically there was a small increase in the difference in life expectancy between the poorest and richest 10 per cent of local authority areas between 1992–94 and 2001–3.[69]

It is important to note that this was because everyone's health was improving; life expectancy in targeted 'spearhead areas' of deep poverty still grew by two to three years over a decade. Mortality rates fell fast in the most deprived areas between 1999–2001 and 2008–10, but they were slightly outstripped by the improving situation everywhere else: the three-year moving mortality average for men, for instance, fell by more than 20 per cent in both targeted areas and (by a point or so more) in the rest of England.[70] To see how this works in practice, we can observe that between 2001 and 2010 *relative* mortality in the most deprived 10 per cent of areas in England went up (from 67 per cent to 82 per cent higher) when compared with the least deprived decile. But *absolute* age-adjusted mortality actually fell rapidly in the poorest areas, from 1,995 per 100,000 people to 1,610. Conversely, after Labour left office, mortality stagnated, with little progress made anywhere, but the gap between richest and poorest areas fell a little – back down from 82 per cent to 76 per cent. Residents of England's most deprived areas would likely prefer the progress of the 2000s, when the alternative was the stagnation of the 2010s.[71] And reductions in inequality may also have been subject to a lag similar to that between increasing funding and performance: we again need to move the clock forward to see the impact of these far-reaching policies. If we look at life expectancy in the most deprived 20 per cent of England's local authorities as against the rest during the period 2004–12, there was a small fall of nearly a month every year in the gap between them. In the period 1983–2003, that figure had been going up, not down, as it did again as austerity took hold in 2013–15.[72]

So this push towards more equal health outcomes involved both successes and failures, including many missed opportunities but also encompassing probable falls in inequality when it came to infant mortality and also possible reductions to differences in long-term life expectancy. Even so, the ambitious aim of sharply narrowing inequalities proved beyond the Government. The record on 2003's 'headline indicators' was mixed. Some progress was made on the narrowing of inequalities in terms of road accidents, child poverty, education, housing, flu vaccinations, teenage pregnancy and some of the major killers such as cancer and heart disease. But little had been done to narrow inequalities on access to primary care, diet or school sport. In 2008 the Department of Health had to admit that 'the health of the most disadvantaged has not improved as quickly as that of the better off. Inequalities in health persist and, in some cases, have widened.'[73] The Government's ten-year review of *Tackling Health Inequalities* concluded similarly that 'the gap is no narrower than when the targets were first set'.[74]

Overall, equity in terms of access to healthcare (as opposed to equality in results) mirrored the results of the Government's efforts to narrow social and economic divides as a whole. As the rising tide of funding opened up the NHS to everyone, not just poorer citizens, the effect on equity was small. Contradictions, unintended consequences and trade-offs abounded. It seems likely, for instance, that GPs spent more of their time dealing with ostensibly 'healthy' patients, as the Government's emphasis on prevention and public health dictated. But this, of course, meant that the *share* of access available to the long-term sick (and likely less wealthy) patient might decline. Elective inpatient admissions climbed for people coming in from neighbourhoods with high scores on the Economic Deprivation Index, but they rose at a similar rate for those from much less deprived areas.[75]

Yet again, New Labour's policies seem to have moved the country slightly towards equity, though not on any really huge scale. Intervention in detail yielded good results, but they were often not enough to allow them to run up the same down escalator they faced on welfare policy. A Quality of Outcomes Framework (QoF) for GPs was for instance expensive, but provided family doctors with incentives as clinical indicators improved: that seems to have raised the performance of the worst-performing practices (often in deprived areas) faster than elsewhere. Between 2004 and 2007, the median achievement on QoF indicators rose by 4.4 per cent for the least 20 per cent of deprived areas, while it rose by 7.6 per cent for the poorest. That reduced the gap between those groups from 4 per cent to 0.8 per cent.[76] There may also have been a small but measurable improvement in socio-economic equity when it came to non-emergency hospital visits. Breaking down the data into very small areas shows that poorer neighbourhoods saw referrals and access rise more quickly than in the rest of the country, and beyond what measures of demographic and clinical need might have suggested. Better primary care facilities in those areas, coupled with more capacity in the hospital system, likely saw the NHS make progress in low-income neighbourhoods slightly quicker than elsewhere.[77] But none of that came near to meeting the grand targets of *Modernising Health*, *Our Healthier Nation* or *Tackling Health Inequalities*.

Rebuilding trust in the NHS

By the late 1990s and early 2000s, the NHS was clearly a site of deep public concern – despite, or perhaps because of, its status as popular national institution and unifying symbol. The Wanless Report was explicit about this widespread dissatisfaction.[78] Given that dire situation, public opinion for a long time showed little sign of reacting to Labour's changes – as Blair well knew. In June 2001 he circulated his staff saying that they should be 'under no illusion: within 6 months, it must be clear: change is underway; we are through the winter without an NHS crisis'.[79] Deep doubt about the NHS's future clearly persisted in the public's mind. In 2002, 30 per cent of voters told Ipsos MORI that they thought that the NHS would get much better over the following few years; 30 per cent expected it to stay the same, while 25 per cent thought the NHS would get worse. Two years later, in 2004, those figures had not moved much at all: they were respectively 26 per cent, 35 per cent and 26 per cent.[80] The same set of findings showed that public satisfaction had been relatively static for some time, responding as much to political perceptions as 'real' performance. Net satisfaction with the NHS stood at −1 in 1991, +6 in 1994, −16 in 1997, +6 in 1998, +3 in 2000, but still only −1 in 2002. More than a decade of reforms had shifted public opinion precisely nowhere.[81]

By 2005, figures from the pollsters YouGov showed that only 26 per cent of voters thought that 'the Government has the right policies for the NHS'. In 2006, 29 per cent of voters thought the NHS was still underfunded; 64 per cent thought that the NHS was now adequately resourced, but that it wasted too much. Only 4 per cent of respondents believed that the NHS was both well-funded and efficient. On the other hand, a great deal of these doubts were down to a kind of inherent general pessimism, and New Labour would become familiar with the dichotomy between voters who thought things were getting worse but who could actually see the situation getting better all around them. Patients' actual experiences were lifting the mood about the care that individuals received: again in 2006, the numbers satisfied with their local hospital (68 per cent to 14 per cent) and with their last visit to hospital (81 per cent to 9 per cent) were impressive, though in the latter case that number had hardly changed at all since the same question was asked in 2001.[82] A more narrowly defined concept of 'satisfaction', linked to what voters themselves saw and experienced – or heard about from others – did gradually filter through into more general perceptions. When the BSA asked people 'How satisfied or dissatisfied would you say you are with the way in which the National Health Service runs nowadays?' the 'very' or 'quite' satisfied line surged upwards after 2001: from under 40 per cent to 70 per cent by 2010.[83] The backdrop of worry about an NHS that the public so idealised, but could never quite perform the way they wanted, could be blanked out by a foreground of better, quicker and more successful treatment.

The 2001 election does seem to have marked some sort of watershed, because for instance on Gallup's figures the Government's net rating on the NHS thereafter rose markedly, from a disastrous −43 in February to a merely unpopular −18 in August, following Brown's big-spending NHS Budget and Spending Review.[84] By 2008, 51 per cent of patients reported that they were 'very' or 'quite' satisfied with the NHS, a figure that had risen 17 percentage points since 1997.[85] The public were extremely hard to please in this area of public policy, as Blair himself conceded they had every right to be: but the Conservatives' failure to make progress on the issue showed that Labour were at least neutralising the issue. William Hague's 2001 general election campaign failed to put up any real case at all on the NHS, though the Conservatives did mount a spirited campaign on the NHS in 2005, focusing on individual cases of postponed operations and the prevalence of the MRSA 'superbug' in NHS hospitals. Labour's lead over the Conservatives declined between 1997 and 2005, to be sure, but they at least managed to hold the line: a lead of fifty-four points at the 1997 election became twenty-eight points in 2001, and twenty-one points in 2005.[86]

Voters told pollsters again and again that they liked and wanted more choice. But that does not necessarily mean that they saw it as particularly important.

According to one Research Council study, twenty-five out of forty-eight laypeople they asked about this issue were confused as to what patient choice would even mean, a view summed up in the following: 'Patient choice is ridiculous. What good is choice going to make for me? When I am ill I just want to get into a hospital and be tended to by people who know what they are doing.'[87] In one Ipsos MORI survey from 2004, patients listed a choice of 'where and when they were treated' as only the eleventh most important element in NHS care (out of sixteen), behind such variables as car parking. In 2007, when asked to choose between four priorities for the NHS as a whole, just 6 per cent chose 'make sure people have a lot of choice about their treatment and care' as opposed to 78 per cent for 'make sure people who are ill get treatment quickly'.[88]

But the BSA surveys allow us to dig a little deeper, and to confirm the idea that choice could also be highly valued – especially when it came to perceptions of care at individual hospitals. 72 per cent of those who perceived 'a lot' of choice were satisfied with their treatment, but only 55 per cent of those who thought they had been given 'a little' choice, and 49 per cent of those who thought they had none. The finding is even stronger in terms of hospitals that match or exceed expectations, and interestingly more powerful among older Britons, as well as those in lower supervisory, semi-routine or routine jobs.[89] It is also the case that if choice was linked to better service, for instance in the London Patient Choice Project where subjects were asked if they would like more choice if it led to shorter waiting times, then numbers in favour rose enormously. It may also be significant that net satisfaction with the NHS in England was often higher (for instance in the 2004 BSA survey) than in Scotland and Wales, countries where moves towards flexibility and choice were not so pronounced and where performance lagged compared to England.[90]

Lurching towards better health

New Labour had set out to 'save' the NHS, and in fact made enormous strides towards doing just that. From employing 1.1 million people in 1998, the NHS workforce had grown to 1.3 million by 2008. The numbers employed by the NHS went up by 26 per cent, rising by 272,000 in a decade (more than 160,000 of these were clinical professionals). The number of doctors working in the country increased, from below 2 per 1,000 population to over 2.5, passing the United States and closing much of the gap with France.[91] Although starting with one of the worst life expectancies in the EU, that indicator improved more than in most other EU states between 1980 and 2010. Improvements in people's actual health were startling, even though in many cases they were following on from long-term trends. The death rate fell 17 per cent; the number of deaths due to circulatory disease among under-75s per 100,000 fell from 129 to 74. Particularly acute problems showed the same marked improvement. The annual fall in cancer mortality, targeted specifically by Labour in power, had on one reckoning been 0.53 per cent under the Conservatives: under Labour, that progress accelerated to 1.17 per cent per annum.[92] Other figures, for instance those from Cancer Research UK, give similar results: the mean fall in cancer deaths under the Conservatives in the 1980s and early 1990s was 0.2 per cent a year, while from the mid-1990s that progress sped up to 0.9 per cent per year (see Figure 4.6).

Other measures of performance demonstrate strong progress. Waiting times fell to the lowest in NHS history; eventually, all Strategic Health Authorities met the target of an eighteen-week maximum between GP referral and beginning any treatment. The average wait to be treated in hospital declined to only 8.6 weeks.[93] Ambitions for public health policy were also very high: it can hardly be said that ministers did not try to make Britain a healthier place. 2.4 million people gave up smoking, assisted by the ban on smoking in public places that started in 2007. £2.4bn more for physical education in schools meant that nine out of ten were taking the required classes by 2010. School fruit was encouraged under the NHS Plan, and 440 million pieces of fruit or vegetables were being given out to two million children every year. Junk food advertising was barred from children's television in the same year that smoking in public places was banned.[94]

But NHS 'reform' owed more to traditional Westminster models than New Labour rhetoric might allow. It was still directed from the centre rather than being made in any true sense of partnership. The Government always remained in ultimate control – reflecting a political reality that the Conservatives would have to face even after the NHS reforms they forced through in the Coalition years. Those changes went much further in disintegrating the 'national' character of an 'NHS' than New Labour ever had: it would hardly have been a 'national' service at all if they had got all their ideas past their Liberal Democrat coalition partners. But the Government still got the blame when things went wrong.[95] This top-down reality extended to reforms supposedly designed to allow power to leach away from Whitehall to the frontline, as the NHS Plan at least claimed to be. As Arturo Alvarez-Rosete and Nicholas Mays have put it: 'The Government was fundamentally in control of the process, selecting the timing and releasing information to the media to test the public mood towards

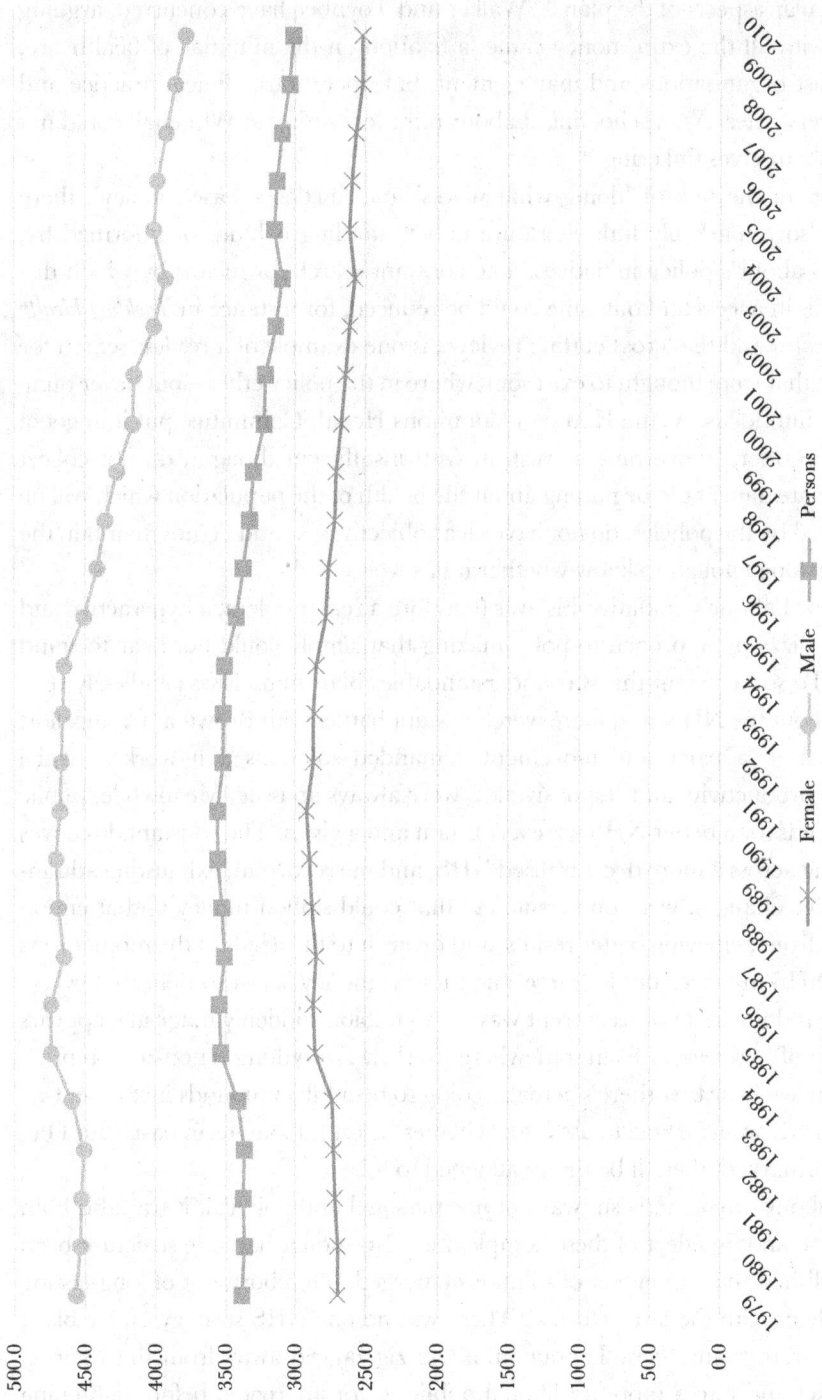

Figure 4.6 Cancer mortality per 100,000, UK (1979–2010)

Source: Cancer Research UK, *Cancer Mortality for All Cancers Combined*, www.cancerresearchuk.org/health-professional/cancer-statistics/mortality/all-cancers-combined#heading-One, accessed 6 March 2025.

particular aspects of the plan.'[96] Walker and Toynbee have concurred, arguing that with all the extra money came 'a fixation on the minutiae of healthcare, not just organisations and management, but operations, clinical practice and recovery rates. As in schooling, Labour ministers sitting in Whitehall could not stop themselves tinkering.'[97]

For all the talk of 'doing what works' and 'evidence-based policy', there was also remarkably little literature either standing behind, or informed by, New Labour's policy initiatives. The constant search for means by which disparities in access and outcome could be reduced, for instance in *Tackling Health Inequalities* and the 'cross-cutting review', is one example of a restless search for 'wins' that were thought to exist somewhere in the policy ether – but never quite came into focus. As the House of Commons Health Committee put it in 2009: 'all too often [g]overnments rush in with insufficient thought, do not collect adequate data at the beginning about the health of the population which will be affected by the policies, do not have clear objectives ... and do not maintain the policy long enough to know whether it has worked'.[98]

New Labour's 'initiative-itis' was therefore a real problem, a hyperactive and often dizzying approach to policymaking that simply could not bear to stand still. To some extent this was understandable. Blair himself was endlessly restless about the NHS, and there were constant battles with Brown as Chancellor; Labour as a party and movement demanded solutions that worked, while NHS productivity and responsiveness were always an issue. Meanwhile, public demands for a better NHS were a constant and a given. The constant directives cutting across a more decentralised NHS, and the recurrent, exhausting administrative changes, were one result. All that could siphon money and attention away from achieving better results, and divert it to the needs of the moment. As one NHS manager put it: 'there's no money, money is just so tight that everything is done in a non-recurrent way ... 10 million suddenly magically appears in sort of ... October from somewhere [but] ... Everything is non-recurrent ... Today we hear that there's actually going to be a billion pounds investment ... maybe ... we'll be able to use it for schemes ... on [a] long-term basis, but I bet it's earmarked, there'll be things attached to it.'[99]

Labour's hyperactivism was not just personal and political: it was also both a cause and an effect of these complexities. No sooner had one structure been established than a new set of solutions emerged, often born out of long-lasting problems with the last 'reforms'. There was no one NHS strategy under Blair: there were many. New Labour ministers zig-zagged away from the Internal Market and into a more traditional public sector approach, before tightening power and influence around the launch of the NHS Plan and then launching out into a world of flexible commissioning and Foundation Trusts. They made only mixed progress towards 'choice', and the narrowing of health inequalities for the most part defeated their best efforts. On the other hand, New Labour's policy moves were increasingly underpinned with vastly more money for the NHS and a focus on quality and fixed charges that lifted performance to all-time highs. All this together helped to deliver a health system for Britain that was never before and has never again been bettered: if we zoom out from all the detail, and consider those overall achievements in a context of an NHS in crisis during both the 1990s and 2020s, none of this era's false starts and manoeuvres seem nearly so important. The simple reality was that patients and public were far better protected by the NHS during these years than they had been in the 1980s and 1990s, and they knew it.

5

'Education, education, education'

Old wine in new bottles?

New Labour's education policies applied and accelerated Conservative ideas from the 1980s and 1990s: there was no question, by this point, of going back on the idea of the National Curriculum brought in by Thatcher during the 1980s, nor of making 'all in' comprehensives the centrepiece of the whole system as both parties had done through most of the 1960s and 1970s. Labour's City Academies also bore a strong flavour of the previous administration's City Technology Colleges, with both enjoying operational independence from the state sector and private or charitable funding. The language of 'standards', discipline, parental choice and school 'values' were all now paramount across the board. Prominent educationalists, such as Sally Tomlinson, have argued that New Labour talked a great deal about 'inclusion', but in fact 'ensured that the education system remains divided and divisive, particularly in socio-economic terms'.[1] As she puts it: 'there was an acceptance of a Conservative faith in choice and competition, with education developing as a market commodity driven by consumer demands ... fuelled by league table publication, school choices, specialist schools and failing schools'.[2]

This approach may, however, underplay the significance of New Labour's ambitious and optimistic view of what the state could achieve, rather than asking parents and teachers alone to take up society's burdens. As so often with Third Way thinking in this era, the state's enabling, convening, networking and inspecting powers might be more radical than they looked – a truth that allowed the character of the new education system introduced during the 1980s to evolve, though perhaps not to be transformed. In this the Third Way was very much of its time. A literature and ethos that came to be known as the School Effectiveness Movement, with its roots in the 1970s, insisted that conservative pessimism rooted in genetics, heredity and a pessimistic view of society was far too gloomy. This outlook became especially influential across the 1980s and 1990s, just as the idea of early intervention and preschool learning also became more fashionable again. Schools *could* make a real difference, it was argued: school leadership, skilled teaching, intellectual challenge, focus and high expectations were all at the centre of work by educationalists such as Michael Rutter and Paul Mortimore. It was these ideas, and the general insights of Giddens around the power of networks, that inspired a tight-knit group of educational enthusiasts including David Miliband, Michael Barber and Andrew Adonis and helped them build a distinctive education agenda within New Labour.[3]

Strong lines of continuity with the Conservatives remained. Key New Labour figures such as Mandelson and Roger Liddle were clear, for instance in their 1996 book *The Blair Revolution*, that 'each school should be made clearly responsible for its own performance and be subject to a mixture of external pressure and support in order to achieve it'. Not only that, but 'New Labour wants to allow schools the maximum freedom to develop their own distinctive ethos and identity'.[4] That was one difference between itself and the Thatcherites that New Labour did articulate: but the provision of far greater resources was important too. Adonis, in his 1997 book *A Class Act* (co-authored with Stephen Pollard), attacked what he regarded as a dual betrayal of young people brought about by Labour's insistence on destroying schools' independence, and the Conservatives refusing to fund the state system to anything like the level it needed. For Adonis, it was 'a sad irony that in destroying the direct grant schools on the altar of equal opportunity, the 1974–79 Labour government succeeded in denying opportunity to many poor children'. All Labour had done, by instating every school fit into one mould, had been to entrench the power of the fee-paying public schools even further. On the other hand, underfunding under Thatcher and Major had led to a situation where, even in 1996, one survey showed that 92 per cent of schools had temporary classrooms and 36 per cent had outside toilets.[5]

Advocates of the Third Way believed that many set-piece battles over grammars versus comprehensives, public versus private and the state versus teachers had already been fought to an exhausted standstill. There might therefore be new opportunities to move beyond all that. Michael Barber, Chief Adviser on School Standards during Blair's first term, for his part believed that a new consensus was emerging around the ways to improve school performance. 'Away from the frontlines of the conflict', he wrote at the time, 'it is hard to see what all the sound and fury are about. Everyone agrees that every child needs, in addition to whatever dialect they speak every day, access to what used to be called BBC English ... the same is true of grammar and spelling. The idea that these should not be considered important is absurd.' For Barber, debates about how schools were governed and organised, teachers' workloads, pay and the curriculum all missed the point of education's main objective: basic standards and an emphasis on the elementary mechanics of how to learn. He argued that complete intolerance for failure, backed by measurement and with constant intervention from outside making sure no school fell behind, could push up standards everywhere. To assume anything else, he believed, was to accept that ability and achievement were fixed and could not be altered – a stultifying and depressing conclusion which educational evidence increasingly contradicted.[6]

At the very beginning of Blair's leadership in the mid-1990s, Labour was more interested in building up a loose framework of principles rather than dictating specific policies. As embodied in her 1994 policy paper, *Opening Doors to a Learning Society*, Shadow Education Secretary Ann Taylor focused on broad principles rather than the endpoint of results: these were listed as access, quality, continuity, accountability and partnership. *Opening Doors* wanted to give power away from the empire successive Secretaries of State had built up through the 1980s and the early 1990s, as they tried to rein in the powers of local authorities. Schools' place in the wider community was central to this vision. Ideas such as the continual use of school facilities by the general public, and of lifelong learning, were at this point central to Labour thought. Council-run local education authorities (LEAs) would return to a key role in planning education places and services for all state schools, giving back at least some of the powers the Conservatives had stripped from them in the 1980s and 1990s.[7]

Taylor, though, was soon replaced by Blunkett, a much more reliable advocate of the 'standards' approach so dear to Miliband, Adonis and Barber. In 1995 a new policy document, *Diversity and Excellence*, promised to replace the Conservatives' semi-independent Grant Maintained (GM) schools with so-called 'Foundation' schools, which in practice might not look so different. Day-to-day schooling would still be in the hands of heads, though LEAs would retain a strategic and enabling role for all schools – including overall responsibility for admissions policy. But Labour was by now in no doubt that 'the whole notion of LEA *control* of schools – on which the drive for GM status started – is history. LEAs do not control schools. Schools do.' LEAs were there to support schools, for instance in the production of Education Development Plans which would 'form the basis of the national drive for rapid and radical improvement in standards and effectiveness'.[8] The shift was initially one more of tone and intent rather than of a battery of concrete policy proposals, in line with New Labour's intention to pose as protector of public service users, not providers. Blair wrote in *The Times* that Labour's platform 'was not devised to please the National Union of Teachers. It was devised to meet the concerns of parents.'[9]

New Labour's education theorists (for instance Barber and Adonis) believed that a new fusion could be achieved: schools would be held accountable for their performance, but given more authority, more respect and more resources. In this way they would play their part in more active and engaged communities. New Labour's Janus face looked in two directions once again. The context of long neglect of many of England's state schools, despite teachers' best efforts, should be taken into account here. The Labour adviser Peter Hyman, later a speechwriter for Blair in Number 10 and a schoolteacher himself, found Brown of the same mind in 1993: at that point the Shadow Chancellor wrote his staff a note about Britain's problems, including as its fourth key point 'a school system that fails to meet the standards we need'.[10] Labour's diagnosis was indeed stark, codified in the 1997 Manifesto: 'Britain has a smaller share of 17- and 18-year-olds in full-time education than any major industrial nation. Nearly two-thirds of the British workforce lack vocational qualifications.'[11] The party promised increased spending on education, nursery places for all 4-year-olds and a reduction in class sizes to under thirty for all five to 7-year-olds, as well as higher standards and new Information Technology for schools. The Conservatives' Assisted Places Scheme, which allowed some low-income children to attend independent schools, would be abolished to recoup some of the costs.[12]

To all these intellectual and political trends we should add one more element, which is the idea of education as investment. This was another constant theme in theories of globalisation current at the time: the idea, familiar in some forms from at least the New Liberal era at the turn of the nineteenth and twentieth centuries, that national economic performance was a race won by the most skilled, educated and adaptable. More control over truly national curricula, and more emphasis on useful 'skills', was therefore called for to raise the country's level of human capital. Education thus became one crucial facet of supply-side reform – one which New Labour believed had been neglected during the 1980s. As Blair told the *New Statesman* in 1995: 'globalisation is changing the nature of the nation state as power becomes more diffuse and borders more porous ... The role of government in this world of change is ... to create a competitive base of physical infrastructure and human skills.'[13] The Blair government's first Education White Paper declared that 'we are talking about investing in human capital in an age of knowledge. To compete in the global economy ... we will have to unlock the potential of every young person.'[14]

Rebuilding schools ... and the system

Once in office, Labour's education record was even more hyperactive than in healthcare, and contradicted at least some of the impression of continuity: between 1997 and 2007 Labour published four White Papers and passed six Education Acts of various types, not to mention launching a host of initiatives, plans and reports. Again, one main element was simply more money. Funding increased to the tune of £19bn even during Labour's relatively lean first three years in office, with more funds (for instance) supporting school playing fields, LEAs' support services and a 'Fresh Start' for struggling schools closed and reopened under different leadership. Labour's initial moves were therefore aimed at repairing some of the damage underfunding had caused, when for instance they dramatically slowed the sell-off of playing fields. Still, the pace of improvement seemed glacial to Number 10, and increasingly it seemed that the party's declared aim of transforming education was not being met. Blair told Brown in January 1999 that 'he had spoken to a number of headteachers ... and school governors in recent weeks and they were all giving him the same message – their budget allocations for next year were not significantly higher than last year and would not be enough to deliver a perceptible improvement in services'. Blair continued:

> The Government had been elected to improve public services. Yet it was becoming increasingly clear that the public did not really notice incremental reform. The problem with the current strategy was that it was not sufficiently 'transforming'. It might be more effective to concentrate over the next year on getting one or two big symbolic things right rather than continuing with the current strategy. For example, we might consider a [Rudy] Giuliani-style drive to completely transform Inner London schools, going through them one by one and sacking all the headteachers who were not up to the job.'[15]

Gradually expenditure increased more steeply, and in real terms rose from £50bn a year when Labour came to power to £90bn per annum when they left office. In 2020/21 prices that meant a rise from £60bn per annum to over £100bn a year (see Figure 5.1). The 1998 Comprehensive Spending Review did not give Education everything it wanted, but the planned increase in funding was from £38bn in 1998/99 to £48bn in 2001/02. That allowed ministers to meet their school class size targets, and to further increase capital spending

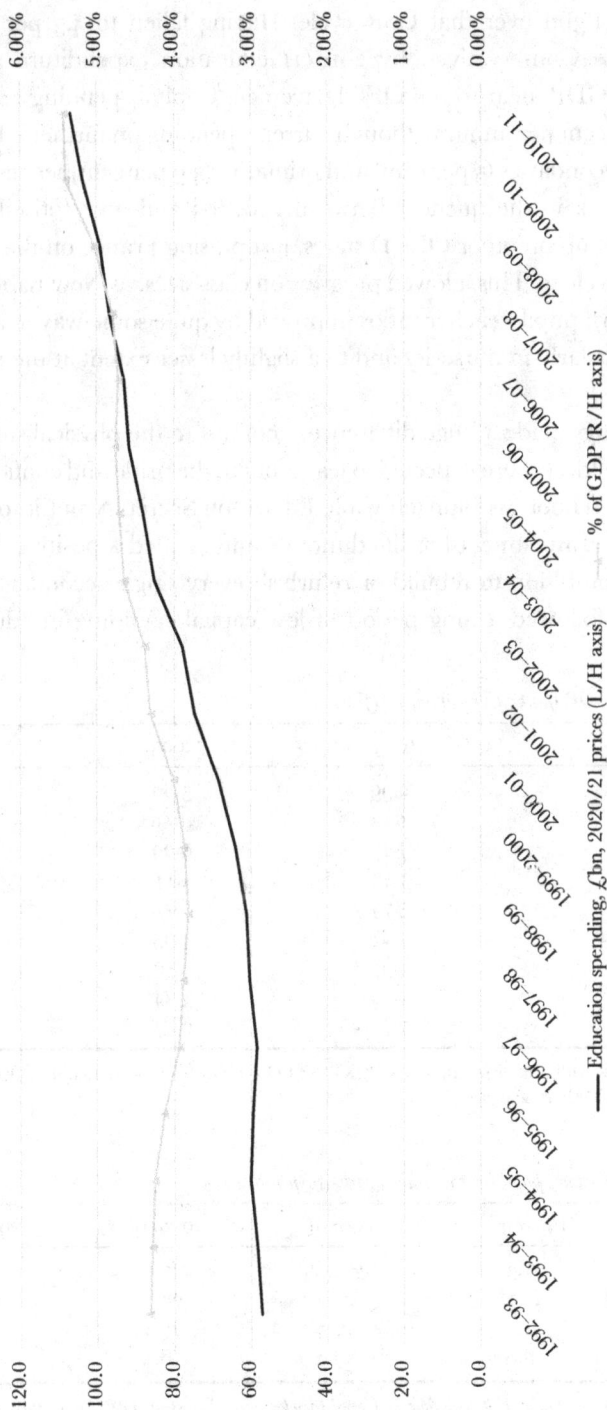

Figure 5.1 UK education spending, 1992/93–2010/11

Source: P. Bolton, *Education Spending in the UK*, House of Commons Library Research Briefing 1078 (November 2021), table 1, p. 26.

by a total of £1.3bn over that CSR cycle. Having fallen to 4.5 per cent of GDP under the Conservatives, by 2010/11 education expenditure reached 6.2 per cent of GDP, near to the OECD average. Capital spending grew rapidly (at 12.9 per cent per annum), though current spending on further education (6.1 per cent), secondaries (5 per cent) and primaries (3.9 per cent) seems to have been further back in the queue.[16] Between 2002/03 and 2005/06 education spending caught up on other OECD states, just passing France on the way, as Table 5.1 makes clear. This allowed progress on class sizes, as New Labour had promised in 1997: pupil–teacher ratios improved by quite some way in all types of school, particularly in nurseries and to a slightly lesser extent at the primary level (Table 5.2).[17]

Better buildings made a huge difference – not just to the physical surroundings in which children were expected to learn, but to the pride and confidence of everyone in the school. As Blunkett while Education Secretary put it to Brown in 1998, 'this first investment has lifted morale and created a positive mood'.[18] New Labour's ambition to rebuild or refurbish every single secondary school in the country followed a long period of low capital spending in education,

Table 5.1 National GDP spent on education, 1995–2010

	1995	2005	2010
Belgium	2.99	5.80	6.44
Germany	4.43	n/a	4.94
Denmark	7.47	8.09	8.56
Spain	4.43	4.14	4.86
France	5.79	n/a	5.66
United Kingdom	4.84	4.93	5.67
Ireland	4.87	4.52	6.05
Italy	4.32	4.24	4.33
Norway	7.70	6.87	6.75

Source: https://data.worldbank.org/indicator/SE.XPD.TOTL.GD.ZS?end=2011&name_desc=false& start=1995, accessed 23 April 2023.

Table 5.2 United Kingdom, pupil–teacher ratios, various types of school

	1995/96	2000/01	2008/09	2009/10
Nursery	21.3	23.1	17.5	17.3
Primary	22.7	22.3	20.7	20.7
Secondary	16.1	16.5	15.4	15.3
All	18.0	17.9	16.4	16.2

Source: DfE, *Education and Training Statistics for the United Kingdom 2011* (London: DfE, 2011), table 1.7, p. 15

and would test the system to its limits. Even by 2001/02, as Adonis told Blair, the capital programme had achieved improvements to 6,000 schools out of 24,000, with 120 schools either new or having been rebuilt: 350 schools had seen their temporary classrooms removed. Coupled with the target of rebuilding or remodelling half of all primary schools, the spending drive took capital spending on school buildings to £8bn a year by 2010/11.[19] This spending surge – unmatched since the demographic bulge of the 1950s and 1960s – definitely bore some fruit. As one primary head in Enfield told Toynbee and Walker, his top year now had their own common room and library, building up their confidence before moving on to secondary school. A new nursery had been built; the playground re-laid.[20]

Beyond the First and Second Ways

Within six weeks of Labour taking office, its 1997 White Paper imagined much more setting and streaming by 'ability', a Standards Task Force to decide on best practice, more specialist schools which could choose students by 'aptitude' (later set at a limit of 10 per cent) and new management or takeovers for 'underperforming' schools. Initial reactions from the teaching profession were positive, if guarded.[21] In some ways, this was an acceleration of Whitehall's agenda under the Conservatives. When they left office there were 210 technology colleges, 50 specialist language schools, 17 based around sports and 13 schools emphasising the arts – 290 in all. But there were 992 specialist schools in England by 2003.[22] There probably were advantages to specialist status in kudos and confidence, though one of the main and crucial benefits was added by Blair and Brown: the extra money that central government provided to bolster schools' emphasis on technology, sport and so on. As one teacher put it in a former coalmining community studied by the Education Department, 'the fact we're going to be teaching as a Sports College next year: I think that will definitely help … I think there will be money coming into the school next year and that's exciting, I'm looking forward to see how we can use that funding to improve the school a bit more'.[23]

In this way, Labour sought to chart an educational Third Way that was unlike the First Way embodied in the wartime coalition's Education Act of 1944 (which stressed voluntarism and localism), and would adopt some elements from the Second Way represented by the National Curriculum in 1988 – controlling, prescriptive, sometimes punitive. But they added new elements too. New Labour tried to grow a new strategy out of that Second Way, one that stressed greater respect for everyone involved in the sector and investment in caring for children as a whole, not just while they were physically in school. More emphasis on accountability was matched by Sure Start centres for parents and children, that 10 per cent limit on selection by aptitude, and the end of Assisted Places. About a third of the Conservatives' raft of Grant Maintained schools clearly discriminated between potential pupils on the basis of parent or pupil interviews and assessments – elements New Labour for the most part dispensed with. Not only did its new Code of Practice ban interviews (except in Church schools, for religious purposes) – levels of so-called total 'ability', rather than a narrow stream of those selected for a particular field of aptitude, were not to be given priority. This agenda might contain *elements* of change from the 1980s and 1990s, but it also sought to empower local people and communities through new links between school, community, local people and the third sector – all elements that Blair and Blunkett inherited from Taylor. There was a great deal of difference between an educational marketplace, which was the direction the Conservatives were headed in, and a highly regulated quasi-market limited to certain parts of the system with clear minimum standards, though this hardly looked much like a 'traditional' Labour agenda either.[24]

A tough inspection regime was very much of the same character, though it did soften as time went by. Chris Woodhead's approach as the Government's existing, inherited Chief Inspector of Schools was abrasive and confrontational, and Ofsted's methodology – with an emphasis placed on classroom observation – came under fire for being time-consuming, impressionistic and stressful. But that situation did not last, at least in acute form, beyond Woodhead's resignation in 2000. In 2004, David Miliband as Minister for School Standards brought in a 'New Relationship' between Ofsted and schools: improvement was to be much more centred around self-evaluation, and work with a School Improvement Partner in the shape of an apparently 'better' school. Self-evaluation from then on was a rather more collaborative affair, checked by smaller Ofsted teams, than it had been in Woodhead's heyday.[25] The gap between inspections shortened, from a norm of six years to three, but government rhetoric also shifted from confrontation to assistance. Ofsted now emphasised the support it could give schools, and its wish to assemble local and national help before severe measures were needed.[26] Support was increasingly offered alongside judgement: for instance, by 2001 more than 450 Learning Support Units were in place to help urban schools with their particular problems. Collaboration between schools, rather than confrontation with an inspectorate, was one of the best and most consensual ways to build knowledge, confidence and achievement.[27]

There was definitely a more general change in atmosphere, and softening of tone, after Blunkett moved on from Education after the 2001 election. Greater creativity was stressed for the primary sector in the Education Department's *Excellence and Enjoyment* (2003), while its guidance on *Assessment for Learning* (2004) encouraged giving students more supportive guidance all the way through a course, with less final testing at the end – in the jargon, increased formative and reduced summative assessment. In these ways the burdens of the very early and very tough emphasis on 'standards not structures' was reduced, albeit only when New Labour ministers were happier that minimum levels of achievement were much more widespread.[28] Ministers at least imagined themselves turning away from directing and imposing structural change and focused more on deepening quality. As Charles Clarke put it as Secretary of State in the Department's Five Year Strategy, published in 2004, 'we will never apologise for the directive action we took, for instance, on literacy and numeracy in 1997 … but once the basics are in place … we need a new sort of system'.[29]

From 'naming and shaming' to 'freedom'

Many parts of the Conservatives' agenda did indeed continue, though of course New Labour had never promised to row back on most of them. Labour had initially been strongly opposed to Grant Maintained schools in the early 1990s, but Blair's leadership saw the party move towards setting up different types of school, some of which looked rather like their Grant Maintained forebears. These 'Foundation' schools, set up under the 1998 Act, were only supposed to establish a loose affiliation with LEAs, and governors were still responsible for employing staff and owning the premises. Lots of other policies from the Major era were kept, notably the rhetoric about 'failing' schools and a preference for intervention if they did not improve. Soon after taking office, Stephen Byers as Education Minister signalled the continuation and intensification of the Conservatives' 'tough' regime by 'naming and shaming' what he called England's eighteen 'worst performing schools'. 'Special consultants' were to be sent in if they did not improve. Islington had day-to-day control of schools taken away from it and given to the for-profit company Cambridge Education Associates for seven years.[30]

New Labour's wave of relatively independent Academies made their first appearance as City Academies in March 2000, with the first three of these opening in 2002. These self-governing schools attracted up to £25 million from the taxpayer, and the Government hoped to raise a further £2 million from sponsors (who would choose the majority of the governors to run the school). The Government's 2005 White Paper envisaged a massive expansion of the Academies programme, growing from 27 schools to 200; and all new schools would be self-governing trusts, with many of the freedoms enjoyed by Academies. Blair was determined to break free of some of the compromises that political and administrative reality had forced on him during his first two terms, much to the chagrin of Brown in Number 11 – at least until he became Prime Minister himself. As Blair told the 2005 Labour Party Conference, 'every time I've ever introduced a reform in Government, I wish in retrospect I had gone further'.[31] He became restless about the pace of change in this as in other fields, and identified clearly the problems that he felt his first and much of his second term had left unanswered: 'what about failing comprehensives, particularly in the cities, which were the real Achilles heel of the state school system? And failing local education authorities? And the teaching profession?'[32]

Some promised school 'freedoms' did not in fact transpire, partly because they would have proved difficult to implement in practice, and also because Labour MPs were extremely sceptical about an admissions 'free for all'. Even given a myriad of concessions between the publication of the Government's 2005 White Paper and the eventual Bill put before Parliament, forty-six Labour MPs voted against its Second Reading in May 2006. That was the biggest such government rebellion since 1924, and the Bill only went through on Conservative votes.[33] By the time the Education and Inspections Act of 2006 was actually passed, a number of concessions had been made to Labour MPs who wanted to make sure that state schools would still receive pupils from a wide cross-section of society. All secondary schools were required to act 'in accordance with the Admissions Code', rather than simply 'to have regard to it', the formula the Government had initially proposed. Many of these changes were actually in line with the Government's understanding of the international evidence. A Number 10 Strategy Unit report at this time reported that (as in New Zealand) the schools system should avoid 'skimming' 'the cheapest to teach or the most able to learn', by 'using regulation and statutory guidance to prevent unfair selection'.[34] Interviews were still not allowed; LEAs could still set up a new school, though only if the Secretary of State agreed. Even so, the 2006 Act was radical enough, especially in terms of Academy governance. Local business sponsors could now provide up to 10 per cent of the capital costs; their heads and staff appointed the majority of governors, with only one from the LEA and one from parents; they were also to specialise, one more way in which specialism became deeply entrenched in the English school system.[35]

The nature of those bodies drawn in to govern schools did not, however, match the 2006 Act's rhetoric. It proved in the end quite difficult to attract the right number of Academy sponsors from the private sector, and the pool of the schools' backers had to be widened accordingly. This allowed different groups from the charitable, local government and activist sectors to take part in the Academy movement, widening it out a great deal from the initial emphasis on private businesses and entrepreneurs. The Church of England's educational arm, the United Learning Trust, became Academies' biggest sponsor, and in the second tranche of these schools 30 per cent were sponsored by faith groups; the Co-operative Movement sponsored 200 Academies. By 2005 only 27 per cent of Academy sponsors were private businesses.[36] It would be hard to design a more obvious example of New Labour attempts to avoid or get around previous dividing lines about the management of schools, but also their policies' debt to Giddens' idea of a networked 'community'. They had broken with what they chose to define as 'Old' Labour ideas less comprehensively than they wanted to admit.

'Zero tolerance of underperformance'

The principles New Labour deployed across most of the education sector could still be traced to the Barber–David Miliband–Adonis group. As the Education Department put it in 1997, 'intervention will be in inverse proportion to success; there will be zero tolerance of underperformance'.[37] Central government's structures were reshaped to match this agenda. A Standards and Effectiveness Unit was set up within central government, a national project on both literacy and numeracy ran on a multi-year basis and maths and literacy hours were set up. Barber and David Reynolds, respectively responsible for the Literacy and Numeracy Strategies, were themselves advocates of the School Effectiveness approach, stressing the difference schools could make in whatever community they were sited, their need for skilled leadership and the necessity of reducing variation between them. David Hopkins, Barber's replacement at the Department's Standards and Effectiveness Unit after 2001, had a similar perspective.[38] On this basis, Labour committed to 80 per cent of 11-year-olds reaching an expected standard in English (and 75 per cent in mathematics) by 2002.[39] These were quite strongly drawn and above all national programmes. The 'guided reading' recommended in the National Literacy Strategy proceeded at a particular pace, teachers' goals were linked to achievements, and concrete learning objectives were delivered via set learning resources.[40]

There is, again, some evidence that these interventions became more consensual and sensitive with time. New data placing schools performance into context – both in terms of individual children's achievements, and those of the schools overall – was introduced in autumn 1998. These attempts at constructing more nuanced and sensitive metrics initially ran into heads' frustration that schools hitherto thought of as doing 'well' could not now show they were progressing even further on well-established yardsticks. Even so, most heads polled in 2000 approved of the Literacy and Numeracy Strategies. A total of 10 per cent of them thought that the National Literacy Strategy was lifting standards 'a great deal', while 50 per cent answered 'quite a lot' to the same question. Turning to the Numeracy Strategy, 31 per cent of heads were 'confident' it would raise standards, while 59 per cent were 'fairly confident'. Only 7 per cent were 'not confident'.[41] Teachers working in poorer areas often or usually approved of the relentless drive on literacy in particular, and on teaching and learning in general. In one study of eight schools in ex-coalfield areas, one teacher asked: 'if pupils can't read how do we expect them to access the curriculum? Literacy is key'. Another said: 'I think the most important thing that the school has done has focused … all the staff, focused everybody on this issue of teaching and learning.'[42]

Area-based initiatives were another of Labour's answers to the problem of social exclusion. Education Action Zones (EAZ) and an Excellence in Cities programme were good examples of these. By concentrating funding on LEAs with high levels of disadvantage, Labour hoped to build a 'fairness' agenda alongside its emphasis on 'quality'. Each EAZ had plans and strategies laid out by an Education Action Forum containing representatives of schools, parents, the Education Secretary, local communities and businesses. An increase in school hours, designed to create a sense that these were 'community schools' trying to support progress in disadvantaged areas, was trialled first in the National Strategy for Neighbourhood Renewal in 1999, and then expanded as one part of the Excellence in Cities programme.[43] Just like Academies, though, the governance structures involved perhaps less radical change than appeared on the surface: out of twenty-five initial EAZs, all but one were proposed and then managed by LEAs.[44] In this respect they looked a lot like the Academy school movement, heavily influenced not so much by local businesses as by the Church and the Co-op. EAZs were eventually absorbed into the Excellence in Cities programme in 2001.[45] But the ambition to change the profile of government effort, from 'standards' alone towards a more equitable distribution of attention as well as resources, was never far from the surface.

Preschool childcare and nursery provision also bore this New Labour hall-mark of seeking to close the achievement gap between different areas. The pledge of a free place for all 4-year-olds was quickly honoured, while 3-year-olds were promised the same in September 2000. Free education places were provided for all 3- and 4-year-olds (for twelve and a half hours a week, thirty-three weeks a year); a network of 524 local Sure Start programmes and more than 1,100 new neighbourhood nurseries underpinned the effort on day care. Both the National Childcare Strategy of 1998, and the later Ten Year Strategy starting in 2004, concentrated help on poorer areas and low-income families, despite a gradual move towards universal childcare: the aim was to establish a Children's Centre in every one of the 20 per cent most deprived wards in England. The 1998 Strategy announced a million new childcare places, 20,000 after-school projects, and 60,000 new childcare jobs; Sure Start's home visits and mix of different support services backed this up.[46] In 2004 Brown promised that 2,500 children's centres would be open by 2008, with many starting up under the Sure Start banner: 3- and 4-year-olds would receive up to fifteen hours a week free childcare, for up to thirty-eight weeks a year. Overall, spending on Early Years provision rose from £1.2bn a year in 1997–98 to £4.2bn in 2005/06.[47]

Were results 'turned around'?

Improvements in education can be as hard to calculate as productivity in the NHS, but it is likely that these years witnessed some closing of the educational attainment gap as between different social classes. The relationship between parental backgrounds and educational attainment seems to have shrunk mark-edly between the mid-1980s and the mid-2000s: the gap between schools' GCSE results closed too. Though to some extent this was because the statistics now included many vocational qualifications as equivalent to GCSE results, results controlling for this effect still show a modest decline in class inequalities in the late 1990s and early 2000s.[48] Many of New Labour's measures taken together – for instance Fresh Start, Excellence in Cities and Academisation in low-income areas – are very likely to have raised the attainment of certain disadvantaged groups such as working-class boys.[49]

But as in the NHS and as we are to see in Chapter 7 when it comes to housing, every step forward was difficult, matched by half a step back: because even as some struggling schools improved, it was often rather better-off pupils within them (or attracted to them) who took advantage. Progress in some areas was also countermanded by developments further from the Government's control. Even as GCSE results seemed to become more 'equal' in terms of background, for instance, entry to higher education became rather less so as those who might once have only narrowly rejected university were drawn into that system. The dividing line between those who did and did not continue into HE therefore became all the sharper.[50]

The GCSE performance of most 'turned around' secondary schools did improve, though that process usually took some years and secondaries coming out of the Fresh Start programme took longer to improve – unsurprisingly, given that they were seen as underperforming to the extent that a complete new beginning was needed.[51] Qualitative evidence of schools that were progressing fastest, disproportionately sited in highly disadvantaged areas, returned evidence of rapid improvements in behaviour, attitude, attendance and discipline.[52] Some schools did start on a merry-go-round of 'stop–go' intervention, with a number of periods spent under the eye of central government. The limits of defining schools by their 'success' and 'failure' can be instanced by the example of The Ridings in Halifax, a school which at the time was often discussed in the media as an instructive example of a 'failing' institution. By 2003, a raft of government interventions seemed to indicate a brighter future for the school as exam results improved; but by 2005, despite a new headteacher, it was once again judged to be 'Inadequate' and was returned to special measures. In the end, the Ridings closed (as part of a wider reorganisation) in 2009.[53] Even so, the general picture was one of partial and piecemeal progress in opening up the potential of secondary education for all.

Teachers, heads and the 'something for something' culture

In general, Labour's approach to the teaching profession mirrored its 'something for something' approach across the public sector: teachers gained higher wages, and more opportunities to progress, but were subject to performance review, annual appraisal and performance thresholds for career advancement. There were more Teaching Assistants to assist staff, constant announcements about 'less' paperwork, and increased resources, but teachers were also supposedly 'held to account' through the published league tables which the media made so much of – a trend ministers' public pronouncements did little to discourage. As the Green Paper *Teachers: Meeting the Challenge of Change* put it in 1998, 'teachers in a modern teaching profession need to have high expectations of themselves, of all pupils, to accept accountability, [and] to take personal and collective responsibility for improving their skills and subject knowledge'.[54] These ideas have been characterised as a shift from teachers' 'individualised professionalism' to a new type of 'managed' or 'networked' professionalism – losing some autonomy in respect of what goes on in actual classrooms, but gaining greater effectiveness and respect as a group.[55]

Labour set up a General Teaching Council in England, to lift the esteem and status of teachers while giving them a say over the development of their own profession: of its sixty-four initial members, twenty-five were to be elected teachers or heads, and nine union appointees. This was supposed to develop as a critical institution giving 'voice' to the profession, to counterbalance the enormous ambitions and powers of the Teacher Training Agency the Conservatives had set up in 1994. The latter body had often focused on the development of 'National Standards' that felt more like systemisation and imposition than a partnership that might draw in expertise and experience from across education.[56] Now, perhaps, the General Teaching Council could counterbalance that one-size-fits-all emphasis on confrontation, and start listening to actual educators – though it proved rather less significant than that in practice. Rank-and-file teachers were furthermore encouraged to access Continuing Professional Development (CPD) on a much deeper and more consistent basis. In short, teachers' career structure and development was reinforced and streamlined, to avoid some of the haphazard and fragmented career paths that had stifled consistent effort and talent in the past. The aim was to bolster the quality and esteem of school leadership at all levels.[57]

That said, the General Teaching Council was an extremely weak version of a professional Council, with few powers of its own: Ofsted continued its controlling and sometimes hostile statements for some time after Labour returned to power, while the attitude of 'something for something' could often mean conforming to national models of 'what works' and a managerialist ethos in return for better pay, conditions and 'respect'. To some extent, this was freedom to do what teachers were told. This could lead to deskilling and demoralisation, as Ofsted noted in 2002 when reporting some very cramped, narrow approaches to the Numeracy Strategy: teachers 'own knowledge of it was weak and they did not see it as a tool for whole-school improvement … [too many teachers still followed] the framework and guidance with too little questioning and reflection'.[58] Given the confusing blizzard of advice and 'development' they were subject to, not to mention public attacks, that was sometimes little wonder.

Nor was 'professionalisation' always a boon for teachers, even in crude terms. The net effect of 'managed' or 'networked' professionalism – so clearly emanating from Giddens and those he influenced within Number 10 – had probably been to raise workloads overall rather than to cut them, though the effect was uneven. The demand to improve yourself and your colleagues, as well as your pupils, was never going to lessen the demands or the stress involved in teaching. On average, primary teachers could work 52–55 hours a week in the early 2000s, with increased paperwork and administration particular points of dispute.[59] Fitting what one has been trained to do into reality might meant obeisance to form and not grasp of substance – a sure recipe for professional frustration and burnout. One primary headteacher in a school with poor results told researchers that he had to deal with twenty-two reports from various inspectors and 'advice': he felt pushed down the depressing route 'of raising standards through paperwork. You know: make sure your planning's right, make sure your assessment's right ... make sure you've got this on the wall, make sure you've got that on the wall.'[60]

Anecdotal evidence and weak statistics

The theory behind New Labour's emphasis on school leadership was not particularly well developed. As one minister put it in a private interview: 'you come to government with anecdotal evidence that heads make a difference ... I don't think we made a decision that we'd concentrate on leadership, there was not a point when that decision was made, it was obvious ...'.[61] This was of a piece with much New Labour policy, which often asserted 'what works' before much research work or observation of reform had actually shown that particular changes had benign effects, necessarily so in many areas when for instance no one could know for sure how a minimum wage, tax credits and Sure Start would play out in the UK. Presupposition and hunch might be proved right in the end, but that validation after the fact was not quite what Blair and Brown's rhetoric promised. In education, any number of examples could be given. By the early 2000s, for instance, researchers noted that the evidence base for improving schools in disadvantaged areas was actually quite limited. The potential for community-based schools with longer hours to make a wider impact via 'engagement' and 'networking' was still unclear, especially as those extra hours often focused on formal education, rather than outreach and engagement with parents and the wider public in those areas.[62]

School Effectiveness research was itself criticised at the time – and has been since – on many fronts. The data could be poor and misused, particularly before a large number of long-running studies had been conducted. In particular, academics argued that this whole research field was reductive, undertheorised and spent its time searching for results in poor and sparse data – most of which only related to other evidence from the same school of thought anyway – in a fruitless attempt to measure the effects of different schooling methods.[63] School 'success' or 'failure' was in this respect still a black box, with experts and practitioners alike trying to work out what schools were doing differently from each other where dissimilar results could not be explained by socioeconomic background, children's prior results or other quantifiable factors. Both the Conservatives and New Labour also used only those parts of the School Effectiveness literature they wanted, playing down for instance the sheer level of complexity involved, or specifically the importance of a balanced intake of pupils.[64]

The emphasis on 'what works', when summed up as 'standards not structures', was clearly not straightforward or an unalloyed positive. In fact some research that emerged as the New Labour reform programme went on very much complicated the picture. Take the vexed issue of parental 'choice'. One 2005 report showed that 70,000 families had not secured their first choice of school: the problem was at its worst in London, but even outside the capital only 85 per cent of parents were able to place children in their first-choice institution. For these parents and children, 'choice' remained mythical. This brought into question even the possibility of squaring the circle between 'excellence' and 'access' with the link between numbers of children on Free Schools Meals and GCSE attainment still yawning wide. City Academies were doing well, but their Free School Meals intake was definitely lower than the schools they replaced as the numbers of children from poorer backgrounds in these schools showed a tendency to fall over time. And there was never a particularly convincing evidence base that they were doing any better, at least in terms of results, than other types of school.[65] Whatever limits New Labour placed on selection, they clearly could not fully counterbalance the pressure on 'good' schools to pick and choose who attended – or address the consequences for those children still left behind.

The university boom

Labour's goals for higher education seemed as clear as they did in the schools sector: here, ministers aimed to boost Britain's stock of economic and social capital via a greater emphasis on advanced skills, increase participation across class boundaries so that approaching half of young people went into HE, and to work more widely with business and the third sector to boost the wider impact of these reforms. These were the key ideas behind Blair's famous aspiration – announced in his 1999 Conference speech, but not achieved in practice while he was in office – that half of all young people should enter HE. First, though, Labour in office had to deal with the mechanics of how to actually boost numbers, as well as react to a report commissioned by the outgoing Conservatives and chaired by the respected administrator and ex-civil servant Ron Dearing. Although Dearing recommended the introduction of a small tuition fee, and the Government did bring in such a fee, they followed almost nothing else Dearing said. They abolished maintenance grants for the poorest students, against Dearing's advice, and instead of a set fee of the same amount for everyone, paid back after graduating, asked for an upfront fee on a means-tested basis (meaning that, by 2003/04 only 43 per cent of students paid the entire fee).[66] This was probably the wrong mix if Labour did indeed intend to expand access to new groups, or to widen HE's funding base. A mix of paying at the point of use, and only bringing in a very small additional amount of money that would not allow the sector to expand, would seem suboptimal from that point of view.

At the same time HE's costs were still rising, and by 2001 one consultancy estimated that the total capital backlog in that part of the sector might add up to £8bn – more than making the case that universities needed another boost to their income.[67] These stresses, combined with the Government's ambitious continuous aims for investment, participation and impact, necessitated a further search for much more cash, leading to a ferocious battle between Brown and Blair. Brown wanted to bring in a time-limited graduate tax based on income, which would of course be more redistributive than fees: Blair and Clarke, Education Secretary between 2002 and 2004, believed that the Treasury's plans were too complicated and too expensive (a view shared by some in the Treasury).[68]

In the end, ministers decided in January 2003 that Number 10's plans would go forward, so in 2003 tuition fees rose again, this time to £3,000 per annum. It is important to remember that these fees were quite different to those later brought in by the Coalition in 2012. The 2003 fees scheme brought in *additional* money, rather than *replacing* state funding, as was the case under the Conservatives and Liberal Democrats. In Denham's words, as the Secretary of State responsible under Brown, 'conceptually th[ese] were two totally different policy approaches'.[69] Even with the extra money, the cost and number pressures in HE meant that core teaching funds in real terms still declined a little between 2003 and 2005/06. Without it, though, funding might have fallen as sharply as it did in the early 2020s. Funding overall rose strongly, indeed doubling from £15bn to £30bn in 2017/18 prices.[70] Numbers were rising even more quickly – a remarkable expansion, but still one that demonstrated strains in the drive towards massification.

The egalitarian thrust was as evident in policy detail as it was in numbers. Widening Participation initiatives were detailed in law for the first time (in the English Higher Education Act of 2004), a measure that was also novel because it specified that there was such a thing as 'underrepresented groups' in HE. An Office for Fair Access was set up to monitor 'access agreements' with universities, which were expected to run schemes to attract new entrants. Initiatives such as AimHigher, working with schools and young people to show them what HE was actually like, were designed to reach out to underrepresented groups. Grants were eventually brought back, alongside bursaries from universities as part of their access agreements. These developments were not without complication or controversy, though, because with different universities running very different access schemes, the data opaque and with low participation rates so deep-rooted, it was hard to assess these schemes' effectiveness – as the NAO pointed out in 2008.[71]

The 2004 Act was attempting to address one paradox of the Government's reaction to Dearing, for New Labour's reforms were not always helpful to students from low-income backgrounds. While the subsidy given to each student fell 35 per cent between 1989 and 2001, because of the run-down and then replacement of grants by loans for almost all students, the reduction in assistance for better-off students was only 2.5 per cent. Students from wealthier backgrounds had never received much help anyway, meaning they hardly noticed the swapping of most grants for loans, while the poorest students were now the most likely to run up the biggest loans. Richer students and their families could always cover their own costs. Access targets and bursaries were to some extent an attempt to right the imbalance inherent in this relative withdrawal of help from those who most needed it, and the rise of numbers across the board shows that it had some effect. But the rising tide did not lift all types of boat equally. Although the raw *numbers* of students from the most disadvantaged social classes going into education of course rose during Labour's time in office, even as the system grew their relative *proportion* stayed the same for a long time, and only grew slightly even by 2009/10.[72] As HE numbers surged upwards, the breakpoint in the labour force between the 'haves' and the 'have nots' could also become the moment of graduation. By altering the very language of higher education, and co-opting it for the Government's emphasis on 'skills' and 'growth' as well as equality, New Labour gave further encouragement to universities' transformation from institutions of learning to training. Those 'left behind', who did not go to university, might fall even further behind in the job market. The difference between graduate and non-graduate earnings did rise slightly in this period, and stayed well above what it had been in the 1980s, though this so-called 'graduate premium' then collapsed again in the 2010s and 2020s as the flood of graduates overwhelmed demand for them.[73]

Numbers grew strongly overall. In 1997/98 there were about 1.65 million students inside HE, while there were 2.025 million by 2002/03. Those entering the HE system annually rose from a quarter of a million to over 400,000 between 1994 and 2010 (see Figure 5.2). In truth, the Government was in part simply accepting a revolution of both social and personal expectations during which many more people expected to go into HE. Even after this rapid new university expansion was well underway, in 2004 34 per cent of the public thought the number of places in HE should be increased a lot or a little (the figure had reached as high as 51 per cent in 1990); only 15 per cent of respondents thought that fewer young people should go on to higher learning. Among professionals, 84 per cent thought it was very or fairly likely that their children would go to university; routine manual workers were not all that far behind, at 65 per cent.[74]

Elsewhere in post-compulsory education, the trendlines were similarly positive, but still mixed. Rates of participation in full-time education between 16 and 18 surged, from 56.4 per cent in 1997 to 70.6 per cent in 2010 – though this again reflected very long-term trends, even more rapidly apparent in the late 1980s and 1990s. This expansion did, however, come at the expense of employer-funded training and work-based learning, which shrank while Labour were in office. Those 16- to 18-year-olds 'Not in Education, Employment and Training' did not in fact go down much, only falling from 8.9 per cent to 7.5 per cent.[75] FE was to this extent replacing training on the job, and as the Department's Five Year Plan accepted in 2004, 'the UK's key weakness is the low participation of 16- to 19-year-olds in education and training', with that indicator notable for trailing the rest of the OECD – unlike most other comparative measures, such as reading and maths proficiency, completion of HE courses and the like.[76] By 2006, the UK was still some way short even of the OECD average for 17-year-olds' participation in education or training, as the Department noted regretfully in its two-year review of the Five Year Plan.[77]

A shake-up of all education between 14 and 19 announced in a 2005 Skills White Paper did create clear vocational pathways to good, respected qualifications that would smooth access to the workplace. But the radical intent of

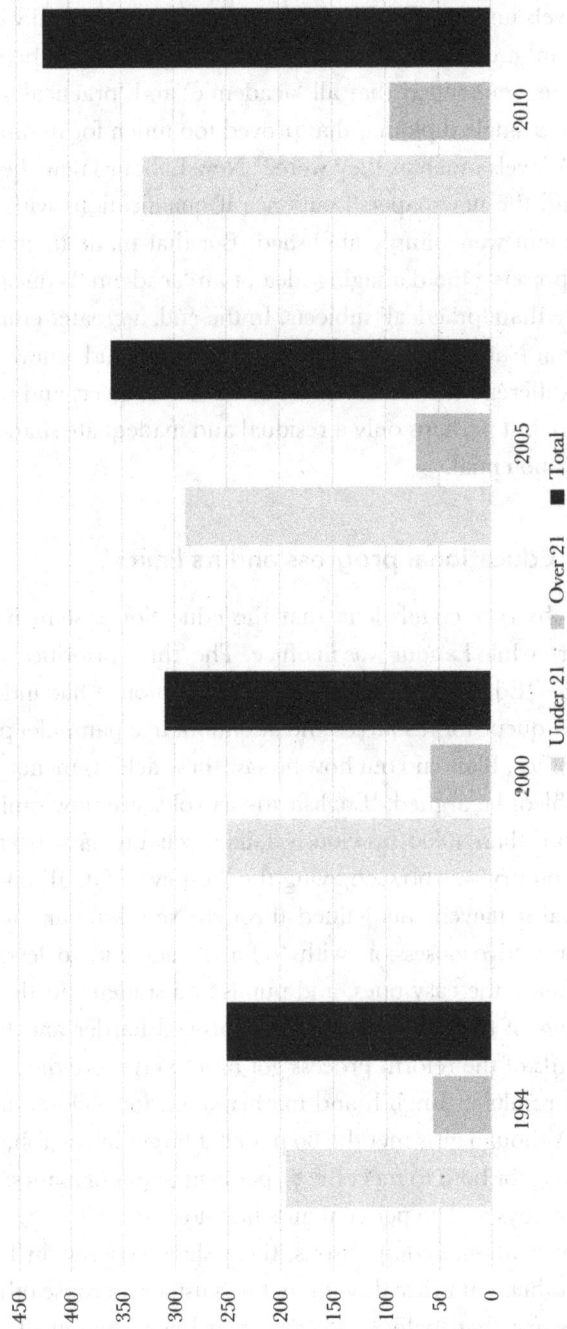

Figure 5.2 Number of students accepted into UK HE

Source: P. Bolton, *Higher Education Student Numbers*, House of Commons Library Research Briefing 7857 (February 2023), 'Summary of applications and accepted applications to Higher Education via UCAS', p. 36.

that White Paper – to absorb all teaching and training into a single post-14 system, if only rhetorically – was in the end stymied by traditionalism. Talk of a wider set of A levels under a 'British baccalaureate' was eventually dropped. Although Mike Tomlinson's 2004 report on reforming education between the ages of 14 and 19 recommended that all 'academic' and 'practical' qualifications be folded into a single diploma, that proved too much for ministers, who kept GCSEs and A levels much as they were.[78] New Labour knew the limits of the electorate's (and the newspapers') patience if qualifications with a strong brand and attachment were simply abolished. But that made them overcautious, and helped preserve the damaging idea of an 'academic' education that was worth far more than 'practical' subjects. In the end, a greater emphasis on practical training via National Vocational Qualifications, and a new Diploma bringing together different 'academic' and 'vocational' subjects and providers, were useful reforms, but perhaps only a residual and inadequate shadow of the Tomlinson report's potential.

Educational progress and its limits

No dispassionate observer could deny that the education system had made large strides forward while Labour was in office. The 'three priorities' Blair had announced in 1996 – 'Education, Education and Education' – had indeed been near the front of the queue for resources and attention. In a pamphlet published in the year he left office, Blair laid out how he saw these achievements. Funding per pupil had doubled, he argued; 'English 10-year-olds are now ranked third in the world'; 'more than 1,500 previously failing schools have been turned around'; and the country was now enjoying the 'best ever' GCSE and A level results.[79] The actual achievements gained through New Labour's additional spending and hyperactive obsession with 'reform' did tend to level off. As ever, the first yards are the easy ones, and pupils and students further 'down' the traditional rungs of the educational ladder proved harder and harder to reach. The last yards of the reform process got more and more difficult. After 2001, Key Stage 2 results in English and mathematics, for children at age 11, began to plateau. Although girls met the 80 per cent target in English, boys did not. It took until 2005 for both to meet the 75 per cent in mathematics: by 2001, 'only' 71 per cent of boys and 70 per cent girls had done so.

If we turn to international comparisons, these show progress in England's ranking as against other countries, though that was usually because other countries were doing worse than before, not due to a huge amount of objective improvement in England. These measures of educational achievement are nec-essarily fragmentary, disputed and controversial among experts, though they are still worth quoting because they are all we have that is concrete and at least a rough guide to policy success or failure. Programme for International Student Assessment (PISA) data show that between 2006 and 2015, when 15-year-olds might have spent the majority of their school lives being taught under Labour, scores for reading in England rose slightly, while performance in Maths and Science declined by a small amount. That said, England was doing something right, or at least less wrong, when compared to Scotland and Wales – where all scores fell and where they fell more quickly in Science and Maths.[80] And there is other evidence, for instance the Trends in International Mathematics and Science Study (TIMSS) tests published by the International Association for the Evaluation of Educational Achievement, that shows Maths and Science scores improved between the mid-1990s and 2007, especially for 10-year-olds (the effect was not so strong among 14-year-olds, though it was still there).[81] The most that could be said here is probably that England was doing quite well in a global context, which is not much of an uplifting political slogan but is still something of an achievement.

GCSE and A level results did continue to rise strongly (see Figures 5.3 and 5.4), and unlike other testing results continuously. The number of GCSE A–C grades in English and Maths also went up, obviously impor-tant to the Government given its Literacy and Numeracy Strategies. Again, though, the picture is complicated. The impression of continual progress we get from the rising number of formal qualifications could be subject to more grade inflation than standardised testing, and in this case their constant improvement at GCSE and A level might not be comparing like for like. The situation here is confused by the inclusion after 1997 of the technical qualifica-tion GNVQs, and from 2004 'other equivalent qualifications', in the GCSE and A level numbers.

Whatever the qualifications we might offer about results, public opin-ion remained relatively sympathetic to the Government's efforts. Education declined as an issue that voters rated 'most important', from 45 per cent in June 1995 to lows of just 26 per cent in December 1998 and 29 per cent in June 1999 and December 2000 – though the number thinking this then rose again, to 35 per cent at the approach of an election in spring 2001.[82] It resumed a slow and slight fall thereafter, which must be some indication that the public thought the issue was being addressed.[83] This was no vast turnaround in public sentiment: in 2005, 26 per cent of voters thought that Labour was handling

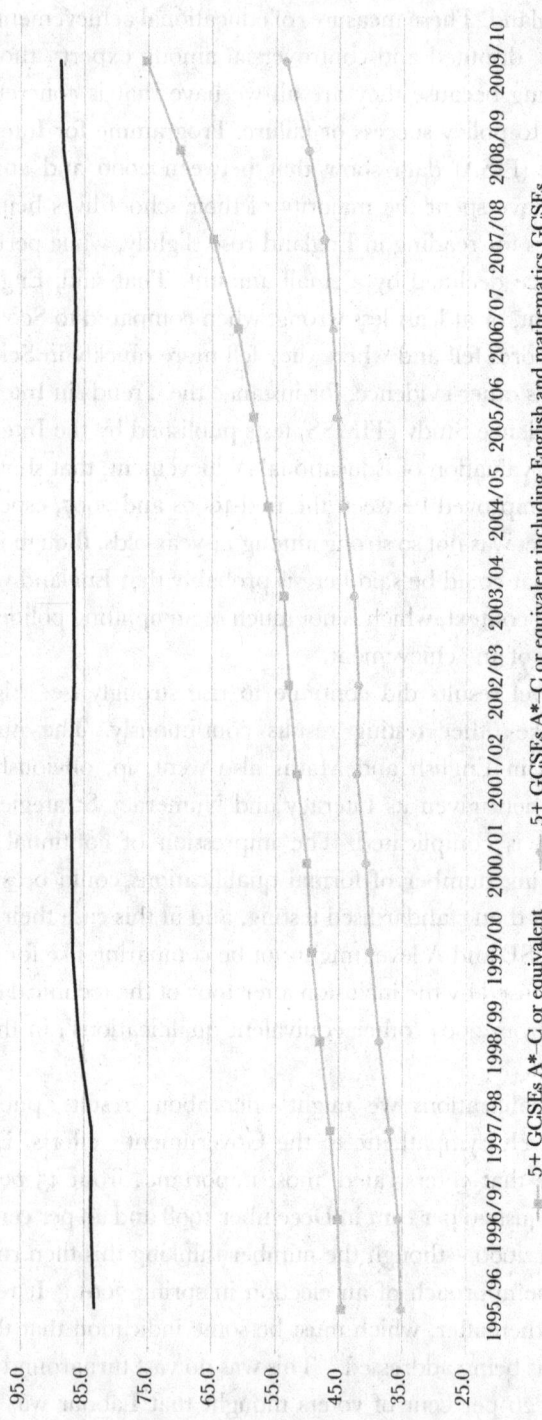

Figure 5.3 GCSE results, 1995/96–2009/10

Source: www.gov.uk/government/statistics/revised-gcse-and-equivalent-results-in-england-2014-to-2015, Main National Table SFR 01/2016, accessed 24 April 2023.

Legend:
- 5+ GCSEs A*–C or equivalent
- 5+ GCSEs A*–C or equivalent including English and mathematics GCSEs
- 5+ GCSEs A*–G or equivalent
- 5+ GCSEs A*–G or equivalent including English and mathematics GCSEs

Y-axis values: 95.0, 85.0, 75.0, 65.0, 55.0, 45.0, 35.0, 25.0

X-axis values: 1995/96, 1996/97, 1997/98, 1998/99, 1999/00, 2000/01, 2001/02, 2002/03, 2003/04, 2004/05, 2005/06, 2006/07, 2007/08, 2008/09, 2009/10

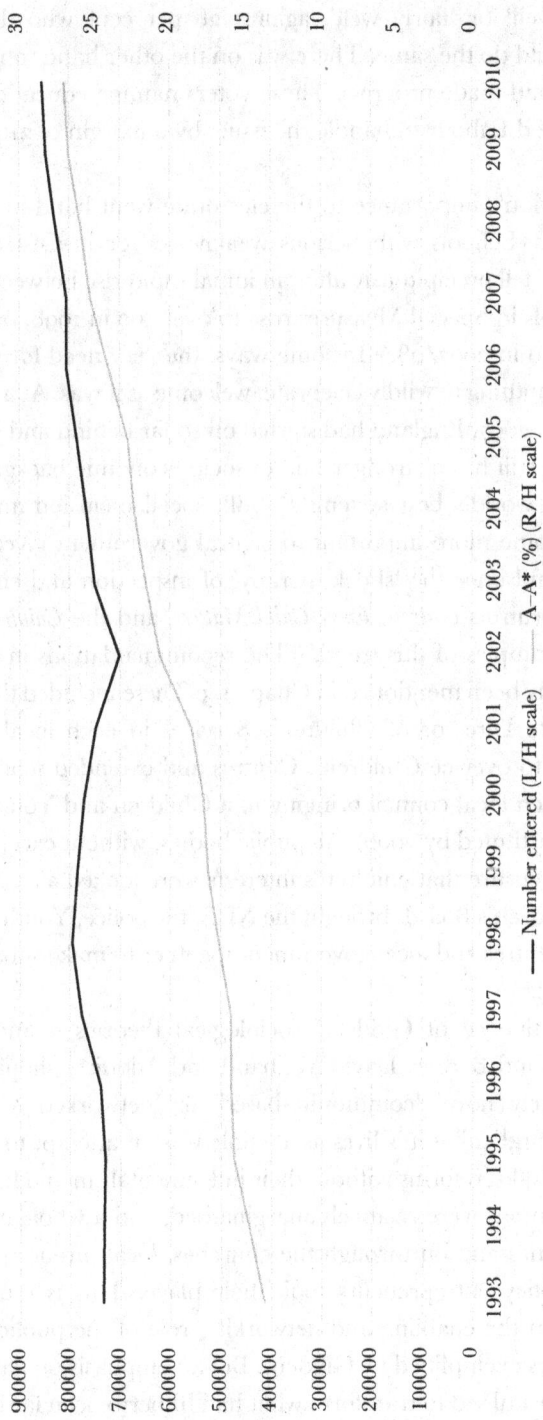

Figure 5.4 A level results, 1993–2010

Source: www.jcq.org.uk/examination-results/ and www.bstubbs.co.uk/a-lev.htm, both accessed 23 April 2023.

Legend: — Number entered (L/H scale) — A–A* (%) (R/H scale)

education 'very well' or 'fairly well', against 26 per cent who thought the Conservatives would do the same. There was on the other hand some recognition that Labour had made progress. Those voters naming education as 'most important' preferred Labour to handle the issue, by a margin of 31 per cent to 11 per cent.[84]

A fall in education's importance to the electorate went hand in hand with real improvements. Schools with 'serious weaknesses' or in Ofsted's Special Measures category fell precipitously after an initial rapid rise between 1997 and 1998. Those schools in Special Measures rose to over 500 in 1998, but fell back later to around 250 in 2007/08.[85] In some ways, the very need for this sort of progress makes it nothing to wildly celebrate, welcome as it was. As a McKinsey study concluded in 2007, England had started off so far behind and so unequal that 'performance still has a stronger link to socio-economic background that is the case in the world's best systems'.[86] Still, social inclusion and equality did gradually become more important to central government given the New Labour agenda, and once the 'shock therapy' of inspection and enforcement had been seen to run its course. *Every Child Matters*, and the *Children's Plan* of 2007, are good examples of this trend.[87] The recommendations in *Every Child Matters* have already been mentioned in Chapter 3. These included the appointment of a separate Director of Children's Services in each local authority, Children's Trusts to oversee Children's Centres and extended school services and hours, and each local council bringing in a Children and Young People's Plan (which was instituted by 2006). All public bodies, without exception, were now mandated to ensure that children's interests were looked after, and Local Safeguarding Children's Boards brought the NHS, the police, Youth Offending Teams, training centres and local government together to make sure standards were better upheld.[88]

Overall, the influence of Giddens' sociological theories – and the like-minded group around Barber, David Miliband and Adonis – should be obvious. Their relatively novel 'community-based' or 'networked' view of the school, education and children's lives as a whole was an attempt to adapt and reuse some of the 1980s reforms without their judgementalism and harsh edges. LEAs and trade unions were relatively marginalised, and a whole host of new actors, from charities and on through the churches, local businesspeople and semi-academic policy entrepreneurs took their place. This is much as one would expect given the enabling and networking role of the public sphere in Third Way theories exemplified by Giddens. But an emphasis on partnerships, and on state power utilised to transform what had hitherto been fairly localised public services, demonstrates in Mark Goodwin's words 'the poverty of … marketisation … as a complete account of the New Labour education project'.[89] The inspection regime, so tight early on, was gradually eased. Schools got more help, not just increased burdens, especially with training and leadership. Contextual data on schools' efforts was added to league tables and the third sector, rather than just private business, grew in strength across the Academy movement.

There was a great deal that was distinctive about the New Labour vision – perhaps for good and ill. Government set much stronger targets and managed the system itself, rather than indirectly, there was far more emphasis on pupil and school support and joint working, and the idea of inclusion rose strongly up the agenda. Coordination, consultation and integration sat alongside increased private sector provision and more expectations placed on parents and children. Many schools of thought also came together to form a unique blend formed out of New Right ideas around 'choice', merged and fused with concerns about universalising quality; 'developmentalism', focusing on social capital and competitive advantage; and a renewed social democracy emphasising better education for all. New Labour's emphasis on school 'choice' and private takeovers of LEAs evoked the first way of thinking. State intervention in the shape of a more respected teaching profession and the National Strategies on literacy and numeracy demonstrated the influence of the second. An emphasis on Early Years, school partnerships, pupil support and Excellence in Cities demonstrated the remaining importance of socialist revisionism.[90]

That list makes clear just how different but how broad were New Labour's inspirations when it came to regenerating the education system in the wake of the Thatcher and Major years. There were continuities in method and rhetoric, but that should not blind us to the new elements in the mix. Blair's language and practice were also very different from those adopted by the Coalition and Conservative administrations that have followed. Those governments have pushed the idea of Academies and Free Schools much further than New Labour ever would have done, reduced the state's role in education overall, shifted from spending surge to stagnation and arrested forward-thinking curriculum reform in favour of traditionalist nostrums. As so often, half-remembered truths from the early 2000s turn out to disguise a far more complicated, interesting – and more progressive – reality.

6

'Tough on crime, tough on the causes of crime'

The remoralisation of the Left

'Tough' policies on crime and punishment were one way in which New Labour sought to remoralise politics. New Labour's overriding view of crime was that it was about ethics as well as evidence, part of a public sphere for which everyone should take responsibility: individuals; families; communities; welfare state professionals; political parties; and local and central government. But the question of where responsibility for crime truly lay would prove a thorny one, and it often lapsed back into just blaming individuals. As Blair wrote when Shadow Home Secretary in March 1993, immediately after the Bulger murder: 'we should be tough on crime and tough on the causes of crime. We should be prepared and eager to give people opportunity. But we are then entitled to ask that they take advantage of it, to grant rights and demand responsibilities.'[1] It was a classic Blairite balancing act: as he told the Police Federation in May 1993, 'if we dare not speak the language of punishment then we deny the real world. If we do not understand the need for social action then we deny the possibility of changing it.'[2]

Blair was not the only one seeking to rebalance their views about crime, for many on the Left had begun to question their earlier views too. A so-called Left Realist view had by now emerged among both criminologists and practitioners. This stressed not just that wrongdoing developed among conditions of deprivation and alienation, but also how much working people were the real victims of most crime. This New Realism emphasised the extent to which any organised and just society should send signals about what it expected through the justice system as well as social policy, though in the light of New Labour's more authoritarian initiatives it should be noted that most New Realist writers were also clear that being more and more punitive might be counterproductive.[3]

Blair's attitude is still similar now: 'when people have drug dealers at the end of the street, they want something done about it. I've always said crime is a working-class issue because the working class suffer.'[4] In the 1990s some Labour-run local authorities, such as Coventry, had already begun to take tougher action against persistent criminals, in Coventry's case trying (and failing) to exclude a particular pair of brothers from areas where they had been menacing local residents. Straw as Shadow Home Secretary was kept in close touch with the Coventry example.[5]

Blunkett, who was Home Secretary between 2001 and 2004, drew on his tough upbringing with a widowed single mother to justify and explain his concern for disadvantaged areas blighted by 'disorder'. Although of course Blunkett was hardly a dispassionate observer, his private correspondence with Blair in 2003 is revealing:

> I know that you are determined, as am I, that we bring about a sea-change in the way that we tackle anti-social behaviour. To do this means not only driving home the hard messages that we mean business and that we are on the side of the victim, but also ensuring that those messages are backed up by realistic actions which will make a difference on the ground. This ranges from tackling gangs of youths hanging around in an intimidating manner on the streets, to ensuring that we deliver more effectively on family support and ... wider preventative measures. I am conscious too, of just how political an issue this is across the Party ... my department has been deluged by letters, e-mails and calls from members of the party in Westminster and at local level. Abuse and violence, people running amok, noise from pubs ruining lives – all these things are blighting communities and those communities are looking to us for leadership and action.[6]

Blair himself was clear: what he thought of as the tolerant liberalism of 'Old' Labour had to be jettisoned in favour of a reimagining of criminal behaviour as 'wrong', a balance of victims' and perpetrators' rights that shifted the balance in favour of the former, and a reconstruction of civil society that stopped crime gaining a hold. This was to some extent another convenient myth about 'Old' Labour, because many of the party's previous Home Secretaries, for instance Callaghan in the late 1960s, had hardly been particularly liberal. But in a keynote speech given at Wellingborough in February 1993, Blair made the Bulger case an example of how bad things he thought things had become since Callaghan's time:

> The news bulletins of the past week have been like hammer blows struck against the sleeping conscience of the country, urging us to wake up and look unflinchingly at what we see. A solution to this disintegration doesn't simply lie in legislation. It must come from a rediscovery of a sense of direction as a country and

most of all from being unafraid to start talking once again about the values and principles but as a community. We cannot exist in a moral vacuum.[7]

This was linked to a wider moral sense of social disintegration and its costs: Blair argued in a collection of Christian Socialist essays in 1992 that 'there is right and wrong. There is good and bad. We all know this, of course, but it has become fashionable to be uncomfortable about such language. But when we look at our world today and how much needs to be done, we should not hesitate to make such judgements.'[8]

This, for Mandelson, was the moment at which Blair 'really broke through as the leading advocate of change in Labour' – in part because he refused to explicitly reference 'how deprivation fed crime', and did not call 'for government to fix the environment which bred it'.[9] Thereafter, Blair made crime and the scourge of 'anti-social behaviour' his signature issue: Ed Balls remembers that, for instance, 'after 2001 Tony wanted to go harder on antisocial behaviour' than Brown.[10] Blair told the *Big Issue* magazine in 1997 that he believed in 'zero-tolerance policy against beggars' because of the 'chain of association between begging, homelessness and petty crime'.[11] Some observers were sceptical of all this moral and religious talk about 'right and wrong', thinking that it was a mere cover for a populist agenda accommodating itself with a right-wing consensus on crime and punishment. Simon Jenkins thought the famous 'tough on crime' soundbite an 'empty phrase … [Blair's] ability to strip words of meaning yet load them with impressionistic effect was extraordinary'. When Nick Cohen phoned Blair about a Conservative minister's proposed hardline speech, toned down on Michael Howard's insistence as Home Secretary, Blair gave him a suitable quote, but still made clear that 'you see, a lot of *Daily Mail* readers would agree with him'.[12]

In this Blair owed a great debt to the more traditionalist, moralising strands within his communitarian outlook – ideas for instance from the Israeli-American sociologist Amitai Etzioni, who often looked back to an imaginary but powerfully attractive 1950s full of stable families and firm parenting, or to Charles Murray and his worries about an emerging 'underclass' – rather than some of the more radical strands of that movement. When they thought of organic, shared social life, European communitarians tended to stress the role of a basic income and a 'common good': but the more severe advocates of this outlook were much happier with a judgemental, conservative view of human nature and society. Blair did lean towards the latter. For Etzioni and his followers, shaming and humiliation could support reintegration for first offenders, enforcing clear lines of behaviour by expressing society's norms and disapproval. Conversely, if the police and state were not strengthened, there was a risk that society would break up, as individuals took justice into their own hands. He stressed obligations over rights.[13] On this subject at least, Blair was showing communitarianism's more conservative face.

Even so, civic duties and punishments were not the be-all and end-all of New Labour's thought about social disorder, as Blunkett's point to Blair about 'family support' made clear. Mandelson and Liddle in *The Blair Revolution* argued that families were society's key institution, 'where the difference between right and wrong is learned, and where a sense of mutual obligation is founded and practiced'. Labour's 1996 policy paper, *Tackling Youth Crime*, also faced both ways on this question: it argued both that 'we will be tougher on the causes of crime by tackling the problems of unemployment and poverty, conditions in which crime breeds', but also that 'the public believes that more responsible parenting is the top priority for improving community safety'.[14] Blair's governments deployed elements of both approaches, though in terms of actual punishment did favour the latter. Papers for the 1997 Cabinet Away Day continued to put the case that 'a decent society means tackling crime ... restoring decent values and a sense of responsibility, supporting family life and showing tolerance to those from all backgrounds'. But they also made clear that 'the key elements of our strategy to crack down on crime' were 'dealing with young offenders, tackling the growing menace of drugs ... and taking tough action on anti-social behaviour with our policy of zero tolerance'.[15]

More police, less crime

The most obvious thing New Labour did in office was to boost police spending and numbers. In raw cash terms, the police budget was £6.45bn in 1994/95; by 2008/09 it had ballooned to £13.7bn. Spending on employing police officers (including pensions) increased by 29 per cent between 1997/98 and 2008/09, rising to £7.8bn.[16] Overall spending on public order and safety rose 47 per cent in real terms between 1997/98 and 2007/08. Police numbers rose by more than 16,000 (or 13 per cent), to an all-time high of more than 142,000. Real spending on criminal justice overall rose by over 3 per cent a year in Labour's first term, nearly 7 per cent in its second, and 3 per cent again between 2005–08. That more than matched spending increases even under Thatcher and Major. The share of GDP spent on these activities rose from just over 2 per cent to 2.5 per cent.[17] This was in stark contrast to the cuts to police spending after

Labour left office in 2010: in 2014/15 prices, Labour increased police spending from £9.7bn to £13.6bn, before the Coalition government cut funding back again to £11.7bn.

New money was matched by new types of policing and public safety measures that were designed to boost the state's knowledge and power while reassuring the public. Any number of examples might suffice, but two in particular are instructive. By 2002 there were 16,000 of a new class of Police Community Support Officers (PCSOs) working alongside their more well-established colleagues; following the launch of Neighbourhood Policing Teams in 2005, 3,600 PCSOs were integrated into those local teams across England's police forces. In rural areas, the Rural Policing Fund (RPF) had a budget of £30 million a year to improve policing in the countryside. Some police forces used the funding to pay for community-based officers or 'beat managers', while others invested in mobile police stations, new telephone and email technology, or rural safety initiatives such as Farm Watch or Rural Watch schemes. All this played some role in both including community groups in attacking crime, as well as boosting confidence in the police, though the RPF was later merged with other initiatives and its impact then faded.[18]

Crime had almost certainly begun falling before Labour came to power, as we can see from Figure 6.1. Between 1995 and 1999, the British Crime Survey recorded a 23 per cent fall in the crime rate, while police figures showed a decline of 20 per cent between 1991 and 1999.[19] In the mid-1990s, Britain's crime rates were the highest in Western Europe, but they then began a long-term fall that seems to have many (endlessly debated) causes. Household goods that were often stolen were becoming relatively less valuable; homes were more secure; this was a time of general prosperity, meaning that the 1990s and 2000s were a time of greater social and political peace than the 1970s and 1980s; and so on.[20] Even the removal of lead from petrol (and exhaust fumes) has been put forward as a possible cause of crime's continued fall.[21] Youth crime – about which so many fears clustered in the 1990s – had also *not* been rising in the way the public feared. On the contrary: between 1987 and 1997 the numbers of those aged 10–17 found guilty of indictable offences fell by 30 per cent. The fear of young people's criminality was more a creation of tabloid editors' imaginations and awful, high-profile causes célèbres than a real phenomenon – though that did not mean that voters did not care about it.[22]

Inside Whitehall, though, the Government was convinced that its interventions were also playing a role – perhaps not explaining the overall trend, but certainly hastening crime's long-term fall. There is little doubt that extra

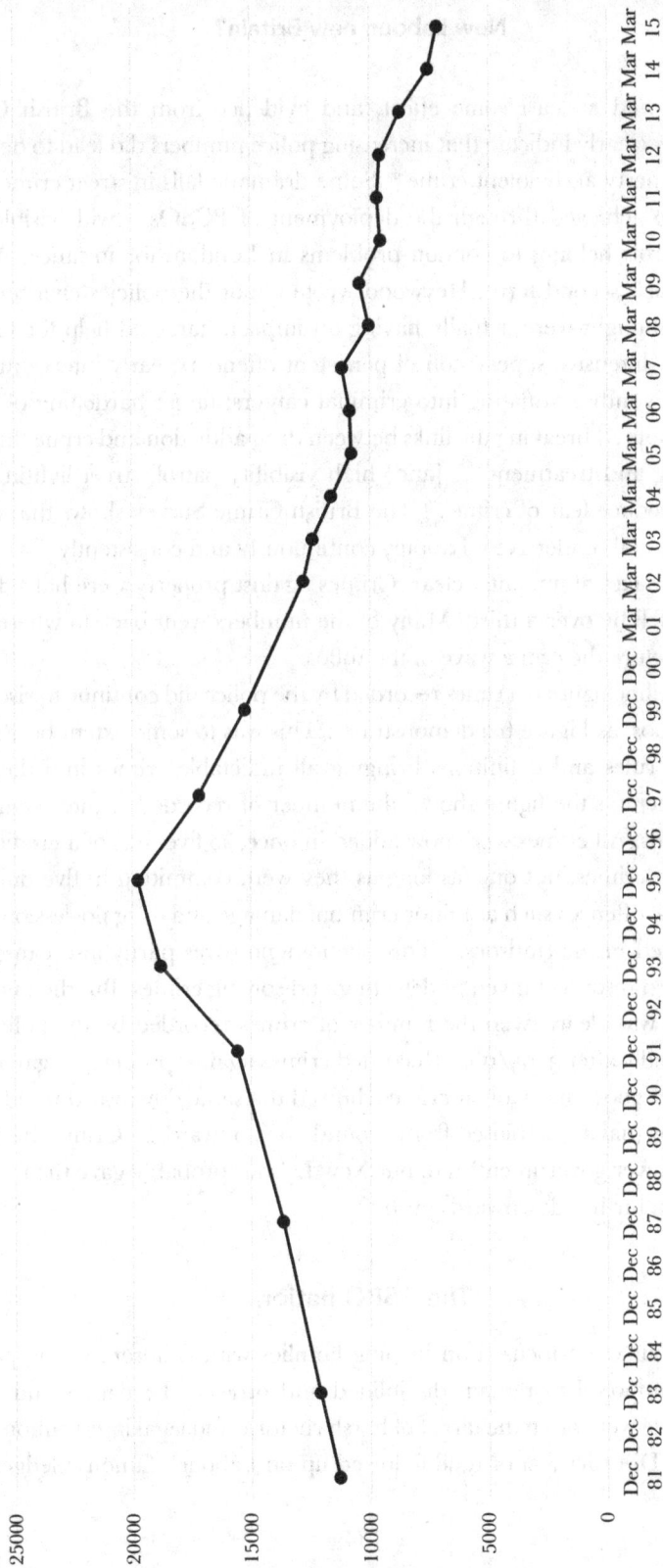

Figure 6.1 Crimes committed overall, England and Wales (Crime Survey), 1981–2015

Source: Crime in England and Wales, www.ons.gov.uk/peoplepopulationandcommunity/crimeandjustice/bulletins/crimeinenglandandwales/yearendingjune2022, accessed 22 March 2023.

investment had at least some effect, and evidence from the British Crime Survey does clearly indicate that increasing police numbers did lead to declines in both property and violent crime.[23] Some dramatic falls in street crime were for instance achieved through the deployment of PCSOs – with visible and regular patrols helping to contain problems in London, for instance. At the start of Blair's second term, Heywood wrote about the policies civil servants and spads thought were actually having an impact: 'targeted help for victims of crime … intensive supervision of persistent offenders; early intervention to stop at-risk youth graduating into criminal careers; target hardening of high-crime hotspots … breaking the links between drug addiction and crime through drug testing and treatment … [and] high visibility patrol, street lighting and CCTV to reduce fear of crime'.[24] The British Crime Survey shows that crime continued to fall under New Labour, continuously and consistently – as again Figure 6.1 makes abundantly clear. Crimes against property were halved; violent crime fell by over a third. Many of the numbers went back to where they had been before the crime wave of the 1980s.

The headline figure of crimes recorded by the police did continue to rise until the mid-2000s, as Figure 6.2 demonstrates. This was to some extent because of changes to rules and definitions bringing all indictable crimes into the data in 1998, when (as the figure shows) the number of recorded crimes seemed to leap upwards. All crimes were now added in once, so five uses of a credit card became five crimes, not one (as long as they were committed in five different outlets): new offences such as minor criminal damage and drug possession were now included in the statistics.[25] This phenomenon was partly also caused by the increased resources given to detecting and solving crimes. But the underlying picture was clear. Even the number of crimes recorded by the police fell away markedly after 2005/06.[26] Recorded crimes against property began to fall quickly after 2004, and violent crimes showed the same downward trend from around 2007 (having stabilised from around 2005 onwards).[27] Crime was likely falling whatever governments did, but New Labour probably gave the number of offences a further downwards push.

The ASBO nation

While Labour often focused on helping families with children, young people were still supposed to remain disciplined and orderly. Teenagers and other young people were often the target of harsh rhetoric and legal intervention. The Crime and Disorder Act of 1998 followed up on Labour's famous pledge card

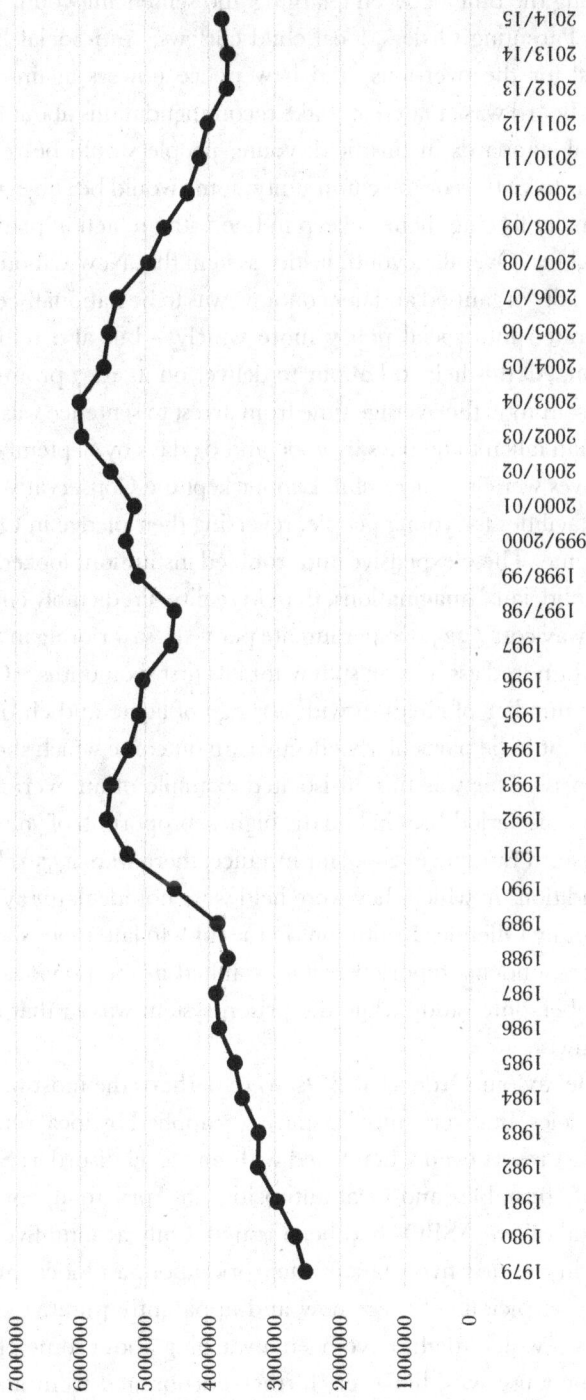

Figure 6.2 Crimes recorded by the police, England and Wales, 1979–2014/15

Source: Historical Crime Data, www.gov.uk/government/statistics/historical-crime-data, accessed 22 March 2023.

promise of halving the time between charging and sentencing young people; it also brought in Parenting Orders, local child curfews, Anti-Social Behaviour Orders (ASBOs) for the over-tens, and new police powers against truancy. A Youth Justice Board was created to make recommendations about best practice and national standards in this field; young people would be required to make reparations to victims or the community; some would be subject to a new Community Penalty forcing them to keep in line with an 'action plan' governing future behaviour. Overall, a youth justice system that New Labour thought of as confused, badly organised and uneconomic was to be nationalised, streamlined and integrated into social policy more widely – but also refocused on crime prevention. All this helped Labour to deliver on its 1997 promise to half sentencing times: in 1996 the average time from arrest to sentence was 142 days, a figure which had fallen to 96 days by 2000 and 63 days by September 2001.[28]

Other initiatives were less successful. Labour kept the Conservatives' idea of secure training facilities for young people, reversing their pledge in Opposition to scrap the scheme. These expensive and troubled institutions looked better in theory, and in politicians' imaginations, than in reality. Predictably enough, the first one at Medway cost £225,000 per inmate per year, saw rioting in 1998, and was the site of a hundred assaults on staff within its first six months.[29] Gathering together a large number of children with a range of acute and chronic problems turned out not to be particularly effective, an outcome which should have come as no surprise. Nor was this an isolated example of an overreliance on incarceration. In this period Britain had the highest proportion of young people locked up in Western Europe: in 2009, for instance, there were 2,556 children in prison. The conditions in which they were held were not ideal, to say the least: one survey of Young Offender Institutions in the mid- to late 1990s showed that 30 per cent of respondents reported being assaulted in the previous month.[30] Expanding numbers in custody while the prison system was in that condition was distinctly unwise.

Anti-Social Behaviour Orders (ASBOs) were perhaps the most well-known of these new policies, but were initially sparingly applied by local officers who saw them as a last resort even when faced with low-level disorder. Straw had to write to chief constables and local authorities in April 1999, complaining that a grand total of five ASBOs had been issued. Only around five hundred were given out in the first five years of their operation, and local authorities were sometimes suspicious of these new and apparently punitive and invasive new powers – which might have been a warning about some of ASBOs' drawbacks.[31] Their use was, however, further encouraged from about 2004 onwards as the Government insisted on the implementation of its 'respect agenda', even dispatching officials to be 'ASBO ambassadors' in each part of the country to make sure that councils applied these powers. This emphasis on ASBOs was codified in the Police Act of 2002, the 2003 White Paper, *Respect and Responsibility: Taking a Stand Against Anti-Social Behaviour* and the subsequent Anti-Social Behaviour Act.[32] The number of ASBOs subsequently rose strongly, rising from 104 in 1999 to over 4,000 in 2005, though those numbers then fell away sharply again as they became seen as hard to manage on that scale.[33]

The use of ASBOs raised the vexed question of arbitrary power, for issuing them could rest on the vagaries of the civil and not the criminal law (though their breach was a criminal matter), as well as on individual police forces. That inevitably meant that their use was even patchier and more variegated than arrest and sentencing. In some areas people were much more likely to be served with these Orders than others: compare the 155 issued in Greater Manchester during the first six months of 2004 to the 27 that were issued on Merseyside. Some cases were almost an absurd caricature of the fears of disorder prevalent at the time. One Order was issued to volunteers manning soup vans giving out food to the homeless in central Manchester when they left a mess; an 18-year-old was arrested for going into a well-run and well-thought-of youth club after he'd been served an ASBO forbidding him to congregate with more than three other young people; a person with substance use disorders faced jail after being forbidden to beg under the Vagrancy Act of 1824.[34]

Nor did these new punishments seem vastly effective. Overall, 70 per cent of 10- to 17-year-olds breached their ASBOs, and 51 per cent of those over 18 did the same: the average number of such breaches was 4.4.[35] Some young people seem to have embraced the labels society put on them, as they reclaimed the judgemental language of others; many more hid the Orders that had been served on them given the shame induced, often further driving them out of the mainstream. Interviews with young people on Merseyside, for instance, found young people ostracised from some of their family and friends: 'all the older ones stopped speaking to me, and you can see them thinking "poor X" [his grandmother], what did she do to deserve another crim in the family'. Another interviewee said: 'you can tell what they're all thinking. People who knew me when I was younger, they all still speak to me, but everything's just about my offending now. I used to be able to talk to mum's mates, you know, about football and things, but it's just "what have you been getting up to?"

"Have you been in any trouble recently?".[36] Rather than *breaking* the link between low-level incivility and crime, then, these Orders could sometimes reinforce them.

Some elements in the Government's ASBO policies did stress reform and recovery. The work of the Youth Service, the advice and guidance service Connexions and intensive fostering were all stressed alongside ASBOs.[37] Denham, who was a Policing Minister between 2001 and 2003, 'was always very keen' on the idea, 'unlike most of the Soft Left ... if they [ASBOs] were used effectively alongside ... youth justice panels and ... as part of a coherent approach to tackling local problems', then they could play a positive role. In Denham's Southampton constituency, for instance, they worked as part of a broader plan: 'you got all the agencies together because you had a gang problem starting in the local precinct'.[38] The Home Office also created a new pathway for young offenders to be diverted from the criminal justice system to community panels which could agree local restitution by those offenders. Youth Offending Teams contained social workers and NHS staff, not just the police and local government. Blair's own public visits, as for instance on a visit to the Blackthorn Estate in Northampton during September 2003, stressed better facilities, improved street architecture and 'developing community activities', such as book clubs and a new playground.[39]

A new view on human rights

Elsewhere in the criminal justice system there was an emphasis on 'rights' rather than 'responsibilities'. The Human Rights Act (HRA) of 1998, which gave 'further effect' to the European Convention on Human Rights in UK law, created positive rights – moving the UK towards a more codified constitution which protected the individual against state action. These rights covered fundamental tenets – rights to life, liberty, a fair hearing, the presumption of innocence, legal assistance, privacy, expression, association, assembly, thought, conscience and religion. But although UK courts under Section 3 of that Act now had to take the European Convention on Human Rights (ECHR) into account when judging legislation, how they did so would strongly depend on the judiciary's outlook.[40] Government and Parliament also remained fairly free to legislate as they wished, which would bring them into conflict with the HRA only later. There was no particular flood of successful HRA cases weakening the Government's anti-crime drive: during the Blair period, seventeen so-called 'declarations of incompatibility' were issued by the courts, most notably that the

Home Secretary's power to determine the term of a prisoner sentenced to life was not compatible with Article 6 of the Declaration.[41]

If many clauses of the continual Crime or Criminal Justice Acts looked to come out of a more conservative past, some pointed to a more liberal future. The 1998 Act, for instance, provided for the treatment of drug offenders and laid down tougher penalties for racially aggravated crimes. The Government also emphasised the importance of intervening in domestic abuse – an area the police had historically been reluctant to work on. The Domestic Violence, Crime and Victims Act of 2004 made defying a non-molestation order a criminal offence. A new forced marriages unit was set up. Straw also took up the Stephen Lawrence case involving the racially motivated murder of a teenage student in 1993, though only after the *Daily Mail* had published a now-famous front page naming those it held responsible for the murder. The shocking nature of the crime, as well as the offence to Middle England's values of fairness and order, was too great for the *Mail* – or Straw – to ignore. The new Home Secretary set up the Macpherson Inquiry into what had happened, and accepted his detection and definition of 'institutional racism' in the Metropolitan Police when its report was published in 1999. Macpherson prompted something of a sea change in how these issues were spoken about, and some practical policies were changed. The Race Relations Act was amended to prevent public bodies discriminating on the basis of race; more black and minority ethnic police officers were recruited.[42]

Building safer communities?

If ideas about policing were changing, its reality was hardly transformed. New Public Management techniques were more slowly applied to policing than other spheres of state activity: so-called Evidence-Based Policing was only really applied during the era of funding restraint after 2008/09. Now was the New Public Management applied as crudely or insensitively as in some other areas. It also proved harder to integrate local police forces into local governance than it did schools or childcare centres, since the police were rightly protective of their separate role in the justice system and because councillors and police officers could often have very different ideas about both ends and means. Those ideas went back a long way. The Morgan Report on Crime Prevention, published in 1991, recommended a statutory duty to organise multi-agency efforts, but the Conservative government of the time rejected the idea, in part because of its distrust of local authorities and higher public spending.[43]

Labour in power enthusiastically embraced the Morgan Report's ideas about joint responsibility, collective working and crime prevention – as they had at the time of Morgan's publication, before Blair became Shadow Home Secretary or leader. The 1998 Crime and Disorder Act placed a statutory duty on the police and local authorities to work together with others to combat crime – in line with Morgan's recommendations from 1991. These interagency Crime and Disorder Reduction Partnerships (CDRPs) were asked to consult about and settle on Crime Reduction Strategies every three years. Partnership working then became more important as time went on. After 2003, and the Green Paper *Building Safer Communities Together*, more emphasis was placed on community policing. Although the eventual White Paper of 2004 still evoked the concepts of 'choice', 'contract' and 'customers', it promised Neighbourhood Policing Teams for every area by 2008, much more flexibility at that level of policing, and much more active local participation.[44] From 2006 CDRPs were supplemented by and included joint working on violent or sex offenders, a framework which eventually became known as Multi-Agency Public Protection Arrangements (MAPPAs). Youth Offender Teams were also formed to work with young people.[45] These Partnerships undoubtedly did a great deal of good work. In 2010 the Audit Commission singled out a number of best practice examples: Brighton and County Durham, for instance, looking at families in difficulty and their neighbours; Liverpool, focusing on students at risk of burglary; and Greater Manchester and Trafford, working to reduce gang and gun violence.[46]

The focus of the CDRPs was never quite clear, however, and although many of them developed into genuine community forums, their ability to respond to local factors was held back by central government. Whitehall was often desperate, not to consult, but to ensure that the Home Office meet the Treasury's PSA targets, as well as benchmarks now set centrally after the Police Reform Act of 2002 and under its Policing Performance Assessment Framework.[47] As one police officer put it: 'front-line officers are focusing their efforts on work that meets the targets set against them as opposed to the needs of the public which offers no kudos to the officer'.[48] CDRPs were also torn between their inclusive brief to promote community safety and some of the Government's harsher instincts about control and punishment. Businesspeople, healthcare professionals and local authority officers alike often found central governments' constant demands used up their energies and cut across their efforts, for instance in regulating the burgeoning night-time economy. And although these partnerships were supposed to push the police into seeing their work in a more holistic way, they often felt they lacked the resources and long-term planning to do so.[49] Once again, an opportunity for a new focus on local leadership was to some extent missed.

Public opinion and crime

The public remained relatively unimpressed with New Labour's record on crime for some years, especially when compared to the strides they thought other services were making. As Figure 6.3 shows, when it came to perceptions of crime rates at a national level, public reactions tended to fluctuate, but stayed rather trendless. Lows of 58 per cent and 61 per cent in respondents thinking that crime was going up overall were followed by highs of 72 per cent in 2002/03 and 75 per cent in 2008/09. There were many reasons for this continuing dissatisfaction, not least the fact that ministers kept emphasising how 'tough' they had to be and that despite the massive increase in manpower, only 11 per cent of policing personnel were visible on the streets at any one time. As the police's role in many types of social problems expanded, technical specialisms abounded, and work on new areas such as counter-terrorism and organised crime burgeoned, work on what voters perceived to be 'ordinary' community policing perhaps relatively suffered. A long-term trend towards scepticism about authority, and the police scandals and miscarriages of justice making headlines at the time, probably also added to the downwards trend of those voters saying they were 'satisfied' with police performance. According to the British Crime Survey (BCS), this measure of public confidence dropped from 92 per cent in 1982 to 79 per cent in 2000.[50]

On the other hand, as Figure 6.3 again makes clear, crime's undoubted decline was being noticed at the local level: after 2002/03, when 54 per cent of those surveyed thought crime was increasing in their vicinity, that number fell all the way to 31 per cent by 2009/10. Persuading voters that the area where they lived was getting safer turned out to be far easier than changing people's minds about the national situation, just as it was when voters could see their local hospital and school was improving – facts they could often see with their own eyes. 21 per cent told the BCS they were themselves worried about becoming the victim of property crime, and 25 per cent violent crime, in 1997: those figures had basically halved to 11 per cent and 13 per cent by 2009.[51] If we look across a range of data measuring concern about crime, rather than just the question of whether it was going 'up' or 'down', we do see a gradual and sustained decline in concern about it after about 2001 – though not in the public's

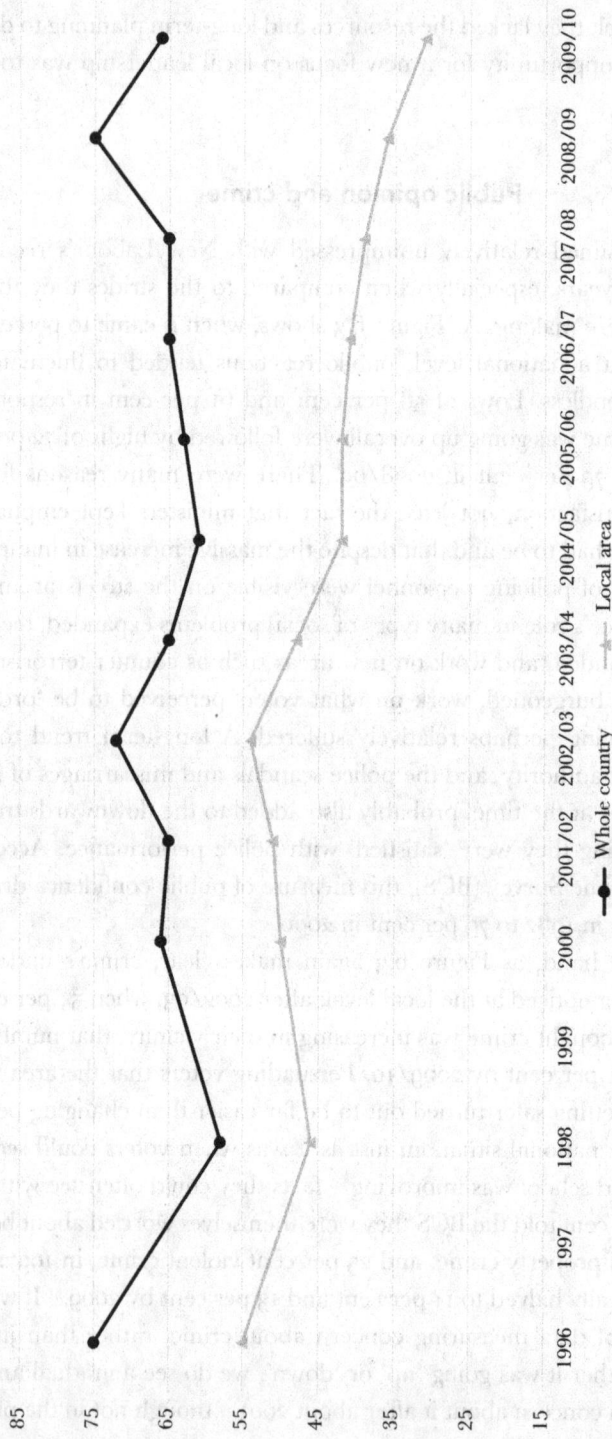

Figure 6.3 Public perceptions of crime (% perceiving more crime), 1996–2010

X-axis labels: 1996, 1997, 1998, 1999, 2000, 2001/02, 2002/03, 2003/04, 2004/05, 2005/06, 2006/07, 2007/08, 2008/09, 2009/10

Y-axis labels: 15, 25, 35, 45, 55, 65, 75, 85

Legend: Whole country · Local area

Source: J. Flatley, C. Kershaw, K. Smith, R. Chaplin and D. Moon, Home Office Statistical Bulletin: Crime in England and Wales 2009/10: Findings from the British Crime Survey and Police Recorded Crime (London: Home Office, July 2010), figure 5.4, p. 111.

punitive outlook, at least until the 2010s.[52] The pattern was the same across the managed economy and the welfare state: understandable initial doubts; grudging acceptance that the situation on the ground seemed better; and then a wider confidence in the Government's ability to deliver.

There is no doubt that the press, particularly the tabloid print media, continually fanned the flames of such concerns. The annual International Crime and Victim Survey, compiled from telephone interviews, was a particular source of lurid headlines. 'England Tops Crime League and We Are the Crime Capital of the World', declared the *Daily Telegraph* in February 2003 – a conclusion that was hardly true on any measure. When street crime rose in 2002, against a backdrop of most crime sharply declining, the *Daily Express* ran a front page headline of 'Scared to Walk Our Streets', echoed by *The Sun* which insisted that 'Muggers Rule Our Streets'.[53] Such campaigns played a key role in Charles Clarke's downfall as Home Secretary in 2006, when the press amplified the scandal that up to 1,000 foreign-born prisoners had not been deported as planned, but had somehow been allowed to disappear within the UK.[54] It might have proved politically dangerous to defy this incendiary language entirely. David Davis, as Shadow Home Secretary, seized on a 9 per cent rise in violent crime, announced during the 2005 election campaign, to 'tell Mr Blair straight: life in Britain is very different outside your security bubble'. He announced a six-point plan to 'make life a misery for criminals'. Labour's plan to recruit more community support officers, and increase the numbers of police officers, helped to neutralise this issue.[55]

However their views were formed, public attitudes to crime and punishment remained relatively punitive. Although some slow and gradual trend towards more liberal attitudes could be discerned in the data, harsh punishments and rapid justice were very popular. Some sense of this can be seen in British Social Attitudes survey data from the period (Table 6.1). In 2006 only a bare majority of the public thought that citizens should have a right to defy the law even in exceptional cases of personal conscience; a mere 27 per cent of respondents disagreed with the statement 'the law should always be obeyed, even if a particular law is wrong'. Only 51 per cent agreed with the statement that it was 'worse to convict an innocent person than to let a guilty person go free'. Those disagreeing with the death penalty 'for some crimes' did rise, from 25 per cent in 1998 to 29–30 per cent in 2009–10. But that left this relatively liberal group still in the minority. Had New Labour listened only to its relatively liberal activists, it would have been moving some way out of the country's mainstream.

Table 6.1 Public attitudes to civil liberties, 1998–2010

	1998	1999	2000	2001	2002	2003	2004	2005	2006	2007	2008	2009	2010
% saying there are exceptional occasions on which people should follow their consciences even if it means breaking the law	NA	NA	NA	NA	NA	NA	NA	NA	54	NA	NA	NA	NA
% saying it is worse to convict an innocent person than to let a guilty person go free	NA	NA	NA	NA	NA	NA	NA	52	51	NA	NA	NA	NA
% disagreeing that 'for some crimes, the death penalty is the most appropriate sentence'	25	27	27	32	32	27	30	28	28	29	25	30	29
% disagreeing that 'the law should always be obeyed, even if a particular law is wrong'	NA	NA	29	26	26	27	26	NA	27	24	26	24	24

Source: E. Clery, J. Curtice and R. Harding (eds), British Social Attitudes 34 (London: National Centre for Social Research, 2016), 'Civil Liberties' chapter, appendix, pp. 63-4.

The many eyes of the surveillance state

In line with the Government's – and the public's – relative illiberalism, surveillance also increased across Britain, with for instance CCTV cameras perhaps numbering over three million by 2009. Crime Reduction Strategies demanded that high-volume, highly visible crime should fall, reducing such crimes as car theft, burglary and disorderly conduct: CCTV was seen as ideal as both a deterrent and a tool to identify suspects. It was also popular with those local residents, businesspeople and local authorities who worked together in the local CDRPs and were keen to improve quality of life in their particular areas. Three-quarters of the Home Office's crime prevention budget was dedicated to CCTV between 1996 and 1998, and the single 'community safety' intervention asked of CDRPs was to set up CCTV cameras.[56] The number of CCTV cameras was seen as pivotal in achieving the Home Office's ambitious crime reduction targets. Once New Labour had won its second term, the fact that 430 more CCTV schemes were due within a year was reported with approval to the Prime Minister himself.[57]

It is important to remember in this respect that, as so often, wider public attitudes were often fairly authoritarian – especially when set against the concerns of the courts and some policymakers, more attuned as they remained to questions of individual liberty. When the Home Office commissioned academics to survey voters in areas about to begin or expand CCTV provision, there was overwhelming support for this idea, especially when it came to city or town centres. Residents in very different areas all approved: in very deprived parts of a northern city nearly 77 per cent were happy; in a mid-range retail and entertainment area in the south, 83 per cent thought more CCTV a good idea; and in an ex-mining town in the Midlands, an even higher share of respondents (93 per cent) were in favour.[58]

The more widespread use of electronic communication also permitted the interception and storage of sensitive personal data, as well as more general information about individuals' communications. This general increase in recording of all types was seen in a relatively relaxed way in both British law and by English and Scottish courts, as was more directed surveillance – the Conservatives' Police Act of 1997, for instance, had given the police more powers to deploy surveillance devices.[59] The march of forensic science posed similar dilemmas about security and confidentiality. The House of Lords decided that the police did not need ever to destroy DNA samples in one 2004 ruling on an ECHR case; only when the idea of a national, permanent DNA database came before the European Court of Human Rights in 2008 was indefinite holding of such material deemed to be contrary to the principle of individual privacy.[60] The UK government was certainly not above gesturing at 'tough' measures that were then struck down by the European courts.

The Blair governments did take or accept some steps to limit these powers, especially given the incorporation of the ECHR into UK law. The Human Rights Act was of course a major milestone, with incalculable long-term effects in British law. The increased, clearer protections around privacy and liberty granted by the Data Protection Act of 1998 – which led to the creation of a Data Protection Commissioner in 2000, monitoring much stricter rules about how people's data could be used – also demonstrated Labour's commitment to a rules-based order which limited government power. It was in part the intervention of the European courts which prompted the creation of at least minimal safeguards, which were still much weaker than in most countries – though, again, Labour made rather more concessions to personal liberty than the Conservatives had done in the 1980s, or probably would have done had they continued in power. Even so, a huge number of bodies, from HMRC to the Food Standards Agency, the Post Office and local authorities were authorised to deploy targeted surveillance. This was not the only time when the incorporation of the ECHR into UK law via the 1998 Act was of questionable utility to citizens. New Labour's domestic statecraft never became particularly liberal, rarely hiding its authoritarian, populist instincts.[61] Public opinion, ministers' conservative views and the courts' rather laissez-faire attitudes all pointed in quite the opposite direction.

More imprisonment, more rehabilitation

Sentencing policies were and are perhaps the most controversial areas in the whole of the crime and justice field. When the Home Office published its conclusions on sentencing frameworks in 2001, in a report known by the name of its author John Halliday, sensible ideas emerged and were implemented. One was a simplification of the panoply of community orders into one coherent system, as well as greater emphasis on help and treatment – for instance, for drug offences. The White Paper and subsequent Criminal Justice Act that followed also aimed at much more coherent and standardised sentencing, in part via the creation of a Sentencing Guidelines Council. But such ideas would again be difficult to implement, because they ran against the tradition of judging each case on its merits: and though the Act stipulated the aims of sentences for the first time (punishment, crime reduction, protection and reparation), these were not ranked by importance, nor clearly defined.[62]

New Labour in power was Janus-faced about sentencing. On the one hand, 'custody-plus' sentences stipulated that custodial sentences of less than a year should not include more than thirteen weeks' confinement, with the rest of the penalty being made up of work and restrictions under a community order. On the other, there were 'community-minus' sentences that would involve immediate incarceration if the terms were breached. This was a harsh, illogical idea which, given rapid reconviction rates, would land perhaps the majority of those convicted back in jail anyway.[63] Most of the Government's direction of travel was towards harsher punishment.[64]

The 2003 Criminal Justice Act brought in a new type of conviction, Imprisonment for Public Protection (IPP), which meant that an adult convicted of a specified serious offence could be incarcerated indefinitely provided they posed 'a significant risk to members of the public of serious harm'. This became something of an object lesson in the unintended consequences of ever-harsher legislation, because ministers had intended this power to be used sparingly, but judges used it far more than the Government had expected. The number of IPPs increased for instance by 31 per cent in 2006 alone – further ballooning the prison population and leaving prisoners languishing there indefinitely.[65] By 2010, there were 6,000 people incarcerated under IPPs. They were made discretionary in 2008, before being abolished in 2012, but this change was not a retrospective one. Even by late 2022, 2,890 of these prisoners remained in prison in England and Wales. Almost all of them had by then passed their normal tariff date for release.[66] As late as 2024 one man, Abdullahi Suleman, was still in prison for an IPP he received for stealing a laptop in 2005. Originally released in 2011, he has since been recalled to prison four times for failing to turn up for the mental health treatment that was a condition of his release.[67] Ministers had not meant such obvious anomalies. But those were the consequences of the overemphasis on punishment that has plagued the British legal system for decades.

Criminal justice interventions that did not involve conviction and sentencing also became harsher, and they too were controversial. So-called 'stop and account' incidents, which involve police interactions with the public under no particular statutory power, rose: from 1.4 million in 2005–06 to 1.87 million the next year. Better regulation and record-keeping, in particular the keeping of written records of these incidents between 2004 and 2009, actually gave this practice a stronger identity as an official legal encounter – not the least of those times when more accountability, regulation and 'rights' might seem to push forward the frontiers of the state as against the individual. Under the Serious Organised Crime and Police Act 2005, powers of arrest without a warrant were expanded to all crimes, not just serious ones or those requiring urgent action. This reform had the knock-on effect of expanding powers of entry and search. The Jean Charles de Menezes case publicly revealed the details of an alleged 'shoot to kill' policy under a 2002-03 Chief Constables' initiative known as Operation Kratos.[68]

Incarceration rates were higher than most other developed countries, and after moving closer to those for instance in France during the late 1980s and the 1990s diverged sharply again after the mid-1990s. In 1975 the prison population of England and Wales had stood at just under 40,000; in the 1980s it peaked near 49,000 before increasing rapidly in the early to mid-1990s, coming down a little and then surging again to nearly 76,000 by 2005 (see Figure 6.4). Prison populations continued to rise through New Labour's time in office, though not quite as quickly as during the Conservatives' final years in office and with the pace of increase slackening somewhat as time went on. The numbers rose to just over 80,000 by 2007, and then 86,000 by the first full year of the Coalition government in 2011.[69]

There were signs of a rethink towards the end of Blair's time in office, in part because the strains on the prison system had simply grown too great to manage. Early release packages, including 'tagged' prisoners who had to wear electronic detection devices, linked together training, job openings and supervision. Efforts were made around that time to stabilise prison overcrowding– through an Intensive Alternatives to Prison initiative, for instance – but Labour still planned to expand the prison estate still further, to 96,000.[70] Martin Narey, Director General of the Prison Service between 1999 and 2005, blunted some of the harsher edges of this expansion with a 'decency agenda' that emphasised the dignity of prisoners, while still confronting them with their behaviour. But as time went on and the prison population continued to expand, these approaches became harder and harder to apply. The sense grew that something was deeply wrong within a prison estate that was simply under too much pressure. Allegations of abuse at the Young Offender Institution at Portland, and the murder of a young Asian inmate at Feltham, both became emblematic of these failures.[71]

Mitigating this punitive turn, at least to some extent, was a new emphasis on the efficacy and usefulness of probation, which was now asked to further concentrate its work on community safety, pushing resources towards lowering

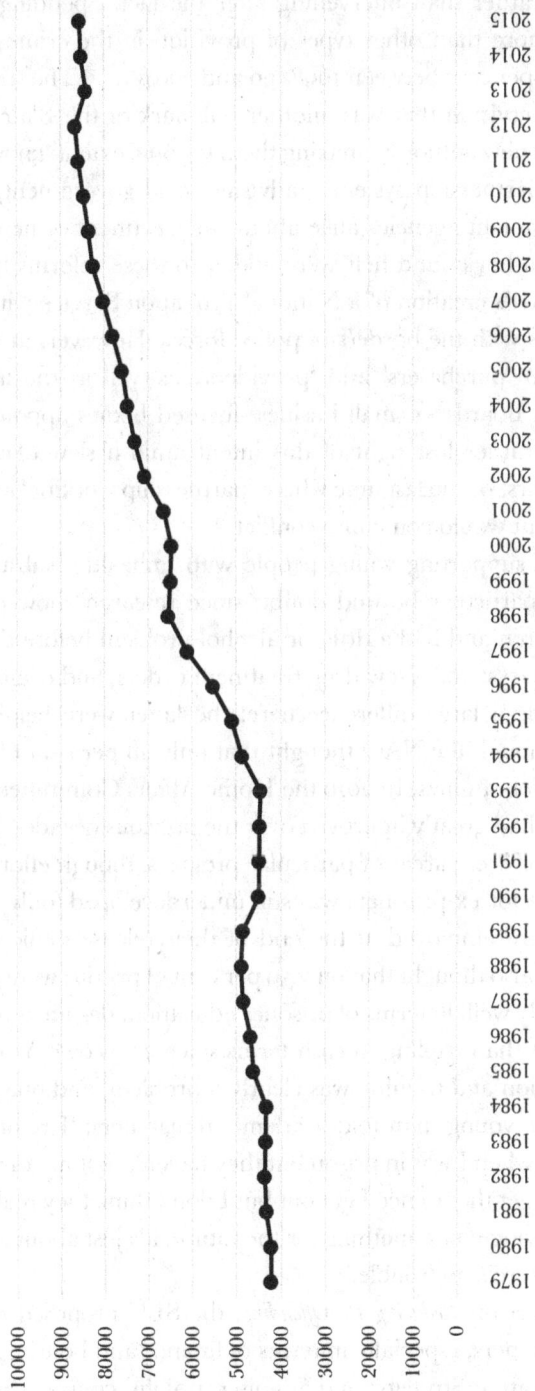

Figure 6.4 Total prison population of England and Wales, 1979–2015

Source: UK Prison Population Statistics, https://commonslibrary.parliament.uk/research-briefings/sn04334/, dataset accessed 22 March 2023; also G. Sturge, *UK Prison Population Statistics, House of Commons Library Briefing Paper* 04334 (25 October 2022), chart, p. 7.

reoffending risks rather than intervening after the fact. Spending on probation rose by far more than other types of provision in the crime and justice field, rising by 160 per cent between 1998/99 and 2004/05.[72] The strengthening of community supervision that was another hallmark of the Blair years gave Probation Officers new authority, making them to some extent 'knowledge brokers' in the new partnership system – advising local government, the police and central government agencies alike about the treatment of newly released prisoners. More authority and heft were added to these reforms by the 2000 Criminal Justice Act's creation of a National Probation Service with forty-two areas, coterminous with the borders of police forces. However, in 2005 a split between probation 'purchasers' and 'providers', as well as the introduction of local Probation Boards as small business-focused bodies appointed by the Home Secretary, rather lost sight of this intent amid a slew of institutional changes – not the first or the last time where 'partnership working' and the New Public Management would come into conflict.[73]

The efficacy of supporting young people with unhealthy substance abuse problems was in particular beyond doubt, since research showed that two-thirds of them on remand had a drug or alcohol problem before they entered the criminal justice system.[74] New drug treatment orders, and drugs teams run by the NHS, made a large difference here: the latter were helping 133,000 people by 2008, though the NAO thought that only 28 per cent of drug users completed their programmes. In 2010 the Home Affairs Committee concluded that these systems had greatly improved over the previous decades. Drug treatment and education were areas of particular progress, though efforts to secure work opportunities for ex-prisoners was still underdeveloped (only 35 per cent of ex-offenders were employed at the end of their release or licence).[75] The Ministry of Justice also thought that only 59 per cent of prisons were performing 'well' or 'reasonably well' in terms of prisoner education, despite funding under that heading more than tripling in cash terms since 2001/02.[76] Young offenders' lack of education and training was clearly a problem, and one they raised themselves. As one young man told academic researchers: 'I retook the ones [GCSEs] I missed when I was in prison but they haven't sent me the results yet. I've been trying to get them since I got out but I don't think they really care. It's not really about giving you something for the future, it's just about keeping you occupied so that there's no trouble.'[77]

In its 2002 report on *Reducing Re-Offending*, the SEU proposed much more support for ex-prisoners, especially in terms of finance and housing; a stronger National Rehabilitation Strategy; and a 'going straight' contract for offenders aged 18–20. All of this would ensure that young people leaving prison, in particular, would have access to education and training, drug treatment and volunteering opportunities. A pilot project, in the South West of England, was announced to test the water.[78] A stronger emphasis on rehabilitation was subsequently included in the *Justice for All* White Paper published in 2002, though by the time the Criminal Justice Bill appeared later that year, some of this emphasis on preventing reoffending via reform had been forgotten.[79] The SEU's ideas about rehabilitation were to some extent stalled by Blunkett's arrival at the Home Office. Clarke was later open about how hard it was to emphasise rehabilitation: 'the media did play a highly significant role … the media made it very difficult to develop alternatives to prison because they were presented as not the "tough" option'.[80]

The Janus faces of New Labour

When it came to crime and punishment, New Labour once again presented a complicated and sometimes paradoxical face to the world. More police were apparently needed, while crime was falling quickly. Young people were out of control, though their reoffending rates were plunging. Prison worked, but also relied on helping offenders to deal with their problems both while they were incarcerated and after they had left. The scale of increased surveillance, the use of administrative rather than judicial structures and populist initiatives such as the DNA database ran counter to the principles of the HRA that New Labour had itself passed. It was a kaleidoscopic mix, though by no means out of line with the paradoxes of New Labour policy on health and education. As one scholar of the field has put it, 'two parallel and contradictory trends emerge: a determination to introduce illiberal legislation based on illiberal populist policies, but an awareness of the human rights context … New Labour appears to wish to have a sound human rights record … But it also wants to appear "tough on crime".'[81]

As in so many other areas, 'New Labour [was] … engaged in a high stakes balancing act. An amalgam of managerialist, communitarian and authoritarian populist ideas had been pulled together under the phrase "modernisation"'. New Labour's rhetoric and strategies enabled the Government 'to look both ways at once', keeping secure training centres for 12- to 15-year-olds but also setting up a host of restorative justice initiatives.[82] Scholars speak of a 'bifurcation' of criminal justice policy, lessening sentences for minor crimes while lengthening them for more serious offences. The Blair governments seem to many like an administration of 'multiple minds', advocating policies and programmes riddled with 'fundamental contradictions' – for instance, between managerialism and the punitive rhetoric of harsh retribution.[83]

There were a number of attempts to square these circles. In one 1998 speech, Straw argued that New Labour was 'trying to develop the concept of the "Active Community" in which the commitment of the individual is backed by the duty of all organisations … to work towards a community of mutual care and a balance of rights and responsibilities'.[84] But this 'active community' was often more honoured in the breach than the observance. New Labour's rhetoric was instead often harshly judgemental, and ignored its earlier emphasis on the social and moral roots of crime. Ministers had sought to effect a paradigm shift in outlooks towards the rights of communities as a whole, as against those of individual lawbreakers. Blair made this clear in the foreword to the revealingly titled White Paper, *Rebalancing the Criminal Justice System in Favour of the Law-Abiding Majority*, published in 2006: 'we must ensure that in a modern world stripped of the bonds of the past … The criminal justice organisations live up to their duty of protecting the rights of victims and communities. We must build a criminal justice system which puts protection of the law-abiding majority at its heart.'[85] To some extent, this outcome was always likely. Laudable talk of 'social exclusion' can itself pathologise and demonise those who fail to respond to 'help'.

One can exaggerate this punitive turn. Community partnerships, local policing, new facilities for young people and help with addition should all be flagged up too. The whole gamut of Labour's economic and social policies – lowering youth unemployment, pushing up wages for the low paid, improving healthcare and education – must also have assisted in crime reduction.[86] Social democratic policies were definitely present. The criminologist Robert Reiner has picked out five hallmarks of social democratic thinking on law and order. Crime is firstly seen as part, but perhaps only a small part, of a range of social problems. It is, second, governed via a mix of social and individual responsibilities and actions. Third, offenders as well as victims are a focus of concern. A fourth social democratic principle is that policing and punishment are only one part of the answer to crime and disorder. A fifth is at least an attempt to avoid extreme language and an exaggeration of crime's place in everyday life, in order to forestall moral panics. This chapter has shown that New Labour could be said to display elements, but only limited elements, of numbers one to four on that list, seeing crime as one social problem among many and its answers as multifarious. On number five, avoiding the damage done by endless 'tough' rhetoric, it surely fell short.[87]

For all its talk of 'evidence-based solutions', and 'doing what works', many examples of which we have unpicked in this chapter, New Labour always thought it simply had to 'out-tough' the Conservatives. It is this sense of political vulnerability that created a false policy auction or bidding war with Michael Howard when he was the Conservatives' hard-line Home Secretary in the mid-1990s, and which continued well into the mid-2000s. It cannot be 'evidence-based' to *always* be on the side of harsher criminal justice measures, and indeed it is arguable that the constant emphasis on punishment emanating from both parties had the effect of making voters growing up during these years even harsher than their forebears. Blair's famous *New Statesman* article from 1993 reflected the New Left Realism's novel ideas, and expressed due concern about the damage crime was doing to working-class neighbourhoods: but he was also clear that middle-class swing voters were watching too. This, he argued, 'is an issue that stretches way beyond our traditional boundaries to the electorate we need to win. Rural England and Tory suburbs are now scarred by almost routine violence ... which local people feel powerless to prevent.'[88]

Ministers' rhetoric about 'doing what works' was not always honoured. Empirical evaluation of ASBOs, for instance, was very limited indeed, despite constant Home Office promises of more data on such interventions' success or failure.[89] Not only did this allow the Conservatives to mount a recovery as the party of civil liberties and compassion, opposing ID Cards while Davis was Shadow Home Secretary and famously promising to 'hug a hoodie' while led by David Cameron: it could also bring the rest of the New Labour strategy into question as its libertarian and social democratic instincts on the HRA or social reform were undermined by its authoritarianism. John Reid's 2006 crime strategy when he was Home Secretary referenced being 'tough' or 'tougher' on crime thirty-four times, but only once did it refer to the causes of crime. New Labour's balancing act had become less than balanced.[90] The legacy of such crude views and one-dimensional solutions would last for a long time: by the 2020s, ministers were having to release prisoners early because jails were overflowing.

Labour ministers justified this, not entirely unfairly, as an expression of democracy and a reflection of the public's complex and mixed views. As Blunkett put it: 'you cannot just ignore what people out there are seeing and what they are reading because they are our task masters ... in a liberal democracy, the sending of signals is important and necessary. If you do not send out signals that you have heard and understood, it leads to people getting disillusioned.'[91] Even Robin Cook, relatively liberal when it came to crime and justice, believed in

2002 that the right-wing populism seen elsewhere in the EU had been deflected by New Labour's success on this issue: 'the phenomenon has caught out a number of our continental sister parties who have not had Blair's skill in turning crime into a strength rather than a weakness for the Left, or Brown's ruthless determination ... to help the poor'.[92] As we have seen, the views of the wider public – not to mention the press – could be deeply conservative when it came to crime, and that was especially true as Blair and Blunkett intuited of many of Labour's own voters. This prevented the party from going further towards 'what works' while in office. Crime fell; policing grew in strength and became more sensitive and more effective; probation, the support offered to offenders and drugs treatment were improved. But the shadow of prison, and of political parties' self-defeating language, still loomed over everything.

7

Housing: chasing demand, falling short

A third way for housing?

It is strange that New Labour's ideas proved hard to apply to housing policy, because that was one of the most varied parts of the mixed economy and a Third Way between public and private should have been applicable most of all to bricks and mortar. In part this was once again down to the initial vagueness of the Third Way itself. As the academic Tim Brown put it in a book published by the Labour Housing Group in 1998 (to which Blair provided a foreword): 'there is a major gap between discussions on these big ideas and housing policies and practices for tackling immediate problems. Much of the literature on the third way and related concepts is … relatively abstract.'[1] Labour's consultative Green Paper *Quality and Choice: A Decent Home for All*, published in 2000, was a very inconclusive document, raising questions and options about housing benefit, social rents and standards in the private rental sector, but without coming to many conclusions. On the other hand, familiar New Labour themes did appear. Local authorities were to take on a more strategic role across the different types of housing stock and tenure; in combination with other agencies, they were to pay much more attention to neighbourhood and community sustainability; tenant participation and 'voice' were to be encouraged wherever possible.[2]

Distinctive new policies could be detected beyond the surface ambivalence. The *Sustainable Communities* White Paper of 2003 argued that housing's effects and importance went beyond local authority boundaries and divides between sectors. It argued that housing should be seen as intricately bound up with other policy areas as varied as crime and transport. Housing should therefore be considered in a much wider frame than it had been previously, and some funding streams (such as those for Housing Associations and local councils) should be merged.[3] The Comprehensive Spending Review of 2000 also led to a large-scale increase in state resources for housing, from £3.55bn in 2001/02 to £4.65bn in 2003/04, though it took most of this period for spending to return to even its early 1990s levels.[4] By 2003 the Government was committing large sums to the effort: £22bn of funding for its new and overarching plan for 'Sustainable Communities' between 2002/03 and 2005/06, including £5bn for more afford-able homes, £1bn of which was for key workers in the public sector. The main Growth Area designed by central government, the Thames Gateway to the East of London, was to receive £446 million; other such areas £164 million (demonstrating the large scale of the Thames Gateway effort). Prescott indeed told Blair in 2003 that the Thames Gateway projects were 'critical to our poli-cies for achieving a step change in housing supply in the South East'.[5]

More joined-up government, and more money, proved as usual no panacea. The New Deal for Communities, launched in 1998, probably spent £1.7bn by 2008, with a further £730 million brought in from the wider public, private and voluntary sectors. In practice, though there were lofty goals about reduc-ing disadvantage through a multi-agency approach, most of this money was spent on housing. On the Aylesbury estate where Blair gave his first speech as Prime Minister, for instance, this New Deal really meant a £243 million plan to demolish the estate and move the tenants into new Housing Association prop-erties. Less large-scale and more traditional architecture, a more mixed com-munity and better design were all thought to hold the keys to a more inclusive future and to offer a solution to housing needs that now needed to replace the way Labour had built during the 1960s and 1970s, the age of mass building and large council estates. The Aylesbury residents, however, disagreed, and voted against stock transfer to the Faraday Housing Association in December 2001. The estate was 'only' partially redeveloped, with one council block demolished and six new buildings put up in which 48 per cent of the dwellings were pri-vately owned. The estate undoubtedly benefited from the investment, but the rebuilding provided fewer social housing units at large expense.[6] Across the whole range of housing policy, it was all very well to recommend partnership, developments from the 'ground up' and a mixed economy: it was much harder to actually reach those aims.

Social housing: two steps forward, one back

It is, as ever, important to put New Labour's advances and setbacks into con-text. By the time Labour returned to power in 1997, the Conservatives had overseen the sale of 1.7 million council houses since their Right to Buy came in.

This scheme first and foremost offered very favourable purchase terms to existing tenants, with discounts of up to 60 per cent of the market value. This had split the housing market in two, with council housing reduced to the status of a residual while owner occupiers enjoyed a boom in prices and landlords reaped the rewards of cheap housing. In 1979, 29 per cent of homes in England were council dwellings; that number had fallen to 14 per cent by the year 2000 (those relative proportions were similar for Britain as a whole). During the 1980s owner occupation became even more of a norm than it had been already and, by 1996, 67 per cent of households lived in owner-occupied housing. If New Labour now wanted to push social housing's share back up, it would have to do so from a low base. Their first steps were cautious, in the shape of limited moves to allow councils to plough house sale profits back into their own stock. Some – though only some – local authority capital spending was unlocked, amounting to £800 million between 1997 and 1999, with increased central government resources for housing then amounting to £3.9bn between 1999 and 2002.[7]

This had important consequences for Blair and Brown's New- or Post-Keynesian regional policy. Given that the new local authority housing in most need of regeneration outside London was most likely to be in the North West, Yorkshire and the Humber and the West Midlands, this in itself amounted to a quiet, unspoken spatial policy that pumped billions into the construction industries of low income areas. The 2003 Local Government Act further allowed councils to spend 25 per cent of their receipts from sales on capital projects. The other 75 per cent was transferred to central government so it could reallocate the money for similar purposes – though, crucially, the money was not ringfenced for housing.[8] Above all, and despite the commitment of some new resources, the numbers of dwellings built for social rent continued to decline right through to 2002/03.[9]

The number of social housing units thus continued to fall, albeit gently, to just over four million by 2004. Housing Association stock made up nearly half that four million by then, as local councils were nearly as distrusted by Labour in office as they had been under the Conservatives. 'High Performing' councils were encouraged to establish Arms Length Management Organisations (ALMOs), spin-off bodies which were permitted to bid for more resources than were their local authority progenitors.[10] Building for social housing did eventually rise slightly (see Figure 7.1). But almost all of those public dwellings, the output of which eventually doubled from a trough around the turn of the century, was predictably built by Housing Associations, not by local councils (see Figure 7.2). And doubling building rates from under 5,000 per quarter to

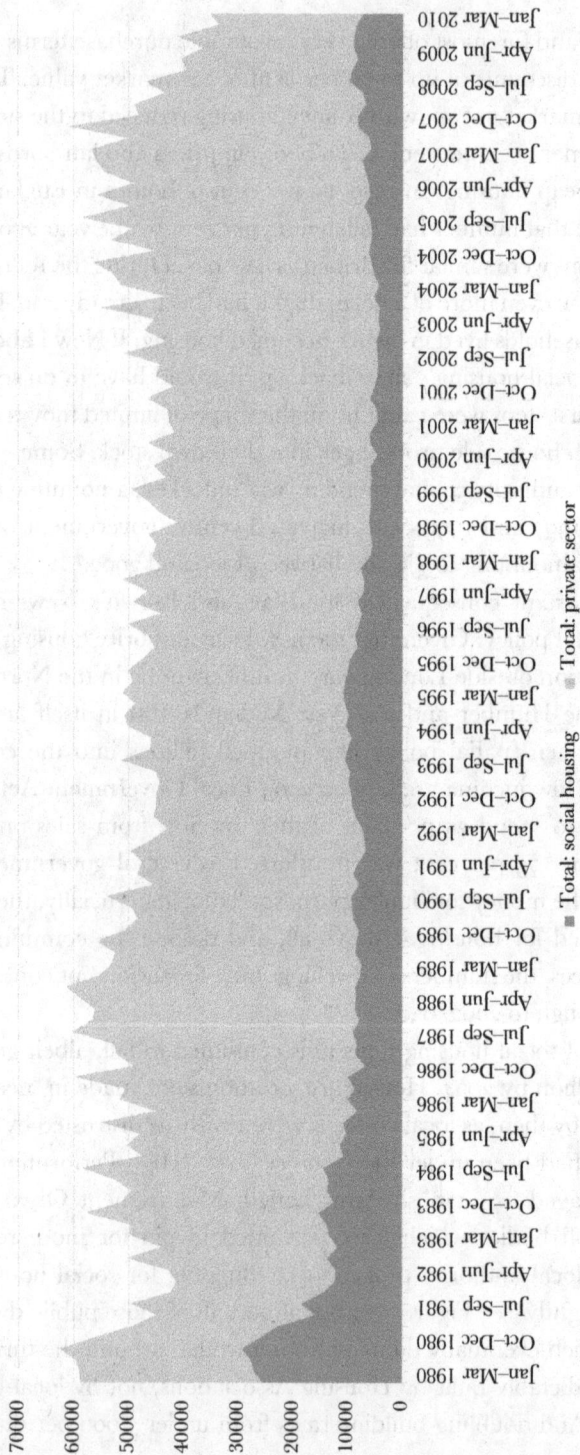

Figure 7.1 Total dwellings completed by quarter, England, 1980–2010

Source: Indicators of House Building, UK, www.ons.gov.uk/peoplepopulationandcommunity/housing/housing/datasets/ukhousebuildingpermanentdwellingsstartedandcompleted, accessed 21 April 2023.

Legend: ■ Total: social housing ■ Total: private sector

X-axis labels: Jan–Mar 1980, Oct–Dec 1980, Jul–Sep 1981, Apr–Jun 1982, Jan–Mar 1983, Oct–Dec 1983, Jul–Sep 1984, Apr–Jun 1985, Jan–Mar 1986, Oct–Dec 1986, Jul–Sep 1987, Apr–Jun 1988, Jan–Mar 1989, Oct–Dec 1989, Jul–Sep 1990, Apr–Jun 1991, Jan–Mar 1992, Oct–Dec 1992, Jul–Sep 1993, Apr–Jun 1994, Jan–Mar 1995, Oct–Dec 1995, Jul–Sep 1996, Apr–Jun 1997, Jan–Mar 1998, Oct–Dec 1998, Jul–Sep 1999, Apr–Jun 2000, Jan–Mar 2001, Oct–Dec 2001, Jul–Sep 2002, Apr–Jun 2003, Jan–Mar 2004, Oct–Dec 2004, Jul–Sep 2005, Apr–Jun 2006, Jan–Mar 2007, Oct–Dec 2007, Jul–Sep 2008, Apr–Jun 2009, Jan–Mar 2010

Y-axis labels: 0, 10000, 20000, 30000, 40000, 50000, 60000, 70000

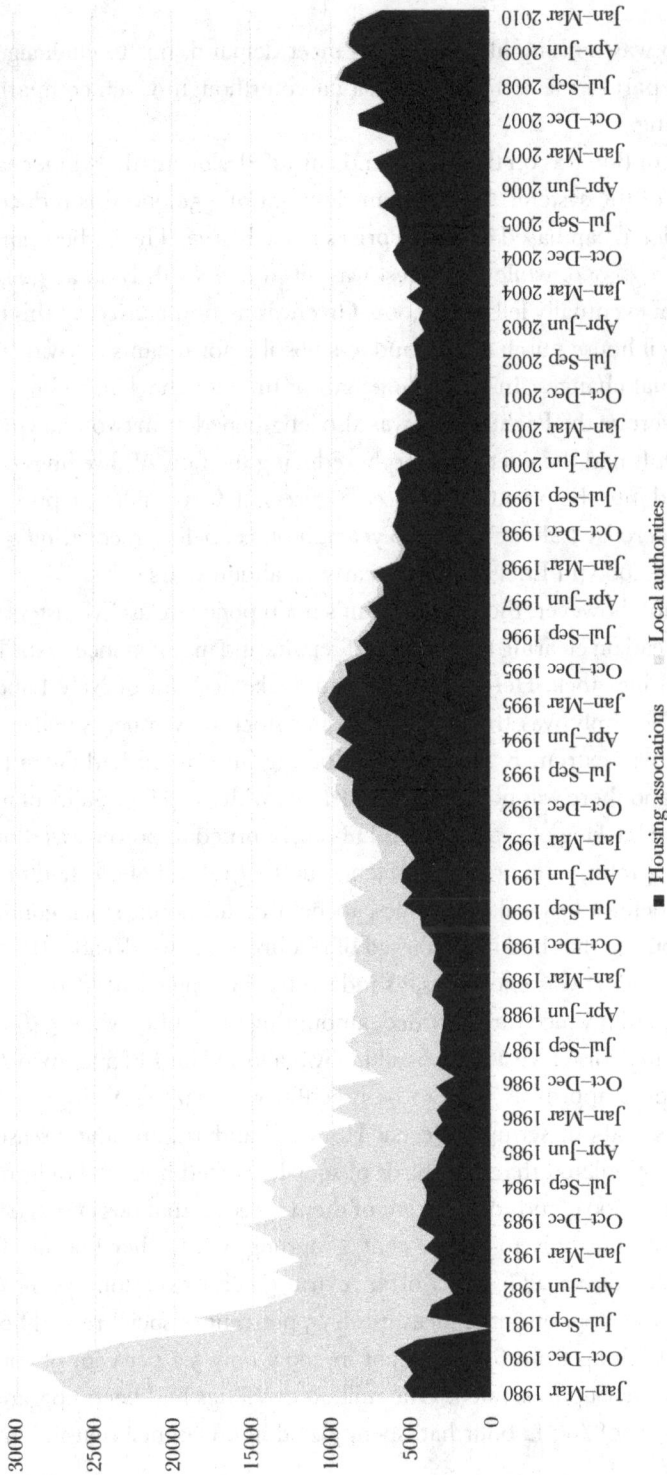

Figure 7.2 Social housing completions, England (quarterly), 1980–2010

Source: Indicators of House Building, UK, www.ons.gov.uk/peoplepopulationandcommunity/housing/datasets/ukhousebuildingpermanentdwellingsstartedandcompleted, accessed 21 April 2023.

nearly 10,000 was nothing like enough to meet demand, nor to challenge the idea that this part of the sector was a residual afterthought when compared to private building.

The Right to Buy was on the other hand curtailed, slowing the winner-takes-all character of the system. A maximum discount of £50,000 was reduced in 1999 to a regional cap based on house prices in each area. The highest limit (in London) was £38,000, while the lowest was set in the North East, at £22,000: that minimum eventually fell to £16,000. Given rising house prices at this time, making council house purchase less and less possible for tenants anyway, these were substantial changes. In 2004 the length of time tenants had to be in any dwelling to exercise the Right to Buy was also lengthened from two years to five. This policy shift had the effect of sharply reducing the flow of dwellings out of the public and into the private sector (see Figure 7.3). Council house purchases fell to nearly zero by Labour's last two years in office, before recovering a little to just under 20,000 (in England) in the early Coalition years.[11]

This was not, however, the Government's main policy thrust. Ministers concentrated instead on clearing the backlog of repairs and maintenance in the local authority housing stock. Here, again, we must take account of New Labour's inheritance. Not only was the council housing stock now much smaller than before, but it was extremely dilapidated. Housing investment had fallen to an all-time low, and there was no strategy for dealing with the poor quality of many dwellings. The backlog of repairs when Labour returned to power was thought to amount to £10bn; estimates later reached up to £19bn. Labour had to provide new guidelines to local authorities, to help them mount stock condition surveys on housing that had been starved of resources for two decades.[12]

The repairs effort was enormous, as indeed by this stage it needed to be. A Major Repairs Allowance was provided, amounting to £1.6bn, while £460 million was allocated for ALMOs, £600 million was allowed for PFI and up to £842 million of capital approvals were to be greenlit by 2003/04. Alongside those new resources, Labour set up a Decent Homes Standard, and the Treasury's Housing PSA stipulated that two-thirds of socially rented homes should reach that standard by 2004, and 100 per cent of them by 2010 (that target was downgraded in 2006, but only to 95 per cent). Funding was further boosted from 2002/03, where direct allocations of an extra £2.8bn over four years were announced.[13] By 2009, on some measures 85.5 per cent of social rented homes met the standard, up from 62.4 per cent in 2002: only 5.2 per cent of council dwellings were not up to scratch. One million dwellings had been upgraded.[14] In the end, by 2008/09 Labour had spent £25.8bn on council housing: much

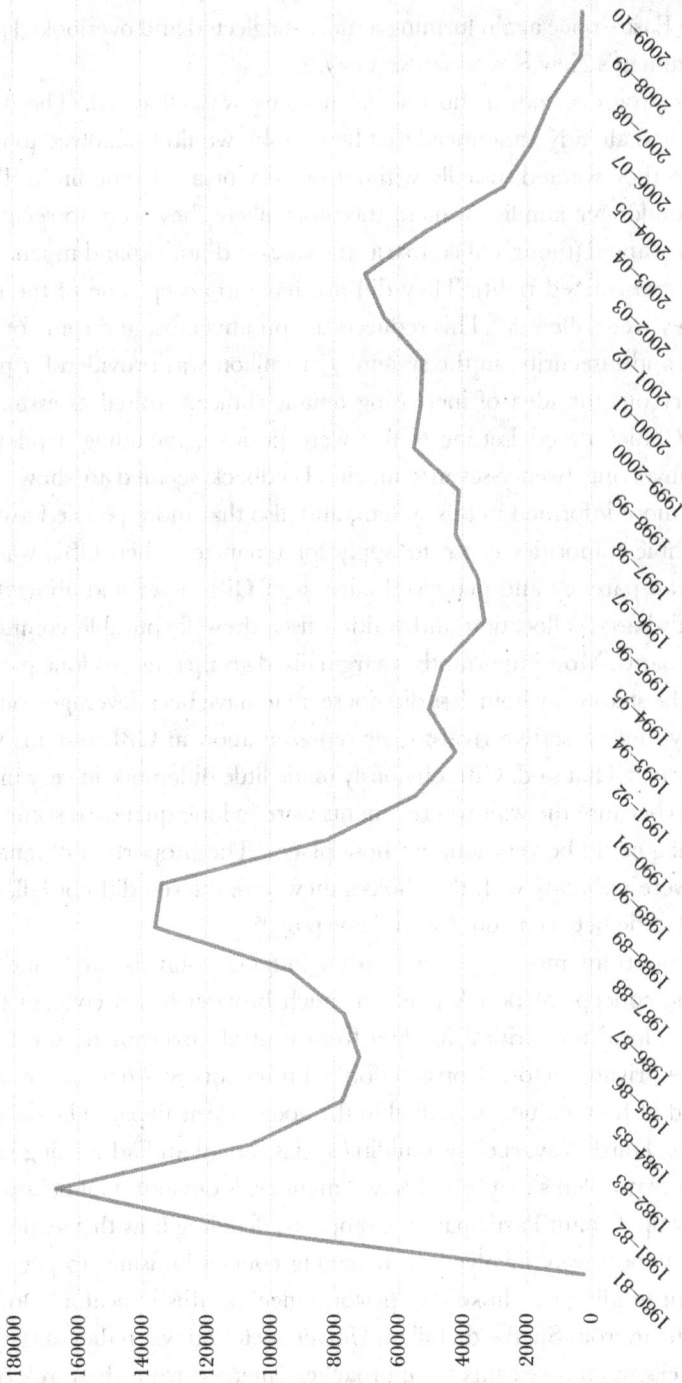

Figure 7.3 Local authority sales, dwellings, England (all types)

Source: Live Tables on Social Housing Sales, www.gov.uk/government/statistical-data-sets/live-tables-on-social-housing-sales#discontinued-tables, accessed 21 April 2023.

of this was disbursed in areas running from Blackpool and Preston in the West, to Hull in the East – once again forming a much-neglected and overlooked part of the Government's New Keynesian strategy.[15]

There was progress, too, in how social housing was allocated. The 2000 Green Paper had already announced that households would be allowed to wait for a dwelling they wanted, usually without penalty or a set time limit. That meant that the longer families waited, the more likely they were to secure a property they wanted (though of course as the stock did not expand much, this was a highly constrained right). They did not have to accept one of the first properties they were offered.[16] This reduced the punitiveness, and some of the sense of rush and insecurity, in the system. £11 million was provided for pilot schemes to try out the idea of increasing tenant choice.[17] Initial assessments of so-called Choice-Based Letting (CBL) were positive, including a pilot of the scheme involving twenty-seven councils. Feedback seemed to show that residents felt more informed in this system, and also that more people in work and more ethnic minorities chose to apply for tenancies when CBL was in effect. The transparency and perceived fairness of CBL, over and above traditional 'needs-based' allocation and waiting lists, drew favourable comment from many tenants. Most importantly, marginalised groups such as lone parent families and the statutorily homeless did not seem to have been leveraged out of the system by more assertive rivals: their representation in CBL systems was similar to others.[18] That said, CBL obviously made little difference in very high-demand areas because the wait where tenants were in long queues to secure or change housing could be very long in those places. The proportion of tenants saying they were unhappy with the choices they were offered did not fall, but rather stayed static between 2001/02 and 2004/05.[19]

Another important move was away from judging councils on 'value for money' to the concept of Best Value – a much broader-based concept that informed both local authorities' funding from central government and their work with the private sector. 'Consultation' with tenants was one of the concepts involved in Best Value, embodied in the 2000 Green Paper. The debt to ideas from the Third Way, such as building social capital and addressing local and community problems in a broad-based manner, is obvious. Councils were asked to draw up Tenant Participation Compacts, detailing how they expected to get residents positively involved in managing council housing: 10 per cent of government funding was linked to 'performance' on this indicator. On the ground, as a team from Sheffield Hallam University found when they surveyed English councils, a complex mix of approaches emerged from these reforms.

Broadly speaking, a blend of traditional 'managerial' attitudes, consumerist ideas about 'customers' and concepts based around rights-based citizenship co-existed and jostled for position with each other. That last approach, which focused on empowering residents to take their full part in decision-making, was however the least noticeable of the different outlooks – as in other sectors, an indicator of how far New Labour had to go to really entrench participation in decision-making. That said, even the 'consumerist' parts of New Labour's programme involved such innovations as citizens' juries, focus groups, work shadowing and 'mystery customer' exercises – not particularly radical, per-haps, but a step forward from the top-down delivery of both the post-war and Thatcher eras.[20]

From public to private

The decline in council housing prior to 1997 was not just a matter of Right to Buy sales, but a concerted drive by Westminster and Whitehall to reduce local authorities' role in housing supply as councils' troubles in managing very large estates from the later 1960s and during the 1970s came back to haunt them. The Conservatives' 1987 Housing White Paper proposed a drive to de-municipalise some local authority housing, and six new Housing Action Trusts were set up – though they proved expensive and complex, with 20,000 proper-ties absorbing £1.1bn over a seven-year period. Elsewhere, early stock transfers were moved over to landlords set up by councils themselves, and run by former staff. Only fifty-four councils transferred some or all of their stock to Housing Associations under the Conservatives.[21] New Labour, also sceptical about the efficiency and responsiveness of local government, redoubled these efforts as they did with PFI, and made much more of an impact. The years 1999 to 2003 were particularly busy in this respect (see Figure 7.4).

By December 2008, 170 local authorities had transferred their entire stock to independent social landlords, known as Registered Social Landlords (RSLs), under the 1996 Housing Act. Six more were about to do so, while 112 councils were continuing with direct management of the homes they owned: 66 other councils had set up ALMOs. Fifteen of this last group had also transferred some dwellings to an RSL. Eventually, half of England's local authorities contained no traditional 'council housing' at all. As the process rolled on, this much broader definition of 'social housing' became not the exception but the norm. The system set up by the Conservatives in the 1990s, under which only the most desirable social housing was transferred as a relatively attractive proposition for

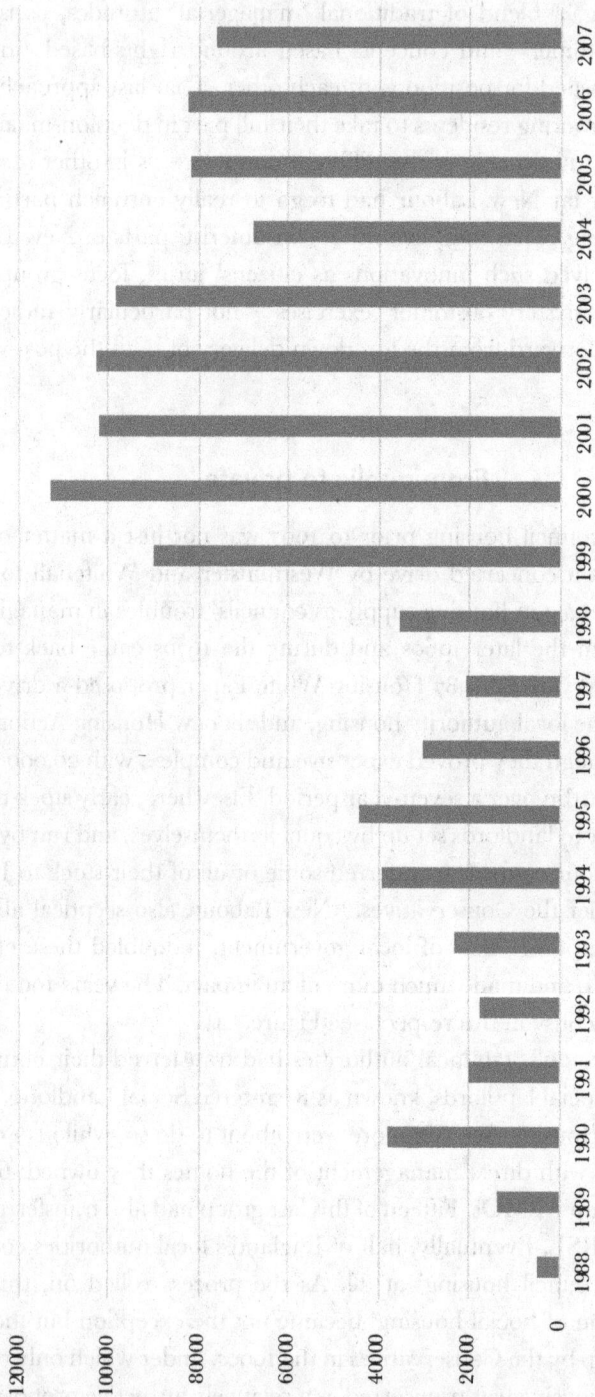

Figure 7.4 Local authority dwellings transferred to Housing Associations, England

Source: Housing Transfer, https://webarchive.nationalarchives.gov.uk/ukgwa/20080908073807/http://www.communities.gov.uk/housing/decenthomes/deliveringdecenthomes/housingtransfer/, accessed 21 April 2023.

new managers, was now reversed as more and more housing was moved away from direct council control. In some ways this was a convenient way for all layers of government to cut off their responsibility for hard-to-manage estates. The unit value of each transferred dwelling plunged from over £14,000 to as little as £2,000 (in 2008 prices). Between 2001 and 2007, 51 per cent of the stock moved over to RSLs failed the Decent Homes Standard, and some authorities handed on an even bigger share needing improvement: Wakefield, for instance (68 per cent), or the Wirral (73 per cent).[22]

Ministers did their best to sell these changes as releasing tenants from the deadening hand of huge local authority landlords. 'The Big Switch', as the process was known for instance in Tameside, Greater Manchester, was, according to Blair, about 'putting New Labour values into action'. For Blair, ministers had 'buried for good the old ideological split between public and private sector'. The 2000 Green Paper looked forward to social landlords being the biggest set of players in this part of the housing market by 2004: large-scale stock transfers from councils to RSLs included Coventry (2000), Sunderland (2001), Bradford, Glasgow and Walsall (all 2003). Only 16 out of 133 tenant ballots returned a 'no' vote between 1999 and 2004.[23] The proportion of social housing provided by 'traditional' local authorities continued to fall, up to the Government's 2004 target and beyond, though Housing Associations did not overtake them. In 1996, councils had run 18 per cent of the total stock, and Housing Associations 5 per cent; by 2006, those figures were 10 per cent and 8 per cent.[24]

These moves had some positive results. Research for the Joseph Rowntree Foundation showed that a large majority of the commitments made by new Housing Association owners were met. Modernisation and investment on elements such as double glazing, central heating, rewiring and security were almost always delivered as promised. Only a tiny number of Housing Association pledges were even delayed: by 2007, about half the transfer associations set up in England up to 2002 could say that more than 90 per cent of their dwellings met the Decent Homes Standard.[25] Some small improvements in tenant satisfaction were reported, over and above those returned by council residents and probably linked to many of these promises being met: when the Government investigated in 2000, they found 85 per cent satisfaction among the tenants of transfer RSLs, as against 79 per cent among local authority tenants as a whole.[26]

Even so, these plans still involved a binary yes or no decision that did involve a kind of choice, but narrowed it to just two paths. This type of 'choice' was also a one-way process, since it could not be rescinded, just as council house sales could not be reversed. Such choices to some extent encouraged an individualistic outlook, especially when linked with financial inducements (such as renovation funding), cutting across the idea of encouraging participation and involvement.[27] Nor is it at all apparent that more than increased funding was behind the marginal improvements in tenants' view of their landlords. Very large amounts of money were made available to smooth the process: up to £1.46bn in 2003/04, for instance. The incentives available, of course – to both councils and tenants – were part of the reason why most of these went through.[28]

In the near term, stock transfer perhaps meant rather less than the bold claims made for it. Existing tenants kept a Preserved Right to Buy, though new ones lost this right. Rents remained controlled, usually fixed at the Retail Price Index plus 1 per cent; a series of conditions were imposed on the new owners at the point of transfer.[29] At the same time, RSLs do seem to have developed a more 'consumer-orientated' approach, as well as increasing their interest in local management and adopting more 'activist', preventive management styles when it came to rent arrears, anti-social behaviour and the like. Encouraged by central government, these new landlords often deployed techniques such as area panels and forums, focus groups and surveys to find out what residents were actually thinking. Some activist tenants found the difference between unresponsive councils and the new more local systems 'like night and day'.[30] Perhaps for these reasons, their eviction rates were lower than the rest of the social rented sector – though transferred areas do not seem to have done any better than local authorities on re-letting times, the speed of maintenance, or indeed general satisfaction about 'opportunities for participation' when tenants were asked about this in surveys. It is possible in the latter case that the undoubted increase in efforts at outreach and involvement as usual reached only a very vocal minority of residents.[31] Many of these moves were significant and did improve housing management, but sometimes they failed to take hold as grassroots reality.

Towards an urban renaissance?

Housing policy must of course go hand-in-hand with the wider planning system, as the Starmer government is finding and which New Labour in power also sought to reorientate. Lord Richard Rogers was for instance commissioned to look at the future of cities. *Towards an Urban Renaissance*, the eventual report of his Urban Task Force, became an extremely influential document, signalling a return of people and confidence to city centres with the same level of impact as the turn towards preservation, improvement and pedestrianisation in the late 1960s. Rogers recommended higher-density building to crowd in many functions from work, living and leisure, as well as making urban areas more efficient and environmentally friendly through shared energy sources and well-designed buildings. Each urban area should be covered by a masterplan, not zoned for particular uses but with their functions treated in three dimensions. Uses would be combined, rather than divided up area by area. RSLs could take the lead in terms of new housing; tax changes, such as zero-rating for VAT for conversions on the same basis as new building, would help encourage a shift in urban economies back towards residential use.[32] Brown did reduce VAT on housing conversions to 5 per cent, and allowed a zero rate on dwellings empty for ten years or more.[33]

In other parts of the country, the problem was not so much what to do with fashionably in-demand areas, but rather how to tackle severe economic and social decline. 'Low demand and abandonment', the Government reckoned, affected about one million properties spread across 120 local authorities in England's North and Midlands (in 2000 many of England's 763,900 empty homes, or 3.6 per cent of the stock, were in these areas).[34] One survey, for instance, estimated that 12 per cent of council dwellings were affected, as against 8 per cent of RSLs and 2.6 per cent of private landlords. The residualisation of council housing and its relegation into the background of housing policy were in this way made even more acute, while there were also plenty of rent-seeking private landlords crowding into those cheap areas and helping to make them even more down at heel and unattractive.[35]

The SEU set up a Policy Action Team to look into this problem in 1998. Its report near the end of 1999 recommended an integrated approach in line with the work of RDAs and the Regional Government Offices. All the government bodies involved were also asked to start working on a mixed and interagency basis across the range of social policies. One further planning reform brought in after this report was also to include empty and dilapidated properties in estimates of available land for development, so these were considered for building before greenfield sites. This, the Government hoped, would encourage rebuilding where possible.[36] Local authorities were also asked to draw up long-term plans, and RSLs were included in Housing Corporation programmes for 'selective acquisition and clearance', so as to manage a thinning out or run down of the most troubled and disliked locales. So a strategy for dealing with very low-demand housing cold spots was at least now in place. The official report on this programme did however warn presciently that 'demolition must be used with care. We found instances where it triggered further decline and broke up communities.'[37]

The National Strategy for Neighbourhood Renewal, launched across the country to some fanfare in 2001, made much of these themes. Nine 'Pathfinder schemes' to tackle decaying areas covered about half the houses thought to be in these low-demand areas, mostly in cities such as Newcastle, Merseyside, Oldham, Manchester and Birmingham. A strategy of 'clearance, refurbishment and new build work' was recommended to revive them, and £500 million was provided for this purpose in the first instance. The most dilapidated dwellings would be torn down, and new, more modern houses built. A strategic action plan for each pathfinder project would draw together government agencies, business and the third sector to work jointly on these problems.[38] This was not without its unintended consequences, and the Government's words of caution about large-scale change on the lines experienced in the 1950s and 1960s were in this respect proved right as in places blight and abandonment spread, despite the policy learning gained from the 'Pathfinder schemes'. Clearance could represent only a relatively cheap way and easy policy shortcut, rather than addressing more deep-seated problems.[39]

Local networking between government agencies, builders, the third sector and councils was less successful than it might have hoped: the Prime Minister was told in 2001 that a 'jumble of local partnerships' had sprung up and that 'we have set up lots of initiatives each of which is run through its own departmental drainpipe'. Local people were therefore forced to sit on a number of bureaucratic committees when they 'need to be freed to take decisions in a more strategic way'. Hence this agenda's relaunch as Local Strategic Partnerships in 2003.[40] By this stage, indeed, Number 10 was frustrated with having spent £5bn with much less to show for it than they had hoped. As Blair was informed in September of that same year:

> Over this period we have turned some estates around ... But others have got markedly worse. Furthermore, some estates in areas like Bexley and Merton where the local authority as a whole is not deprived, have received relatively little help. The estates that have received the most funding are not necessarily those that have thrived ... In short: the gap between deprived and non-deprived areas has probably widened over the past 6 years in respect of crime and health. Educational attainment seems set still to miss the relatively unambitious ... target. Only in housing, employment and child road fatalities have things demonstrably improved. The first is due in part to a lot of cash, and the second owes much to economic recovery.[41]

Most areas targeted for intervention did improve, despite Number 10's continual desire to go further and faster, though some of them had been doing so during the 1990s too. Going 'with the grain', as it were, once again proved more important than the organisation or intensity of intervention. One report for the Joseph Rowntree Foundation drew on staff and residents' views expressed in four surveys of twenty very 'unpopular estates' conducted in 1982, 1988, 1994 and 2005. They found no perceived progress in only four: six had improved throughout the period between 1982 and 2005, while another ten had done better on for instance being 'difficult to let' in the 1990s and early 2000s. Although this is not quite the same category of 'low demand' as the blighted Pathfinder areas, experiences there likely improved too.[42] The NAO in 2009 reckoned that the problem of 'low demand' had more than halved since its peak.[43]

Although the data in this area is uncertain, there is evidence that the number of vacancies in a wider group of unpopular areas fell, and fell most sharply where the problem was at its worst in 2001. More than half of those parts of the country with more than 15 per cent dwellings vacant in 2001 had dipped below that level by 2007/08.[44] The gap in house prices and vacancies between blighted and very low-demand areas did start to close, and the Pathfinder areas did better on average than other local authorities: on the other hand, their performance was very uneven. The Birmingham and Oldham projects had done well in bringing vacancies down; Newcastle and Merseyside had made little progress.[45] Some of this of course will have been due to residents moving into cheaper areas at a time of steeply rising housing costs; but given their position in poorer parts of the country, policy impact seems just as likely.

Critically, given the Government's stress on getting local communities on board, it was also clear from NAO evidence that what was supposed to be 'community engagement' was still being organised on a top-down basis. While each Pathfinder area had a community engagement strategy in place, these likely did not really involve local people early enough or long enough in which the actual redevelopment was taking place. In some areas, such as Oldham, strong community groups emerged to oppose Compulsory Purchase Orders and demolition.[46] Some of the lessons of the 1960s and 1970s, when whole communities had been uprooted by comprehensive redevelopment, had still not been learned. That might seem strange when one considers New Labour's retreat from uniform state provision and (to a lesser extent) its debt to the New Left that also critiqued this type of state power. But that lack of institutional memory was perhaps inevitable given the sheer amount of time that had passed since there had last been a large-scale clearance programme in the 1950s and 1960s.

A red-hot housing market

New Labour gave further encouragement to owner occupation, which was probably not entirely wise. Many elements of detailed policymaking revealed the Government's preference for private purchase: longer-term support for those with mortgages who were moving off benefits into work, for instance, or via the Starter Homes Initiative which subsidised the mortgages of 10,000 key workers from 2001. This is not to say that all policy went in that direction: quite the contrary. Subsidies to owner occupiers were cut, especially at the top end of the income distribution. In Brown's July 1997 Budget, for instance, Mortgage Income Relief at Source (MIRAS – which provided tax relief on some mortgage payments) was reduced to 10 per cent, while Stamp Duty for more expensive homes was increased. As interest rates were fairly low at this time, and MIRAS was paid out on interest charges, this was seen as a good moment to run this tax break down towards zero, when its impact would be fairly limited.[47] All three of Brown's next Budgets, in 1998, 1999 and 2000, raised Stamp Duty: by then the rates were 3 per cent for dwellings sold for between £250,000 and £500,000, and 4 per cent for those over £500,000. MIRAS was meanwhile finally abolished in the 1999 Budget.[48] House prices would have risen even further and faster had not the Treasury applied the brakes in this manner.

House prices nevertheless still surged, more quickly and to even greater heights of unaffordability than they had touched even in the mid- to late 1980s (see Figure 7.5). This was a long-term trend, observable since perhaps the late 1960s, as UK housebuilding simply did not respond to price signals to the same extent as it did in other countries. The three housing booms of the early 1970s, the mid-1980s and the turn of the century pushed up the ratio of house prices to first-time buyers' income from around 2.5 to nearly 3.5.[49] During these years, and before the Great Financial Crisis and its attendant housing crash, more and more strain was put on mortgagees' finances. To take one measure of these massive increases in housing costs as an example, the proportion of an average household's total income needed to service a typical mortgage in England rose from 11.9 per cent in 1997 to 13.7 per cent in 2001, and up to a peak of 22.6 per cent in 2007, before falling back in the recession (the figures for the UK as a whole were 11.6 per cent, 13 per cent and 22 per cent).[50] A Joseph Rowntree Foundation report in 2003 found thirty-three local authority areas where even

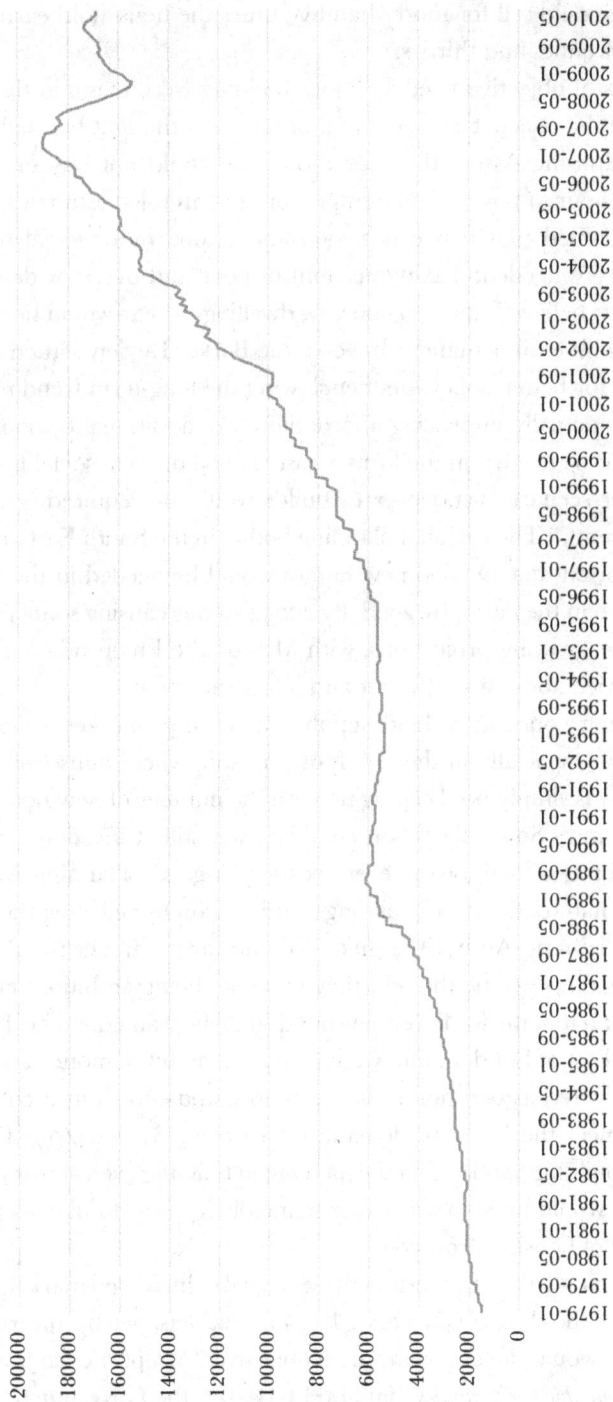

Figure 7.5 Average property price (all property types), UK, 1979–2010

Source: House Price Statistics, https://landregistry.data.gov.uk/app/ukhpi/browse?from=1979-01-01&location=http%3A%2F%2Flandregistry.data.gov.uk%2Fid%2Fregion%2Funited-kingdom&to=2015-01-01&lang=en, accessed 21 April 2023.

a small dwelling could sell for more than five times the household earnings of people in their twenties and thirties.[51]

Few estimates of objective need for more building were made in the 1980s and 1990s, since the concept of 'need' at that time was thought best left to the market, or to Housing Associations for those who could not buy or rent at market rates. Labour in power did attempt more research-led estimates, which for instance reckoned that between 22,000 and 72,000 more social housing units per year were needed. Taking account of poor and overcrowded housing, many experts believed that 250,000 new dwellings a year would be needed just to keep up with total demand.[52] In 2004, the Barker Review settled on two possible options for better policy – either slowing the long-term trend towards higher prices, or actually improving affordability. An additional 87,000 dwellings a year would be needed in the former case (17,000 of them social housing), and in the latter scenario 141,000 extra builds would be required (21,000 of them for social rent).[53] The regional planning bodies in the South East and East of England reported that 720,000 new homes would be needed in the former area, and 478,000 in the latter, by 2026. By 2005 this was causing some political resistance to ever-growing projections, with MPs on the Environmental Audit Committee worried about waste, water and infrastructure.[54]

Given planning constraints, land supply was clearly one key element of these price rises – especially in the South of England, where housebuilding in the early 2000s was simply not keeping up with the number of new households formed. In England's South East, housebuilding was still at this point running 40,000–50,000 units a year below even existing targets.[55] Planning Minister Nick Raynsford had tried to raise building in this region by rejecting the South East Regional Planning Authority's guidance and targets in 2001 and asking them to think again, since he thought they were not being ambitious enough. Raynsford still had to settle for fewer new builds than he wanted.[56] The Thames Gateway to the East of London, into which a huge amount of money and hope was poured, delivered 24,000 homes between 2001 and 2005, but it could not even begin to meet the levels of demand on its own. By 2004/05, Thames Gateway housebuilding was lagging the increase in building even across the rest of the region. It would have to accelerate markedly if it was to play its part in any step-change of housing provision.[57]

Barker recommended that governments set a goal of increased market affordability as part of the Treasury's PSAs. Regional targets, set by the regional planning bodies, would dovetail with these objectives.[58] In part encouraged by the ideas in *Sustainable Communities*, but also by Barker, the Government did go some way towards these ideas, by instituting Regional Spatial Strategies for each region, encouraging local authorities to build more, and also setting up a £350 million Planning Delivery Grant to support planners in their efforts.[59] This would be paid out increasingly on the basis of performance (chiefly judged by speed in taking decisions), and between 2003/04 and 2007 disbursed around £68 million a year. All that said, performance in this regard seems to have remained extremely variegated.[60]

Many of the Government's targets were met. Before the housing crash that came with the Great Recession, the Government felt it was 'on track' to deliver on some higher building targets, and annual net additions to the stock did rise from under 150,000 at the turn of the century to over 200,000 on the eve of the crash. The Housing Corporation actually exceeded its target of building 27,000 social or affordable housing units by 2004/05 (it actually built nearly 29,000). There was some optimism about meeting the target of 1.1 million new dwellings in the South East by 2016, 160,000 of which would be in the Thames Gateway, though of course this was deeply vulnerable to market fluctuations. However, blurred lines of communication between central government, the regions and local authorities were already causing the housing acceleration to slow down by 2005. In particular, local authorities found it hard to deal with private developers from whom they wanted 'community benefits' in order to green light projects: the feelings of frustration were often mutual.[61]

As some targets were reached, however, both the planning system and demographics were making it harder and harder for the Government to keep up. The house price crisis that was to become most acute in the later 2010s and the 2020s definitely had its roots in these years, a fact which gradually became clear at the time. Mulgan advised Blair in 2004: 'current plans for about 1.1 million homes over the next 12 years won't be enough (and are already falling behind ... [while] investment in new social housing remains very low'.[62] Given high demand at the top end of the market, too many large three- and especially four-bedroom houses were also being built, particularly in the South and East. The main need in terms of household formation was for smaller properties, but developers would make less profit from those and so their number fell behind actual needs. The population of the UK was also growing, from around 58 million in 1997 to 61 million by 2007. Moving forward ten more years, those trends accelerated, which was always a risk: the UK population had reached 66 million and then over 67.5 million by 2022.[63] Given this imbalance between demand and supply, measures designed to help homebuyers, especially first-time buyers, could only pump up the market even further, not damp it down.

Homebuy, launched in 1999 to provide interest-free loans towards the purchase of social housing by their tenants, can be seen in this light: so can the Starter Homes Initiative.[64]

Affordability for first-time buyers continuously deteriorated, especially in the South East of England and London, and the overall earnings to prices ratio jumped under Blair – surging in England from 3.54:1 in 1997 to 7.15:1 in 2007. That ratio then deteriorated more slowly, creeping up to just over 8:1 in the early 2020s.[65] So in this case the real crisis, one of affordability, developed during the Blair years and not afterwards. In the end, Barker's ambitious target of increasing housebuilding to 240,000 units a year was never met: the real annual average until the 2020s was more like 190,000. New Labour did take some account of Barker's views. Ten of her thirty-six recommendations were implemented, while ten were partially applied. Labour for instance brought in some regional targets and made sure local authority financial settlements at least partly reflected future housing growth. Many of those policies were disassembled once Labour left office: five out of the twenty agreed with in total or in part were reversed.[66]

New Labour can hardly be taken to task for later mistakes, nor the later surge in the population beyond what they might have foreseen. But overall it was during these years that the present lack of houses for sale began to become apparent, and there was simply not enough drive behind the Government's approach to push housebuilding up as far as it needed to go. Developers were not forced as they might have been to develop infrastructure, or pay for it; there were to be no New Towns on the 1940s model; there was no binding social housing target. In the end, the deficit between Barker's targets and reality has left England some 900,000 homes short of the number needed. Some estimates looking right back to the 1940s are even higher, estimating that the UK as a whole is lacking over four million dwellings when compared with the building rates of other Western European countries.[67]

For a while easier financing, which had become cheaper and simpler to access since the 1980s, lubricated the whole system and allowed people to keep buying. But housing inequality kept growing in terms of both buyers' wealth and age, and as regards ownership – quite contrary to the state's intentions. If we look at the period between 2006 and 2016, just after this study ends, the third quartile of the population gained 22 per cent in housing wealth, but the lowest only 7 per cent. Home ownership, which peaked at just under 70 per cent at the end of the 1990s, now began to fall.[68] Governments simply did not want to intervene, in part because house price rises were popular with homeowners.[69]

Housing: chasing demand, falling short

During Brown's period as Prime Minister, one official (perhaps apocryphally) is supposed to have replied to calls for more housebuilding: 'if we did that it would hit house prices and we should lose the election'. Some of Brown's colleagues privately appealed to the financial journalist William Keegan to write about the issue, to increase pressure on the Government to act.[70]

House price rises also underpinned consumption, and those assets might also provide for citizens' future income – particularly in old age. Academics have come to term this phenomenon 'asset-based welfare', the process by which citizens are remade 'into people who will be willing and able to care for themselves in an open and financialized economy', in particular spending their housing wealth on care in their later years. The New Labour government is often thought to have 'encouraged and sought to facilitate the growth of the financialised individual'.[71] A culture of more and more socially acceptable borrowing and home improvement did undoubtedly emerge at this time, though it is at least as arguable that voters' preferences simply reflected economic reality. Voters told the British Social Attitudes survey that the fact that buying was a 'good investment' was the most important cause of its desirability, and interest rates were at this time fairly low and stable compared to previous peaks and troughs. While house prices fell in the 1990s, fewer respondents recommended buying 'as soon as possible': this number reached a low of 54 per cent in 1996. As prices rose once more, that figure rose again to 71 per cent.[72]

The house price boom eventually helped to destabilise the economy as a whole. At a time when wage growth fell far behind house price rises, many households found the ability to tap into the value of their home invaluable to keep up their standard of living. By 2006 the capital gains accruing from house price rises were on average equivalent to two-thirds of pre-tax earnings, fuelling an unsustainable level of consumption and debt as unseen dangers were piling up inside the financial system – especially the US mortgage market. This was another way in which money was pumped into the economy, alongside public spending increases.[73] Mortgage credit flooded into consumers' bank accounts even more quickly than in the 1980s. The mortgage market (including for buy-to-lets) expanded to such a point that up to, or even more than, 100 per cent of a house's value could be released. Mortgage debt as a whole rose to 129 per cent of total disposable income.[74] Between 2002 and 2007, home equity withdrawal amounted to 4 per cent of GDP: in 2003 this source of income peaked at £63bn, or 9 per cent of consumer spending. The value of the stock was by this stage extremely high: £3,152bn, of which £2,185bn was unmortgaged equity.[75]

All this eventually led property wealth to dominate the banking system, and of course in the end to threaten to bring it down during the Great Financial Crisis – a slide that could only be prevented at vast expense to the taxpayer. There is little doubt that, given their time again, ministers might act to restrain the housing market, but given the attractions of the Treasury's bulging coffers, sequential election victories and the extent to which families' welfare and life savings were invested in that system, that has always been easier said than done. The planning system has remained impervious to meaningful reform up to the present day, although, as we have seen, New Labour in office did take a more strategic view of growth points and the demographic and population pressures that became even more acute in the years to come. It seemed to make sense, for a while, to let the market do its job, at the eventual cost of the type of house price crash that had also hit the British economy in the 1970s and 1980s.

The attack on homelessness and rough sleeping

There was however one area where New Labour did intervene strongly, putting in place vigorous new policies: the widespread problem of homelessness, and the narrower but no less acute problem of rough sleeping that had become so visible on Britian's streets during the 1980s and 1990s. In 1997 homeless house-holds were given priority on council housing lists – a benefit the Conservatives had removed in the 1996 Housing Act. In 2002 the Homelessness Act gave local authorities a statutory duty to draw up comprehensive homelessness reduction strategies. At the same time, the new Act removed time limits on using council housing as temporary accommodation, and also made councils responsible for homeless families for as long as they were not in permanent housing.[76] For a while that may have made the numbers in what became defined as 'tempo-rary housing' worse, especially in the South East of England, as the council stock absorbed families coming off the street and temporary housing was used as more of a high-volume but short-term option (see Figure 7.6). Eventually, though, the situation turned a corner during 2004 and 2005. By 2004, the Government was able to announce that no more families with children would be housed in bed and breakfast accommodation, except in emergencies.[77]

The previous government's Rough Sleepers Initiative had already spent £200 million, or an average of £33 million a year, between 1990 and 1996. Immediately upon coming to power, the Government announced another £17.2 million of funding for the RSI, with an extra £2 million for a Homeless Mentally Ill Initiative; a further £1.5 million was announced in February 1998. The first

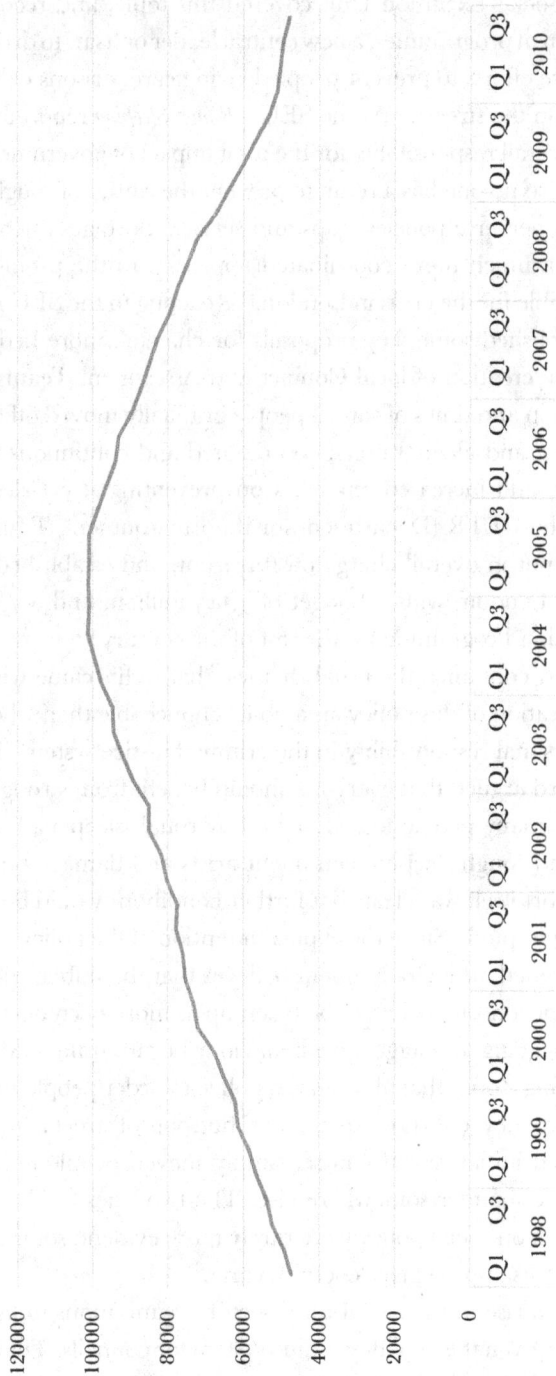

Figure 7.6 Households in temporary accommodation, England (1998–2000)

Source: Housing: Live Tables on Homelessness, https://webarchive.nationalarchives.gov.uk/ukgwa/20120910151917/http://www.communities.gov.uk/housing/housingresearch/housingstatistics/housingstatisticsby/homelessnessstatistics/livetables/, accessed 21 April 2023.

report of Blair's Social Exclusion Unit covered this topic, and recommended better coordination of programmes, a new central leader or 'tsar' to drive through progress, and more efforts to prevent people leaving care, prisons or the armed forces ending up on the streets.[78] As the SEU's *Rough Sleeping* report argued, 'no department has overall responsibility for the total impact of government policies on rough sleepers; so no one has a remit to prevent the causes of rough sleeping, or make sure that perverse policies, gaps and service shortages are addressed'. There should be a much more coordinated approach to the problem, and a new body responsible for the crisis in London.[79] Reacting to the SEU report, the Government established some 'key proposals for change': more bedspaces for rough sleepers; the creation of local Contact and Assessment Teams; different levels of intervention and times of stay as people gradually moved off the streets; more help for drug and alcohol users; coordinated and continuous routes out of rough sleeping; and increased emphasis on preventing street sleeping, not just 'solving' it. The DETR (Department for the Environment, Transport and the Regions) was put in overall charge on this front, and established a Rough Sleepers Unit for London, with a budget of £145 million, and a £34 million Homelessness Action Programme for the rest of the country.[80]

The SEU report contained the usual rhetoric that rights came with responsibilities, a moralisation of this policy area no less noticeable than when it came to insisting on personal responsibility in the criminal justice system. The Prime Minister's foreword argued that everyone should benefit from stronger policies on homelessness: 'many people feel intimated by rough sleepers, beggars and street drinkers, and rough sleeping can blight areas and damage business and tourism'. The report itself was clear that further conditions would be placed on help if it was not accepted. 'Since the explicit intention of the policy is to deliver clear streets', it argued, 'the Government believes that the public will feel they have a right to expect hostel places to be taken up as more become available.'[81] Crackdowns on begging and aggressive behaviour began, using ASBOs, fines, Controlled Drinking Zones that allowed the police to order people to stop consuming alcohol, and new efforts to 'design out' hotspots of street activity. Many of these area-based initiatives, of course, simply moved people on to behave in exactly the same manner somewhere else. The two sides of New Labour's Janus-faced outlook on social policy were rarely more evident: some academics have characterised its approach as 'coercive care'.[82]

There was also a rise in the use of third sector organisations to fight homelessness, especially given the new Best Value system for councils. That tendency increased as New Labour's time in office went on. Surveys of these groups however uncovered a large range of attitudes to that work: housing associations and large professional charities were sometimes uncomfortable with the tasks they were asked to perform, while smaller voluntary groups were much more wary of being drawn into the state's orbit, as well as less able to help with actual shelter. As a result, many of the benefits of third sector provision, theoretically a warmer, smaller-scale kindness and sense of personal service, could be lost. Smaller groups, perhaps small faith-based local charities, could provide companionship and emergency emotional or financial help, but were less likely to be integrated into large-scale work with rough sleepers. On the other hand, more professional and standardised practices filtered out through the system, while homelessness workers were far better financed and joined up with each other, particularly under a Supporting People programme announced late in 1998 and finally launched in 2003. This created a single budget for homelessness work conducted by voluntary associations.[83]

Following the 2002 Homelessness Act, early success in reducing rough sleeping allowed the Government to turn towards the problem of homelessness overall. The 2004 Spending Review targeted a reduction in the use of temporary accommodation for the homeless of 50 per cent by 2010: the use of short-term housing just to place roofs over people's heads then tailed off (Figure 7.6).[84] Best Value indicators were deployed to make councils set up 'housing options' schemes, mobilising interviews to see if any interventions could work before families were labelled statutorily homeless. The results were remarkable. In just two and a half years, officially recorded homeless numbers fell by over 40 per cent. In the third quarter of 2003 just under 80,000 claims were processed by local authorities; that number had fallen to about 50,000 by the first quarter of 2006.[85] Having peaked around 2002–03, the number of people who were homeless on local authorities' definitions was cut by two-thirds (see Figure 7.7).

These numbers are of course open to dispute, and the complex overlap between 'rough sleeping' and homelessness always makes the former hard to quantify. Emergency accommodation remained hard to get into, and of variable quality, making for constant movement between the two groups. Pressure on the system remained high, despite the Government's launch of a Homelessness Action Programme in 1999 (with £134 million allocated to 113 towns and cities across Britain) and then its turn towards reducing homelessness overall during 2003. Joint working across agencies, despite being heavily encouraged, happened much more in some areas than others, and only in those parts of the country was the situation entirely clear.[86]

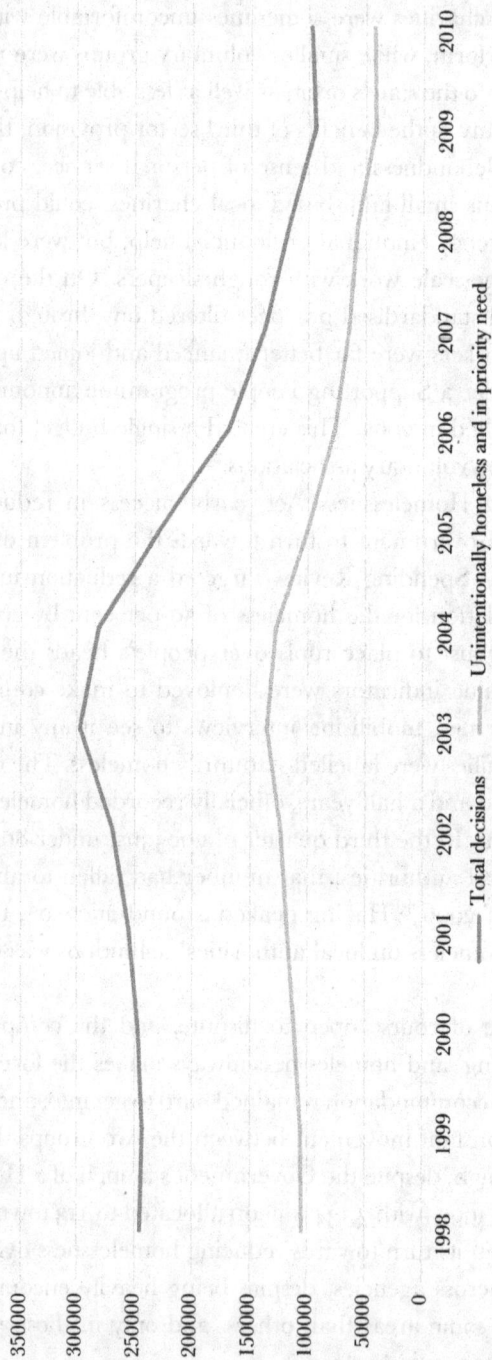

Figure 7.7 Homelessness in England (local authority definitions), 1998–2010

Source: Housing: Live Tables on Homelessness, https://webarchive.nationalarchives.gov.uk/ukgwa/20120919151917/http://www.communities.gov.uk/housing/housingresearch/housingstatistics/housingstatisticsby/homelessnessstatistics/livetables/, accessed 21 April 2023.

Most local authorities did not monitor rough sleeping when Labour returned to power in 1997. For these reasons official numbers were likely to be under-estimates, though the trend upwards over the 1980s and 1990s was clear. The number of homeless people was of course much greater than those sleeping on the streets. Shelter estimated this number at 0.75 million in the winter of 1997/98, and we could if so minded add to that number all those people living in dwellings judged unfit for human habitation (1.47 million) or statu-torily overcrowded (478,000 in 1996).[87] The official counts of those 'homeless' depended on a statutory definition of those unintentionally without a home, in priority need (for instance with children), and perhaps with a local connection. Only in 2005/06 did the responsible Department, the Office of the Deputy Prime Minister, bring in an indicator of 'households who considered themselves homeless' as part of its Best Value programme. This too was riddled with prac-tical difficulties, but at least pushed the Government's knowledge and under-standing a little further forward.[88]

By 2010 one official count of people sleeping on the streets in England had fallen to only 440 (see Figure 7.8). That was also very likely a severe underesti-mate, and when the numbers were adjusted in the early days of the Coalition – to include every single local authority in the country, and everyone not just bedded down but looking like they could be – they came to 1,768.[89] However, that very low figure of 440 did at least reflect a sharp fall on the numbers counted in the same way in the late 1990s, just as the situation in the tempo-rary accommodation world and in terms of homelessness more generally was sharply improving by the second half of the 2000s. That progress has not been sustained. During the autumn of 2023, there were nearly 4,000 people sleeping rough on England's streets.[90] There were 109,000 families in temporary accom-modation as legally defined, which was higher even than its peak under New Labour during 2004 and 2005.[91] The charity Shelter estimated that there were 309,000 homeless people in total. [92] All those indices seem to have got worse and worse after 2010: the numbers of people sleeping on the streets or in temporary accommodation more than doubled between that year and 2023.[93] As home-lessness and rough sleeping mounted up again in the 2020s, the New Labour era – for all its problems – came to seem like something of a relative success.

Was housing still the 'wobbly pillar'?

The one single and very clear failing in this policy area was the runaway house price boom, which ran faster and faster through to the 2007–08 financial crisis

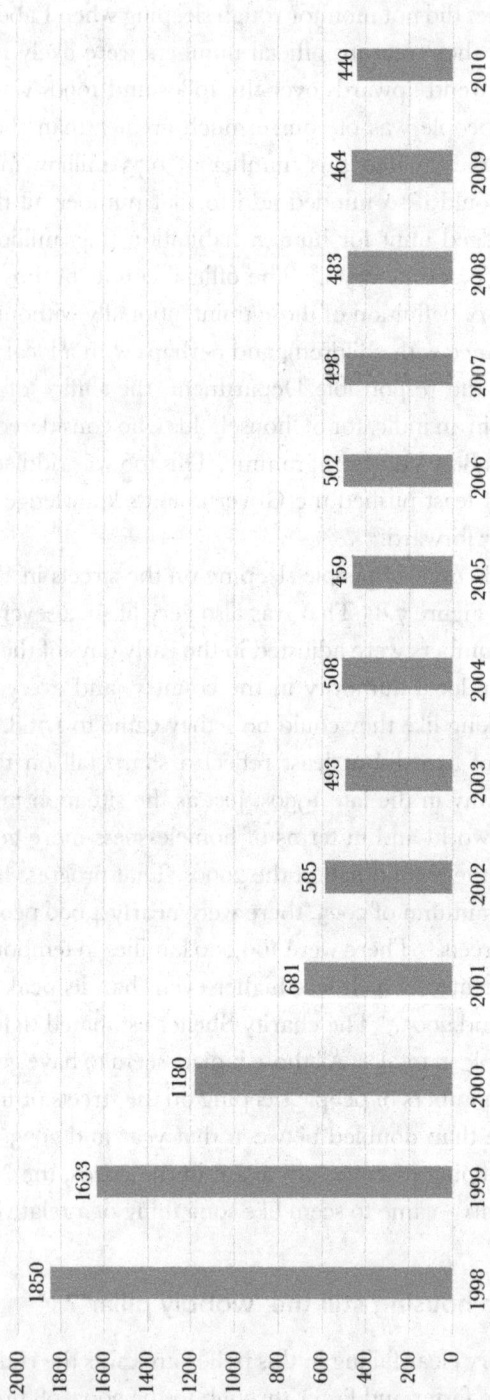

Figure 7.8 People sleeping rough in England, 1998–2010

Source: Housing: Rough Sleeping in England, https://webarchive.nationalarchives.gov.uk/ukgwa/20120919163559/http://www.communities.gov.uk/housing/housingresearch/housingstatistics/housingstatisticsby/homelessnessstatistics/roughsleepingcounts, accessed 21 April 2023.

even though the Government tried to restrain it by intensifying strategic house-building. Brown's insistence that the UK's housing market had not converged with that of the Eurozone, and that the UK could not join the Euro, probably avoided even further disaster. If interest rates had been lower, as they would have been had the UK joined the Euro, the boom – and then the correction – would have been all the greater. That was not much comfort to those voters who had been told that 'boom and bust' was over, or mortgage holders who overextended themselves, but it was something of a non-decision or negative policy success. Unfortunately, that happy accident was more than eclipsed by the poor design of monetary policy and regulation divided between the Bank of England and the FSA.

Basic presumptions that had long held back British housing policy were never challenged. The default building-block of most housing policy remained owner-occupation: as Brown put it in April 2005, a 'Britain of ambition and aspiration is a Britain where more and more people must and will have the chance to own their own homes'.[94] Councils were to continue to play less and less of a role as landlords, while 'choice' and diversity were to be entrenched in each part of the system. All this to some extent disarmed further govern-ment intervention, and prevented a full-on attack on overall housing need. Local authorities never took the strategic lead on the housing sector that Labour imagined in the 2000 Green Paper; instead, power passed to a whole range of local bodies, along with the regional planning institutions favoured by the Treasury. Stock transfers from public to private or third sectors prob-ably did provide benefits for tenants. But on the other hand the shift from what the writer Lynsey Hanley labels 'providing' to 'enabling' better housing further stigmatised and disadvantaged council housing, yet again weaken-ing one of the columns that could have held up a general housing drive.[95] Strategies aimed at preventing 'social exclusion' came with the usual ques-tion of exactly what homeless people, or citizens in housing stress, should be 'included' within – and a heavy dose of moralising 'conditionality' if they were to be helped off the streets or into better dwellings. Social cohesion can indeed mean social control.[96]

There were multiple successes in terms of building up more coherent and holistic housing policies. Right to Buy sales continued, but at a lower level as New Labour tightened up the rules. City centres were revived: by the end of 2005 the centre of Manchester had 25,000 residents, in an area where only ninety people had lived in the early 1990s. The Sustainable Communities programme had delivered much-needed funding to cities, while attracting follow-on money from the private sector. By this point 70 per cent of new development was on brownfield sites: that figure had been 56 per cent in 1997.[97]

New Labour's efforts were more double-edged than critics allow. The market was not seen as the be-all and end-all in housing policy, and it was not treated as such. The complex and multiple needs of rough sleepers were highlighted and addressed in new and more profound ways. The skills of people working with the homeless were far more advanced than they would have been. Voluntary working was far better connected up to state services, while accountability and standards rose.[98] What the Government actually did or recommended might be heavily loaded with certitudes about both the 'right' way to conduct policy and indeed live, but they also built up better access to counselling, GPs, councils' resettlement services and follow-on day centres. Punitive enforcement measures such as ASBOs were undoubtedly harsh on street dwellers, and could be counterproductive: but surveys of rough sleepers and support providers alike demonstrated that these interventions could work if sensitively approached, only slowly building up to sanctions while providing a range of help.[99]

The British housing system was full of long-standing weaknesses, and they were accentuated not created by this new house price boom and the sheer levels of rising demand. Chief among these problems was the lack of an overarching strategy. A list of the endless switchback of Britain's housing policies might suffice to make the point. Attlee's Labour did not have a particularly well-developed housing strategy when it took power in its own right in 1945.[100] Labour struggled to get its council house drive off the ground in the later 1940s, amid economic turbulence and austerity. Once the Conservatives had broken the back of total demand in the early 1950s, they scaled back the council housing programme and used it for slum clearance.[101] Council house building peaked in the late 1960s and then declined precipitously: governments had spent their time since the 1960s and 1970s trying to encourage Housing Associations. All of this created an overreliance on owner occupation. To some extent, New Labour's preference for the private sector was simply reflecting the political reality of a public used to that system, and not some imaginary alternative one. The British Social Attitudes survey showed in 2004 that residents in every type of housing tenure returned at least a plurality who wanted to be owner-occupiers, though among council tenants not by a large amount (46 per cent to 39 per cent who wanted to stay as they were).[102]

So the paradox or strangeness of a Third Way government struggling to manage a mixed economy of housing, while finding it easier to govern much more nationalised sectors such as health and education, is perhaps easier to understand than it might at first seem. Unlike mostly nationalised services, housing remained a key part of the market economy as a popular savings pot as well as a place for people to live. It was therefore far more difficult to provide for or control than, for instance, health or education. New Labour's more vigorous regional policy, increased strategic planning and attempts to build quasi-markets and at least some amount of 'choice' into social housing did allow public and private sectors to come rather closer together and to be seen as such. But council housing and the housing associations together remained what one academic has termed a 'wobbly pillar' only just about holding up the system, as indeed it had always been.[103] As the economy expanded, the British once again invested in their own dwellings above all, inflating an asset boom that was always going to end in tears. Blair and Brown had always praised individual ambition and voters' desire to own their own homes: but one irony of their tenure was that system eventually imploded, exposing their brand of politics to defeat and derision.

'We were all New Labour now'

Landslide nation

The Blair governments were extremely popular by any standards, and they remained so for a long time. The party's 1997 election success outranks all of the other huge landslides in modern British history – 1895, 1906, 1945, 1983 and 2024. Excluding the National Government's success in 1931, which saw a recent Labour leader in Ramsay MacDonald leading an all-party coalition to an almost complete triumph, those four landmarks saw the Conservatives in 1895 gain an overall majority of 152, the Liberals of 1906 win by 124 seats, and Labour returned with absolute majorities of 146 and 174 in their really big wins under Attlee and Starmer. Thatcher was meanwhile able to win a majority of 144 in 1983, against the backdrop of a recovering economy and victory in the Falklands conflict. Blair's Labour eclipsed all those achievements in 1997, at least in terms of seats, winning a huge majority of 178 over all the other parties. It was no wonder that he said a new dawn had broken.

Labour advanced everywhere, among all social classes, and in almost every part of the country. What is more, the party picked up votes where it had traditionally been weakest – for instance in the South and South East of England – and outperformed Wilson and Kinnock's more limited progress among professional and managerial workers.[1] It did all this while holding on to its working-class base, an electoral trick that was going to get much harder in the first decades of the twenty-first century. Labour under Blair kept most of its 'own' voters loyal, but also grasped and profited from the fact that party loyalties had become more fluid, less matters of identity and more of choice, from the 1970s onwards. New Labour both understood and emphasised that voters were ready to be convinced by new offers and ways of thinking, ideas untied to the battles of the 1980s and 1990s. In 1997, Blair managed to capture a majority of the non-manual workforce (at 40 per cent, as against 38 per cent for the

Conservatives) while still holding on to 58 per cent of the manual workforce. It was a remarkable achievement given that Wilson, self-consciously casting himself as a tribune of the trained and technical 'black-coated worker', managed only 22 per cent among non-manual workers in 1964: Blair's victory among the manual workforce was also down only six points (from 64 per cent) on 1964, the last time Labour had won a majority straight out of Opposition.[2]

Although some Conservatives attempted to explain their enormous defeat by virtue of the intervention of small anti-European parties, or abstentionism on the part of their supporters, there is little evidence to support that. In fact, Labour – and to a lesser extent the Liberal Democrats – simply convinced large numbers of ex-Conservative voters to come over to their 'side', at least as an experiment.[3] Nearly two million voters had switched straight from the Conservatives to Labour. Philip Gould worked long and hard with focus groups across the South of England to instil a sense of what mainstream, though persuadable, Conservative voters thought and felt about politics. He was ecstatic when that work paid off, bringing voters from the suburbs where he had grown up into the Labour fold, many for the first time. He recalled his own upbringing in Woking, Surrey (where Labour had increased its vote by 7.6 per cent and over 2,500 votes):

> I thought of my father who had hoped for this moment, but doubted it would come. Most of all I thought of the quiet suburban street that I came from, and felt pride that people from that street, and millions like them, had dared to vote Labour … The suburbs had changed, but this time Labour had changed with them.[4]

Conservative abstentionism was clearly not the main factor in this election, though the presence of minor anti-European groups such as the Referendum Party did make a marginal difference to Conservative performance. Labour simply did not enjoy particularly high swings towards it where the Conservatives' raw vote count fell the most. Its advance was very similar whether the turnout fell by less than 4 per cent, or more than 8 per cent. A roll call of some of the suburban seats where Labour now mounted a challenge make these two points eloquently and together: in Crosby, for instance, scene of the great Social Democratic Party's (SDP's) by-election triumph of 1981, turnout was down about 5 percentage points, but that did not make much difference to the huge 18 per cent swing to Labour. In Spelthorne, on the border between Surrey and London, there was a 14.5 per cent swing to Labour (who got within 3,500 votes of the Conservatives) while turnout fell 6.7 per cent.[5] Labour surged almost everywhere across England (except perhaps the South West, where the Liberal Democrats were usually best placed to beat the Conservatives): they won ten seats from third place, jumping over Paddy Ashdown's party to win the constituency themselves.[6]

Labour had by that point endured eighteen years out of office, and at several points in the mid-1980s and early 1990s it had seemed as if it might never gain an overall majority again. That gave the 1997 result even more significance. Sympathisers were delighted, while opponents seemed ready to give New Labour the benefit of the doubt. Mattinson, later to become a key adviser to Gordon Brown and at one point Director of Strategy for Starmer, recorded the mood as she waited for her children at their school:

> As we waited, a teacher walked from one building to another in front of us. Halfway across she stopped suddenly and leapt in the air, tossing her bag up, and letting out a joyous whoop. She then walked briskly on to the classroom. I didn't know any of the other parents but we all smiled at her and at each other. There was even a small scattering of applause. We enjoyed sharing the moment. We all knew how she felt. We were all New Labour now.[7]

New Labour's first victory helps us understand more deeply why it stayed so popular for years afterwards. The party possessed a rare ability to reach out to new parts of the electorate and new areas of the country, while holding onto strongholds. Blair's own leadership, a sense of hope, optimism and dynamism, as well as the Conservatives' deep unpopularity, were all elements within that renewed appeal. All of them would help the party stay in power and reshape the country for a decade and more.

New Labour's extraordinary popularity

What, though, did Labour's apparent electoral hegemony really mean, beyond the raw fact of that it was able to win power and then dominate its opponents? There is no perfect test or ideal type against which to test their electoral dominance, but we can turn to historical polling figures to show that the Blair effect allowed New Labour to gain and retain a remarkable amount of public support, which it held onto for years. That long-lasting popularity could be measured on any number of metrics, though four may suffice if we look in detail at the numbers. First of all, as we can clearly see in Figures 8.1 and 8.2, the Blair governments climbed initially to heights of public approval that no other government in Britain has managed in recent history. Labour's lead over the main Opposition peaked at nearly 37 percentage points in June 1997, very

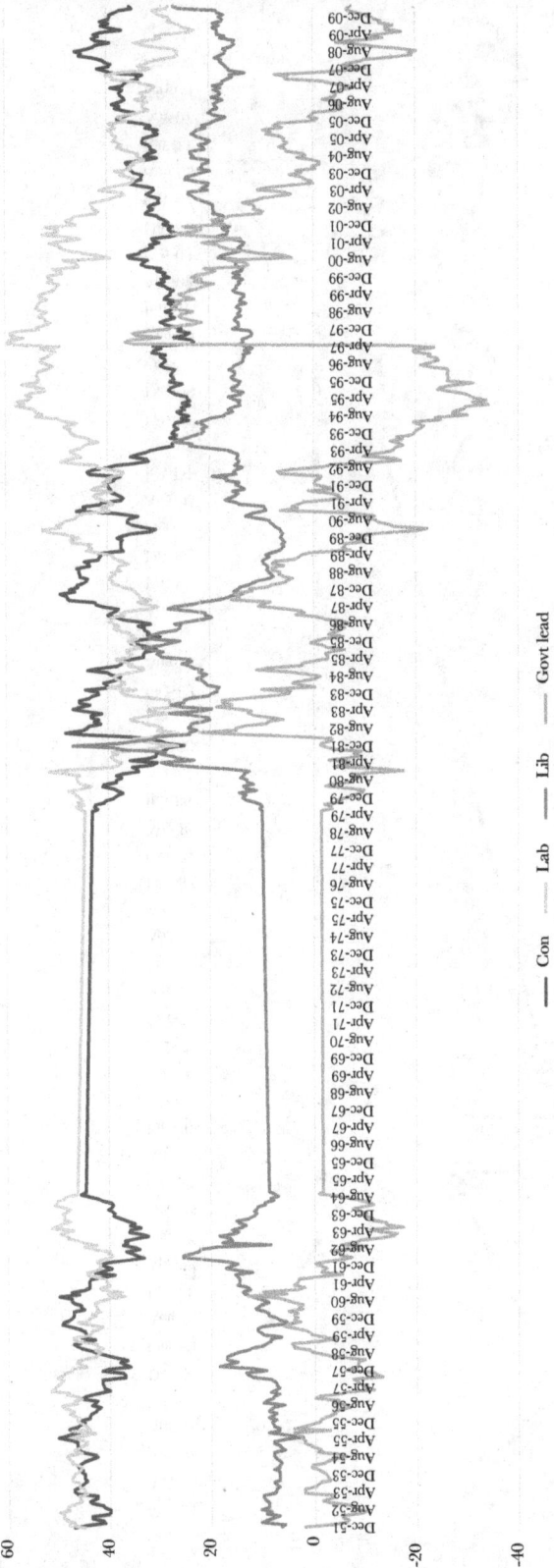

Figure 8.1 Government polling lead over the main Opposition, 1951–2010 (selected)

Source: Mark Pack PollBase data at www.markpack.org.uk/opinion-polls/, accessed 19 April 2023.

Con ——— Lab ——— Lib ——— Govt lead

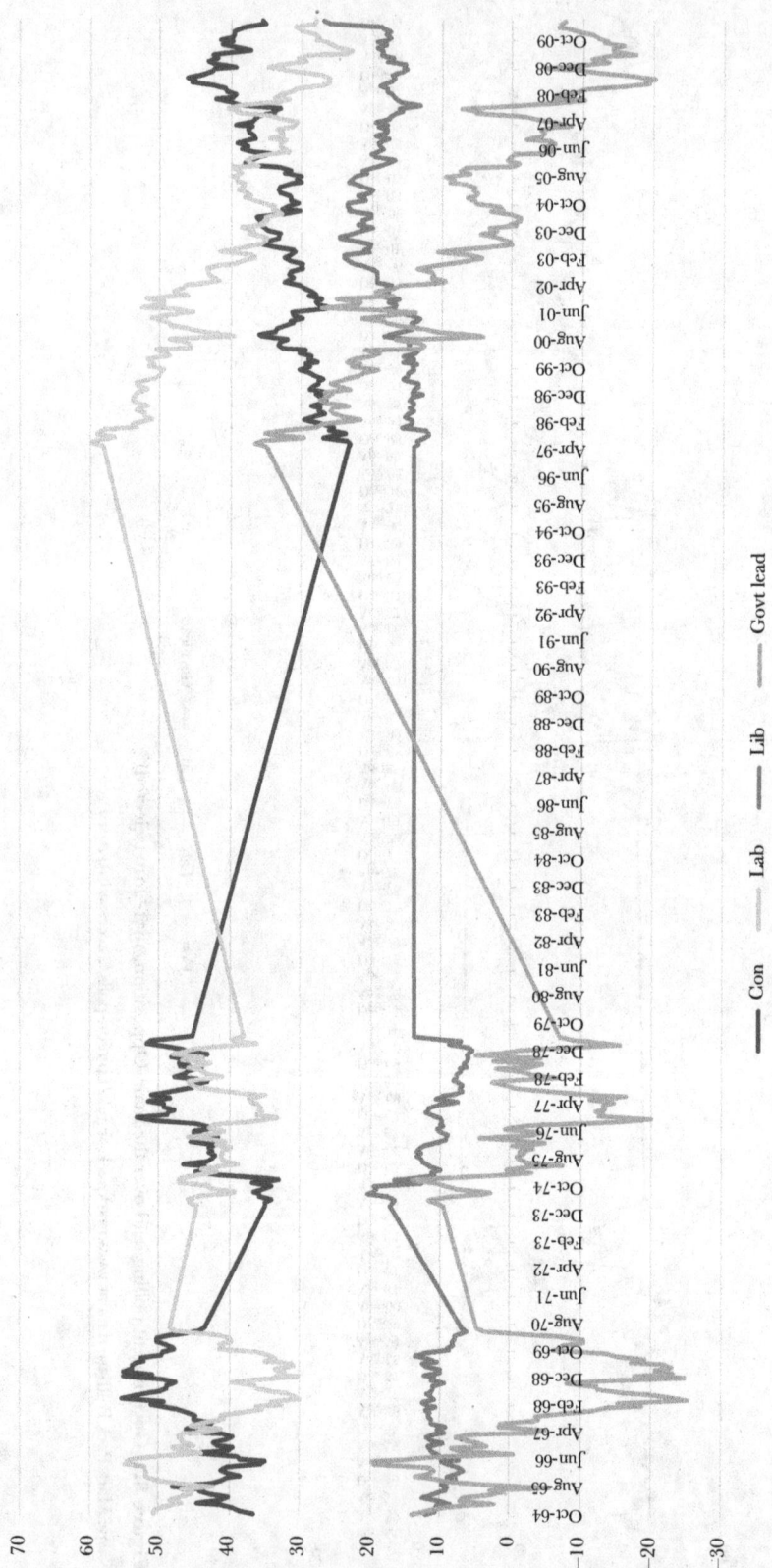

Figure 8.2 Labour leads during three periods in office, 1964–2010

Source: Mark Pack PollBase data at www.markpack.org.uk/opinion-polls/, accessed 19 April 2023.

early in Blair's Premiership and during a remarkable honeymoon period, but was as high as 27 points as late as August 2001 and following New Labour's second landslide victory. By contrast, the Thatcher government for instance could 'only' lead Labour by 22 points at the height of its popularity at the end of the victorious Falklands conflict (in June 1982). At no other time did the Conservatives stretch their lead to more than 20 points, though they still led Labour in early 1989, ten years after coming to power.

That evidence of long-lasting strength in the polls takes us to a second measure of Labour's success with the electorate: the length of time it took to fall behind its main rival for public support. Apart from poor numbers in the Augusts of both 1965 and 1966, Figure 8.2 shows that it took until the spring of 1967 for Harold Wilson's Labour to trail the Conservatives – over thirty months into his time in Number 10. By contrast, during the first six months after Thatcher took up residence in Downing Street, the Conservatives actually trailed Labour by between 1.4 per cent and 5.3 per cent; the Conservative-Liberal Democrat Coalition administration of 2010–15 lagged behind Ed Miliband's Labour within seven months of agreeing to enter government together.

It took much longer for Blair and Brown's government to be challenged on anything like this scale. Even the famous fuel protests of September 2000, which for a moment seemed as if they might knock the Government completely off course, failed to drag Labour down into second place if we look at the monthly averages from September and October 2000 (during which months Blair's party was 4 per cent and 5.2 per cent ahead, respectively). The first real challenge to New Labour's electoral hegemony came after the Second Iraq War, and during Michael Howard's leadership of the Conservatives between 2003 and 2005. Howard was a somewhat more plausible figure than the Leaders of the Opposition he succeeded, William Hague and Iain Duncan Smith, even if he was not exactly popular. He managed to take the Conservatives into the lead in February, April and May 2004 – but only by 0.5 per cent, 1.2 per cent and 1.3 per cent. He was also assisted in gaining that tiny lead by the popularity of the Liberal Democrats under Charles Kennedy, whose anti-war stance helped to take his party to between 21 and 22 per cent in the polls. But by that time, New Labour had been in power for nearly seven years, in fact between 82 and 85 months to be precise: they had put in an extraordinarily long and indeed unique run of poll leads.

On a third measure – the depths of the Government's unpopularity after a long period in office – the New Labour years look more 'normal', or at least more usual for UK governments in the second half of the twentieth century.

Since only the Conservatives' electoral dominance of 1951–64 and 1979–97 saw any single party remain in office for anything like as long as Blair and Brown served as Prime Minister, this is the comparison which seems most relevant. After just over eleven years in power, the Conservatives reached their polling nadir under Harold Macmillan in March 1963, a month in which they were 16 points behind Labour in the polls. Another historic low point was reached under John Major in January 1995, after nearly sixteen years of that long-lasting government. By that point the Conservatives were much further behind Blair's Labour Party: they trailed by more than 34 points, with their own average polling score below 24 per cent.

Similarly, Brown's period as Prime Minister was marred by a large surge in unpopularity during 2008, more intense than Macmillan's though nowhere near as bad as Major's. Labour lagged the Conservatives by some 20 points at their worst point in that electoral cycle (in August 2008). The worst moment for Labour's polling during Blair's leadership came right at the end of his Premiership, in March 2007, when he was already committed to standing down within the year: Labour was an average of 8.4 points behind the Conservatives at that point. These figures seem unremarkable, at least in terms of what historic examples we have, and speak to a government's popularity degrading under events and inevitably divisive decisions – the so-called 'costs of governing'.[8] If New Labour changed electoral dynamics and broke records between 1994 and 2001, later in its life it fell back towards a more humdrum, workaday reality.

Fourth and last in our popularity tests comes the Prime Minister's own personal ratings (Figure 8.3). Here again, New Labour's early years in office saw Blair return unprecedented polling numbers before a return to something closer to the norm. By this measure, his approval ratings stayed extremely high for five years, though they had certainly sagged to more 'normal' levels by 2003–07. Even after the Second Iraq War Blair enjoyed moments when his popularity recovered to fairly high levels. Periods like this, such as the summer of 2005 when Britain won its bid to host the 2012 Olympics and London endured bomb attacks on the Underground on what became known as '7/7', did however become few and far between (see Figure 8.3). Interestingly, just as New Labour's poll rating came to look more like that of the Conservatives during the 1990s, so Blair's numbers more and more tracked those of Mrs Thatcher. If a heady fusion of elements had seen Labour seize and keep office, much of the spell seemed to have worn off by the end of Brown's short honeymoon as Prime Minister in the late summer and early autumn of 2007.

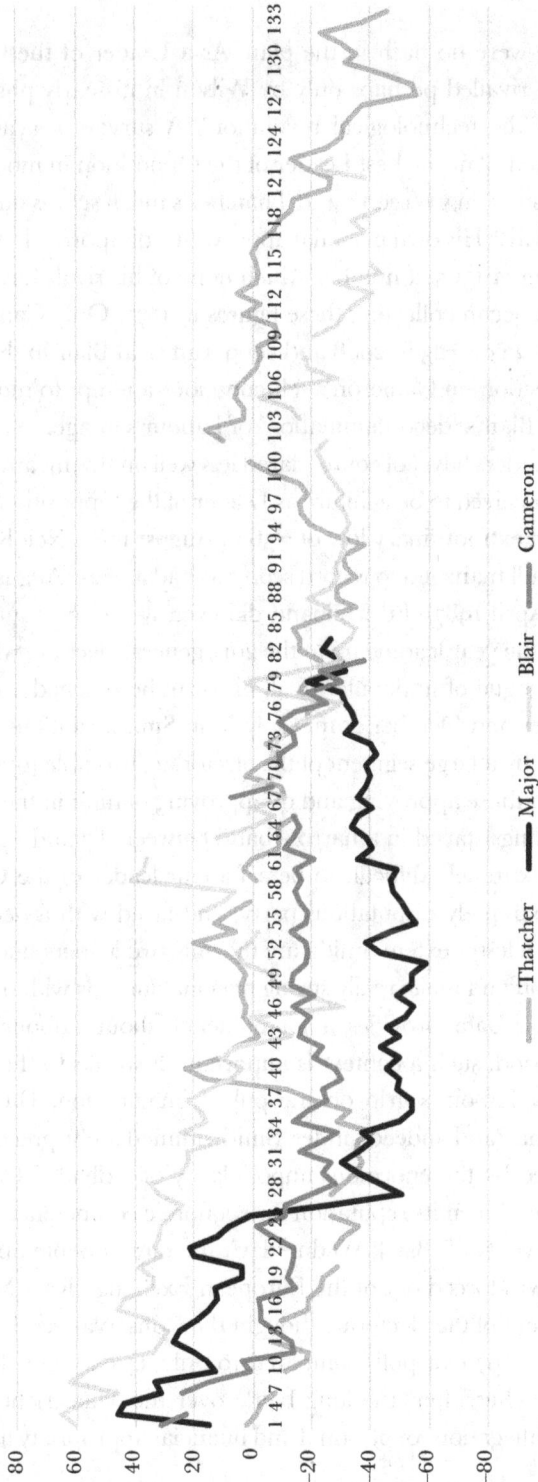

Figure 8.3 The personal ratings of four Prime Ministers, 1979–2016 (by months in office)

Sources: Political Monitor: Satisfaction Ratings, www.ipsos.com/en-uk/political-monitor-satisfaction-ratings-1977-1987, www.ipsos.com/en-uk/political-monitor-satisfaction-ratings-1988-1997 and www.ipsos.com/en-uk/political-monitor-satisfaction-ratings-1997-present, accessed 19 April 2023.

These numbers were no flash in the plan. As a Leader of the Opposition, Blair was peerless, rivalled perhaps only by Wilson in his early phase evoking the 'white heat of the technological revolution'. A survey of academics has indeed recently rated Blair the best Leader of the Opposition in modern British history, at 8.4, outstripping Wilson's and Thatcher's mean scores out of ten (7.3 and 6.6) by some way.[9] His own personal approval-to-disapproval score peaked at +30 in the spring of 1995, a number which none of his rivals have managed since Ipsos MORI began collecting these figures in 1977. Only Cameron, with ratings as high as +22 or +23 in 2008 and 2009, can rival Blair in this respect – an interesting reflection on Cameron's self-conscious attempt to model himself and his project on Blair's 'decontamination' of Labour's image.

Other Labour leaders have, of course, fared less well on this measure. Michael Foot was widely perceived to be a failure as Leader of the Opposition: his figures bottomed out at an extraordinary low of −56 in August 1982. Neil Kinnock did better, though he still managed to record scores as bad as −25 (August 1985) and −30 (March and April 1987). Ed Miliband did even worse, his rating between −26 and −44 over the year leading up to the 2015 general election, while Jeremy Corbyn was in a league of unpopularity all his own: he touched a record −60 rating in September and October 2019. Only John Smith, cautious but seen as trusted and serious by a large segment of the electorate, was able to stay roughly in balance between those approving and disapproving of him: in the last year of his life, Smith's ratings stayed in a narrow band between +7 and −4. All in all, it is and remains extremely difficult to be a Labour leader of the Opposition, 'followed' by an extremely disputatious party, and faced with a deeply hostile press. Blair, and to a lesser extent Smith, are the only two leaders since the 1960s to defy that situation and make really strong personal inroads with the public.[10]

Although all this data provides a lot of detail about Labour's electoral strength in this period, such a context is important: it speaks to the huge scale and scope of New Labour's grip on the public imagination. During Blair's years in Opposition (and indeed under Smith immediately preceding him), Labour was assisted by the enormous unpopularity of a divided Conservative Government that had seen its reputation for economic competence completely destroyed by the events of 'Black Wednesday', the day in September 1992 on which the pound was forced out of the European Exchange Rate Mechanism. A massive 84 per cent of the electorate thought the Conservatives divided when they answered the 1997 exit poll, compared to only 34 per cent thinking the same of Labour.[11] Thereafter, the long battle over the Maastricht Treaty on European Union, allegations of personal and financial impropriety and Major's own image as a weak and vacillating leader all damaged the Conservatives' image beyond short- or even medium-term repair. Labour opened up huge leads in the polls (Figure 8.4). Consider these words from a self-employed bricklayer in 2000, during the lead-up to the 2001 election:

> We had the ERM debacle, interest rates went doolally, the building industry couldn't operate. I had to take a 50 per cent pay cut overnight and my mortgage went up £150 a month. I went to Germany looking for work but that didn't pan out very well so, for a time, we had to rent out the home and move in with [my wife's] parents just to hang on to [our home]. She took a job as a cleaner to help make ends meet. So that's why I finished with the Tories, and it's never again so far as I'm concerned.[12]

We can see this effect when we compare Figure 8.1 with Figure 8.3, since Labour's lead over the Conservatives, with some interruptions during 2003 and 2004 immediately after the Second Iraq War, lasted long after Blair's own popularity had been reduced to something more normal for a long-serving Prime Minister. Although the British public's extremely high regard for the Prime Minister had long since melted away, their acceptance of – and indeed liking for – New Labour's electoral dominance *over the Conservatives* had not. Labour's absolute ratings gradually declined throughout this period, but their relative ranking as against Duncan Smith's and Howard's party was usually still favourable. Labour were trusted less and less: but the Conservatives were not yet seen as a credible alternative.

Labour positives and Conservatives negatives

Blair's long dominance of the electoral landscape was not, however, simply a matter of the weakness of his opponents – important as that was. His staff and allies were extremely focused, indeed pitiless, in exploiting the weaknesses and divisions that might have been less ruthlessly exploited by a more amateur or less enthusiastic team. Labour's recovery from the internecine strife of the 1980s, their professional campaigning, and their ability to react quickly to attacks, certainly played a role in their day-to-day dominance. Given they were a small cadre of enthusiasts who tried to move the Labour Party decisively in their direction, Blairites strangely resembled the Corbynites between 2015 and 2020, though both extremes in Labour's endless civil war would no doubt reject the comparison. Some of the sense of dynamic zeal and both experienced and claimed 'authenticity', which saw Labour mount a stirring campaign during the general election of 2017, was possessed by both camps. Most importantly

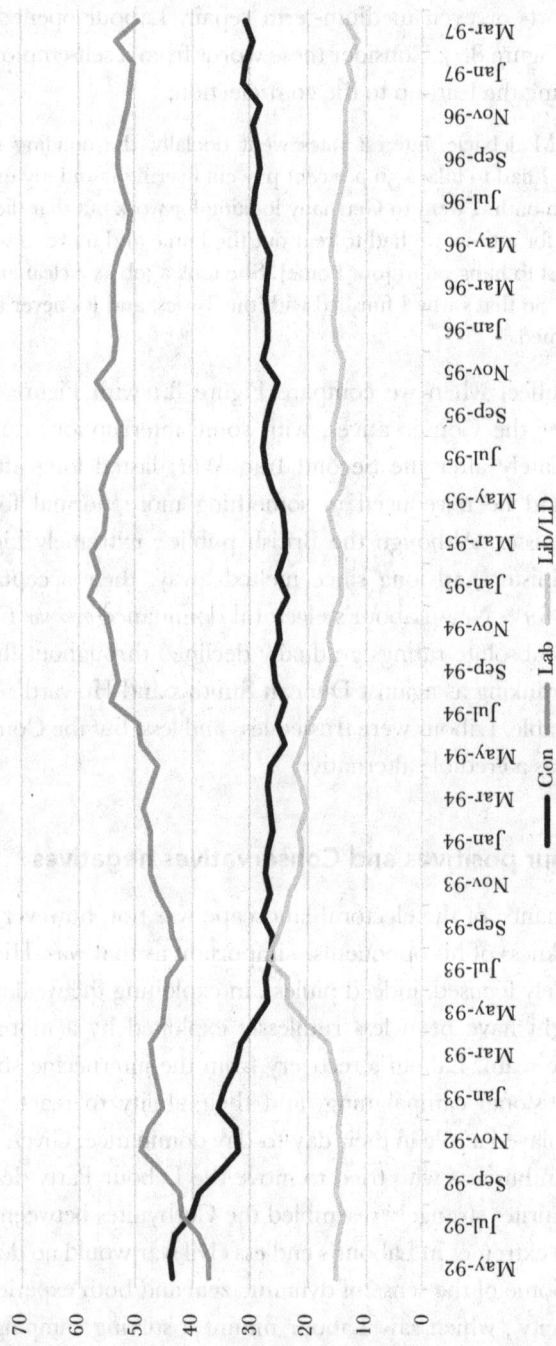

Figure 8.4 Opinion polling in the 1992–97 Parliament

Source: Mark Pack PollBase data at www.markpack.org.uk/opinion-polls/, accessed 19 April 2023.

during the 1990s and 2000s, the intensity and drive of figures such as Campbell and Mandelson demonstrated New Labour's desire for power. The atmosphere within the Blair team was summed up by Campbell:

> In the long build-up to the campaign I felt physically and mentally like a race-horse. I felt like we were testing the whole time, training, trying things out, building up stamina, finding out the things that could be rejected, and working out the things that had to be developed ... If you had a camera in there people wouldn't have dreamed of voting for us – it was ridiculous, circular conversations – and yet there was discipline in the end.[13]

The effects of this narrow focus on electability can be seen in Labour's image on economic policy, on which they would place huge emphasis during Blair's time in office. In 1992, the party had lagged the Conservatives badly on 'pocketbook' issues. A mix of concern over potential tax rises stoked by Labour's declared intention to raise taxes on high earners, Kinnock's poor personal ratings and a deep recession that dissuaded many voters from the risks of change all hurt Labour. In the lead-up to the 1992 contest, Gallup figures showed that Labour trailed the Conservatives by 14 percentage points on the economy. By 1997, that picture had been transformed, and Labour led with Gallup on the economy by 11 points (the exit poll of that year gave them a smaller 2 point advantage).[14] Here again, Conservative decline was skilfully matched by Labour's messaging. The two Budgets of 1993 had ushered in the largest peacetime tax rises since the Second World War, as the Conservative Chancellors Norman Lamont and Kenneth Clarke attempted to return spending towards balance after the recession. Labour then constantly evoked the '22 Tory Tax Rises' of 1992–97, emphasising that in 1992 the Conservatives had said they had no need or plans to raise taxes. They forced the Government to reduce an increase in Value Added Tax on fuel and power from 17.5 per cent to eight per cent; and they promised to cut it further, to 5 per cent, once in office.[15]

This was a skilful appeal to a very visible part of pensioners' weekly budget; combined with Brown's January 1997 promise not to raise Income Tax, and to stick to government spending plans for two years, Conservative negatives were turned into Labour positives. Blair and Brown were at this point speaking to fundamental questions about trust in politics, and also answering questions in the voters' minds about the whole nature of the Labour Party and its attitude to spending. Given the Conservatives' demolition of their own promises on tax, any sense of trust was at a low ebb: instead of making big promises, perhaps matched by some increases in contributions, the Labour team decided to focus on narrow, believable and deliverable goals. This was the origin of the 'Road to the Manifesto' document of 1996, to be voted on by the party's own members – and the famous 'pledge card', which invited voters to hold Labour to the five promises printed on the pocket-sized card. According to Gould, 'people wanted smaller policies that they could believe in, not larger ones that seemed incredible'.[16] The evidence suggests that this narrowcasting was, for a while at least, fairly successful.

A dominant project

In an even deeper and perhaps more positive sense, Blair's appeal flowed from that communitarianism which we have already identified as the key to his whole approach – the idea of governance as contractual, not in a narrow or legalistic sense, but in a way that gave some emotional heft to the experience of globalisation's uncertainties. On so-called social or moral issues, this allowed him to take up a relatively (though not intensively) socially conservative stance, while on the other hand appearing to be mildly though not dangerously radical about the living standards of lower-income voters, redistribution and spending on public services. This latter tone gave him appeal on the Left, as well as among more centrist or conservative voters. In effect, Blairism filled the entirety of the country's news bandwidth by posing and answering its own questions in surprising ways. The techniques that won the 1997 landslide allowed Blair to dominate the political landscape, allowing him to avoid clear definition on a Left-to-Right spectrum. They helped him bridge across from socially liberal Labour voters in swing seats to more conservative Labour supporters in what the party still thought of as its 'heartlands'. The strange duumvirate of the Blair-Brown years, during which time the country sometimes appeared to have two leaders who emphasised different parts of the New Labour agenda, helped rather than hindered in this respect. Essentially unopposed by a Conservative Party lacking public attention and even sometimes self-respect, New Labour even had a right-leaning and a left-leaning leader and provided its own official Opposition from within.[17]

Another factor here, often forgotten but of enormous importance at the time, was a tacit alliance with the Liberal Democrats under Ashdown. The Liberal Democrats made a great deal of the electoral running in polls and local elections between 1992 and mid-1994, when Labour was still staking out a cautious manifesto under Smith (see Figure 8.4): in August 1993, though only briefly, Ashdown's party actually overtook the Conservatives and moved narrowly into second place in the polls. The Liberal Democrats also won three famous by-election victories with huge swings at Newbury, Christchurch and Eastleigh.[18] Blair was at ease with the idea of a broad coalition for 'change', ousting the Conservatives after a long period of electoral dominance. That helped to identify him with that renewed Liberal surge, which in both polling and by-elections echoed the smaller party's forward movements as the Liberals and the SDP-Liberal Alliance in 1972–73 and 1981–82. It also saw Blair steal many of the smaller party's ideas and rhetoric, as well as their voters: in 1994 Ashdown confided to his adviser, Richard Holme, that 'I have been building the Party to fill a certain gap in politics, which I know is there … But then along comes Blair with all the power of Labour behind him, and fills exactly the space I have been aiming at for the last seven years!'[19] Watching Blair's 1996 Conference speech, Ashdown exclaimed: 'same words, same notions, same sentiments, same policies as I have been trying to get on to the agenda now for eight years. And he comes along and takes it off me in one!'[20]

Important figures within New Labour such as Liddle, as well as Adonis, had come to the party via the SDP: their influence, and Blair's own friendship with the Liberal Democrats' elder statesman Roy Jenkins as one of his mentors, brought the two parties closer together than they had been since perhaps the Edwardian period. Mandelson and Liddle argued, in *The Blair Revolution*, that New Labour was 'a concept which joins the left to the centre of British politics'. Shorn of its statist view of nationalisation and converging on similar views around 'community', social exclusion and education, Labour looked like a much more natural partner for the Liberal Democrats than the Conservatives.[21] In a series of private meetings, Blair came close to offering a full coalition to Ashdown. There was also heady talk of a two-stage referendum on Proportional Representation which would first see the principle of change established, before moving on to the details in a second vote. Labour later retreated from this position a little, to offer a Commission on PR which would recommend the shape of any changes, but again the signal of a Labour-Liberal Democrat alliance was sent.[22] That helped Blair to occupy their ideological space, detoxify Labour with some voters worried about the Left, and to present himself as leading a broad coalition. Extraordinarily for commentators who remembered Labour's struggles in the 1980s, Labour's vote increased most among right-leaning voters in 1997, squeezing out any potential Liberal Democrat advance in that part of the electorate.[23]

This identity of interests and ideas also allowed Labour to concentrate on those swing seats where they could beat the Conservatives, leaving Liberal Democrat-Conservative marginals to be contested by the smaller party. Tactical voting, tacitly encouraged by both Blair and Ashdown, could then take care of the rest. Ashdown's abandonment of 'equidistance' between the two larger parties in May 1995, and his emphasis on removing the Conservatives from office, caught Major and then, to a lesser extent, Hague in a pincer movement from which they could not escape. Though it is hard fully to disentangle the effects of tactical voting, it clearly occurred in 1997 on a scale not seen since pollsters began asking about it in 1983: 10 per cent of voters said they had voted tactically.[24] It might be that Labour gained an extra 3 per cent of the vote in those seats where they were second to the Conservatives, compared to elsewhere – and these votes came largely from the Liberal Democrats. This allowed Labour to win an extra 15–21 seats than they would otherwise have done, expanding their landslide majority. In effect, the policy of at least wary non-aggression between Blair and Ashdown turned a very large victory into a rout.[25]

'It's the economy, stupid'

Added to this ideological domination of Labour's opponents, and to the crowding out of rivals to the margins, was of course the successful economy that Britain enjoyed during the entirety of Blair's time in Number 10. This was a period of sustained low inflationary growth and job creation, as well as ongoing real wage growth, and allowed ministers to keep talking in the same hopeful, optimistic tones that had proved so popular in 1997. None of those factors were in place consistently in the eras immediately before and after Blair's period in office, and the electorate gave the Government credit for it. From a position where the parties were neck and neck on the economy in 1997, Labour took a strong lead over the Conservatives on pocketbook issues into both the 2001 and 2005 general elections.[26] In 2005, Labour actually led the Conservatives on the economy by 36 points, while Conservative promises to cut taxes were ignored: 60 per cent of voters thought that Howard's party would actually raise taxes.[27] Only once the debacle of 1992–97 was well behind them, and they had refocused their entire image during Cameron's leadership and the Global Financial Crisis, would the Conservatives be listened to on the economy.

These factors remained and remain critical to the maintenance of any electoral coalition – simply put, success breeds success. Clinton's mantra – 'It's the economy, stupid', both impressed itself on Blair's mind given the Democrats' return to the White House in 1993, and allowed Labour to avoid some of the cultural conflicts that were later to bedevil it in Opposition after 2010.[28] A long period of low inflation and high employment helped reinforce the image of the rhetoric and methods being wielded at the time. One of the secrets here was that, during Blair's period in office, all the measures of economic progress were going in the right direction. Inflation was low; unemployment fell to extremely low levels, not seen since the 1970s; wage growth was strong, especially (in conjunction with tax changes) for the low paid. Getting all three indicators in the right place, once compared by Macmillan to a child's toy which one could solve on two sides but not all three, does explain some of Labour's long-lasting popularity. The link between economic progress and political success may have become weaker since its heyday in the 1950s and 1960s, but it did not disappear, and indeed was still in action early in the twenty-first century. Wages were falling when Theresa May was humiliated by the electorate in 2017, while they were rising at the time of Boris Johnson's electoral triumph in December 2019.[29]

There can be no doubt that the years of popular affluence around the turn of the century were of central importance to Labour's popularity, as the party's collapsing poll rating during the Global Financial Crisis and Great Recession help to demonstrate. Even so, it was Labour's political strategy during these years that allowed the party to take credit for the boom, providing a narrative for both its longevity and social purpose (in the shape of higher spending on better public services). Economic expansion was not sold just as prosperity, but justified in terms of spreading personal and collective opportunities. Given widespread prosperity and large increases in public spending, most of the public thought Brown's Budgets 'fair': the lowest number agreeing with that proposition was 55 per cent after the Budget of 2000, while 82 per cent and 71 per cent said the 1997 and 2001 Budgets were equitable. Large majorities thought Labour's first-term Budgets were 'good for the country', while most voters thought that Labour looked after the interests of *both* 'the working class' and 'the middle class'. Those last numbers fell as time went on, especially in terms of 'looking after' the 'working class': but they remained positive during Labour's early years back in power. Labour had in effect established a new consensus – not challenged by Cameron in Opposition – that increased government spending should be privileged over tax cuts.[30]

This was clearly not the be-all and end-all of Labour's appeal. The Conservatives even during the period of strong economic growth in the mid-1980s had not enjoyed continual polling leads of the length and extent of Labour's in the late 1990s and early 2000s. Major's popularity did not boom along with the economy in the mid- to late 1990s, though he did recover from the extraordinary lows that he plumbed during 1993 and 1994. One of the secrets to New Labour's popularity was that the ongoing economic expansion allowed them to meet many of their pledges, at least to some or an arguable extent. Class sizes did fall; NHS waiting lists did shrink; a Windfall Tax was introduced; and so on. In particular, the last bullet point on New Labour's pledge card at the 1997 election – 'no rise in Income Tax rates, cut VAT on heating to 5 per cent and inflation and interest rates as low as possible' – was more than delivered. Consumer Price Inflation stayed below 2 per cent for all of Labour's first term, and only rose above that level after Blair's third election victory. Having initially risen in 1997 and the first three-quarters of 1998, interest rates then fell back again.

New Labour in decline

New Labour in office did, for a while, reverse at least a little of the damage the flood of scandals and 'sleaze' had done in the mid-1990s. Trust in politicians is not exactly a mass phenomenon, but the numbers of people who did believe they generally told the truth rose from 14 per cent in 1993 to 23 per cent in 1999. That number stuck at a slightly higher level until the expenses scandal of 2009.[31] That said, New Labour's popularity did wane as time went on. Not only is that clear in the opinion polls, which threatened to turn against Labour – for instance in 2004 – and dramatically deteriorated for the party after the autumn of 2007; general election results bear this out too. Labour's share of the vote in Great Britain fell from 44.3 per cent in 1997 to 42 per cent even in 2001, an election they won easily. It then fell much further in 2005, to 36.1 per cent, before bottoming out at 29.7 per cent in the 2010 election, which Labour lost. Not only that, but the absolute number of voters choosing Labour declined rapidly too. 13.5 million Labour supporters in 1997 became 10.7 million in 2001, 9.5 million in 2005 and just 8.6 million in 2010. Labour had lost 14.6 per cent of the vote and 5.1 million voters in thirteen years of government, though Blair himself 'only' lost 7.2 per cent or four million voters in his three elections as leader.[32]

To some extent, of course, the end of the long boom and the onset of the Great Recession called the whole New Labour project into question. The factors that brought Labour to power in 1997 now went into reverse, to some extent proving their influence in the first place. From a position of unalloyed dominance in 2005, the Conservatives could now contest the economy on level terms with Labour: they enjoyed a small lead on economic questions going into the 2010 general election. There can be little doubt that negative views of Labour's economic management played a role in causing many voters ultimately to desert the party.[33] While economic issues had faded slightly into the background during the expansion of the late 1990s and early 2000s, now they were clearly the most important issue facing the country: YouGov data showed that it led the next most important issue, immigration and asylum, by a huge margin of 70 per cent to 49 per cent. The issue was, however, complicated by the Conservatives' perceived inexperience, the idea that they would cut public services quickly and mercilessly, and by Brown's long history of success as Chancellor and decisive moves during the worst of the downturn. During the 2010 campaign, Brown himself actually enjoyed a slight lead over Cameron when pollsters Populus asked voters about the leader 'who knows how to get our economy strong'. Those answering the question preferred Brown by 41 points to 36.[34] The impact of the Global Financial Crisis was by no means straightforward.

In fact, Labour's retreat went back much further, and was caused by a gradual uncoupling of voters from leaders. A key reason for the slow deterioration in Labour's position – despite the record levels of popularity they still enjoyed, right up to the 2007–08 crash – was disengagement with politics as a whole. This was first and foremost notable in the declining turnout at general elections. The number of voters actually casting a ballot crashed most notably between 1997 and 2001. It fell by 12 percentage points to 59.4 per cent between those two elections, hitting the lowest level since the Second World War. One explanation put forward for that low turnout in 2001, both at the time and subsequently, has been the public's apathy when the campaigns talked endlessly about Europe (a low priority singled out by only 26 per cent of voters in one poll) and when the outcome was not seriously in doubt. Put that together with general approval of Blair's record (56 per cent thought that he was doing a 'good' or 'excellent' job) as well as the perception of the election as a foregone conclusion, and a sluggish turnout might have been expected.[35]

The malaise was actually more profound, a reality demonstrated by the fact that turnout recovered only slightly (to 61.2 per cent) in 2005 when the election was more hotly contested.[36] First of all, the electorate's evident dissatisfaction spoke to a fundamental dealignment of lower-income voters with Labour under Blair and Brown. These voters did not at first move towards the United Kingdom Independence Party (UKIP) or the Conservatives, but initially sat out some elections altogether. The fall in turnout, particularly notable in some traditionally working-class seats that had long been regarded as *being* 'Labour' rather than voting Labour, was an ominous sign that the wide coalition of 1997 could not be maintained. Moving into the centre had its costs, and Labour's Left flank had been exposed. Fewer and fewer voters saw a large difference between Labour and the Conservatives: while 56 per cent did so in 1992, only 33 per cent said the same in 1997, 17 per cent in 2001 and 21 per cent in 2005.[37]

The growing centralisation and professionalisation of politics, especially in England without a devolution settlement of its own, also made voters feel as if 'politics' itself took place a long way away from their neighbourhood – as did the increased targeting of marginal seats and falling spending on 'safe' Labour areas. The emergence of a professional 'governing class' among Labour's spads fast-tracked from Oxbridge, like Ed Miliband and Andy Burnham, alienated some other working-class voters. Labour's superb media operation, working for the most part on television, also allowed local links and canvassing to atrophy – especially as Labour's membership numbers fell away during its time in office, another sign of waning popularity (see Table 8.1). The 1987 British Election Study showed that 47 per cent of voters had received a visit from party workers: in 2001 that figure was only 23 per cent, and by 2010 it had shrunk to 11 per cent.[38]

Overall, the calculation that Labour could move off in search of middle-class votes without suffering among less prosperous communities was shown in the long run to be flawed, as more working-class voters felt increasingly alienated. Mattinson has admitted, for instance, that in all her decades of work for the

Table 8.1   Labour Party membership, 1992–2010

	Members	% Increase/decrease
1992	279,530	7.0
1993	266,270	−4.7
1994	305,189	14.6
1995	365,110	19.6
1996	400,465	9.7
1997	405,238	1.1
1998	387,776	−4.3
1999	361,000	−6.9
2000	311,000	−13.9
2001	272,000	−12.5
2002	248,294	−8.7
2003	214,952	−13.4
2004	201,374	−6.3
2005	198,026	−1.6
2006	182,370	−7.9
2007	176,891	−3.0
2008	166,247	−6.0
2009	156,205	−6.0
2010	193,961	24.2

Source: H. Pemberton and M. Wickham-Jones, 'Labour's Lost Grassroots: The Rise and Fall of Party Membership', British Politics 8, 2 (2013), 181–206, table 1, p. 189.

Labour Party 'other than the occasional by-election, at no point ... did we ever consider running focus groups or polling in any of the Red Wall seats [across the North of England]. Their reliability was seen as a given – quite frankly, they were taken for granted'. Mattinson's more recent focus groups in the North East detect a palpable ambivalence and unease about Blair in particular as a politician who was both 'the last decent leader that they [Labour] had', but also in the words of Darlington's Conservative MP Peter Gibson between 2019 and 2024 a 'man who used the region and its safe seat to develop his career'. Turnout in 2001 fell the most in the North West of England and Scotland, also areas where Labour was seen to have taken voters for granted.[39] This disengagement between Labour and 'its voters' was of course to endanger any chance Labour had of winning a majority.

Trust was secondly damaged by the question of the Second Iraq War, initially fairly popular with the public but thereafter a running sore for the government. Blair had made a case for that war which dissipated amid a welter of unproven claims and a vicious civil war within Iraq itself. At the start of the war, the public backed action against Saddam Hussein's regime by a margin of 53 per cent to 39 per cent; when Baghdad fell to allied forces, that approval had risen to a net +37 (66 per cent to 29 per cent). But thereafter, with no sign of the much-vaunted Weapons of Mass Destruction (WMD) and with Iraq descending into chaos, the public's view of military action, and of the Government itself, soured markedly. Opinion was relatively finely balanced during 2004, but by 2005 a large majority of the public disapproved of Britain's action alongside the Americans. During the 2005 general election campaign, 53 per cent were against Britain's involvement, and only 35 per cent were in favour. By that time, Blair's own handling of the war was supported by only 25 per cent of the electorate, with 63 per cent against.[40]

From a position where Blair's approval and disapproval ratings were relatively in balance during the first half of 2002 (and +2 when Baghdad fell to American forces in April 2003), Figure 8.3 shows that his personal numbers fell to −35 by the autumn of that year. Although they recovered strongly in the build-up to the 2005 general election, enormous damage had been done to long-term views of Blair and the trust he had sought to build up early in his tenure. Blair had linked himself in the public mind to a very unpopular US President in the shape of George W. Bush, as well as shattering the public's regard for his probity. During the 2005 election campaign, 65 per cent of voters told YouGov they believed Blair had either lied or exaggerated about evidence of WMD in Iraq. At the time of the 2001 election, 51 per cent of electors believed the

Government to be 'honest and trustworthy'. Only 26 per cent said the same by the time of the 2005 contest.[41] By this stage, the Prime Minister was a polarising figure, and may even have been a net negative for his party. Mattinson's focus groups had long before turned against Blair on this issue: 'he just wants to prove himself abroad – at any cost', they believed. Or alternatively: 'the US just has to say "Jump" and Tony Blair asks "How high?"'[42]

Blair and Labour were only saved from further electoral damage by the fact that the Conservatives had been, if anything, even more enthusiastic about the Iraq War. When the Attorney-General's March 2003 legal advice to the Cabinet was leaked during the 2005 election campaign, Howard argued that Blair had 'told lies to win elections'. Kennedy's retort was a strong one, calling the Conservatives' arguments 'clap-trap' coming from 'the principal cheerleaders for … this war in the first place'. Even at that stage, though, Labour strategists thought that they lost five days of the campaign to the subsequent row, along with two to three points of their vote share.[43] In the short term, it was the Liberal Democrats who benefitted most from the Iraq issue: for one thing, they took twelve seats from Labour in 2005, as against a net loss of two to the Conservatives. But the most notable long-term effect was probably the hidden, hard-to-capture damage done to Labour's reputation overall. By 2016, 53 per cent of voters were saying that they could 'never forgive' Blair for the war; only 8 per cent thought he did nothing wrong.[44]

Immigration was a critical third element in this process, threatening Labour's relationship with its voters in all sorts of ways. As we saw in Chapter 2, immigration rose strongly in the New Labour years, in part because Blair was committed to a pro-European agenda, to some extent because of a failure to understand the implications of EU enlargement, and also because of an influx of workers drawn in by the UK's booming economy. In Western Europe, only Germany and Spain rivalled the UK for their increase in migrant numbers.[45] As so often, Labour in office chose to pursue a radical policy while playing down (or refusing to talk about) its consequences. Ministers felt they had little choice: the EU was hardly popular with the British public, let alone a large-scale influx of migrants from its other twenty-seven members. In the autumn of 2007, 34 per cent of UK respondents thought EU membership a 'good thing', while 28 per cent thought it a bad idea: across the rest of the EU, the figures were 58 per cent for 'good', and only 13 per cent for 'bad'.[46]

Although voters were relatively used to immigration given the post-war arrival of new Britons from the Empire and Commonwealth, the speed and spread of the influx, and the lack of consultation it was thought to involve, proved a recruiting ground for discontent. The arrival of Eastern European migrants keen to take up jobs in parts of the country which had previously experienced little immigration – Lincolnshire, for instance – was later shown to be correlated with very high votes in the 2016 Brexit referendum.[47] Immigration shot up, and stayed high, in surveys of issue salience to voters. Ipsos MORI's regular Issues Index provides one example, as Figure 8.5 demonstrates. Respondents picking immigration as either the most or another important issue facing Britain rose and rose until the onset of the Global Financial Crisis for a while eclipsed it in voters' minds. From a range of 3 to 7 per cent in 1997–98, voters naming immigration as a key concern rose to highs of 16–18 per cent in the leadup to the 2001 election, 39 per cent in May 2002, 40 per cent in February 2005, 45 per cent in August 2006 and 46 per cent in December 2007.

Controversies over immigration shook working-class loyalties to Labour, in the long run perhaps fundamentally damaging its relationship with the communities it had once sprung from. This issue on its own helps to explain much of the class realignment that was to become more obvious after Brexit in 2016. The number of working-class voters saying that immigration needed to be reduced 'a lot' was 45.6 per cent in 1995, but 60.6 per cent in 2011; the number of middle-class voters saying the same rose 'only' from 37.4 per cent to 41.6 per cent. As that gap opened up, it allowed Labour to be characterised as an elite party of high-income graduates, since only 28.6 per cent of graduates agreed with reducing immigration 'a lot'. When YouGov asked voters at the European Parliament elections in 2009 who Labour wanted to help, working-class voters were much more likely to think 'immigrants and non-white Britons' than 'ordinary working people', and they even – though by a much smaller margin – thought that Labour favoured 'the rich' more than 'working people'.[48] Labour was some way from most of its voters on issues of race and ethnicity throughout this period. They were further out of line with 'their' voters on these questions in 1992 than were the Conservatives and Liberal Democrats, but that dichotomy grew further with time. By 2010, Labour voters from 2005 gave the party a net score of −35 on immigration, as compared with −28 among the public as a whole.[49] Immigration in this respect was a corrosive acid, dissolving the bonds between Labour and its supporters.

The same issue threatened Labour in less tangible ways, too. In the influential reading of political scientists Pippa Norris and Ronald Inglehart, many voters felt Labour's improvements to public services were threatened by new arrivals from overseas. Some Britons worried, too, about the threat to 'British values' and way

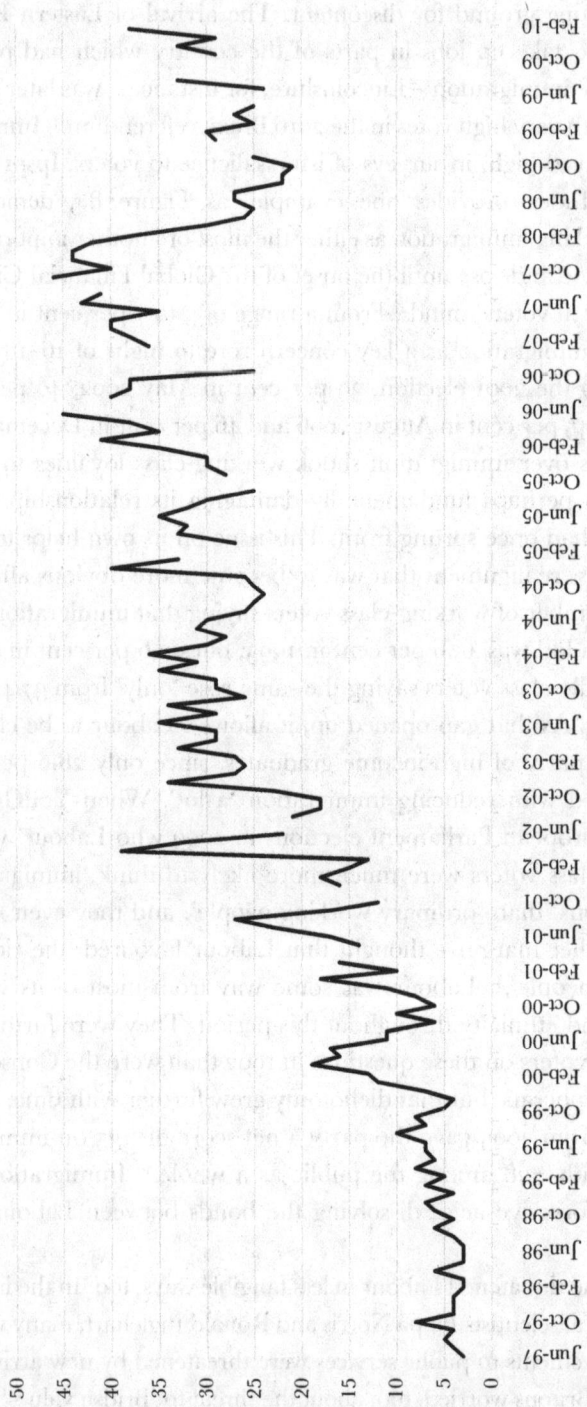

Figure 8.5 Voters naming race/immigration as first or other important issue

Source: *Issues Index*, www.ipsos-mori.com/en-uk/issues-index-1997-2006 and www.ipsos.com/en-uk/issues-index-2007-2017, accessed 20 April 2023.

of life given the numbers arriving. Resentment about the economic effects of immigration – 'taking jobs', for example – were a long-standing part of the British electoral landscape. But social and cultural issues do seem to have become more acute as immigration now increased again, while world events spread fear of outsiders in general and Islam in particular.[50] Many white working-class voters came to feel outnumbered, excluded, looked down on and discriminated against.[51]

That threatened New Labour's contract with the electorate in two ways. The long hoped-for improvement in schools and hospitals was thrown into doubt, while the communitarian or solidaristic ideals behind the popularity of more public spending could also be brought into question. Government could also seem remote, aloof and far from real problems. As Denham put it to me in 2024, 'with the accession states it was just two things. The change was massive. But the second thing about … migration was utter denial at every level of government that this was happening':

> That was the second thing, that had Tony Blair said round about 2005, 2006, f*** me there's a lot of Poles around, there might be people who said they get it because it wasn't a xenophobic response. The government was unable to acknowledge that it had been responsible for a dramatic change in the nature of communities up and down the country. Now at the end of the day, it's not an issue anymore. These communities have been absorbed. Nobody goes around talking about Eastern European migrants anymore. It's not an issue twenty years on but it was the inability of the government to even acknowledge that something had happened, for which it was largely responsible.[52]

For a long time, controversies around immigration looked manageable, in electoral terms at least. Voters told pollsters during the 2001 election that although asylum and Europe *would* be important issues, they still thought that health and education *should* be far more central to the campaign.[53] The openly anti-immigrant British National Party (BNP), along with UKIP, registered only about 2 per cent in the opinion polls between 2005 and 2009. Although the Conservatives made an issue of immigration in the 2005 general election, as part of their 'Are You Thinking What We're Thinking?' campaign, their appeal to nativist sentiments did not seem particularly successful. Even so, it is noticeable that the largest fall in Labour's share of the vote in 2005 was among social classes C2 and DE – exactly as we would expect given the evidence of discontent about Labour's immigration policies among those voters.[54] That trend continued in 2010, with a 7.5 per cent swing from Labour to the Conservatives among C2 voters, and a 7 per cent swing in the DE category (the figures for AB and C1 were 'only' 2 per cent and 3 per cent).[55]

Even further beneath the surface of national politics, the BNP and UKIP were making strong progress in those local elections in which they stood candidates. As social and cultural issues became more strongly linked to ideas about both access to public services and identity, so insurgent parties on the Right began to prosper. In 2002 the BNP stood only 66 candidates and gained 29,000 or so votes; by 2010 those two numbers were 716 and over 346,500. UKIP grew its vote from only 19,000 in 2002 to 314,000 in 2009 and 226,500 in 2010. The BNP gained 564,000 votes in the 2010 general election, while UKIP were able to secure 920,000.[56] Given Labour's problems with trust, at exactly the same time as the Conservatives continued to be unpopular, the electoral battlefield was becoming more fragmented, as well as becoming increasingly friendly to the populist Right or even the Far Right. Even setting the Nationalist parties in Scotland and Wales to one side, the percentage of the electorate in Great Britain voting for 'others' rose continuously from 0.4 per cent in 1987 to 5.8 per cent in 2005 and 7.6 per cent in 2010.[57] A sense of general unhappiness and discontent was, perhaps, looking for a cause to latch on to.

Margaret Hodge, the Labour MP for Barking who fought a long-running battle against the BNP, commissioned Mattinson to work on these questions in her East London seat after the 2001 election. What Mattinson discovered while talking with focus groups was instructive. In Barking, as elsewhere, housing and immigration were two crucial issues that Labour was not thought to have addressed. As Hodge put it in the *Guardian*:

> Issues in a Labour area like Barking are different from those that appear crucial in middle England. Poor housing has the biggest impact on the lives of the people we spoke to, but it is perceived as having disappeared from the national agenda. Although there was some feeling that schools had got better, the lack of facilities for young people, the lack of open spaces for play, the arrival of a considerable number of asylum seekers and the breakdown of community networks all combined to make voters feel that the quality of their lives was awful and nothing had changed since Labour came to office.[58]

Barking voters still resented the Thatcher government's policy of selling off council housing stock, which had made some residents rich – but on a totally random basis. Other voters described 'the appalling conditions that many Labour voters were living in, and how public housing had become a "Cinderella" issue'.[59] But large-scale immigration gave their resentments another focus.

When the academic Justin Gest visited Barking and Dagenham to ask voters about these issues, the interplay between cultural concerns, the provision of and access to shared public spaces, and long-term issues around communality and trust, sprung crystal clear out of residents' responses. Such views tended to also be coded in more or less racialised terms. As one older voter active in the Tenants and Residents Association told Gest:

> A lot of the new communities don't want to mix in. I think we can learn a lot from each other, but they don't want to learn … Immigration should have been stopped years ago, and now people are thinking the worst: 'They're taking our jobs', and things like that. We don't go out hardly, and I can't get settled [financially]. This house is a rental, and we've been on the Council's [housing waiting] list for three years. We just had so much debt that we had to sell our old house before it got repossessed or fell apart around our ears![60]

Another cause of voters' abstentionism and drift away from formal politics was an undertow of worry about New Labour as 'spin' and not substance. Underneath the surface of New Labour's success, qualitative surveys such as those conducted by Mass Observation revealed a fundamental concern among voters that New Labour was all about 'spin', containing little substance beyond its public relations exercises. This was a concern across class lines, and above and beyond existing loyalties of Left or Right. As one floating voter leaning towards the Liberal Democrats put it in her diary late in 1996: 'I don't believe the promises of either side. I'm fed up of Blair's smile and prefer Major's simplicity.' And then again, in March 1997: 'still no real policies to argue about. All sound bites from Blair while his Left keeps silent.'[61] Gould's focus groups used almost the same words to express unease about Blair as a slick, but perhaps dishonest, front man: 'Tony Blair is all right, but what about the rest of the Party? They don't agree with him; they are biting their tongues, biding their time.' Newspaper mentions of Blair reflected latent concerns about the apparent Prime Minister in waiting. They were more likely to negatively mention his trustworthiness or honesty, and to characterise him as arrogant or smug, than they were Major.[62]

That unease with the New Labour project was to become a burgeoning cynicism during the party's time in office, in part because the hopes evoked by 1997 were impossible to live up to, to some extent because Blair and Brown moved only quite slowly and cautiously towards rebuilding the public realm, and also because some of the causes of inequality and poverty required long-term action. A fourth factor in Labour's slow decline was therefore the public's impatience with the pace of change in public services. From the NHS in Chapter 4 to housing in Chapter 7, this book has made clear that individual parts of the welfare state and public services were improving, and thought to be improving: but the *overall* impression could still be threadbare compared to the amounts of money Brown was pouring in. In December 2003 YouGov found that 69 per cent of voters thought they paid too much tax, and that 79 per cent thought much government spending was wasted. In 2003 the same pollster found that 71 per cent agreed with the view that 'Labour is failing to deliver on the major public services, like the NHS and education', while in 2004 46 per cent thought that public services had got worse under Blair and Brown. Only 22 per cent believed that they had got better.[63] Add to that the corrosive and interlinked effects of working-class abstentionism, Iraq and immigration, and it is to some extent a surprise that Labour remained as popular as it did, for as long as it did.

A unique moment

Not every event worthy of comment requires a series of large-scale explanations. Many possible futures are always in constant flux: the so-called 'great forces' often thought to run through history, replete with 'structural developments' and 'long-term trends', can be overplayed. Many small events can be just as powerful as supposedly huge changes 'beneath the surface'. New Labour's remarkable and singular electoral success between 1994 and (although fraying) right up to the Global Financial Crisis of 2008, in fact require a range of explanations along these less ambitious lines. Some are proximate and easily identified, some are more general and harder to pinpoint, and some can only be felt as a vague impression or mood. But they all matter. Important elements include the Conservatives' perceived mismanagement of the economy in the 1990s, as well as that party's chronic civil war and the idea that the Government of 1979–97 was simply past its sell-by date. Also vital to New Labour's success were Blair's implicit alliance with the Liberal Democrats, Labour's focused and ruthless dominance of political arguments, even providing its own internal opposition, and Blair's own political skill and personal charisma. Once in office, Labour's control of almost every element of the electoral battlefield was entrenched by seeming to provide for *both* a strong economy *and* better public services.

We can reinforce these points by demonstrating Labour's decline as an electoral force after 2007. Each of the trends helping New Labour now ran in the opposite direction. In 2005 the Conservatives found a relatively popular and energetic leader, who seemed to unite that party round his own agenda: by then the Tories had been out of power for a decade, while some of the toxic memories of 1992–97 had faded. New Labour's fellow-feeling with the Liberal Democrats broke down under Kennedy's leadership and given his opposition to the Second Iraq War. Labour lost control of many elements of public discourse – for instance on immigration, housing and some public services. Trust in Blair and his ministers rather drained out of the system. Public scepticism and apathy now chipped away at New Labour's coalition. Trust had ebbed away over the Iraq War. It proved impossible in the end to manage the Blair-Brown duumvirate, with the tensions between the two bursting out into the open. Blair himself was replaced by the more maladroit Brown, unable himself to adapt to the day-to-day business of politicking while still Prime Minister. Then, given Labour's reversion to a more 'normal' political picture affected by the simple costs of governing, the economy experienced its worst crisis since the early 1980s, calling into question the entire Third Way model.

Voters with more conservative social values were long kept within the New Labour tent by strong language and action on crime, and by tough words (sometimes not matched by action) on immigration. But the wider and wider gap between liberals and more authoritarian citizens that was emerging could not be avoided forever, and Blair and Brown's attempts to bridge that gulf became less successful as time went on. For Blair, the main answer to worries about immigration was ID cards: but whether or not that could have worked, they never happened. There was also at the very least a failure to make a coherent case for the scale of change immigration was causing. In his interview for this book, Phil Wilson said 'we didn't have a counter-argument [...] to say that we need these people to work in our industries ... We were never able to get that point over.'[64] In the opening years of the twenty-first century, trust in national governments and parliaments deteriorated everywhere across the EU. In Britain, too, there seems to have been a rapid and sustained fall in loyalty to the established pattern of political life. The numbers of voters stressing the importance of democracy fell perhaps faster there than in any other post-industrial democracy among so-called 'Generation Xers' and 'Millennials' born in the 1970s and 1980s – and therefore coming to political maturity and the vote during New Labour's time in office.[65] The party could never have reached the broad, sunlit uplands briefly visible in 1997. But the suspicion lingered that it might have achieved more than it did.

9

New Labour as history

When the historian Peter Hennessy came to sum up the post-war Labour government led by Clement Attlee, he wrote that Britain by 1951 'was a kinder, gentler and a far, far better place in which to be born, to grow up, to live, love, work and even to die. Such an epitaph cannot be placed with conviction on the plinths of any of the eras to come.'[1] Now there had been another Labour government with a long list of successes on the home front, during which the British people mainly prospered, enjoyed a time of low unemployment, benefited from better public services and saw poverty reduced. It was likely better 'to be born, to grow up, to live, work and even to die' in 2007 than 1997. NHS services got far better as waiting lists collapsed; schools became much more successful, especially where their pupils had suffered from low expectations; crime fell; a new emphasis on supporting children and families helped more and more people live a healthier, happier, more satisfying life; the numbers sleeping on the streets went down; trust in the state's ability to make people's lives better recovered.

The public's faith in their local hospitals and schools picked up, and their fear of crime hitting their own house or street declined. Gradually, as voters began to notice their local services and communities improving, even trust in public life more generally recovered a little from its mid-1990s nadir. Data from Ipsos shows that trust in politicians as a whole peaked in 1999, at 23 per cent. That outstripped any number for trusting politicians they had previously recorded since they started collecting that data in the 1980s. Trust in ministers hit a similar peak in 2008 (though it only reached 25 per cent). By 2023, only 10 per cent of the public trusted ministers, and a mere 9 per cent of the public trusted politicians as a group. The parliamentary expenses scandal of 2009, public sector austerity and cuts and all the unmet promises of Brexit had taken their toll.[2] Better hospitals, schools, children's services and more help making work pay all played a role. It took a long time for the public realm to recover from its travails

214

during the 1980s and 1990s, but New Labour was skilful enough, and successful enough, to effect at least a small recovery in the reputation of politics itself. As Blair put it in one 2004 speech, 'polling evidence on public perception of the services we offer reveals a paradox. While people's own experiences are generally positive and improving, this is not reflected in their perception of services as a whole.'[3] But the public sector's recovery did have a marked effect. It was foreign policy, and most of all the Second Iraq War, that crystallised all voters' doubts about New Labour, while a slow-burning discontent about immigration also built up under the surface.

This is hardly to write off the failings and reverses Blair and Brown suffered – or imposed on themselves. Their continual compromises with the rich and powerful were born out of the experiences of successive defeats in the 1980s and early 1990s, but they were surely not all necessary. The balance of power between the Labour Party, the Conservatives and the press had been completely transformed since 1992. Endless accommodations offered too many hostages to fortune. During the 1997 general election, for instance, Blair wrote a Eurosceptical opinion piece for *The Sun* which promised to 'SEE OFF EURO-DRAGONS' on St George's Day. His gestures towards Euroscepticism would come back to haunt the country later, as Euroscepticism boomed and it became harder and harder to sell the EU's positive benefits.[4] Intellectual uncertainty also plagued the New Labour project. Without many of the fixed points of Labourism or parliamentary social democracy, timid as they could be, the search for the 'new' in New Labour was often frenetic. Blair sometimes appeared rootless, grasping at each passing idea. Robin Cook spent one long car journey in the summer of 2001 'discussing the complexity of Tony's character and the psychological ease with which he picks up political theories, only to drop them when they have outlived their novelty. Whatever happened to the Third Way, which only Anthony Giddens now writes about?'[5]

Just as New Labour's reforming fervour often exposed insecurity, so its policies could fail too. Crime and housing represented particularly missed opportunities. Both were fields where notable successes could easily just be listed. Local policing, cooperation with local councils, drug rehabilitation and probation all deepened and improved in the late 1990s and early 2000s. Housing policy aimed at improving the quality of the social housing stock while reducing homelessness and rough sleeping, and many of those policies worked well too. But if we zoom back from the particular to the general, the constant talk of 'toughness', the endless deployment of 'crackdowns', judgement and prison, detracted from the balance Blair had more carefully struck while Leader of the

Opposition. If we turn to housing, building increased, but only very slowly; the number of new social housing starts crept up. But the quantitative effect overall was not commensurate with need then, let alone the housing shortage to come. House prices surged, and took the dream of home ownership that Blair and Brown promoted out of the reach of many young people. None of that can be counted a success.

Economic policy, which seemed for years to have discovered the secret of sustainable growth, eventually ended up looking threadbare. As Colm Murphy has made clear, 'even if it was the realistic path to take at the time, New Labour's abandonment of the restoration of manufacturing, and its consequent reliance on the City, had repercussions. Without tighter and deeper regulation, its vulnerability to any financial crisis increased. Labour's ... dependency on a successful financial sector spiked its growth model with a particularly strong spirit.'[6] We need to be clear that the debacles of 2007–09 emerged from inside the US banking system and the subprime mortgage sector there, and were made far worse than they need have been by the US administration of the time. The UK was a helpless bystander to much of that. Anatole Kaletsky has argued, perhaps with a touch of exaggeration, that 'had the Bush administration dealt with Lehman in 2008 as the Brown government managed Northern Rock a year earlier – then the global economic catastrophe of 2008–9 would never have occurred'.[7]

But without the vast house price boom, extreme financialisation of the economy, and the poor organisation of monetary policy, the UK would have been better equipped to stand up to the aftershocks of banks' actions. The disaster did emanate from the US, but that is not to say that every country was at the same level of preparedness, or that there had been no room to build up defences before it hit. Economies with a more sober banking system, such as Canada, stood up far better to the storm; those such as Sweden, which had already experienced a banking crisis in the 1990s, emerged more quickly and more strongly than did the UK.[8] Alistair Darling, Chancellor when the crisis broke, later reflected that the Treasury and FSA failed to work well together as the true scale of the problem emerged, and more widely that '"light-touch" regulation came to influence the whole climate in which these institutions operated. If there was money to be made, they did not hold back. There was a general assumption that ... the good times would continue to roll.'[9] New Labour's divide between monetary policy and regulation, which the Bank of England had warned against in 1997, turned out to be one of its key weaknesses.

Many of the hopes that had been raised in 1997 were always unlikely to be fulfilled: the sheer size of Labour's victory raised expectations that were simply impossible to meet, at least quickly or without invidious trade-offs. Cherie Blair remembers that 'Tony was now being seen as the instrument of ... change and there was a huge expectation that, with a change of government, we would have a change of culture: that the country would change practically overnight. It was completely unrealistic.'[10] Blair's own image, as salesman and persuader, hardly helped here, and the mood music turned gradually towards a sense that the public were not being told the full truth. His style of decision-making, often caricatured as 'sofa government' after the sofa in the small room next to the Cabinet Room where he made key decisions, did not help with this gathering sense of tricky impermanence. Blair's style of government sometimes seemed over-personal, casual, quixotic. Even as the economy grew, public services improved and crime fell, many voters simply did not believe in those developments: they were dismissed as 'spin'. To quote Mattinson again:

> Early in 2004 we conducted a series of focus groups in Radlett, Edgware and Sale ... They confirmed the disillusionment with the government. I wrote in my debrief notes, 'The dream of 1997 has been replaced with the nightmare of 2004'. And that 'the feeling of hope and belief has turned to anger and betrayal'. Much of this antipathy was directly squarely at Tony Blair, who was losing support ... Projective exercises revealed that the animal he was most like was a fox, a snake or a cheetah. As a drink he might be cava: 'lots of bubbles but it's fake, not the real thing'.[11]

Then, too, there were the infamous 'TB–GBs': the division of a government that would surely have been stronger had both principals worked more harmoniously together. Brown's conviction that he had agreed to Blair becoming leader only if he stepped aside at some point in the future hung over the internal workings of the Government like a pall. Even on the night of New Labour's electoral triumph in 1997, many in Brown's team were gloomy. One source familiar with the mood remembered: 'they were bad times for Gordon and his senior allies. They weren't celebratory because of what was going on behind the scenes, the battles with Tony.' Long-running feuds over (for instance) Brown's press secretary Charlie Whelan, who claimed a semi-independent briefing role with the media between 1997 and his resignation in 1999, distracted and drained the Government. By early 2005 the Blair–Brown relationship had reached its nadir, with the public revelation in a book by Robert Peston that Brown had told Blair he could never trust him again.[12]

That problem can be exaggerated, for as difficult as relations became, the Prime Minister and Chancellor were still fundamentally close. Macpherson has put it like this: 'the only person who Blair ever treated as a grown-up was Brown. And it kind of worked ... because of the strength of the relationships.'[13] Phil Wilson, close to Blair throughout this period, believes that 'maybe those arguments were knocked out of proportion', because the two men always had shared interests and ideas.[14] Looking back, Blair now thinks that for all the difficulties 'there were ... advantages, in the sense that it allowed you to thrash out the debate in what was sometimes a very tough way, but always a very honest way. ... And Gordon was managing the economy in a way that took [away] a lot of things I didn't have to worry about, because he was worrying about them.'[15] Diamond thinks there were other pluses amid the minuses:

> There were some areas of policy where almost the rivalry between Number 10 and Number 11 made the government more ambitious. I mean one example would be around child care and early years policy which both Blair and Brown got very interested in ... [that] basically led to a position where for the first time in post-war British history ... children and the welfare of younger children and early intervention and importance of reducing disparities in the life chances of children from highly disadvantaged households was almost at the centre of the government's agenda.[16]

Many of the problems that eventually eroded New Labour's power and influence actually ran far deeper. Because New Labour had closed down some of the avenues for *political* choice, the idea of inevitable, predetermined and therefore necessary *economic* choices gained a vice-like grip on the policy imagination. Blair appealed to what Mark Bevir has termed 'inexorable social forces' – globalisation most of all, but also technical progress and the march of individualism.[17] In the words of the writer Richard Power Sayeed, Blair 'viewed the globalization of markets as a historical juggernaut, as inevitable, and his political programme required that both the British government and its citizens – its workers, its consumers – should unquestionably adapt to such an unstoppable force'.[18] Blair's rhetoric spoke of globalisation as an ineluctable, unstoppable force in and of itself. He lodged a claim to understand it as a force of nature, while choosing not to foreground the huge businesses and investors who were in part driving those changes. Economic globalisation became an abstract actor – the only idea that could not be challenged or even analysed.

This was all part of the unfortunate technocratic impression these governments often gave, even if in reality research often followed and did not precede new policies. That held back the idea of political choices and new directions too.

Everything was quantified and intricately measured, understandable as central government came to realise how little it knew and understood between the 1960s and 1990s, but still confining and stifling imagination. New techniques, and more technology, were not always the answer. The project to build the NHS a single computer system was an unnecessary fiasco.[19] Ministers now had an obsession with 'good' and 'better' schools, but they had not always thought about the true quality of what everyday life in those schools might look like or what teachers would do if their set texts and structured resources did not work. New Labour lionised education, but as a means of increasing social and human capital, not always as the truly transformative experience it could be. NICE may have taken some decisions on drug treatment out of their hands, but it did not help them avoid the attendant controversy. The idea of all governance as somehow about *economics*, which rarefied the central but still limited insight of choice about how to use scarce resources under constraints, became in short more important than it might have been: a set of guiding principles, not a tool-box of techniques. For Alan Finlayson, although 'elements of reheated New Liberalism, communitarianism and Christianity are mixed in with the Third Way ... they do not take priority'. Instead, New Labour simply took the world as it was and accepted it: a retreat from the reformism of both the Liberal Party and 'Old' Labour.[20]

Apparently laudable attempts to create a sense of local civic involvement were linked to the way in which New Labour avoided large-scale political rethinking, instead narrowing everything down to management. Schools governed by parents and headteachers, hospital trusts with elected members on their boards, citizens' juries and inclusive tenants' groups were all ways to encourage an active citizenry who would take control into their own hands. But none of them quite caught on. Perhaps this was because they were not really forms of grassroots governance at all, only permitting participants the freedom to manage the settlement central government handed down. This is exactly what Roy Hattersley, hardly a left-wing firebrand, argued in his 1987 book *Choose Freedom*. There Hattersley had made clear that no government could allow such groups to take over most of the decisions voters wanted ministers to make. That would mean the Government insisting on guardrails: national guidelines against discrimination, national standards on preschool provision, allocation rules for tenancies in social housing and so on.[21] So localism would always, necessarily and inevitably, remain an aspiration not a reality – a fact that came as no surprise to 'Old' Labour social democrats and revisionists such as Hattersley.

Voters could then switch off. As we saw in Chapter 8, some of Labour's core vote drifted away during the Blair years – many to not voting at all. The fall in turnout that was so obvious between 1992 and 2005, taking five million people out of the electorate, was most concentrated among white school leavers with no further qualifications.[22] Labour gained 50 per cent of the vote among skilled manual workers in 1997: that had drifted down to 40 per cent by 2005, and then fell to 29 per cent in 2010.[23] Cook noted in 2002 that 'Tony seems incapable of recognising that right now the wing of the [New Labour] coalition that is crumbling is among the core voters, not the aspirational voters.'[24] Futurism, management, technocracy and localism – ladled with charismatic leadership and more spending – could only take New Labour so far.

Stepping back from the minutiae, what Blair actually wanted was to make the whole labour movement, including the trade unions, a looser alliance of progressives – all the better to draw in more voters, but also a recognition that the strength of the state might weaken in this new age of global capital and rapid change. Phil Wilson phrases it like this: 'people are prepared to accept your principles and where the Labour Party is standing. As long as you do it in such a way that you're not ramming it down the[ir] throats that it's an ideology, there's a set of principles where we better off working together.'[25] But that openness, and the desire to build a broad tent, often came on the terms Blair wanted, and could sometimes lapse back into narrower or partisan thinking. Blair's own scepticism about devolution, his government's monitoring of the social markets it created and the control it exercised over schools and hospitals, as well as its attempt to control political life from the central executive of Cabinet Office and Treasury, all pointed in the other direction – towards a closed vision, not a truly pluralistic one. He did not, for example, take the crucial step of accepting the 1998 Jenkins Commission Report on proportional representation, a measure that would truly have made British politics more pluralist, and may also have enabled a 'progressive' majority. The search for a progressive alliance was not very rigorous.

It is even so far too easy, and ridiculously one-dimensional, to write about Blairism as just one more type of neoliberalism, however we define that loaded term. In fact, the picture was far more mixed. It is clear that neoliberalism was one strand within New Labour's DNA, particularly when it came to governing techniques and especially how to deliver change in how the public sector was run. Arms-length management, constant centralising pressure for 'improvement' and endless targets, embodied both in Number 10's Delivery Unit but also in the Treasury's PSAs, undoubtedly did reflect neoliberal thinking.

These concepts were economistic, determinist, one-dimensional. But a deep commitment to social justice ran alongside those elements in Third Way thinking, even if it was to be achieved in new ways. That was obvious in the New Deal for Young People, the Working Families Tax Credit, Sure Start and higher child benefit, though Labour's commitment now was obviously an attack on *poverty*, without any deep commitment to increased overall *equality*. All those families who thrived and held together in part because they were helped by Sure Start, or who lived in areas that were less plagued by crime because of its influence, were hardly being abandoned to the whims of the market, neoliberal or otherwise.

Full employment was also still an aim, though it was to be achieved via increased childcare, training and 'active labour market policies' rather than countercyclical budgeting and spending more to escape from economic slow-downs. Labour rights and protections recovered a little from their low point in the 1990s, though most of the anti-trade union laws from the Thatcher era remained. Solidarity remained important, but was made concrete in better public services and a huge increase of in-work benefits for young families, not comprehensive social insurance. Huge gains still resulted for working people on low incomes. The benefits system worked far better for low-income families than it had in 1996, 1989 or even 1978.[26] The share of national income paid in wages rose in the first years of Blair's government, from its trough of 50 per cent to around 55 per cent, though it did not return to its post-war average of about 70 per cent.[27]

During the 1990s and 2000s Labour's ideas, so often staid and unsurprising, also span off in genuinely new directions. Since its ideas were so multiple, what they ended up producing was extremely diverse, often blended together, complicated or at variance with promises made in Opposition, though that is in the nature of taking and using power. As Blair said to me in 2024: 'Tony Giddens had the Third Way concept ... to combine the public and private sector most effectively. And so that conceptual thinking helped ... with the work that Will Hutton did around stakeholders ... But when you get into government, you realize that the conceptual framework has its limitations, because in the end, it's about the practical application. And that's always the toughest thing.'[28] Diamond remembers 'different views within the prime minister's own team about how much time he should be devoting to, having dialogues with Anthony Giddens ... or whoever it is as you can imagine. So there isn't a lot of I guess fine-grained discussion of the positions of different sort of public intellectuals'.[29]

New Labour still developed some innovative and prescient approaches, which emerged more from political pressure and the experience of actually governing than from theorising. The importance of the family was definitely one novel theme. Better child protection, Every Child Matters, far stronger Early Years provision and parental leave are all examples of this trend. This government's policies also saw women benefit more than others, and their interests were certainly served by New Labour in office, sometimes through the example of better conditions in the public sector. Equal pay, childcare and better welfare services were all to the fore. This was hardly a radical embrace of the politics of gender inequality overall, and was limited to helping 'women as women', sometimes in a stereotypical manner: but it was undoubtedly a large-scale move forward from where Old Labour had stood. Working mothers, and women working part time, gained a great deal, with the latter closing the pay gap on men: women without children working full time did less well.[30]

New Labour was also more 'European' than its forebears, taking its cue for instance from the West German Social Democrats' updated Basic Programme in 1989 or Norwegian Labour's 'Freedom Debate' between 1986 and 1988. In Diamond's words, 'there was ... a lot of learning from Europe. So the welfare reform programmes that have been done in the Nordic countries ... the Dutch government's reform of welfare and Social Security and some of the reforms in health also had some feedback into the UK.'[31] The Human Rights Act incorporating the ECHR is another example of this 'Europeanisation'. So are adopting the Social Chapter of the Maastricht Treasury; setting up an independent central bank, which had been running monetary policy in Germany (if on rather different lines) since the 1950s; and asking a Low Pay Commission to set the National Minimum Wage. These European-style elements in New Labour's programme also possessed the ability to snowball, and to become more and more important as time went by. Along with devolution, these elements of New Labour statecraft were in practice dynamic, gathering pace as they went. The Human Rights Act has built up key precedents through a series of landmark rulings, the Bank of England's authority grew with practice and successive governments have increased the level at which the NMW is set.

For New Labour's more sympathetic historians, such as Steven Fielding, its 'approach to poverty and equality remains comparable with that of both its predecessors and its counterparts in contemporary European social democracy'.[32] New Labour redistributed income fiercely: their successors chose to go down a quite different path. As we saw in Chapter 3, it was the poorest who gained most from New Labour's policies, and with every move up the income ladder taxpayers contributed more. After 2010, the picture changed entirely. The poorest 10 per cent of the population did worst out of the Coalition and Conservative years (though the richest 10 per cent were the next worst hit), and the second, third and fourth deciles were also made worse off in real terms than they would have been under the rules in place when Labour left office.[33] Under Blair and Brown the abolition of MIRAS helped to pay for tax credits which, complex and frustrating as they were, boosted the income of the working poor; there were massive increases in health and education spending; social housing was re-equipped and rebuilt; health inequalities were named, researched and targeted.

It is vitally important, given all these policies and initiatives, not to read the whole history of modern British governance as 'neoliberal', or to see it as all of one piece. There were key differences between New Labour and the Coalition and Conservative governments that followed it in office: between the massive capital spending cuts implemented by George Osborne in the early 2010s and New Labour's record of investment; between networked governance and every part of the public sector being left to fend for itself; between an organised NHS armed with a ten-year plan and a chaotic mess of a health 'system'; between schools acting as inspiration and community hubs and just instilling knowledge and discipline; between £3,000 and £9,250 university fees; between an ordered higher education system and a zero-sum game setting universities against each other. A stronger regional policy, the work of the Social Exclusion Unit, increased community policing, Crime and Disorder Reduction Partnerships, the New Deal for Communities and Best Value not lowest cost rules for councils were all adaptations of ways Labour had previously thought about the country and then governed – and which left behind their own legacy. Take the Braunstone Estate in Leicester, where a plaque on the Health and Social Care Centre recalls the fact it was built under the New Deal for Communities which invested £49.5 million in the estate. That sign hangs on a building which is not just bricks and mortar, but the home of b-inspired, a community business which is a real, living legacy of that New Deal.[34] New Labour's stronger state was a deep intervention in the country's collective life, and that was not all about economic liberalisation or the market. To pretend otherwise is to lose all specificity and potential for analysis.

The Labour Party's own history is nowhere near as straightforward as its internal warriors would have us believe. As Murphy has recently reminded us, there have always been many meanings of 'modernisation', and they have never been limited to the Labour Right. Wilson had championed the 'modernisation' of Labour's internal structures and its electoral appeal from the 1950s onwards. Ken Livingstone spoke of a more modern and popular Labour Party in the 1980s. *Marxism Today* had always made a similar case. The radical economist Stuart Holland and the feminist writer Beatrix Campbell similarly tried to rethink socialist aims in the new conditions of the late twentieth century, albeit in very different ways.[35] It had been Callaghan, the very essence of so-called 'Old' Labour, who had talked first about school standards with his 'Great Debate' of 1976; not only that, but as one of Labour's most prominent social conservatives he had made clear the need for public services, particularly local authorities, to be more responsible to citizens – especially when it came to the management of public housing. It was Callaghan, not Blair, who first consulted with the Liberals and became a convert to Scottish and Welsh devolution.[36] It was not Blair, but Kinnock from the Soft Left, who first reduced the importance of nationalisation as one of the party's objectives, and who first defined state intervention in the economy as a means, not an end.[37] New Labour absorbed and amplified all these meanings of the 'modern', not just the globalised market.

Blair was always at pains to include most wings of the Labour Party, which again militates against a simplistic reading of his Premiership. A government including left-leaning MPs such as Cook, Michael Meacher and Clare Short as well as (for a time) Chris Mullin and Tony Banks does not lack for at least some left-wing support. Diamond remembers a government that was more representative of Labour in the country and Parliament than sometimes imagined: 'sometimes we underappreciate that New Labour government was a coalition of politicians many of whom had views that were somewhat different to Tony's but ... also had their own political supporters ... I think we are at risk of the Blair-Brown dynamic obscuring the fact that there were also some other extremely important and influential politicians who exerted a lot of influence over policy.'[38] Indeed, Mullin noted in his diary during June 1994 that Blair wanted his government to 'be broad-based. "I am not bothered about left or right as much as competence".' Later that same year, Blair told Mullin that he wanted 'sensible radicals' in his government, as opposed to those Mullin termed 'impossibilists' and those Blair thought of as 'conservatives', 'whose idea of being radical is to defend the *status quo*'.[39]

This ecumenicalism arose in part because Blair intended to run the Government from the centre, surrounded by an able and committed team of loyalists and equipped with new machinery such as the Performance and Innovation Unit. His belief in ability and hard work, rather than outlook, were obvious if oft-neglected parts of his technocratic outlook. When Blair left office in 2007, only three ministers were seen as particularly 'Blairite': John Reid at the Home Office, John Hutton at Work and Pensions and Adonis, by that time a junior minister at Education.[40] Blair continues to stress this point today, emphasising the value of a strong team (like his) around any leader. As he told me: 'you have to go and search ... and get the best people. It's all about the people in the end. I think virtually anyone who's ever run anything will tell you that in the end it's about the quality of the people ... I was very lucky to have that group.'[41] One chapter in Blair's recent book *On Leadership* ended with the clear instruction: 'Make the centre STRONG!'[42]

There are many ways of understanding this broad church politics. For the Labour MP John Cruddas, who retired from the Commons in 2024, New Labour involved a 'blending of competing approaches to justice ... a merger of traditions ... Blair rehabilitated early ethical concerns along with the spirit of New Liberalism to anticipate the renewal of a nation'. Through an 'embrace of ethics and morality', of a renewed New Liberalism and a utilitarian approach to the public good, Blair rode the wave of turn-of-the-century prosperity.[43] Each of those elements in his thinking would of course become less cohesive and convincing as time went on, as the Government's morality was challenged, as it became less liberal, and then when the economic boom faded. But the last strand in the Blair government's DNA was perhaps the oldest element of all in socialist politics: Christian Socialism. In the 1993 Christian Socialist pamphlet *Reclaiming the Ground*, Blair argued explicitly that he wanted 'to reunite the ethical code of Christianity with the basic values of democratic socialism': that, in fact, 'the Christian message is that self is best realised through communion with others. The act of Holy Communion is symbolic of this message.'[44] In one speech to the Christian Socialist movement delivered in 2001, Blair used the word 'community' or 'communities' more than twenty times. The influence of Catholic social teaching, the decline of which was soon to be bemoaned by theologians interested in Blue Labour such as John Milbank, was unmistakable – stressing as it does the role of the collective social good, community and solidarity.[45]

Many Third Way thinkers thought differently: Giddens, for instance, focused much more closely on economic and technological change in the creation of a newly self-reliant, self-starting and assertive type of individual citizen. 'A politics of self-actualisation', he called it, a politics which sought 'to further the possibilities of a fulfilling and satisfying life for all'.[46] Blair's ideas were more small-c conservative than Giddens, though the two men's thinking overlapped when it came to the idea of reinventing the state to help people throughout their lives, rather than just bail them out in crises. Communitarianism, in its more conservative guises such as those adopted by Blair, posited a single moral vision and set of common values and interests, rather than the real world's conflicts, compromises and contested half-measures. An emphasis on 'social cohesion' meant that everyone should 'cohere' – but to what? Blair and his adherents believed in a society of strong identity and fellow-feeling, the emotional bonds of which were inherently likely to produce good outcomes. But their authoritarianism, their attempts to *enforce* and *police* those feelings, perhaps inevitably did not feel communitarian at all.

Blair often quoted the communitarian thinker John Macmurray, but in many ways he was not truly in alignment with Macmurray's views. For as Macmurray wrote, 'the personal life ... demands a relationship with one another in which we can be our whole selves and have complete freedom to express everything that makes us what we are'. This was a moral and not contractual communitarianism, in which giving and sharing were natural, positive and liberating *in their own right*, not because they gave rise to desirable social outcomes.[47] The concepts of control and direction are present in Macmurray's work as the idea of justice, which sets external limits on action and makes everyone subject to rules decided by the community. But for Macmurray, those rules were rather undesirable, a necessary negative as it were, designed to ensure freedom through constraint but to be avoided if possible. In his terms, what Blair was really talking about all the time was *society*, which existed to organise common purpose and imposed many of those rules, not a *community*, which exists in 'the sharing of a common life' which is 'our nature' and helps people to feel and act truly as themselves.[48] Blair's communitarianism was far more strict, judgemental and conservative than this, and therefore in some ways not communitarian at all. Nor was the Blairites' insistence on the individualism of the market particularly communitarian when weighed against Macmurray's concept of the truly engaging humanity of sharing or Giddens' self-reliant citizen.[49]

These rarefied concepts and debates became more and more important when it came to policy, because arguments about what 'the nation' was and is became more and more acute. Ideas of community and nation were of course challenged by large-scale immigration, and as with Britain's lack of preparation for any financial crash many New Labour partisans later came to believe that their handling of this issue represented a serious blunder. Not that there wasn't significant progress on this front either. The Blair governments succeed in defusing much of the refugee 'crisis' that had risen up the political agenda in the 1990s, as the UK's systems were adapted to cope with and run down the backlog that had developed under Major. The PSA target on asylum contained in the 2002 Spending Review, that 75 per cent of claims be processed within two months, was met, though at some cost to the quality of those decisions: soon a fifth of appeals were upheld. The asylum crisis that had been building since the late 1980s, with the numbers applying rising eightfold and a backlog of 52,000 cases building up, was halted and reversed.[50]

That did not stop immigration as a whole climbing further up the agenda, nor stop the public worrying about it. One of the papers circulated in the build-up to the Government's international Progressive Governance Conference and Summit in 2003 was clear about this problem: 'growing fears of mass migration, asylum seekers, and illegal immigration have accompanied increased economic insecurity aggravating the potential for xenophobia and racism … [but] at the same time it is clear that Europe needs both highly skilled and unskilled migrants to fill labour shortfalls'.[51] New Labour built an economic model that relied on migration, but then struggled with the implications of that dependence. Mattinson witnessed it all in her focus groups: 'we described it as a "vortex" issue, one which sucked all other issues in – the NHS is struggling? That's because it's crowded with immigrants. Can't get a job? That's because immigrants have undercut your rates.'[52]

Such feelings were definitely widespread, but immigration was rising during a period of rapid economic growth, not stagnation, and numbers were nowhere near what they would reach after Brexit. 600,000 people coming into the country (in 2010) is hardly the same as 1.2 million (in the calendar year 2023).[53] This period may indeed have set the scene for a populist reaction against rapid social change. Many people across the Labour Party from most intellectual traditions, including the influential centre-left group Labour Together, believe that Blair was nearly as guilty as Corbyn when it came to 'hollowing out' the party and breaking its connection with past Labour voters.[54] But the situation only became truly poisonous in the decade after Blair and Brown left Downing Street. In 2010 Labour's vote collapsed to a mere 29 per cent among skilled manual voters, but they were still only eight points behind the Conservatives: by 2019 their vote share among that part of the electorate had not moved much at 32 per cent, but they were 15 points behind. Similarly, among voters in social classes D and E (semi-skilled and unskilled workers) Labour had 40 per cent and a lead of nine points over the Conservatives in 2010; they could only win 39 per cent, and were two points behind, by 2019. The working-class movement away from Labour was most marked in the years 2015–19: that seems not to have abated much in 2024, in part because of the rise of Reform UK.[55] Blair had a point when he told Amol Rajan in a 2024 interview that 'I am very happy to take full responsibility for the more than ten years I was British Prime Minister, and for the decisions I took. What I won't do is take responsibility for the time when I wasn't Prime Minister.'[56] Although Blair's governments may have helped create some of the *conditions* for populist reaction, they did not make it actually *happen*. That honour belongs to others. Far larger numbers of migrants were still to come, and the public reaction was to become even more heated.

A great deal that Blair built or tried to preserve was torn down in the 2010s and 2020s. But one cause of that political recession may have been a failure of language, and of confidence, which turn-of-the-century's Cool Britannia could not mask for long. As late as the summer of 2000 one minister told the journalist Andrew Rawnsley that 'every day is a panic. We're so neurotic.' Another adviser said 'Wilson said he wanted to make Labour the natural party of government. He failed. We have failed.'[57] New Labour declined to talk about many of its achievements, for fear of worrying Middle England, and much of the redistribution being conducted was hidden from view. The party remained in terror of and in thrall to powerful newspaper proprietors and the 'feral media' Blair only really challenged right at the end of his time in office. Labour Party members, according to Cook, 'never hear Tony talking to them in terms of how we have dramatically reduced child poverty, and greatly widened job opportunities'. That fundamentally undermined his support on Britain's Left.[58] Constantly talking about benefit fraud meant that the public increasingly agreed that 'large numbers falsely claim benefits', even while the percentage of fraud and error in the welfare system fell. In the journalist Lewis Goodall's words, the government's reticence 'allowed ... internal opponents to cast it as a dull technocrats and themselves as the true inheritors of the party's radical flame'.[59]

Labour's radical critics are still in danger of what the political scientist Andrew Hindmoor calls 'left miserablism', focusing only on the gap between the high hopes of campaigning and the mundane realities of governing. This is not just or even really about defending or attacking New Labour, which at best amounts to a tedious back-and-forth depending on observers' prior views and perspective and can reduce any government to the Good or Bad of day-to-day newspaper commentary. It is about seeing the later 1990s and early 2000s in the round, and the Blair governments in context, just as we would any other past political movement or government. That is new and important work. As Hindmoor says, 'New Labour's legacy ... has been reduced to its foreign policy failures and the 2007/8 financial crisis.'[60]

That is an impoverished way of understanding these years. In reality, New Labour in power had an analysis of the world around them, a plan and a core team dedicated to carrying it out, despite its inevitable flaws and contradictions. In Blair's second and third terms, Sam Freedman has judged that 'Number 10 got as close to being a functional centre of government as we have seen before or since'.[61] One might approve or not approve of the Blair group's objectives: but at least they *had* a strategy. As Blair told me: 'you've got to keep a strategic clarity and momentum, and if you do that, I think everything else in the end can be relegated beneath that, whereas if you don't have that then all of these things, these problems, whether it's scandals, crises, they dominate and they define'.[62] The same could not be said for the periods of Conservative rule between 1993 and 1997 or 2015 and 2024, both filled with civil war over Europe and distinguished by neither long-term planning or leadership. Without mythologising the Blair era too much, or lapsing into nostalgia, New Labour's record bears more than comparison with what came before and after its time in power.[63]

New Labour has often been lambasted for implementing only piecemeal reforms, which were easily reversed after they left office. After 2010 RDAs became Local Enterprise Partnerships, which were later abolished; Sure Start faded; local government initiatives on homelessness and crime were swept away once funding was cut while police numbers dwindled. But major legacies were *not* destroyed, sometimes to the Conservatives' frustration. There has been no return to the mass unemployment of the 1980s, in part because of the massive Keynesian intervention mounted in 2007–10. The Minimum Wage remains, and has only become more generous. Osborne's attempts to cut tax credits during 2015 were a failure. New and remodelled schools and hospitals still stand. Maternity and paternity leave and pay remain important. The share of young people going to university continued to rise until recently. The Human Rights Act is still in force and the UK is still subject to the jurisdiction of the European Court of Human Rights, despite Conservatives' attempts to write a 'British' Bill of Rights. Right-wing Conservative MPs such as Miriam Cates (who lost her seat in 2024) in fact endlessly bemoan Blair's influence. Cates wrote in January 2024 that 'Tony Blair is still ruining Britain' – over sixteen years after he left office.[64]

The UK government's recent record has been far less impressive than New Labour's. No one who has led the country since has been able to deliver on the voters' key priorities. Nor have they been able to fuse together the country's belief in hard work, its constant demand for better public services and its increasing social liberalism. The aftershocks of the Great Financial Crisis, and the blows inflicted in quick succession by Brexit, Covid and then Russia's war in Ukraine, of course make the comparison rather unfair. But the numbers are still very stark. Blair's early years saw the asylum backlog mainly cleared; by 2024, that system was in disarray. Child poverty declined under Labour; once they were gone, children's relative poverty rose once more. By 2022/23, half of all Labour's progress on that measure was wiped out.[65] Spending on disability benefits, cuts to which caused the Starmer government so much trouble in 2025, tumbled while Blair was in office. But they began to increase again sharply after the shock of the Covid pandemic.[66] While NHS waiting lists fell between 1997 and 2007, now they rose and then surged, in part because of the disastrous 'reforms' launched by Andrew Lansley in 2012.[67] Universities boomed under Blair and Brown; by 2025 they were teetering on the edge of a severe financial crisis.[68] Number 10 helped to tackle the crisis of rough sleeping that the 1980s and early 1990s had created. But that progress too was soon squandered.[69]

New Labour could achieve all that exactly because it appealed to so many different types of voter. It was a collage, a mosaic, or in the jargon an 'assemblage', that covered almost all the British people's many outlooks.[70] Although it sounded dubious at the time, this was also the meaning of Blair's assertion that New Labour was 'the political wing of the British people'. His policies helped you find work, but insisted you looked for it; gave public sector workers such as teachers more pay and respect, but asked them to implement the Government's vision; expanded surveillance, but brought in a Data Protection Commissioner; used prison more, but also stressed rehabilitation. Blair's views blended elements of socially conservative communitarianism, liberal individualism, Christian Socialism, Catholic Social Teaching, social democracy, the outlook and ethos of the SDP, Labour revisionism, the women's movement, Europeanisation and Marxist cultural thought from the 1980s and 1990s. And those were just the organising concepts. Beneath those overarching ideas crowded more specific theories: neo-Keynesianism; networked governance; New Public Management; regional economic clusters based around universities and knowledge industries; the School Effectiveness Movement; social capital as investment; the New Left Realism developing within criminology; and so on. If we see New Labour from these multiple angles, rather than in one simple spotlight, Murphy is surely right when he asserts that 'any characterisation of the Labour Party as primarily "neoliberal" by the 1990s and 2000s becomes unsustainable'.[71]

It is those Janus faces of New Labour, not any individual guise it wore, that will reward our attention and repay our study. In part because of that complexity, this book has been only a reconnaissance, not a sustained exploration. It has missed out, in particular, on a Four Nations approach to contemporary British history: the way in which England, Scotland, Wales and Northern Ireland were moving apart or together will be another line of enquiry that will no doubt bear much fruit. But there is a pressing need for practitioners and experts to analyse and understand the good, the bad and perhaps even the ugly in New Labour's ideologies and practices. New Labour personnel are again present in government at all levels, from Liz Lloyd as a Minister in the Lords to Michael Barber as an adviser on Starmer's five 'national missions'. But a consistent and not a personal, individual or impressionistic look at these problems is required. At a time when Starmer has been actively taking advice from Blair, a balanced but also thorough and consistent assessment of the Blair years is urgent, and will remain so for some years.[72] That work should be undertaken with all the precision, consistency and speed we can muster, and it should start now.

List of figures

List of figures

List of tables

Bibliography

A complete bibliography is available at https://www.manchesterhive.com/nlnb-bibliography.

Acknowledgements

This book is the work of many hands, because it simply could not have been written without the vital contributions of friends, colleagues, collaborators and interviewees. I am as ever enormously grateful to all of them. Although a simple mention in this last section of *New Labour, New Britain?* does absolutely no justice to their huge generosity, skill and knowledge, it is right that their part in making this book should be recorded formally.

Academic colleagues across the sector have offered good company, sharp comment and some key facts and readings I had missed. I am indebted to the assistance of Priya Atwal, Laura Beers, Joanne Begiato, Lawrence Black, Lise Butler, Richard Carr, Michelle Clement, Jim Cooper, Tom Crook, Robert Evans, Steve Fielding, Eunice Goes, Ben Griffin, Ben Jackson, Alysa Levene, Peter Mandler, Rohan McWilliam, David Nash, Helen Parr, Christiana Payne, Andrew Roe-Crines, Tom Robb, Laura Sandy, Rob Saunders, Richard Sheldon, Peter Sloman, Andrew Spicer, Sarah Spooner, John Stewart, Florence Sutcliffe-Braithwaite, Simon Szreter and Richard Toye.

Many others have helped deepen and widen my understanding of New Labour, and indeed British politics as a whole: thanks must also go to Will Barber-Taylor, George Dibb, Ben Dubow, Ceci Flinn, Amir Girnary, Dan Girnary, Robert Massey, Daniel Sleat, Emily Stacey, Iselin Theien and Nathan Yeowell. Lyndsay Grant helped build my understanding of policy in general and the education field in particular, and helped reshape the text at a crucial late stage.

My colleagues on the Arts and Humanities Research Council-funded project 'In All Our Footsteps: Tracking, Mapping and Experiencing Rights of Way in Post-War Britain' were very understanding as I constantly talked about New Labour. Tom Breen, Abbi Flint and my Co-Investigator, Clare Hickman, went above and beyond while I tried (and often failed) to balance two or three

Acknowledgements

projects at once. Fellow members of the similarly AHRC-backed programme 'Spaces of HOPE: The Hidden History of Community-Led Planning in the UK' were also a great help. That team were and are more than impressive, and I very much enjoyed working with Sue Brownill, Geraint Ellis, Matthew Groves, Debbie Humphry, Andy Inch, Michael Howcroft, Loraine Leeson, Martha Mingay, Glyn Robbins, Francesca Sartorio and Jason Slade.

At Manchester University Press, Emma Brennan, Tom Dark, Jonathan de Peyer, Alun Richards and Kim Walker have all been exemplary in the care and attention they have paid the book. As Covid, lockdowns and upheavals in higher education threatened its progress, they stood by the project. I am immensely grateful for that.

Last of all, the book was made immeasurably better by five interviewees who added their own insights: Sir Tony Blair, Stefan Czerniawksi, John Denham, Patrick Diamond and Phil Wilson. Robin Curtis and Carol Brown helped greatly with the preparation of University Ethics forms for those interviews. All errors and inaccuracies, of course, remain my own.

Notes

Chapter 1

1 'Dawn Comes Up Like Thunder', *New Statesman*, May 1997 special edition, p. 3.
2 J. Walsh, 'Power and Glory', *Time*, 12 May 1997, p. 22.
3 Mass Observation Project 1981–1997 Online (hereafter AMD Digital), Module 2, B1665's response to 1996 Autumn/Winter directive part 3 & 1997 Spring directive part 2, response reference SxMOA2/1/49/3/1/24, 26 August 1997, www.massobservation-project.amdigital.co.uk/, accessed 9 April 2021.
4 D. Cowling, 'A Landslide Without Illusions', *New Statesman*, May 1997 special edition, p. 12.
5 K. Jefferys, *Finest and Darkest Hours: The Decisive Events in British Politics from Churchill to Blair* (Atlantic Books, 2003), p. 303.
6 R. McKibbin, 'Homage to Wilson and Callaghan', *London Review of Books* 13, 20 (1991), pp. 3–5.
7 K. Pike, *Getting Over New Labour: The Party After Blair and Brown* (Agenda, 2024), p. 115.
8 D. Harvey, *A Brief History of Neoliberalism* (Oxford University Press, 2007), p. 2.
9 M.B. Steger and R.K. Roy, *Neoliberalism: A Very Short Introduction* (Oxford University Press, 2010), pp. 11–15.
10 C. Hay, *The Political Economy of New Labour: Labouring Under False Pretences?* (Manchester University Press, 1999), pp. 126–7.
11 R. Heffernan, *New Labour and Thatcherism: Political Change in Britain* (Palgrave Macmillan, 2000), p. 73.
12 F. Faucher-King and P. Le Galès. *The New Labour Experiment: Change and Reform under Blair and Brown* (Stanford University Press, 2010), pp. 7, 59; see A. Hindmoor, *Haywire: A Political History of Britain Since 2000* (Allen Lane, 2024), pp. 176–8.
13 A. Weiss, 'Management Consultancy and the British State, *c.*1960–*c.*2010', PhD thesis, Birkbeck, University of London, 2017, pp. 247–50, 259, table 12 and figure 19, pp. 261–2, 269–70, 278–90 and table 14, p. 283.
14 A. King and I. Crewe, *The Blunders of Our Governments* (OneWorld, 2014), pp. 204–14.
15 S. Jenkins, *Thatcher and Sons: A Revolution in Three Acts* (Penguin, 2007), p. 224.
16 S. Hall, 'New Labour's Double-Shuffle', *Review of Education, Pedagogy, and Cultural Studies* 27, 4 (2005), pp. 320–1.
17 N. Cohen, *Pretty Straight Guys* (Faber, 2004), pp. 7, 18.

Notes

18 S. Fielding, *The Labour Party: Continuity and Change in the Making of 'New' Labour* (Palgrave, 2003), p. 101.

19 N. Cohen, *What's Left?: How the Left Lost its Way* (Fourth Estate, 2007), p. 201.

20 A. Blick, *People Who Live in the Dark: The History of the Special Adviser in British Politics* (Politico's, 2004), pp. 284–9; N. Jones, *Soundbites and Spin Doctors: How Politicians Manipulate the Media – and Vice Versa* (Indigo, 1996), pp. 161–76.

21 S. Whale, 'Living in the Dark: The Truth About Special Advisers', *Politics Home: The House*, 2 June 2020, www.politicshome.com/thehouse/article/living-in-the-dark-the-tr uth-about-special-advisers, accessed 10 October 2024. See A. Finlayson, *Making Sense of New Labour* (Lawrence and Wishart, 2003), e.g. p. 15.

22 L. Minkin, *The Blair Supremacy: A Study in the Politics of Labour's Party Management* (Manchester University Press, 2014), pp. 148–50, 333–5.

23 Cohen, *Pretty Straight Guys*, p. 47.

24 D. Kogan, *Protest and Power: The Battle for the Labour Party* (Bloomsbury, 2019), p. 105; T. Bower, *Broken Vows: Tony Blair, The Tragedy of Power* (Faber, 2016), pp. 52–61.

25 A. Rawnsley, *The End of the Party: The Rise and Fall of New Labour* (Viking, 2010), pp. 357–61, 126.

26 Bower, *Broken Vows*, pp. 45–6.

27 C. Mullin, *A View from the Foothills: The Diaries of Chris Mullin* (Profile, 2009), diary entry for 1 October 2004, p. 5000.

28 L. Harding, 'How Tony Blair Advised Former Kazakh Ruler after 2011 Uprising', *Guardian*, 6 January 2022; 'Sir Tony Blair's Institute Continued to Receive Saudi Arabian Money after Murder of Jamal Khashoggi', *Sky News*, 12 August 2023, https://news. sky.com/story/sir-tony-blairs-institute-continued-to-receive-saudi-arabian-money-after- murder-of-jamal-khashoggi-12939029, accessed 7 October 2024.

29 D. Edgerton, *The Rise and Fall of the British Nation: A Twentieth-Century History* (Penguin, 2018), p. 519.

30 L. Abse, *The Man Behind the Smile: Tony Blair and the Politics of Perversion* (Robson Books, 1996), pp. 56, 57, 59, 68, 82–3.

31 M.E. Smith, *Renegade: The Lives and Tales of M.E. Smith* (Viking, 2008), pp. 232–3.

32 C. Clarke, *Warring Fictions: Left Populism and its Defining Myths* (Policy Network, 2019), pp. 47–8.

33 Kogan, *Protest and Power*, p. 168.

34 T. Bale, *Five Year Mission: The Labour Party Under Ed Miliband* (Oxford University Press, 2015), pp. 74–6; I. Watson, *Five Million Conversations: How Labour Lost an Election and Rediscovered Its Roots* (Luath Press, 2015), p. 60; P. Wintour, 'Ed Miliband Makes High-Risk Speech to Labour Conference', *Guardian*, 27 September 2011.

35 L. Byrne, *The Inequality of Wealth: Why It Matters and How to Fix It* (Bloomsbury, 2024), p. 189.

36 A. Nunns, *The Candidate: Jeremy Corbyn's Improbable Path to Power* (OR Books, 2016), p. 122.

37 T. Heppell and T. McMeeking, 'The Election and Re-election of Jeremy Corbyn as Leader of the Labour Party', in A.S. Roe-Crines (ed.), *Corbynism in Perspective* (Agenda, 2021), p. 28.

38 G. Radice, *Southern Discomfort* (Fabian Society, 1992), pp. 5, 10.

39 'Blair's October Revolution', *Economist*, 8 October 1994, p. 15.

40 BBC Radio 4, 'The Reunion: The Blair Government's First 100 Days', 18 August 2024, www.bbc.co.uk/programmes/m00223nc, accessed 27 September 2024.

41 H. Harman, *A Woman's Work* (Allen Lane, 2017), p. 171.

Notes

42 G. Radice and S. Pollard, *Any Southern Comfort?* (Fabian Society, 1994), p. 11.

43 D. Mattinson, *Talking to a Brick Wall: How New Labour Stopped Listening to the Voter and Why We Need a New Politics* (Biteback, 2010), p. 38.

44 C. Blair, *Speaking for Myself: The Autobiography* (Little, Brown, 2008), p. 219.

45 A. Crosland, *The Future of Socialism* (Cape, 1956), p. 216.

46 The National Archives, Kew, London (hereafter TNA) PREM 49/3052, Diamond to Blair, 'The Third Way Progressive Agenda: next steps for new challenges', 20 December 2002.

47 A. Giddens, *Beyond Left and Right: The Future of Radical Politics* (Polity, 1994), pp. 152–5; Giddens, *The Third Way: The Renewal of Social Democracy* (Polity, 1998), pp. 102–4, 116–22.

48 A. Wallace, *Remaking Community? New Labour and the Governance of Poor Neighbourhoods* (Routledge, 2010), p. 21.

49 Author interview, John Denham, 22 July 2024.

50 Author interview, Sir Tony Blair, 16 July 2024.

51 Author interview, Stefan Czerniawski, 9 July 2024.

52 Author interview, Sir Tony Blair, 16 July 2024.

53 Finlayson, *Making Sense*, p. 119.

54 TNA PREM 49/3564, Straw to Blair, 'Free movement of workers/access to benefits', 10 February 2004.

55 S. Berg, 'Blair was Urged Not to Let in New EU Workers Too Quickly, Files Reveal', *BBC News Online*, 31 December 2024, www.bbc.co.uk/news/articles/cz7q5j24qzjo, accessed 31 January 2025.

Chapter 2

1 P.G. Cerny and M. Evans, 'Globalisation and Public Policy under New Labour', *Policy Studies* 25, 1 (2004), pp. 55–8; J. Cronin, *New Labour's Pasts: The Labour Party and its Discontents* (Routledge, 2016), pp. 426–7; Fielding, *Labour Party*, pp. 150–1.

2 Cm. 4176, *Our Competitive Future* (DTI, 1998), p. 9.

3 D.T. Dye, 'New Labour, New Narrative? Political Strategy and the Discourse of Globalisation', *British Journal of Politics and International Relations* 17, 3 (2015), pp. 531, 541–2.

4 A. Hindmoor, *What's Left Now?: The History and Future of Social Democracy* (Oxford University Press, 2018), p. 26.

5 Jenkins, *Thatcher and Sons*, pp. 253, 255.

6 T. Blair, 'The Economic Framework for New Labour', in F. Capie and G.E. Wood (eds), *Policy Makers on Policy* (Routledge, 2nd edn., 2020), pp. 161, 162–3, 164.

7 R. Toye, '"The Smallest Party in History"? New Labour in Historical Perspective', *Labour History Review* 69, 1 (2004), pp. 89–90.

8 E. Balls, *Speaking Out: Lessons in Life and Politics* (Arrow, 2017), p. 110.

9 C. Hay, 'New Labour and "Third Way" Political Economy: Paving the European Road to Washington?', in M. Bevir and F. Trentmann (eds), *Critiques of Capital in Modern Britain and America: Transatlantic Exchanges, 1800 to the Present Day* (Palgrave, 2002), p. 207.

10 R. Carr, *March of the Moderates: Bill Clinton, Tony Blair and the Rebirth of Progressive Politics* (I.B. Tauris, 2019), pp. 136–7.

11 A. Gamble and G. Kelly, 'Stakeholder Capitalism and One Nation Socialism', *Renewal* 4, 1 (1996), pp. 23–32.

Notes

12 W. Hutton, *The State We're In* (Vintage, 1996), pp. 255–6, 262–5.

13 C. Murphy, *Futures of Socialism: 'Modernisation', the Labour Party and the British Left 1973–1997* (Cambridge University Press, 2023), p. 114.

14 G. Davies, 'Tony Blair Puts Meat on the Stakeholder Bones', *Independent*, 15 January 1996.

15 P. Norris, 'New Labour and the Rejection of Stakeholder Capitalism', in G.R. Taylor (ed.), *The Impact of New Labour* (Macmillan, 1999), pp. 28–31; see N. Thompson, *Left in the Wilderness: The Political Economy of British Democratic Socialism since 1979* (Cambridge University Press, 2013), pp. 237–44.

16 D. Cobham, C. Adam and K. Mayhew, 'The Economic Record of the 1997–2010 Labour Government: An Assessment', *Oxford Review of Economic Policy* 29, 1 (2013), pp. 7, 2.

17 D. Garcia-Macia and J. Korosteleva, 'Tracing Productivity Growth Channels in the UK', *Research Policy* 54, 1 (2025), tables 8–9, p. 8.

18 D. Corry, A. Valero and J. Van Reenen, 'UK Economic Performance Since 1997: Growth, Productivity and Jobs', *London School of Economics Centre for Economic Performance Special Paper* 24 (December 2011), table 2, p. 13 and figure 7, p. 17. On catch-up and convergence see M. Abramovitz, 'Catching Up, Forging Ahead, and Falling Behind', *Journal of Economic History* 46, 2 (1986), pp. 385–406.

19 G. Brown, *My Life, Our Times* (Bodley Head, 2017), p. 131.

20 J. Davis and J. Rentoul, *Heroes or Villains? The Blair Government Reconsidered* (Oxford University Press, 2019), pp. 175–6.

21 Faucher-King and Le Galès, *New Labour Experiment*, p. 17; M. Moran and E. Alexander, 'The Economic Policy of New Labour', in D. Coates and P. Lawler (eds), *New Labour in Power* (Manchester University Press, 2000), p. 113.

22 P. Diamond, *The British Labour Party in Opposition and Power 1979–2019: Forward March Halted?* (Routledge, 2020), pp. 78, 84.

23 Fielding, *Labour Party*, p. 153.

24 TNA PREM 49/175/1, Blunkett to Brown, 21 November 1997.

25 S. Wren-Lewis, 'Aggregate Fiscal Policy Under the Labour Government, 1997–2010', *Oxford Review of Economic Policy* 29, 1 (2013), figures 1–2, p. 33 and table 1, p. 34.

26 Davis and Rentoul, *Heroes or Villains?*, pp. 244–5.

27 P. Toynbee and D. Walker, *The Verdict: Did Labour Change Britain?* (Granta, 2010), pp. 78–9; Wren-Lewis, 'Fiscal Policy', pp. 36–8.

28 TNA PREM 49/176, Butler to Blair, Wallace to Blair, both 4 May 1997.

29 TNA PREM 49/177, Wallace record of Blair meeting with George, 1 August 1997.

30 P. Sinclair, 'The Treasury and Economic Policy', in A. Seldon (ed.), *Blair's Britain 1997–2007* (Cambridge University Press, 2007), p. 199.

31 Cm. 8012, *A New Approach to Financial Regulation: Building a Stronger System* (The Stationery Office, February 2011), pp. 4–5, 15.

32 M. Watson, 'The Split Personality of Prudence in the Unfolding Political Economy of New Labour', *Political Quarterly* 79, 4 (2008), pp. 580–1.

33 William Keegan, *The Prudence of Mr Gordon Brown* (Wiley & Sons, 2004)?, pp. 168–9; Brown, *My Life*, p. 122; Davis and Rentoul, *Heroes or Villains?*, pp. 187–8.

34 Balls, *Speaking Out*, pp. 148–9.

35 D. Cobham, 'Monetary Policy under the Labour Government: The First 13 Years of the MPC', *Oxford Review of Economic Policy* 29, 1 (2013), table 1, p. 55.

36 Keegan, *Prudence*, pp. 200–1, 210–11, 223.

Notes

37 O. Daddow, 'New Labour: A Witness History', *Contemporary British History* 29, 1 (2015), p. 113.

38 Cobham, 'Monetary Policy', figure 2, p. 51.

39 P. Arestis and M. Sawyer. 'Macroeconomic Policy in the UK under New Labour: The End of Boom and Bust?', in P. Arestis, E. Hein and E. Le Heron (eds), *Aspects of Modern Monetary and Macroeconomic Policies* (Palgrave, 2007), pp. 261–2.

40 Faucher-King and Le Galès, *New Labour Experiment*, p. 23.

41 D. Farnham, 'New Labour, the New Unions and the New Labour Market', *Parliamentary Affairs* 49, 4 (1996), p. 588.

42 P. Cressey, 'New Labour and Employment, Training and Employee Relations', in M. Powell (ed.), *New Labour, New Welfare State?: The 'Third Way' in British Social Policy* (Policy Press, 1999), pp. 171–2.

43 W. Brown, 'International Review: Industrial Relations in Britain under New Labour, 1997–2010: A Post Mortem', *Journal of Industrial Relations* 53, 3 (2011), pp. 402–6.

44 Farnham, 'New Labour Market', p. 590.

45 T. Casey and A.Q. Howard, 'New Labour and the British Model of Capitalism', in T. Casey (ed.), *The Blair Legacy: Politics, Policy, Governance, and Foreign Affairs* (Palgrave, 2009), p. 142.

46 Cm. 4176, *Our Competitive Future*, p. 12.

47 Corry et al., 'Economic Performance', p. 36; Fielding, *Labour Party*, p. 161.

48 H. Mercer, *Constructing a Competitive Order: The Hidden History of British Anti-Trust Policies* (Cambridge University Press, 1994), pp. 92–5, 99–103.

49 TNA PREM 49/1410, Hewitt to Roche, 19 October 1999.

50 E. Consterdine, *Labour's Immigration Policy: The Making of the Migration State* (Palgrave, 2018), pp. 127–8, 130.

51 W. Somerville, *Immigration Under New Labour* (Policy Press, 2007), pp. 30–2 and figure 1.1, p. 32.

52 W. Somerville, 'The Politics and Policy of Skilled Economic Immigration Under New Labour, 1997–2010', in T. Triadafilopoulos (ed.), *Wanted and Welcome?: Policies for Highly Skilled Immigrants in Comparative Perspective* (Springer, 2013), pp. 260–1, 265.

53 Carr, *March of the Moderates*, p. 237; Migration Advisory Committee, *Review of the UK's Transitional Measures for Nationals of Member States that Acceded to the European Union in 2004* (MAC, 2009), figure 2.1, p. 17.

54 Davis and Rentoul, *Heroes or Villains?*, p. 305.

55 Consterdine, *Labour's Immigration Policy*, p. 201.

56 ONS, *Long-Term International Migration, Provisional: Year Ending June 2024*, www.ons.gov.uk/peoplepopulationandcommunity/populationandmigration/internationalmigration/bulletins/longterminternationalmigrationprovisional/yearendingjune2024, accessed 11 February 2025.

57 TNA PREM 49/2330, Smith to Brown, enclos. report, 9 February 2000.

58 TNA PREM 49/178, Prescott to Robinson, 13 June 1997, Prescott to Robinson, 3 November 1997.

59 TNA PREM 49/178, Finch to Jacobs, 23 June 1997; TNA PREM 49/1663, Barder to White, enclos. report, 3 February 2000; TNA PREM 49/2330, Smith to Brown, enclos. report, 9 February 2000.

60 P. Hare, 'PPP and PFI: The Political Economy of Building Public Infrastructure and Delivering Services', *Oxford Review of Economic Policy* 29, 1 (2013), pp. 96–8.

61 TNA PREM 49/1818, Memorandum on 'Private/voluntary sector engagement in Education', (June?) 2001.

62 Hare, 'Public Infrastructure', p. 108.

63 Sinclair, 'Treasury and Economic Policy', pp. 205–7.

64 B. Jefferys and S. George, 'PFI Contract Makes School Pay Thousands to Cut Grass', *BBC News Online*, www.bbc.co.uk/news/education-68207051, accessed 14 May 2024.

65 N. Timmins, 'An Unhealthy End Looms for the Private Finance Initiative', *King's Fund Policy, Finance and Performance Blog*, 16 February 2024, www.kingsfund.org.uk/insight-and-analysis/blogs/unhealthy-end-looms-private-finance-initiative, accessed 13 May 2024.

66 Hare, 'Public Infrastructure', p. 107.

67 Davis and Rentoul, *Heroes or Villains?*, p. 224.

68 C. Giles, 'PFI Discredited by Cost, Complexity and Inflexibility', *Financial Times*, 26 September 2017; J. Kraindler, Z. Firth and A. Charlesworth, 'False Economy: An Analysis of NHS Funding Pressures', *Health Foundation*, May 2018, www.health.org.uk/publication/false-economy, accessed 13 May 2024.

69 Hare, 'Public Infrastructure', figure 1, p. 99.

70 J. Harrison, 'The Political-Economy of Blair's "New Regional Policy"', *Geoforum* 37, 6 (2006), pp. 935–6.

71 M.R. Quinn, 'New Labour's Regional Policy and its Impact on the East Midlands', PhD dissertation, University of Leicester, 2012, e.g. p. 7. See A.L. Saxenian, *Regional Advantage: Culture and Competition in Silicon Valley and Route 128* (Harvard University Press, 1994), e.g. p. 161; M. Storper, *The Regional World: Territorial Development in a Global Economy* (Guildford Press, 1997), pp. 210, 218.

72 HM Treasury/DTI, *Productivity in the UK 3: The Regional Dimension* (HM Treasury, 2001), chart 1.1, p. 3.

73 Britain's Growing Regional Divides project, interview with Gordon Brown, 10 May 2022, https://sites.harvard.edu/uk-regional-growth/directory/gordon-brown/, accessed 28 February 2024.

74 J. Adams, P. Robinson and A. Vigor, *A New Regional Policy for the UK* (IPPR, 2003), p. 45.

75 M. Sandford, *The New Governance of the English Regions* (Palgrave, 2005), pp. 99–100, 106–7, 109–12, 116–17.

76 TNA PREM 49/2200, Gallagher et al. to Blair, 25 May 2000, Virley to Blair, 10 May 2000, Gallagher to Blair, 5 June 2000, Prescott to Blair, 13 February 2001, Miliband to Blair, 14 February 2001.

77 TNA PREM 49/3294, Hurst to Blair, 14 April 2003; TNA PREM 49/3295, McGowan to Blair, 16 May and 3 June 2003, TNA PREM 49/3296, Raynford to English Regional Policy Committee members, 17 October 2003.

78 'North East Votes "No" to Assembly', *BBC News Online*, 4 November 2004, http://news.bbc.co.uk/1/hi/uk_politics/3984387.stm, accessed 2 February 2024.

79 TNA PREM 49/2371, Byers to Heywood, 6 February 2001; TNA PREM 49/2466, Treasury/ DfES paper, 'Developing workforce skills: piloting a new approach', April 2002.

80 Sandford, *English Regions*, pp. 113–14.

81 E. Balls, 'Britain's New Regional Policy: Sustainable Growth and Full Employment for Britain's Regions', in E. Balls and J. Healey (eds), *Towards a New Regional Policy: Delivering Growth and Full Employment* (Smith Institute, 2000), pp. 14–16.

82 Adams, Robinson and Vigor, *New Regional Policy*, pp. i, 3, table 1.1, p. 5.

Notes

83 HM Treasury/DTI, *Regional Dimension*, box 4.3, p. 48.

84 Author interview, John Denham, 22 July 2024.

85 D. Turner, N. Weinberg, E. Elsden and E. Balls, *Why Hasn't UK Regional Policy Worked? The Views of Leading Practitioners*, Mossavar-Rahmani Center for Business and Government Associate Working Paper Series 216, Harvard Kennedy School (October 2023), pp. 32–9.

86 M.R. Quinn, 'New Labour's Regional Experiment: Lessons from the East Midlands', *Local Economy* 28, 7–8 (2013), p. 745.

87 Balls, 'New Regional Policy', pp. 9, 11; Turner et al., 'Why Hasn't UK Regional Policy Worked?', figure 1, p. 7.

88 N. Weinberg, D. Turner, E. Elsden, E. Balls and A. Stansbury, *A Growth Policy to Close Britain's Regional Divides: What Needs to be Done*, Mossavar-Rahmani Center for Business and Government Associate Working Paper Series 225, Harvard Kennedy School (February 2024), pp. 4, 18, 21–2, 31, 36–7, 42, 52.

89 Brown interview, 10 May 2022, https://sites.harvard.edu/uk-regional-growth/directory/gordon-brown/, accessed 28 February 2024.

90 R. Martin, 'Uneven Regional Growth: The Geographies of Boom and Bust under New Labour', in N.M. Coe and A. Jones (eds), *The Economic Geography of the UK* (Sage, 2010), figure 3.1, p. 34, figure 3.7 and table 3.2, p. 43.

91 Simon Lee, *Boom and Bust: The Politics and Legacy of Gordon Brown* (OneWorld, 2009), pp. 68–9; Thompson, *Wilderness*, p. 255.

92 D. Coates, 'Chickens Coming Home to Roost? New Labour at the Eleventh Hour' *British Politics* 4, 4 (2009), pp. 424–5, 427–8.

93 G. Parker and J. Pickard, 'Tony Blair Think-Tank Revenues Hit $140m as Governments Pay for Advice', *Financial Times*, 22 December 2023.

94 J. Hopkin and D. Wincott, 'New Labour, Economic Reform and the European Social Model', *British Journal of Politics and International Relations* 8, 1 (2006), table 1, p. 56 and figure 2, p. 58.

95 Michael Sheen and Tony Blair, '"I Tried to give Britain a Different Narrative": Tony Blair and Michael Sheen in Conversation', *New Statesman*, 23 March 2022, www.newstatesman.com/politics/a-dream-of-britain/2022/03/tony-blair-michael-sheen-interview, accessed 30 January 2024.

96 Casey and Howard, 'British Model', table 9.1, p. 137.

97 M. Wickham-Jones, 'New Labour in the Global Economy: Partisan Politics and the Social Democratic Model', *British Journal of Politics and International Relations* 2, 1 (2000), pp. 12, 16.

98 A. Gamble and G. Kelly, 'Labour's New Economics', in S. Ludlam and M.J. Smith (eds), *New Labour in Government* (Macmillan, 2001), pp. 167, 176.

99 J. Van Reenen, 'Productivity Under the 1997–2010 Labour Government', *Oxford Review of Economic Policy* 29, 1 (2013), figure 5, p. 124 and figure 6, p. 125.

100 Diamond, *British Labour Party*, p. 240.

101 Toynbee and Walker, *Verdict*, p. 74; Corry et al., 'Economic Performance', pp. 2, 11 and figure 6, p. 15.

102 A. Giddens, 'The Rise and Fall of New Labour', *New Statesman*, 17 May 2010, p. 26.

Chapter 3

1 D. Dorling, 'New Labour and Inequality: Thatcherism Continued?', *Local Economy* 25, 5/6 (2010), p. 407.

2 G. Irvin, *Super Rich: The Rise of Inequality in Britain and the United States* (Polity Press, 2008), p. 4.

3 R. Lister, 'From Equality to Social Inclusion: New Labour and the Welfare State', *Critical Social Policy* 18, 55 (1998), p. 222.

4 E. Shaw, *Losing Labour's Soul?: New Labour and the Blair Government 1997–2007* (Routledge, 2007), pp. 44–5, 48–9, 54–5.

5 J. Macleavy, 'The Language of Politics and the Politics of Language: Unpacking "Social Exclusion" in New Labour Policy', *Space and Polity* 10, 1 (2006), p. 89; R. Levitas, *The Inclusive Society?: Social Exclusion and New Labour* (Macmillan, 2nd edn., 2005), pp. 22–5.

6 TNA PREM 49/164, Mulgan to Blair, 12 November 1997.

7 D. Backwith, *Social Work, Poverty and Social Exclusion* (Open University Press, 2015), p. 33.

8 N. Ellison and S. Ellison, 'Creating "Opportunity for All"? New Labour, New Localism and the Opportunity Society', *Social Policy and Society* 5, 3 (2006), p. 337.

9 Dorling, 'Thatcherism Continued?', p. 414.

10 S. Meredith, 'Mr Crosland's Nightmare? New Labour and Equality in Historical Perspective', *British Journal of Politics and International Relations* 8, 2 (2006), pp. 239–40.

11 A. Deacon, 'Levelling the Playing Field, Activating the Players: New Labour and the Cycle of Disadvantage', *Policy & Politics* 31, 2 (2003), pp. 125, 132–3.

12 S. Driver, 'North Atlantic Drift: Welfare Reform and the "Third Way" Politics of New Labour and the New Democrats', in S. Hale, W. Leggett and L. Martell (eds), *The Third Way and Beyond* (Manchester University Press, 2018), pp. 31–2.

13 Author interview, Sir Tony Blair, 16 July 2024.

14 R. Plant, 'Crosland, Equality and New Labour', in D. Leonard (ed.), *Crosland and New Labour* (Palgrave Macmillan, 1998), pp. 32–3.

15 M. Hill, 'Social Security: Welfare Reform or Piecemeal Adjustment?', in S. Savage and R. Atkinson (eds), *Public Policy Under Blair* (Palgrave, 2001), pp. 192–3.

16 Harman, *Woman's Work*, pp. 195, 203, 207.

17 TNA PREM 49/161, Field to Blair, 9 June 1997.

18 Hill, 'Welfare Reform', p. 195.

19 TNA PREM 49/165, White to Blair, 17 December 1997.

20 TNA PREM 49/161, Harman and Field memorandum, 23 May 1997.

21 TNA PREM 49/164, Miliband to Blair, 5 November 1997, White to Blair, 28 November 1997.

22 TNA PREM 49/162, Powell to Blair, 14 July 1997.

23 TNA PREM 49/163, Powell to Miliband, 2 October 1997.

24 Author interview, John Denham, 22 July 2024.

25 Author interview, Stefan Czerniawski, 9 July 2024.

26 TNA PREM 49/162, White to Blair, 5 September 1997.

27 TNA PREM 49/165, White to Blair, 15 December 1997, Heywood to White, 8 December 1997.

28 Department of Social Security (DSS), *New Ambitions for Our Country: A New Contract for Welfare* (TSO, 1998), pp. 20, iii and 81–5.

29 F. Field, 'Welfare Reform: A Lost Opportunity', *Political Quarterly* 77, 1 (2006), p. 60.

30 TNA PREM 49/161, Darling to Harman, 12 June 1997, 25 June 1997, Darling to Prescott, 24 June 1997; TNA PREM 49/162, White to Blair, 18 July 1997.

31 Ibid., Wallace to Blair, 20 June 1997, Harman to Darling, 21 May 1997, Harman to Prescott, 20 June 1997.

32 Author interview, Stefan Czerniawski, 9 July 2024.

33 'Blair Suffers in Benefits Revolt', *BBC News Online*, 11 December 1997, http://news.bbc.co.uk/1/hi/uk/38656.stm, accessed 20 December 2023.

34 Brown, *My Life*, pp. 144–5.

35 T. Sefton, J. Hills and H. Sutherland, 'Poverty, Inequality and Redistribution', in J. Hills, T. Sefton and K. Stewart (eds), *Towards a More Equal Society?* (Policy Press, 2009), p. 22.

36 S. McKay and K. Rowlingson, 'Social Security and Welfare Reform', in M. Powell (ed.), *Modernising the Welfare State: The Blair Legacy* (Policy Press, 2008), figure 4.1, p. 57.

37 Brown, *My Life*, pp. 146–7.

38 Field, 'Welfare Reform', p. 55.

39 Low Pay Commission, *20 Years of the National Minimum Wage: A History of the UK Minimum Wage and its Effects* (LPC, 2019), pp. 9–12.

40 Ellison and Ellison, 'Opportunity Society', p. 339.

41 Department for Communities and Local Government, *The New Deal for Communities Experience: A Final Assessment, Final Report Volume 7* (DCLG, 2010), figure 3.2, p. 23 and figure 3.3, p. 25.

42 M. Stafford et al., 'Evaluating the Health Inequalities Impact of Area-Based Initiatives Across the Socioeconomic Spectrum: A Controlled Intervention Study of the New Deal for Communities, 2002–2008', *Journal of Epidemiology and Community Health* 68, 10 (2014), figure 1, p. 984.

43 P. Alcock, 'Poverty and Social Exclusion', in T. Ridge and S.E. Wright (eds), *Understanding Inequality, Poverty and Wealth: Policies and Prospects* (Policy Press, 2008), p. 46; Toynbee and Walker, *Verdict*, pp. 200–1.

44 TNA PREM 49/164, Blair to Prescott, 20 November 1997.

45 TNA PREM 49/162, Young, Mulgan and Miliband memorandum to Blair, (August?) 1997.

46 TNA PREM 49/164, Mulgan to Blair, 27 November 1997.

47 K. Stewart, 'Equality and Social Justice', in Seldon (ed.), *Blair's Britain*, figure 19.4, p. 431.

48 P. Gregg, 'New Labour and Inequality', *Political Quarterly* 81, s1 (2010), figure 2, p. S23.

49 Cressey, 'New Labour and Employment', p. 177.

50 R. Blundell, H. Reed, J. Van Reenen and A. Shephard, 'The Impact of the New Deal for Young People on the Labour Market: A Four-Year Assessment', in R. Dickens, P. Gregg and J. Wadsworth (eds), *The Labour Market Under New Labour: The State of Working Britain 2003* (Palgrave, 2003), table 1.3, p. 24 and p. 27.

51 Driver, 'North Atlantic Drift', p. 39.

52 M. Hewitt, 'New Labour and the Redefinition of Social Security', in M. Powell (ed.), *Evaluating New Labour's Welfare Reforms* (Policy Press, 2002), p. 199.

53 TNA PREM 49/163, Wallace to Blair, 22 October 1997.

54 S. Driver, 'New Labour and Social Policy', in M. Beech and S. Lee (eds), *Ten Years of New Labour* (Palgrave, 2008), p. 53; M. Hewitt, 'New Labour and Social Security', in Powell (ed.), *New Welfare State?*, pp. 158–9.

55 T. Hyland and D. Musson, 'Unpacking the New Deal for Young People: Promise and Problems', *Educational Studies* 27, 1 (2001), pp. 56–7, 64.

56 A. Gray, 'Making Work Pay: Devising the Best Strategy for Lone Parents in Britain', *Journal of Social Policy* 30, 2 (2001), p. 191.

57 B. Rieger, 'British Varieties of Neoliberalism: Unemployment Policy from Thatcher to Blair', in A. Davies, B. Jackson and F. Sutcliffe-Braithwaite (eds), *The Neoliberal Age?: Britain Since the 1970s* (UCL Press, 2021), pp. 122–3; A. Jones, 'Looking Back on New Labour: What Got Better?', *Local Economy* 25, 5–6 (2010), p. 363.

58 Brown, *My Life*, p. 129.

59 TNA PREM 49/82, Blair memorandum, 28 December 1997.

60 DSS, *New Contract for Welfare*, pp. iii and 23; see Hewitt, 'New Labour and the Redefinition of Social Security', p. 189.

61 B. Jessop, 'From Thatcherism to New Labour: Neo-Liberalism, Workfarism and Labour-Market Regulation', in H. Overbeek (ed.), *The Political Economy of European Employment* (Routledge, 2004), p. 146.

62 T. Shildrick and R. MacDonald, *Poverty and Insecurity: Life in Low-Pay, No-Pay Britain* (Policy Press, 2012), p. 64.

63 F. Green, 'Job Quality in Britain under the Labour Government', in P. Gregg and J. Wadsworth (eds), *The Labour Market in Winter: The State of Working Britain* (Oxford University Press, 2011), p. 120 and figure 8.6, p. 121.

64 R. Blundell and B. Etheridge, 'Consumption, Income and Earnings Inequality in Britain', *Review of Economic Dynamics* 13, 1 (2010), figure 2.3, p. 80.

65 P. Gregg and J. Wadsworth, 'Workless Households and the Recovery', in Dickens, Gregg and Wadsworth (eds), *The Labour Market Under New Labour*, table 2.1, p. 34, figure 2.2 and table 2.2, p. 35 and table 2.4, p. 37. The point about the targeting of 'assistance and support' is the present author's own inference.

66 G. Pascall, 'Gender and New Labour: After the Male Breadwinner Model?', in T. Maltby, P. Kennett and K. Rummery (eds), *Social Policy Review 20* (Policy Press, 2008), p. 219.

67 Deprivation here is defined as lacking three or more socially perceived necessities: see J. Bradshaw and G. Main, 'Child Poverty and Deprivation', in J. Bradshaw (ed.), *The Well-Being of Children in the UK* (Policy Press, 2016), figure 3.7, p. 48.

68 Arestis and Sawyer, 'Macroeconomic Policy', table 13.6, p. 263.

69 TNA PREM 49/161, Harman speech to IPPR, 11 June 1997.

70 Harman, *Woman's Work*, p. 123.

71 J. Waldfogel, 'Family-Friendly Policies', in Gregg and Wadsworth (eds), *The Labour Market in Winter*, pp. 145–8; Pascall, 'Gender and New Labour', pp. 223–5.

72 TNA PREM 49/2465, Milburn to Hewitt, 31 January 2002, Hewitt to Prescott, 15 January 2002. For progress in the police, prisons and probation service, see TNA PREM 49/2467, Blunkett to Hewitt, 18 April 2002.

73 Green, 'Job Quality', figure 8.2, p. 117 and figure 8.3 (a) and (b), p. 118.

74 Gray, 'Lone Parents', p. 195.

75 T. Rutherford, *Historical Rates of Social Security Benefits*, House of Commons Library Standard Note SN/SG 6762 (November 2013), Annex 1, p. 11.

76 D.P. Dolowitz, 'Prosperity and Fairness? Can New Labour Bring Fairness to the 21st Century by Following the Dictates of Endogenous Growth?', *British Journal of Politics and International Relations*, 6, 2 (2004), 213–230, p. 224; Hopkin and Wincott, 'New Labour, Economic Reform and the European Social Model', p. 62.

77 J. Hills, *Inequality and the State* (Oxford University Press, 2004), table 9.1, p. 214.

78 J. Waltman, 'Reformulating Social Policy: The Minimum Wage, the New Deal, and the Working Families Tax Credit', in Casey (ed.), *Blair Legacy*, p. 128.

79 N. Parton, *The Politics of Child Protection: Contemporary Developments and Future Directions* (Bloomsbury, 2014), p. 35.

80 L.A. Karoly, *Investing in Our Children: What We Know and Don't Know about the Costs and Benefits of Early Childhood Interventions* (Rand, 1998), pp. 37–47.

81 J. Lewis, 'What is New Labour? Can it Deliver on Social Policy?', in J. Lewis and R. Surender (eds), *Welfare State Change: Towards a Third Way?* (Oxford University Press, 2004), p. 219.

82 J. Millar and T. Ridge, 'Parents, Children, Families and New Labour: Developing Family Policy?', in Powell (ed.), *Evaluating*, table 5.1, p. 87 and p. 96; Gray, 'Lone Parents', p. 197 and table 1, p. 201.

83 Parton, *Child Protection*, pp. 45–60.

84 E. Melhuish, *The Impact of Sure Start Local Programmes on Seven Year Olds and Their Families*, Department for Education Research Reports DFE-RR220 (DfE, 2010), Executive Summary, Conclusions and tables 3.2–3.3, pp. 26–7.

85 J. Hall, P. Sammons, R. Smees, K. Sylva, M. Evangelou, J. Goff, T. Smith and G. Smith, 'Relationships Between Families' Use of Sure Start Children's Centres, Changes in Home Learning Environments, and Preschool Behavioural Disorders', *Oxford Review of Education* 45, 3 (2019), pp. 369–70, tables 5–6, pp. 379, 381, and text on p. 381.

86 P. Carneiro, S. Cattan and N. Ridpath, *The Short- and Medium-Term Impacts of Sure Start on Educational Outcomes*, Institute for Fiscal Studies Report R307 (April 2024), figures 5.1–5.3, pp. 25–7.

87 P. Carneiro, S. Cattan, G. Conti, C. Crawford, E. Drayton, C. Farquharson and N. Ridpath, *The Effect of Sure Start on Youth Misbehaviour, Crime and Contacts with Children's Social Care*, Institute for Fiscal Studies Report R338 (October 2024), figure 5.3, p. 31 and figure 5.9, p. 38.

88 K. Mason, A. Alexiou, D.L. Bennett, C. Summerbell, B. Barr and D. Taylor-Robinson, 'Impact of Cuts to Local Government Spending on Sure Start Children's Centres on Childhood Obesity in England: A Longitudinal Ecological Study', *Journal of Epidemiology and Community Health* 75, 9 (2021), p. 863.

89 Stewart, 'Equality and Social Justice', table 19.1, p. 415.

90 Bradshaw and Main, 'Child Poverty and Deprivation', figure 3.2, p. 38.

91 Toynbee and Walker, *Verdict*, p. 211.

92 D. Piachaud and H. Sutherland, 'Child Poverty in Britain and the New Labour Government', *Journal of Social Policy* 30, 1 (2001), table 3, p. 103 and pp. 95–6.

93 Lee, *Boom and Bust*, p. 254.

94 Stewart, 'Equality and Social Justice', figure 19.2, p. 420; R. Joyce and L. Sibieta, 'An Assessment of Labour's Record on Income Inequality and Poverty', *Oxford Review of Economic Policy* 29, 1 (2013), figure 7, p. 191.

95 J. Browne and D. Phillips, *Tax and Benefit Reforms under Labour*, Institute for Fiscal Studies Election Briefing Note 1 (IFS, 2010), table 3.1, p. 19.

96 Sefton, Hills and Sutherland, 'Redistribution', table 2.2, p. 28.

97 M. Evans and L. Williams, *A Generation of Change, A Lifetime of Difference?: Social Policy in Britain Since 1979* (Policy Press, 2009), figure 10.3, p. 203.

98 MacLeavy, 'Language of Politics', p. 96.

Notes

99 R.M. Page, 'Without a Song in Their Heart: New Labour, the Welfare State and the Retreat from Democratic Socialism', *Journal of Social Policy* 36, 1 (2007), pp. 19–20, 22–3.

100 S. Wilson and B. Spies-Butcher, 'After New Labour: Political and Policy Consequences of Welfare State Reforms in the United Kingdom and Australia', *Policy Studies* 37, 5 (2016), pp. 413, 417.

101 D. Marron, 'Governing Poverty in a Neoliberal Age: New Labour and the Case of Financial Exclusion', *New Political Economy* 18, 6 (2013), pp. 788, 790, 793.

102 McKay and Rowlingson, 'Welfare Reform', table 4.1, p. 54.

103 Hewitt, 'New Labour and Social Security', p. 167.

104 Waltman, 'Reformulating Social Policy', p. 130.

105 T. Sefton, 'Moving in the Right Direction? Public Attitudes to Poverty, Inequality and Redistribution', in Hills, Sefton and Stewart (eds), *Towards a More Equal Society?*, table 11.2, p. 226.

106 Hindmoor, *What's Left Now?*, figure 6.11, p. 142 and figure 6.12, p. 146; Blundell and Etheridge, 'Earnings Inequality', figure 1.1, p. 7; M. Daly and R. Valletta, 'Cross-National Trends in Earnings Inequality and Instability', *Economics Letters* 99, 2 (2008), figures 1–3, pp. 217–18; B. Francis-Devine and S. Orme, *Income Inequality in the UK*, House of Commons Library Research Briefing 7484 (April 2023), p. 14.

107 O. Bargain, 'The Distributional Effects of Tax-Benefit Policies under New Labour: A Decomposition Approach', *Oxford Bulletin of Economics and Statistics* 74, 6 (2012), table 1, p. 867.

108 Blundell and Etheridge, 'Earnings Inequality', figure 7.2, p. 100; Dorling, 'Thatcherism Continued?', figure 2, p. 410. For long-term figures see Hills, *Inequality and the State*, table 2.6, p. 27.

109 D. Dorling, *Inequality and the 1%* (Verso, 2019), p. 90; Hindmoor, *What's Left Now?*, p. 126.

110 Hindmoor, *What's Left Now?*, figure 6.9, p. 139.

111 A. Chakelian, 'Liam Byrne: "New Labour Economics is History"', *New Statesman*, 1 February 2024, www.newstatesman.com/politics/politics-interview/2024/02/liam-byrne-new-labour-economics, accessed 2 February 2024.

112 Lee, *Boom and Bust*, p. 254.

Chapter 4

1 A. Alvarez-Rosete and N. Mays, 'Understanding NHS Policy Making in England: The Formulation of the NHS Plan, 2000', *British Journal of Politics and International Relations* 16, 4 (2014), p. 625.

2 Brown, *My Life*, p. 162.

3 Alvarez-Rosete and Mays, 'NHS Policy Making', p. 626.

4 TNA PREM 49/179, Dobson to Brown, 20 June 1997.

5 A. Seldon, *Blair* (Free Press, 2005), p. 434.

6 J. Stewart, *Taking Stock: Scottish Social Welfare After Devolution* (Policy Press, 2004), pp. 103–34.

7 T. Blair, *A Journey* (Arrow, 2011), pp. 263, 265.

8 Alvarez-Rosete and Mays, 'NHS Policy Making', p. 632.

9 TNA PREM 49/1641, Hill to Blair, 9 March 2000, Heywood to Blair, 10 March 2000.

10 J. Le Grand, 'The Labour Government and the National Health Service', *Oxford Review of Economic Policy* 18, 2 (2002), p. 138.

11 R. Klein, 'The New Model NHS: Performance, Perceptions and Expectations', *British Medical Bulletin* 81, 1 (2007), p. 42 and table 43, p. 46; on GP numbers (1997–2003) see P. McGregor, P. McKee and C. O'Neill, 'Structural Change in the NHS and GP Utilization in England under New Labour, 1997–2003', *Public Administration* 91, 3 (2013), table 1, p. 635.

12 TNA PREM 49/1818, Stevens to Blair, 6 July 2001.

13 M. Warner and B. Zaranko, *The Past and Future of NHS Waiting Lists in England*, IFS Report R302 (February 2024), https://ifs.org.uk/publications/past-and-future-nhs-wai ting-lists-england, accessed 6 March 2025.

14 TNA PREM 49/2432, Adonis to Blair, 7 January 2002.

15 TNA PREM 49/82, Miliband memorandum, 16 July 1997. On 'contestability' see C. Ham, 'Contestability: A Middle Path for Health Care', *British Medical Journal* 312, 7023 (1996), pp. 70–1.

16 Klein, 'New Model NHS', pp. 41–2; D. Richards, 'Delivery of Public Services', in A. Geddes and J. Tonge (eds), *Britain Decides: The UK General Election 2005* (Palgrave, 2006), p. 250.

17 L. Mayhew and D. Smith, 'Using Queuing Theory to Analyse the Government's 4–H Completion Time Target in Accident and Emergency Departments', *Health Care Management Science* 11, 1 (2008), figure 10, p. 19, and discussion on p. 20.

18 M. Warner and B. Zaranko, 'Is There Really an NHS Productivity Crisis?', *Institute of Fiscal Studies: Comment*, 17 November 2023, https://ifs.org.uk/articles/there-really-nhs-productivity-crisis, accessed 6 March 2025.

19 C. Propper and M.-A. Venables, 'An Assessment of Labour's Record on Health and Healthcare', *Oxford Review of Economic Policy* 29, 1 (2013), pp. 210–11.

20 Ibid., p. 210.

21 C. Paton, 'Blair and the NHS: Resistible Force Meets Moveable Object?', in Casey (ed.), *Blair Legacy*, p. 117.

22 Brown, *My Life*, p. 168.

23 G. Bevan and C. Hood, 'What's Measured is What Matters: Targets and Gaming in the English Public Health Care System', *Public Administration* 84, 3 (2006), pp. 518, 525.

24 R. Klein, 'Transforming the NHS: The Story in 2004', in M. Powell, L. Bauld and K. Clarke (eds), *Social Policy Review 17* (Policy Press, 2005), p. 62.

25 N. Timmins, N. Rawlings and J. Appleby, *A Terrible Beauty: A Short History of NICE* (HITAP, 2016), e.g. pp. 60–2, 12.

26 M. Exworthy and D.J. Hunter, 'The Challenge of Joined-Up Government in Tackling Health Inequalities', *International Journal of Public Administration* 34, 4 (2011), p. 205.

27 N. Perkins, K.E. Smith, D.J. Hunter and C. Bambra, '"What Counts is What Works"? New Labour and Partnerships in Public Health', *Policy & Politics* 38, 1 (2010), p. 101.

28 Ibid., p. 103.

29 TNA PREM 49/2435, Heywood to Blair, 14 April 2002.

30 Alvarez-Rosete and Mays, 'NHS Policy Making', pp. 633–4, 637.

31 Blair, *Journey*, p. 273; Seldon, *Blair*, p. 634.

32 Paton, 'Blair and the NHS', p. 114; C. Paton, 'The NHS After 10 Years of New Labour', in Powell (ed.), *Modernising*, p. 28.

33 Paton, 'NHS After Ten Years', p. 19.

34 Alvarez-Rosete and Mays, 'NHS Policy Making', p. 627; R. Cookson, M. Laudicella, P. Li Donni and M. Dusheiko, 'Effects of the Blair/Brown NHS Reforms on Socioeconomic

Equity in Health Care', *Journal of Health Services Research & Policy* 17, 1 (2012), p. 57; Klein, 'Transforming the NHS', p. 7.

35 Driver, 'New Labour and Social Policy', p. 60.

36 P. Cowley and M. Stuart, 'A Rebellious Decade: Backbench Rebellions under Tony Blair, 1997–2007', in Beech and Lee (eds), *Ten Years of New Labour*, p. 210.

37 Blair, *Journey*, p. 491.

38 Davis and Rentoul, *Heroes or Villains?*, pp. 230–1.

39 I. Greener, 'Who Choosing What? The Evolution of the Use of "Choice" in the NHS, and its Importance for New Labour', in C. Bochel, N. Ellison and M. Powell (eds), *Social Policy Review 15* (Policy Press, 2003), pp. 56–7.

40 Cm. 5503, *Delivering the NHS Plan: Next Steps on Investment, Next Steps on Reform* (The Stationery Office, 2002), p. 22.

41 Klein, 'Transforming the NHS', p. 52.

42 I. Greener, 'The Three Moments of New Labour's Health Policy Discourse', *Policy & Politics* 32, 3 (2004), pp. 305–10.

43 Greener, 'Who Choosing What?', p. 59.

44 J. Appleby and A. Alvarez Rosete, 'The NHS: Keeping Up with Public Expectations?', in A. Park, J. Curtice, K. Thomson, L. Jarvis and C. Bromley (eds), *British Social Attitudes: The 20th Report: Continuity and Change Over Two Decades* (Sage, 2003), table 2.1, p. 31.

45 J. Clarke, J. Newman and L. Westmarland, 'The Antagonisms of Choice: New Labour and the Reform of Public Services', *Social Policy and Society* 7, 2 (2008), p. 251.

46 Klein, 'Transforming the NHS', p. 57.

47 S. Ruane, 'Health Policy under New Labour: Not What it Seems', in I. Greener, C. Holden and M Kilkey (eds), *Social Policy Review 22* (Policy Press, 2010), p. 59.

48 TNA PREM 49/1663, Hill to Blair, 28 May 1999.

49 Cookson et al., 'Effects of the Blair/Brown NHS Reforms', p. 56.

50 'Independent Sector Treatment Centres', King's Fund Briefing Note (October 2009), p. 2 and table 1, p. 3; Toynbee and Walker, *Verdict*, p. 56; W. Beckert and E. Kelly, 'Divided by Choice? For-Profit Providers, Patient Choice and Mechanisms of Patient Sorting in the English National Health Service', *Health Economics* 30, 4 (2021), p. 821.

51 W. Beckert, M. Christensen and K. Collyer, 'Choice of NHS-Funded Hospital Services in England', *Economic Journal* 122, 560 (2012), p. 403.

52 Toynbee and Walker, *Verdict*, p. 56.

53 Beckert, Christensen and Collyer, 'Choice', p. 401, table 2, p. 410, p. 408 and figure 1, p. 408; Propper and Venables, 'Assessment of Labour's Record', p. 222.

54 Propper and Venables, 'Assessment of Labour's Record', p. 223.

55 C. Propper, S. Burgess and K. Green, 'Does Competition Between Hospitals Improve the Quality of Care? Hospital Death Rates and the NHS Internal Market', *Journal of Public Economics* 88, 7–8 (2004), table 2, p. 1262.

56 Beckert, Christensen and Collyer, 'Choice', p. 404.

57 A. Dixon and J. Le Grand, 'Is Greater Patient Choice Consistent with Equity? The Case of the English NHS', *Journal of Health Services Research & Policy* 11, 3 (2006), p. 164.

58 I. Greener and M. Powell, 'The Changing Governance of the NHS: Reform in a Post-Keynesian Health Service', *Human Relations* 61, 5 (2008), pp. 629–30; Clarke, Newman and Westmarland, 'Antagonisms of Choice', p. 249.

59 TNA PREM 49/139, Dobson to Blair, 13 June 1997.

60 Sir Donald Acheson, *Independent Inquiry into Inequalities in Health* (HMSO, 1999), Part 2, 'List of Recommendations', pp. 75–82; NHS recommendations are found on pp. 81–2.

Notes

See A. Oliver and D. Nutbeam, 'Addressing Health Inequalities in the United Kingdom: A Case Study', *Journal of Public Health* 25, 4 (2003), p. 282.

61 Le Grand, 'Labour Government', table 5, p. 143.

62 J.P. Mackenbach, 'Can We Reduce Health Inequalities? An Analysis of the English Strategy (1997–2010)', *Journal of Epidemiology & Community Health* 65, 7 (2011), p. 568.

63 M. Exworthy, L. Berney and M. Powell, '"How Great Expectations in Westminster May be Dashed Locally": The Local Implementation of National Policy on Health Inequalities', *Policy & Politics* 30, 1 (2002), pp. 81–2.

64 Oliver and Nutbeam, 'Addressing Health Inequalities', p. 283.

65 Ibid., p. 284; Mackenbach, 'Can We Reduce Health Inequalities?', p. 569.

66 B. Barr, J. Higgerson and M. Whitehead, 'Investigating the Impact of the English Health Inequalities Strategy: Time Trend Analysis', *BMJ* 358, j3310 (2017), p. 1.

67 F. Sassi, 'Health Inequalities: A Persistent Problem', in Hills, Sefton, and Stewart (eds), *Towards a More Equal Society?*, figures 7.1 and 7.2, p. 142 and figure 7.4, p. 144; also D. Dorling et al., 'Inequalities in Mortality Rates under New Labour', in E. Dowler and N.J. Spencer (eds), *Challenging Health Inequalities: From Acheson to Choosing Health* (Policy Press, 2007), figure 3.2, p. 39.

68 T. Robinson, H. Brown, P.D. Norman, L.K. Fraser, B. Barr and C. Bambra, 'The Impact of New Labour's English Health Inequalities Strategy on Geographical Inequalities in Infant Mortality: A Time-Trend Analysis', *Journal of Epidemiological and Community Health* 73, 6 (2019), table 1, p. 566.

69 M. Shaw, G.D. Smith and D. Dorling, 'Health Inequalities and New Labour: How the Promises Compare with Real Progress', *BMJ* 330, 7498 (2005), table, p. 1019.

70 Mackenbach, 'Can We Reduce Health Inequalities?', figure 1, p. 571 and commentary on p. 572; Propper and Venables, 'Assessment of Labour's Record', figure 11, p. 218.

71 Figures calculated from The Health Foundation, *Age-Standardised Mortality Rates per 100,000 of Population, by Deprivation Decile: England, 2000–2020*, www.health.org.uk/evide nce-hub/health-inequalities/inequalities-in-age-standardised-mortality-rates, accessed 26 January 2022.

72 Barr, Higgerson and Whitehead, 'Impact of the English Health Inequalities Strategy', table 1, p. 7.

73 Exworthy and Hunter, 'Joined-Up Government', p. 205.

74 P. Mackenbach, 'Has the English Strategy to Reduce Health Inequalities Failed?', *Social Science & Medicine* 71, 7 (2010), p. 1250.

75 Cookson et al., 'Effects of the Blair/Brown NHS Reforms', figure 1, p. 58 and discussion on p. 59.

76 T. Doran, C. Fullwood, E. Kontopantelis and D. Reeves, 'Effect of Financial Incentives on Inequalities in the Delivery of Primary Clinical Care in England: Analysis of Clinical Activity Indicators for the Quality and Outcomes Framework', *Lancet* 372, 9640 (2008), figure 1, p. 731 and commentary on p. 732.

77 R. Cookson, M. Laudicella and P. Li Donni, 'Measuring Change in Health Care Equity Using Small-Area Administrative Data: Evidence from the English NHS 2001–2008', *Social Science & Medicine* 75, 8 (2012), figures 1–2, pp. 1517–18 and table 1, p. 1519.

78 K. Syrett, 'A Technocratic Fix to the "Legitimacy Problem"? The Blair Government and Health Care Rationing in the United Kingdom', *Journal of Health Politics, Policy and Law* 28, 4 (2003), p. 716.

79 TNA PREM 49/1818, Blair to Powell, Campbell, Heywood and Hunter, 23 June 2001.

80 Klein, 'Transforming the NHS', p. 53.

81 Appleby and Alvarez Rosete, 'Keeping Up with Public Expectations?', table 2.1, p. 31.

82 Klein, 'New Model NHS', table 2 and discussion, p. 44; TNA PREM 49/1819/2, Bellulo, Brown and Donovan paper to Strategy Unit, (August?) 2001.

83 J. Morris, L. Schlepper, M. Dayan, D. Jefferies, D. Maguire, L. Merry and D. Wellings, *Public Satisfaction with the NHS and Social Care in 2022: Results from the British Social Attitudes Survey* (King's Fund, 2023), figure 1, p. 8.

84 A. King, 'Tony Blair's First Term', in A. King (ed.), *Britain at the Polls, 2001* (Seven Bridges Press, 2002), table 1.3, p. 24; J. Bartle, 'Why Labour Won – Again', in A. King (ed.), *Britain at the Polls, 2001* (Chatham House, 2002), p. 181.

85 Toynbee and Walker, *Verdict*, p. 63.

86 Bartle, 'Why Labour Won', p. 181; P. Whiteley, D. Sanders, H. Clarke and M. Stewart, 'The Issue Agenda and Voting in 2005', in P. Norris and C. Wlezien (eds), *Britain Votes 2005* (Oxford University Press, 2005), table 2, p. 154.

87 A. Wallace and P. Taylor-Gooby, 'New Labour and Reform of the English NHS: User Views and Attitudes', *Health Expectations* 13, 2 (2010), p. 215.

88 J. Curtice and O. Heath, 'Does Choice Deliver? Public Satisfaction with the Health Service', *Political Studies* 60, 3 (2012), p. 486, table 1, p. 491 and discussion on p. 491.

89 Ibid., table 3, p. 493 and table 4, p. 495.

90 Alvarez-Rosete and Mays, 'NHS Policy Making', table 5.10, p. 127 and p. 117; I. McLean, 'The Politics of Fractured Federalism', in J. Bartle and A. King (eds), *Britain at the Polls, 2005* (CQ Press, 2006), p. 117.

91 Propper and Venables, 'Assessment of Labour's Record', figure 8, p. 214.

92 Toynbee and Walker, *Verdict*, p. 46; Propper and Venables, 'Assessment of Labour's Record', figure 9, p. 215 and figure 10, p. 216.

93 Ruane, 'Health Policy Under New Labour', p. 55.

94 Toynbee and Walker, *Verdict*, pp. 47–9.

95 On the chaos threatened before Lansley's plans were 'paused' and watered down, see R. Klein, 'The Twenty-Year War over England's National Health Service: A Report from the Battlefield', *Journal of Health Politics, Policy and Law* 38, 4 (2013), p. 859.

96 Alvarez-Rosete and Mays, 'NHS Policy Making', p. 640.

97 Toynbee and Walker, *Verdict*, pp. 44–5.

98 Mackenbach, 'English Strategy', p. 1250.

99 Oliver and Nutbeam, 'Addressing Health Inequalities', p. 265.

Chapter 5

1 S. Tomlinson, 'New Labour and Education', *Children & Society* 17, 3 (2003), pp. 195–6.

2 S. Tomlinson, *Education in a Post-Welfare Society* (Open University Press, 2nd edn., 2005), p. 90.

3 C. Chitty, 'The School Effectiveness Movement: Origins, Shortcomings and Future Possibilities', *Curriculum Journal* 8, 1 (1997), pp. 50–5; A. Smithers, 'Education Policy', in A. Seldon (ed.), *The Blair Effect: The Blair Government 1997–2001* (Little, Brown, 2001), p. 407.

4 P. Mandelson and R. Liddle, *The Blair Revolution: Can New Labour Deliver?* (Faber, 1996), pp. 92, 94.

5 A. Adonis and S. Pollard, *A Class Act: The Myth of Britain's Classless Society* (Penguin, 1998), pp. 39–40, 53.

Notes

6 M. Barber, *The Learning Game: Arguments for an Education Revolution* (Indigo, 1997), pp. 173, 195–202; see M. Barber, *Instruction to Deliver: Fighting to Transform Britain's Public Services* (Methuen, 2008), pp. 22–30.

7 Labour Party, *Opening Doors to a Learning Society: A Policy Statement on Education* (Labour Party, 1994), pp. 9–11, 15–16, 29.

8 Labour Party, *Diversity and Excellence: A New Partnership for Schools* (Labour Party, 1995), p. 14.

9 Blair, *Journey*, p. 99.

10 P. Hyman, *One Out of Ten: From Downing Street Vision to Classroom Reality* (Vintage, 2005), p. 43.

11 A. Heath, A. Sullivan, V. Boliver and A. Zimdars, 'Education under New Labour, 1997–2010', *Oxford Review of Economic Policy* 29, 1 (2013), p. 227.

12 C. Chitty, *New Labour and Secondary Education, 1994–2010* (Palgrave, 2013), p. 81.

13 M. Cole, 'Globalisation, Modernisation and Competitiveness: A Critique of the New Labour Project in Education', *International Studies in Sociology of Education* 8, 3 (1998), p. 315.

14 Tomlinson, *Post-Welfare Society*, p. 96.

15 TNA PREM 49/1122, Heywood to Scholar, 26 January 1999.

16 TNA PREM 49/561, Schofield to Wardle, 7 July 1998; Heath et al., 'Education under New Labour', table 1, pp. 229–30 and p. 230.

17 D. Butler and D. Kavanagh, *The British General Election of 2001* (Palgrave Macmillan, 2001), p. 92.

18 TNA PREM 49/535, Blunkett to Brown, 30 January 1998.

19 TNA PREM 49/1818, Adonis to Blair, 6 July 2001; Department for Education and Skills (DfES), *The Five Year Strategy for Children and Learners: Maintaining the Excellent Progress* (DfES, 2006), p. 14.

20 Toynbee and Walker, *Verdict*, p. 18.

21 Chitty, *Secondary Education*, pp. 85–7.

22 Tomlinson, *Post-Welfare Society*, p. 102; A. West and H. Pennell, 'How New is New Labour? The Quasi-Market and English Schools 1997 to 2001', *British Journal of Educational Studies* 50, 2 (2002), p. 211; Tomlinson, *Post-Welfare Society*, p. 126.

23 A. Harris, C. Chapman, D. Muijs, J. Russ and L. Stoll, 'Improving Schools in Challenging Contexts: Exploring the Possible', *School Effectiveness and School Improvement* 17, 4 (2006), p. 414.

24 S. Power and G. Whitty, 'New Labour's Education Policy: First, Second or Third Way?', *Journal of Education Policy* 14, 5 (1999), pp. 537–8, 541.

25 D. Muijs and C. Chapman, 'Accountability for Improvement: Rhetoric or Reality?', in C. Chapman and H.M. Gunter (eds), *Radical Reforms: Perspectives on an Era of Educational Change* (Routledge, 2008), p. 30.

26 House of Commons Committee of Public Accounts, *Improving Poorly Performing Schools in England: Fifty-Ninth Report of Session 2005–2006* (House of Commons, 2006), figure 2, p. 9.

27 Cm. 5050, *Schools: Building on Success* (The Stationery Office, 2001), p. 13; M. Ainscow, A. Dyson, S. Goldrick and M. West, 'Making Schools Effective for All: Rethinking the Task', *School Leadership & Management* 32, 3 (2012), pp. 8–10.

28 M. Bottery, 'New Labour Policy and School Leadership in England: Room for Manoeuvre?', *Cambridge Journal of Education* 37, 2 (2007), p. 160.

29 Cm. 6272, *The Five Year Strategy for Children and Learners* (The Stationery Office, 2004), p. 4.

30 J. Dunford and C. Chitty, 'Introduction', in J. Dunford and C. Chitty (eds), *State Schools: New Labour and the Conservative Legacy* (Woburn Press, 1999), p. 7; P. Toynbee and

Notes

D. Walker, *Did Things Get Better?: An Audit of Labour's Successes and Failures* (Penguin, 2001), pp. 46–7.

31 A. Dyson, K. Kerr and M. Ainscow, 'A "Pivotal Moment"? Education Policy in England, 2005', in L. Bauld, K. Clarke and T. Maltby (eds), *Social Policy Review 18* (Policy Press, 2006), p. 49.

32 Blair, *Journey*, p. 210.

33 S.J. Ball and K. Clarke, '"Going Further?" Tony Blair and New Labour Education Policies', in K. Clarke, T. Maltby and P. Kennett (eds), *Social Policy Review 19* (Policy Press, 2007), p. 15.

34 Prime Minister's Strategy Unit, *School Reform: A Survey of Recent International Evidence* (DfES/PMSU, 2006), pp. 5, 35–8.

35 Ball and Clarke, '"Going Further?"', p. 19.

36 P.A. Woods, 'Academies: Diversity, Economism and Contending Forces for Change', in A. Green (ed.), *Blair's Educational Legacy: Thirteen Years of New Labour* (Palgrave, 2010), pp. 151–6.

37 H.M. Gunter and C. Chapman, 'A Decade of New Labour Reform of Education', in Chapman and Gunter (eds), *Radical Reforms*, p. 3.

38 P. Sammons, 'Zero Tolerance of Failure and New Labour Approaches to School Improvement in England', *Oxford Review of Education* 34, 6 (2008), p. 654.

39 M. Galton, 'New Labour and Education: An Evidence-Based Analysis', *FORUM For Promoting Comprehensive Education* 49, 1 (2007), p. 159.

40 G. Moss, 'Assessment, Accountability and the Literacy Curriculum: Reimagining the Future in the Light of the Past', *Literacy* 51, 2 (2017), p. 58. I owe this reference to Dr Lyndsay Grant.

41 M. Barber, 'High Expectations and Standards For All, No Matter What', in M. Fielding (ed.), *Taking Education Really Seriously: Four Yours Hard Labour* (Routledge, 2001), figures 2.7–2.8, pp. 26–7.

42 Harris et al., 'Improving Schools', p. 416.

43 A. Dyson and C. Raffo, 'Education and Disadvantage: The Role of Community-Oriented Schools', *Oxford Review of Education* 33, 3 (2007), p. 299.

44 J. Tooley, 'The Good, The Bad and the Ugly: Four Years of Labour Education Policy', in Fielding (ed.), *Seriously*, p. 58.

45 Chitty, *Secondary Education*, p. 97.

46 Tomlinson, *Post-Welfare Society*, p. 106.

47 S.J. Ball and C. Vincent, 'The "Childcare Champion"? New Labour, Social Justice and the Childcare Market', *British Educational Research Journal* 31, 5 (2005), pp. 559–60; DfES, *Five Year Strategy: Maintaining the Excellent Progress*, p. 6.

48 Heath et al., 'Education under New Labour', pp. 239–40.

49 J. Tipaldy, 'Did the Rising Tide of State Education Lift All Boats? An Investigation into the Secondary Education and Attainment Policy Towards White Working-Class Boys in England, 1997–2010', PhD Thesis, University of Hull, 2023, pp. 180–1.

50 P. Johnson, 'Education Policy in England', *Oxford Review of Economic Policy* 20, 2 (2004), pp. 186–7, 194–5.

51 On 'Fresh Start' see Tipaldy, 'Rising Tide', pp. 77–81, 180.

52 Q. Gu, P. Sammons and P. Mehta, 'Leadership Characteristics and Practices in Schools with Different Effectiveness and Improvement Trajectories', *School Leadership and Management* 28, 1 (2008), pp. 53, 62.

53 Muijs and Chapman, 'Accountability for Improvement', pp. 32–3.

Notes

54 G. Welch and P. Mahony, 'The Teaching Profession', in J. Docking (ed.), *New Labour's Policies for Schools: Raising the Standard?* (David Fulton Publishers, 2000), pp. 144–5.

55 J. Furlong, 'New Labour and Teacher Education: The End of an Era', *Oxford Review of Education* 31, 1 (2005), pp. 120–2.

56 Welch and Mahony, 'Teaching Profession', pp. 145–6.

57 P. Downes, 'Changing Pressures in the Secondary School', in Chitty and Dunford (eds), *State Schools*, pp. 41–3.

58 K.J. Brehony, 'Primary Schooling under New Labour: The Irresolvable Contradiction of Excellence and Enjoyment', *Oxford Review of Education* 31, 1 (2005), p. 37.

59 Galton, 'New Labour and Education', pp. 163–4.

60 Bottery, 'School Leadership', p. 166.

61 H. Gunter and G. Forrester, 'New Labour and School Leadership 1997–2007', *British Journal of Educational Studies* 56, 2 (2008), pp. 145–6, 148.

62 Harris et al., 'Improving Schools', p. 410; Dyson and Raffo, 'Education and Disadvantage', pp. 299–300, 306.

63 S. Gorard, 'Serious Doubts about School Effectiveness', *British Educational Research Journal* 36, 5 (2010), pp. 748–57.

64 H. Goldstein and G. Woodhouse, 'School Effectiveness Research and Educational Policy', *Oxford Review of Education* 26, 3–4 (2000), pp. 356–9.

65 S. Gorard, 'Are Academies Working?', in H.M. Gunter (ed.), *The State and Education Policy: The Academies Programme* (Continuum, 2011), pp. 120–32.

66 A. Ryan, 'New Labour and Higher Education', *Oxford Review of Education* 31, 1 (2005), p. 91; Driver, 'New Labour and Social Policy', p. 62.

67 Ryan, 'Higher Education', p. 94.

68 Brown, *My Life*, pp. 236–7; TNA PREM 49/1819/1, Adonis to Blair, 28 October 2001.

69 Author interview, John Denham, 22 July 2024.

70 P. Bolton, *Higher Education Finance Statistics*, House of Commons Library Briefing Paper 5540 (June 2019), table 1, p. 17.

71 National Audit Office, *Widening Participation in Higher Education* (NAO, 2008), e.g. pp. 7–10, 23, 25–6.

72 C. Callender, 'The Costs of Widening Participation: Contradictions in New Labour's Student Funding Policies', *Social Policy and Society* 1, 2 (2002), pp. 87–9; R. Lupton and P. Obolenskaya, *Labour's Record on Education: Policy, Spending and Outcomes 1997–2010*, London School of Economics Social Policy in a Cold Climate Working Paper 3 (2013), table 11, p. 45.

73 G. Giupponi and S. Machin, *Labour Market Inequality: The Deaton Review* (IFS/Nuffield Trust, 2022), figure 19, p. 29.

74 T. Wragg and M. Johnson, 'Higher Education: A Class Act', in A. Park et al. (eds), *British Social Attitudes, the 22nd Report: Two Terms of New Labour* (National Centre for Social Research, 2005), tables 4.7–4.8, pp. 96–7.

75 Heath et al., 'Education under New Labour', table 2, p. 238.

76 Cm. 6272, *Five Year Strategy*, p. 14 and figure, p. 15.

77 DfES, *Five Year Strategy: Maintaining the Excellent Progress*, figure, p. 17.

78 Working Group on 14–19 Curriculum and Qualifications Reform, *Final Report of the Working Group on 14–19 Reform* (DfES, 2005), pp. 20–8.

79 Gunter and Chapman, 'Decade of New Labour', p. 3.

80 National Foundation for Educational Research, *Key Insights from PISA 2015 for the UK Nations* (NFER, 2015), pp. 4–6.

81 S. Freedman, *Lessons Learnt?: Reflecting on 20 Years of School Reform in England* (Sutton Trust, 2024), figures 7–10, pp. 31–3.

82 S. Ward, 'Environment and Transport: A Conspiracy of Silence?', in A. Geddes and J. Tonge (eds), *Labour's Second Landslide* (Manchester University Press, 2002), table 9.2, p. 176.

83 P. Cowley and J. Green, 'New Leaders, Same Problems: The Conservatives', in Geddes and Tonge (eds), *Britain Decides*, figure 4.5, p. 64.

84 Whiteley et al., 'The Issue Agenda and Voting in 2005', figure 2, p. 153 and table 2, p. 154.

85 Sammons, 'Zero Tolerance', figures 1–2, pp. 656–7; see NAO, *Improving Poorly Performing Schools in England* (NAO, 2006), figure 7, p. 7.

86 S.J. Ball, 'New Class Inequalities in Education', *International Journal of Sociology and Social Policy* 30, 3–4 (2010), p. 157.

87 Cm. 7280, *The Children's Plan: Building Brighter Futures* (The Stationery Office, December 2007).

88 Tomlinson, *Post-Welfare Society*, p. 133; Cm. 6272, *Five Year Strategy*, p. 28.

89 M. Goodwin, 'Schools Policy, Governance and Politics under New Labour', *Political Studies Review* 13, 4 (2015), p. 536.

90 L. Paterson, 'The Three Education Ideologies of the British Labour Party, 1997–2001', *Oxford Review of Education* 209, 2 (2003), p. 166.

Chapter 6

1 T. Blair, 'Why Crime is a Socialist Issue', *New Statesman and Society*, 29 January 1993, republished online by *New Statesman*, 29 April 2017, www.newstatesman.com/archive/2017/04/1997-election-archive-tony-blair-why-crime-socialist-issue, p. 4, accessed 1 April 2023.

2 J. Sopel, *Tony Blair: The Moderniser* (Bantam, 1995).

3 I. Brownlee, 'New Labour, New Penology? The Punitive Rhetoric of Managerialism in Criminal Justice Policy', *Journal of Law and Society* 25, 3 (1998), pp. 319–21.

4 Author interview, Sir Tony Blair, 16 July 2024.

5 E. Burney, *Making People Behave: Anti-Social Behaviour, Politics and Policy* (Willan, 2013), pp. 21–2.

6 TNA PREM 49/3081, Blunkett to Blair, 28 January 2003.

7 Cohen, *Pretty Straight Guys*, p. 7.

8 J. Petley, 'New Labour, Old Morality', *Index on Censorship* 36, 2 (2007), p. 135.

9 P. Mandelson, *The Third Man* (HarperPress, 2011), p. 152.

10 Davis and Rentoul, *Heroes or Villains?*, p. 250.

11 Faucher-King and Le Galès, *New Labour Experiment*, p. 125.

12 Jenkins, *Thatcher and Sons*, pp. 216–17; Cohen, *Pretty Straight Guys*, p. 10.

13 G. Hughes, 'Communitarianism and Law and Order', *Critical Social Policy* 16, 49 (1996), pp. 18–23, 29–32; D. Lassalle, 'Policing the Margins: Anti-Social Behaviour and the "Underclass Discourse"', in S. Pickard (ed.), *Anti-Social Behaviour in Britain* (Palgrave, 2014), p. 194.

14 Levitas, *Inclusive Society?*, p. 12.

15 TNA PREM 49/82, 'What is the Government Trying to Do?' and 'Questions Asked by Journalists', (July?) 1997.

16 M. Burton, *The Politics of Public Sector Reform* (Palgrave, 2013), p. 179.

17 E. Solomon, C. Eades, R. Garside and M. Rutherford, *Ten Years of Criminal Justice under Labour: An Independent Audit* (Centre for Crime and Justice Studies, 2007), figures 1–2, pp. 18–19.

18 R. Yarwood, 'Policing Policy and Policy Policing: Directions in Rural Policing under New Labour', in M. Woods (ed.), *New Labour's Countryside* (Policy Press, 2008), pp. 209–10, 214.

19 J. Young, 'Winning the Fight against Crime? New Labour, Populism and Lost Opportunities', in R. Matthews and J. Young (eds), *The New Politics of Crime and Punishment* (Willan, 2013), p. 33.

20 Short summaries of some of the literature can be found at G. Farrell, G. Laycock and N. Tilley, 'Debuts and Legacies: The Crime Drop and the Role of Adolescence-Limited and Persistent Offending', *Crime Science* 4, 1 (2015), pp. 1–4 and M. Tonry, 'Why Crime Rates are Falling Throughout the Western World', *Crime and Justice* 43, 1 (2014), pp. 48–54.

21 A. Higney, N. Hanley and M. Moro, 'The Lead-Crime Hypothesis: A Meta-Analysis', *Regional Science and Urban Economics* 97, 103826 (2022), pp. 1–18.

22 E. McLaughlin and J. Muncie, 'The Criminal Justice System: New Labour's New Partnerships', in J. Clarke, S. Gewirtz and E. McLaughlin (eds), *New Managerialism, New Welfare* (Sage, 2000), pp. 171, 177.

23 B. Vollaard and J. Hamed, 'Why the Police Have an Effect on Violent Crime After All: Evidence from the British Crime Survey', *Journal of Law and Economics* 55, 4 (2012), table 4, p. 916.

24 TNA PREM 49/1819/2, Heywood to Blair, 24 August 2001.

25 G. Berman, *Changes in Crime Recording Practices*, House of Commons Library Standard Note SN/SG/2607 (October 2008), p. 5 and table 1, p. 6.

26 Diamond, *British Labour Party*, pp. 250–1; Toynbee and Walker, *Verdict*, pp. 171–2.

27 O. Marie, *Reducing Crime: More Police, More Prisons or More Pay?* (Centre for Economic Performance Policy Analysis, 2010), figure 2, p. 3.

28 Solomon et al., *Ten Years of Criminal Justice*, pp. 58–9.

29 Cohen, *Pretty Straight Guys*, pp. 18–19.

30 C. Goldsmith, '"You Just Know You're Being Watched Everywhere: Young People, Custodial Experiences and Community Safety', in P. Squires (ed.), *Community Safety: Critical Perspectives on Policy and Practice* (Policy Press, 2006), pp. 13, 18; M. Vanstone, 'New Labour and Criminal Justice: Reflections on a Wasteland of Missed Opportunity', *Probation Journal* 57, 3 (2010), p. 283.

31 S. Hodgkinson and N. Tilley, 'Tackling Anti-Social Behaviour: Lessons from New Labour for the Coalition Government', *Criminology and Criminal Justice* 11, 4 (2011), p. 287.

32 Cm. 5778, *Respect and Responsibility: Taking a Stand Against Anti-Social Behaviour* (The Stationery Office, March 2003), pp. 9, 11, 29–31, 59–63; P. Squires, 'New Labour and the Politics of Antisocial Behaviour', *Critical Social Policy* 26, 1 (2006), pp. 144–5.

33 Burney, *Making People Behave*, pp. 102–3.

34 On ASBOs generally see K.D. Ewing, *Bonfire of the Liberties: New Labour, Human Rights, and the Rule of Law* (Oxford University Press, 2010), pp. 28–30; also Lassalle, 'Policing the Margins', p. 197.

35 Hodgkinson and Tilley, 'Tackling Anti-Social Behaviour', p. 290. Not dissimilar figures can be found in Burney, *Making People Behave*, table 5.1, p. 106.

36 J. Jamieson, 'New Labour, Youth Justice and the Question of "Respect"', *Youth Justice* 5, 3 (2005), p. 188; see Goldsmith, 'Young People', p. 27 for similar sentiments.

37 TNA PREM 49/3082, Clarke to Prescott, 4 March 2003, Acton to Blair, 26 February 2003.

38 Author interview, John Denham, 22 July 2024.

39 TNA PREM 49/3083, Flint to Hodge, 31 July 2003, Casey to Heywood, enclos. draft Action Plan, 22 July 2003 and 9 September 2003, Garvey to Blair, 3 September 2003.

40 H. Fenwick, *Civil Rights: New Labour, Freedom and the Human Rights Act* (Longman, 2000), pp. 17, 22–3.

41 M. Bevir and R. Maiman, 'Judicial Reform and Human Rights', in Casey (ed.), *Blair Legacy*, pp. 156–7.

42 R.P. Sayeed, *1997: The Future That Never Happened* (Zed Books, 2017), pp. 84, 91–2, 98–100.

43 N. Brain, *A History of Policing in England and Wales Since 1974: A Turbulent Journey* (Oxford University Press, 1974), pp. 189–90.

44 E. McLaughlin, 'Forcing the Issue: New Labour, New Localism and the Democratic Renewal of Police Accountability', *Howard Journal of Criminal Justice* 44, 5 (2005), pp. 479, 482.

45 S. Chapman and S.P. Savage, 'Controlling Crime and Disorder: The Labour Legacy', in Powell (ed.), *Modernising*, pp. 117–18; P. Senior, C. Crowther-Dowey and M. Long, *Understanding Modernisation in Criminal Justice* (McGraw Hill, 2007), p. 131.

46 House of Commons Home Affairs Committee, *The Government's Approach to Crime Prevention, Tenth Report of Session 2009–10, Volume II: Oral and Written Evidence* (House of Commons, 2010), pp. 93–4.

47 D. Gilling, 'Celebrating a Decade of the Crime and Disorder Act? A Personal View', *Safer Communities* 7, 3 (2008), p. 42; T. Hope, 'The New Local Governance of Community Safety in England and Wales', *Canadian Journal of Criminology and Criminal Justice* 47, 2 (2005), p. 377.

48 B. Loveday, 'Policing Performance: The Impact of Performance Measures and Targets on Police Forces in England and Wales', *International Journal of Police Science and Management* 8, 4 (2006), p. 283.

49 P. Hadfield, S. Lister and P. Traynor, '"This Town's a Different Town Today": Policing and Regulating the Night-Time Economy', *Criminology and Criminal Justice* 9, 4 (2009), pp. 478–9; G. Marnoch, J. Topping and G. Boyd, 'Explaining the Pattern of Growth in Strategic Actions Taken by Police Services during the New Labour Years: An Exploratory Study of an English Police Service', *Policing and Society* 24, 3 (2014), p. 304.

50 TNA PREM 49/1819/2, Prime Minister's Forward Strategy Unit, 2001.

51 Marie, 'Reducing Crime', table 1, p. 4.

52 P.K. Enns, J. Harris, J. Kenny, A. Roescu and W. Jennings, 'Public Responsiveness to Declining Crime Rates in the United States and England and Wales', *British Journal of Criminology* 62, 5 (2022), figure 10, p. 1106 and figure 12, p. 1110; M. Tiratelli, 'Attitudes to Crime and Punishment in England and Wales, 1964–2023: A Reinterpretation of the 1980s and a Model of Interactions Between Concern, Punitiveness and Prioritization', *British Journal of Criminology* 65, 2 (2025), pp. 387–404.

53 Young, 'Winning the Fight', pp. 36–7, 44.

54 J. Silverman, *Crime, Policy and the Media: The Shaping of Criminal Justice, 1989–2010* (Routledge, 2012), pp. 79–80.

55 D. Butler and D. Kavanagh, *The British General Election of 1997* (Macmillan, 1997), p. 78.

56 P. Fussey, 'New Labour and New Surveillance: Theoretical and Political Ramifications of CCTV Implementation in the UK', *Surveillance and Society* 2, 2/3 (2004), pp. 254, 259; P. Squires, 'Introduction: Asking Questions of Community Safety', in Squires (ed.), *Community Safety*, p. 3.

57 TNA PREM 49/1818, Russell to Blair, 6 July 2001.

58 A. Spriggs, J. Argomaniz, M. Gill and J. Bryan, *Public Attitudes Towards CCTV: Results from the Pre-Intervention Public Attitude Survey*, Online Report 10/05 (Home Office, 2005), table 2.15, p. 18.

59 E. Carrabine, M. Lee and N. South, 'Social Wrongs and Human Rights in Late Modern Britain: Social Exclusion, Crime Control, and Prospects for a Public Criminology', *Social Justice* 27, 2 (2000), p. 203.

60 Ewing, *Bonfire*, pp. 55, 61–3, 80–4.

61 The Act as originally passed is available at www.legislation.gov.uk/ukpga/1998/29/contents/enacted, accessed 27 March 2023.

62 N. Hutton, 'Sentencing Guidelines', in M. Tonry (ed.), *Confronting Crime: Crime Control Policy Under New Labour* (Routledge, 2013), pp. 121–6.

63 M. Tonry, *Punishment and Politics: Evidence and Emulation in the Making of English Crime Control Policy* (Willan, 2012), pp. 7–10.

64 S. Farrall and E. Gray, *The Politics of Crime, Punishment and Justice: Exploring the Lived Reality and Enduring Legacies of the 1980s Radical Right* (Routledge, 2024), pp. 128–9.

65 M. Cavadino, J. Dignan and G. Mair, *The Penal System: An introduction* (Sage, 5th edn., 2013), p. 105; Chapman and Savage, 'Controlling Crime', p. 109.

66 J. Beard, *Sentences of Imprisonment for Public Protection*, House of Commons Library Research Briefing 6086 (17 January 2023), p. 5.

67 A. Matthews, 'Man Still in Jail 20 Years after Laptop Robbery', *BBC News Online*, 2 August 2024, www.bbc.co.uk/news/articles/c1e5154j4zoo, accessed 28 March 2025.

68 Ewing, *Bonfire*, pp. 20–3, 36–41, 17–18.

69 Cavadino, Dignan and Mair, *Penal System*, table 1,1, p. 13; G. Sturge, *UK Prison Population Statistics*, House of Commons Library Briefing Paper 04334 (25 October 2022), chart, p. 5.

70 P. Carter, 'Penal Policy – A Journey', in N. Seddon (ed.), *Reform: The Next Ten Years* (Reform, 2012), p. 93; Sturge, *Prison Population*, chart, p. 3.

71 T. Morris, 'Crime and Penal Policy', in Seldon (ed.), *Blair Effect*, p. 364.

72 Solomon et al., *Ten Years of Criminal Justice*, table 1, p. 21.

73 L. Burke and S. Collett, 'People are not Things: What New Labour has done to Probation', *Probation Journal*, 57, 3 (2010), 232–49, p. 234.

74 Goldsmith, 'Young People', p. 16.

75 Ministry of Justice, *National Offender Management Service: Annual Report and Accounts 2010–2011* (TSO, 2011), p. 10.

76 House of Commons Home Affairs Committee, *The Government's Approach to Crime Prevention, Tenth Report of Session 2009–10, Volume I: Report* (House of Commons, 2010), pp. 38–42.

77 Goldsmith, 'Young People', p. 26.

78 Social Exclusion Unit, *Reducing Re-Offending by Ex-Prisoners* (SEU, 2002), pp. 131–3; Home Office, *Reducing Re-Offending: National Action Plan* (Home Office, 2004), pp. 4, 6.

79 Cm. 5563, *Justice for All* (The Stationery Office, July 2002), e.g. pp. 107–11.

80 Silverman, *Crime, Policy and the Media*, pp. 67–8.

81 Fenwick, *Civil Rights*, p. 420.

82 McLaughlin and Muncie, 'New Partnerships', pp. 169, 183.

83 Hutton, 'Sentencing Guidelines', pp. 117–18; Tonry, *Punishment and Politics*, p. 4; Brownlee, 'New Penology', p. 333. See Carrabine, Lee and South, 'Social Wrongs', pp. 197–8.

84 Burney, *Making People Behave*, p. 33.

85 Chapman and Savage, 'Controlling Crime', p. 112.

86 D. Downes, 'New Labour and the Lost Causes of Crime', *Criminal Justice Matters* 55, 1 (2004), p. 4; D. Downes, 'What Went Right: New Labour and Crime Control', *Howard Journal of Criminal Justice* 49, 1 (2010), p. 395.

87 R. Reiner, 'Policing and Social Democracy: Resuscitating a Lost Perspective', *Journal of Police Studies* 25 (2012), pp. 94–5.

88 Blair, 'Crime is a Socialist Issue', p. 2.

89 Hodgkinson and Tilley, 'Tackling Anti-Social Behaviour', p. 289.

90 N. Lawson, '"Reid"ing the Riot Act: New Labour, Crime and Punishment', *Renewal* 14, 3 (2006), pp. 1–2.

91 Silverman, *Crime, Policy and the Media*, p. 63.

92 R. Cook, *The Point of Departure: Diaries from the Front Bench* (Pocket Books, 2004), diary entry for 23 April 2002, p. 140.

Chapter 7

1 T. Brown, 'The Third Way', in T. Brown (ed.), *Stakeholder Housing* (Pluto Press/Labour Housing Group, 1998), pp. 9, 21.

2 See DETR, *Quality and Choice: A Decent Home for All: The Housing Green Paper* (DETR, 2000), pp. 10–14, and on local authorities' management of housing pp. 56–7, 68–9.

3 D. Mullins and A. Murie, *Housing Policy in the UK* (Palgrave, 2006), pp. 76–7.

4 J. Ford, 'Housing Policy', in N. Ellison and C. Pierson (eds), *Developments in British Social Policy 2* (Palgrave Macmillan, 2003), table 8.2, p. 148; P.A. Kemp, 'Housing Policy Under New Labour', in Powell (ed.), *New Welfare State?*, p. 143.

5 Office of the Deputy Prime Minister, *Sustainable Communities: Building for the Future* (ODPM, 2003), p. 4 and table, p. 7; TNA PREM 49/3295, Prescott to Blair, 28 May 2003.

6 J. Broughton, *Municipal Dreams: The Rise and Fall of Council Housing* (Verso, 2018), pp. 221–4, 228; see also B. Lund, 'Housing Policy: Coming in and Out of the Cold?', in Powell (ed.), *Modernising*, pp. 36–7.

7 D. Cowan and A. Marsh, 'New Labour, Same Old Tory Housing Policy', *Modern Law Review* 64, 2 (2001), pp. 262–3; H. Armstrong, 'A New Vision for Housing in England', in Brown (ed.), *Stakeholder Housing*, p. 124.

8 A. Murie, *The Right to Buy: Selling Off Public and Social Housing* (Policy Press, 2016), p. 41.

9 S. Metcalfe, *From the Ground Up: How the Government Can Build More Homes* (Institute for Government, 2024), figures 8–9, pp. 36–7.

10 H. Pawson, 'Restructuring England's Social Housing Sector Since 1989: Undermining or Underpinning the Fundamentals of Public Housing?', *Housing Studies* 21, 5 (2006), p. 772.

11 Murie, *Right to Buy*, pp. 41, 44; A. Diner and H. Wright, *Reforming Right to Buy: Options for Preserving and Delivering New Council Homes for the Twenty-First Century* (New Economics Foundation, 2024), text and figure 1, p. 9, figure 7, p. 20.

12 DETR, *Quality and Choice: A Decent Home for All: The Way Forward for Housing* (DETR, 2000), p. 6; Ford, 'Housing Policy', pp. 145, 151.

13 NAO/Comptroller and Auditor General, *The Decent Homes Programme* (NAO, 2009), p. 6; ODPM, *Sustainable Communities: Building for the Future*, p. 15.

14 NAO/Comptroller and Auditor General, *Decent Homes*, figures 4–5, pp. 18–19; Diamond, *British Labour Party*, p. 213.

15 Iain Wright, oral answers, 'Decent Homes Programme', Hansard, HC (series 5) vol. 493, cols 158–9 (2 June 2009). See J. O'Shea, 'Reassessing New Labour's Political Economy: A Study of Housing and Regional Economic Policy', PhD Dissertation, University of Cambridge, 2023, figure 18, p. 158 and text on p. 159.

16 DETR, *Quality and Choice: A Decent Home for All*, pp. 81–3; see D. Cowan, 'From Allocations to Lettings: Sea Change or More of the Same?', in D. Cowan and A. Marsh (eds), *Two Steps Forward: Housing Policy into the New Millennium* (Policy Press, 2001), p. 139.

17 DETR, *Quality and Choice: A Decent Home for All*, p. 40.

18 S. Fitzpatrick and H. Pawson, 'Welfare Safety Net or Tenure of Choice? The Dilemma Facing Social Housing Policy in England', *Housing Studies* 22, 2 (2007), p. 174 and table 5, p. 175; see TNA PREM 49/1819/2, Strategy Unit Paper, August 2001, pp. 16, 24–5.

19 Lund, 'Housing Policy', p. 40.

20 P. Hickman, 'Approaches to Tenant Participation in the English Local Authority Sector', *Housing Studies* 21, 2 (2006), p. 210, table 1, p. 212 and p. 217.

21 P. Malpass and D. Mullins, 'Local Authority Housing Stock Transfer in the UK: From Local Initiative to National Policy', *Housing Studies* 17, 4 (2002), pp. 675–6; Ford, 'Housing Policy', p. 153.

22 H. Pawson and K. Jacobs, 'Policy Intervention and its Impact: New Labour's Public Service Reform Model as Applied to Local Authority Housing', *Housing, Theory and Society* 76, 1 (2010), p. 77; H. Pawson and D. Mullins, *After Council Housing: Britain's New Social Landlords* (Palgrave, 2010), pp. 197–8.

23 DETR, *Quality and Choice: A Decent Home for All*, p. 61; N. Ginsburg, 'The Privatisation of Council Housing', *Critical Social Policy* 25, 1 (2005), p. 116, table 2, p. 120 and p. 121.

24 Pawson and Mullins, *After Council Housing*, table 2.1, p. 31.

25 H. Pawson, E. Davidson, J. Morgan and R. Edwards, *The Impact of Housing Stock Transfers in Urban Britain* (Joseph Rowntree Foundation/Chartered Institute of Housing, 2009), table 2.1, p. 22; Pawson and Mullins, *After Council Housing*, table 7.1, p. 200 and p. 201.

26 Ginsburg, 'Privatisation', p. 126.

27 P. Malpass and C. Victory, 'The Modernisation of Social Housing in England', *International Journal of Housing Policy* 10, 1 (2010), p. 13.

28 Ford, 'Housing Policy', table 8.2, p. 148.

29 D. Mullins and H. Pawson, 'The Evolution of Stock Transfer', in P. Malpass and R. Rowlands (eds), *Housing, Markets and Policy* (Routledge, 2010), p. 90.

30 H. Pawson and R. Smith, 'Second Generation Stock Transfers in Britain: Impacts on Social Housing Governance and Organisational Culture', *European Journal of Housing Policy* 9, 4 (2009), p. 422.

31 Pawson and Mullins, *After Council Housing*, pp. 209–10, figure 7.4, p. 211 and table 7.3, p. 217; Pawson et al., *Impact of Housing Stock Transfers*, table 4.5, p. 53.

32 Urban Task Force, *Towards an Urban Renaissance: Final Report of the Urban Task Force* (UTF, 1999), pp. 68–70, 73, 152–3, 255.

33 A. Seely, *VAT and Construction*, House of Commons Library Briefing Paper 587 (October 2019), p. 11.

34 House of Commons Transport, Local Government and the Regions Committee, *Empty Homes: Sixth Report of Session 2001–2002, Vol. I* (House of Commons, 2002), p. 10.

35 G. Bramley and H. Pawson, *Low Demand Housing and Unpopular Neighbourhoods* (DETR, 2001), table 5, pp. 404–5 and table 2, p. 399.

36 Social Exclusion Unit, *National Strategy for Neighbourhood Renewal: Policy Action Team Audit* (SEU, 2001), p. 98.

37 DETR, *National Strategy for Neighbourhood Renewal: Report of Policy Action Team 7, Unpopular Housing* (DETR, December 1999).

38 ODPM, *Sustainable Communities: Building for the Future*, pp. 25, 28.

39 G. Bramley and H. Pawson, *Low Demand Housing and Unpopular Neighbourhoods: Technical Appendix* (DETR, 2001), pp. 412–13.

40 TNA PREM 49/2371, Emmerich to Blair, 9 March 2001.

41 TNA PREM 49/3296, Hurst to Blair, 19 September 2003.

42 R. Tunstall and A. Coulter, *Progress on Twenty 'Unpopular' Estates, 1980–2005*, Joseph Rowntree Foundation Report (Joseph Rowntree Foundation, November 2006).

43 R. Lupton, A. Fenton and A. Fitzgerald, *Labour's Record on Neighbourhood Renewal in England: Policy, Spending and Outcomes 1997–2010*, LSE Social Policy in a Cold Climate Working Papers 6 (July 2013), p. 19.

44 A. Fenton and R. Lupton, *Low-demand Housing and Unpopular Neighbourhoods Under Labour*, LSE Social Policy in a Cold Climate Research Note Series RN006 (April 2013), pp. 7–8.

45 NAO, *Department for Communities and Local Government: Housing Market Renewal* (NAO, 2007), p. 7 and table 13, p. 21; Toynbee and Walker, *Verdict*, p. 140.

46 Ibid., pp. 6, 26–7.

47 TNA PREM 49/174, Scott to Blair, 25 June 1997; TNA PREM 49/538, Scott to Blair, 22 December 1998.

48 O'Shea, 'Reassessing New Labour's Political Economy', p. 160.

49 K. Barker, *Review of Housing Supply: Final Report: Recommendations* (HMSO, 2004), charts 1.1, 1.2, pp. 13, 15.

50 S. Wilcox and H. Pawson (eds), *UK Housing Review 2010/11* (Chartered Institute of Housing and Council of Mortgage Lenders, 2011), table 2.3.2, p. 63.

51 Toynbee and Walker, *Verdict*, pp. 138–9.

52 P. Durden, 'Housing Policy', in S.P. Savage and R. Atkinson (eds), *Public Policy Under Blair* (Palgrave, 2001), p. 145.

53 Barker, *Review of Housing Supply*, table 1.1, p. 21.

54 House of Commons Environmental Audit Committee, *Housing: Building a Sustainable Future: First Report of Session 2004–2005, Vol. I* (House of Commons, 2005), pp. 24, 27–8.

55 ODPM, *Sustainable Communities: Building for the Future*, map, p. 10 and p. 32.

56 Metcalfe, *From the Ground Up*, p. 67.

57 NAO, *The Thames Gateway: Laying the Foundations* (NAO, 2007), p. 5 and figures 20–21, pp. 32–3.

58 Barker, *Review of Housing Supply*, pp. 24, 34–5.

59 ODPM, *Sustainable Communities: Building for the Future*, pp. 32–3.

60 P. Allmendinger, *New Labour and Planning: From New Right to New Left* (Routledge, 2011), pp. 119 and e.g. table 6.2, p. 122.

61 NAO, *Building More Affordable Homes: Improving the Delivery of Affordable Housing in Areas of High Demand* (NAO, 2005), p. 20, figure 4, p. 21 and pp. 11–12, 52–4; NAO, *Thames Gateway*, p. 12.

62 Diamond, *British Labour Party*, p. 213.

63 ONS, *Census 2021: United Kingdom Population Mid-Year Estimate*, www.ons.gov.uk/people populationandcommunity/populationandmigration/populationestimates/timeseries/ ukpop/pop, accessed 14 May 2024.

64 Metcalfe, *From the Ground Up*, box 1, p. 38.

65 ONS, *Housing Affordability in England and Wales: 2024*, 24 March 2025, www.ons.gov. uk/peoplepopulationandcommunity/housing/bulletins/housingaffordabilityinenglan dandwales/latest, accessed 9 April 2025.

66 House Builders Federation, *Beyond Barker: A Two-Decade Review of England's Housing Policies and Progress* (HBF, 2024), pp. 8, 15–20.

67 Ibid., pp. 5, 9; S. Watling and A. Breach, *The Housebuilding Crisis: The UK's 4 Million Missing Homes* (Centre for Cities, 2023), table 3, p. 44.

68 B. Christophers, 'A Tale of Two Inequalities: Housing Wealth Inequality and Tenure Inequality', *Environment and Planning A: Economy and Space* 53, 3 (2019), pp. 574, 578, 581.

69 M. Watson, 'Constituting Monetary Conservatives via the "Savings Habit": New Labour and the British Housing Market Bubble', *Comparative European Politics* 6, 3 (2008), p. 289.

70 W. Keegan, *'Saving the World'?: Gordon Brown Reconsidered* (Searching Finance, 2012), p. 19.

71 A. Finlayson, 'Financialisation, Financial Literacy and Asset-Based Welfare', *British Journal of Politics and International Relations* 11, 3 (2009), pp. 400, 416.

72 A. Humphrey and C. Bromley, 'Home Sweet Home', in A. Park, J. Curtice, K. Thomson, C. Bromley, M. Phillips, and M. Johnson (eds), *British Social Attitudes, the 22nd Report* (Sage, 2005), table 3.5, p. 70, table 3.2, p. 67 and table 3.8, p. 73, respectively.

73 C. Hay, 'Good Inflation, Bad Inflation: The Housing Boom, Economic Growth and the Disaggregation of Inflationary Preferences in the UK and Ireland', *British Journal of Politics and International Relations* 11, 3 (2009), p. 469 and figure 6, p. 470; for 'privatised Keynesianism' see C. Crouch, 'Privatised Keynesianism: An Unacknowledged Policy Regime', *British Journal of Politics and International Relations* 11, 3 (2009), pp. 382–3.

74 J. Ryan-Collins, 'The Demand for Housing as an Investment: Drivers, Outcomes and Policy Interventions to Enhance Housing Affordability in the UK', *UCL Institute for Innovation and Public Purpose*, Policy Report 2024/13 (UCL, 2024), figures 2, 4 and 5, pp. 18, 20–1; Crouch, 'Privatised Keynesianism', p. 391.

75 J. Montgomerie and M. Büdenbender, 'Round the Houses: Homeownership and Failures of Asset-Based Welfare in the United Kingdom', *New Political Economy* 20, 3 (2015), p. 394; P. Malpass, 'Housing and the New Welfare State: Wobbly Pillar or Cornerstone?', *Housing Studies* 23, 1 (2008), p. 11.

76 B. Lund, *Understanding Housing Policy* (Policy Press, 3rd edn., 2017), p. 163.

77 ODPM, *Sustainable Communities: Building for the Future*, p. 31.

78 Kemp, 'Housing Policy Under New Labour', pp. 137–8.

79 Social Exclusion Unit, *Rough Sleeping: Report by the Social Exclusion Unit* (HMSO, 1998), pp. 13, 18–20; see A. Taylor, '"Hollowing Out" or Filling In? Taskforces and the Management of Cross-Cutting Issues in British Government', *British Journal of Politics and International Relations* 2, 1 (2000), pp. 63–4.

80 Rough Sleepers Unit, *Coming in from the Cold: The Government's Strategy on Rough Sleeping* (HMSO, 2000), pp. 11–19; Durden, 'Housing Policy', p. 151.

81 S. Fitzpatrick and A. Jones, 'Pursuing Social Justice or Social Cohesion? Coercion in Street Homelessness Policies in England', *Journal of Social Policy* 34, 3 (2005), pp. 393–4.

82 M. Whiteford, 'New Labour, Street Homelessness and Social Exclusion: A Defaulted Promissory Note?', *Housing Studies* 28, 1 (2013), pp. 13, 15.

83 D. Christie, '"A Hand Up, Not a Hand Out": New Labour and Street Homelessness, 1997–2010', PhD thesis, University of Birmingham, 2023, pp. 184–90.

84 Pawson and Jacobs, 'Local Authority Housing', p. 81.

85 H. Pawson and E. Davidson, 'Fit for Purpose? Official Measures of Homelessness in the Era of the Activist State', *Radical Statistics* 93 (2006), p. 9.

86 J. May, P. Cloke and S. Johnsen, 'Shelter at the Margins: New Labour and the Changing State of Emergency Accommodation for Single Homeless People in Britain', *Policy and Politics* 34, 4 (2006), pp. 715, 718–19, table 2, p. 721; Lund, *Understanding Housing Policy*, figure 7.3, p. 165.

87 P. Cloke, P. Milbourne and R. Widdowfield, 'Making the Homeless Count? Enumerating Rough Sleepers and the Distortion of Homelessness', *Policy and Politics* 29, 3 (2001), pp. 269, 273, 262–3.

88 Pawson and Davidson, 'Official Measures of Homelessness', pp. 11–12, 22–3.

89 DCLG, 'Rough Sleeping Statistics England – Autumn 2010 Experimental Statistics', *Housing Statistical Releases*, 17 February 2011, pp. 1–5.

90 Department for Levelling Up, Housing and Communities, *Rough Sleeping Snapshot in England: Autumn 2023*, February 2024, www.gov.uk/government/statistics/rough-sleeping-snapshot-in-england-autumn-2023/rough-sleeping-snapshot-in-england-autumn-2023, accessed 14 May 2024.

91 Department for Levelling Up, Housing and Communities, *Statutory Homelessness in England: July to September 2023*, 30 April 2024, www.gov.uk/government/statistics/statutory-homelessness-in-england-july-to-september-2023/statutory-homelessness-in-england-july-to-september-2023, accessed 13 May 2024.

92 Shelter, 'At Least 309,000 People Homeless in England Today', 14 December 2023, https://england.shelter.org.uk/media/press_release/at_least_309000_people_homeless_in_england_today, accessed 15 May 2024.

93 J. Burn-Murdoch, 'Data Points: Why Britain is the World's Worst on Homelessness', *Financial Times*, 17 May 2024.

94 Humphrey and Bromley, 'Home Sweet Home', p. 63.

95 L. Hanley, *Estates: An Intimate History* (Granta, 2012), pp. 144–5.

96 R. Dobson and J. McNeill, 'Homelessness and Housing Support Services: Rationales and Policies under New Labour', *Social Policy and Society* 10, 4 (2011), pp. 582–3; Fitzpatrick and Jones, 'Social Justice or Social Cohesion?', pp. 390–2, 403–4.

97 Urban Task Force, *Towards a Strong Urban Renaissance* (UTF, 2005), p. 2.

98 Christie, 'Street Homelessness', pp. 198–200.

99 S. Fitzpatrick and S. Johnsen, 'The Use of Enforcement to Combat "Street Culture" in England: An Ethical Approach?', *Ethics and Social Welfare* 3, 3 (2009), pp. 294, 300.

100 P. Malpass, 'The Wobbly Pillar? Housing Policy and the British Postwar Welfare State', *Journal of Social Policy* 32, 4 (2003), pp. 597, 600.

101 S. Merrett, *State Housing in Britain* (Routledge, 1979), pp. 244–50, including table 9.2, p. 247 and graph 9.1, p. 250.

102 Humphrey and Bromley, 'Home Sweet Home', table 3.1, p. 66.

103 Malpass, 'Housing and the New Welfare State', pp. 3–4, 9; Malpass, 'The Wobbly Pillar', p. 589; Pawson and Jacobs, 'Local Authority Housing', p. 77.

Notes

Chapter 8

1 P. Norris, 'Anatomy of a Labour Landslide', in P. Norris and N.T. Gavin (eds), *Britain Votes 1997* (Oxford University Press, 1997), table 3, p. 9, figures 4–5, pp. 10–11 and table 6, p. 16.

2 D. Sanders, 'The New Electoral Battleground', in A. King (ed.), *New Labour Triumphs: Britain at the Polls* (Chatham House, 1998), table 8.1, p. 220.

3 A.F. Heath, R.M. Jowell and J. Curtice, *The Rise of New Labour: Party Policies and Voter Choices* (Oxford University Press, 2001), figure 6.11, p. 119.

4 P. Gould, *The Unfinished Revolution: How the Modernisers Saved the Labour Party* (Abacus, 1999), pp. 390, 392.

5 www.electionpolling.co.uk/constituencies/uk-parliament/spelthorne, accessed 10 July 2025.

6 D. Broughton, 'The 1997 General Election in England: A Landslide Without Illusions?', *Regional and Federal Studies* 7, 3 (1997), p. 185, and table 1, p. 187; C. Pattie, R. Johnston, D. Dorling, D. Rossiter, H. Tunstall, and I. MacAllister, 'New Labour, New Geography? The Electoral Geography of the 1997 British General Election', *Area* 29, 3 (1997), table 1, p. 255.

7 Mattinson, *Brick Wall*, p. 30.

8 For this model, see J. Green and W.J. Jennings, *The Politics of Competence: Parties, Public Opinion and Voters* (Cambridge University Press, 2017), e.g. chapter 6, pp. 167–96.

9 M. Gill and K. Theakston, 'The League Table of Post-War Leaders of the Opposition According to Academics: Corbyn Not the Worst and Starmer Trending Below Kinnock', *LSE British Politics and Policy Blog*, 13 July 2021, https://blogs.lse.ac.uk/politicsandpolicy/post-war-leaders-of-the-opposition/, accessed 19 July 2021.

10 www.ipsos.com/en-uk/political-monitor-satisfaction-ratings-1977-1987, www.ipsos.com/en-uk/political-monitor-satisfaction-ratings-1988-1997 and www.ipsos.com/en-uk/political-monitor-satisfaction-ratings-1997-present, accessed 19 April 2023.

11 Butler and Kavanagh, *General Election of 1997*, p. 231.

12 Bartle, 'Why Labour Won', p. 188.

13 Gould, *Unfinished Revolution*, pp. 261–2.

14 M. Wickham-Jones, 'How the Conservatives Lost the Economic Argument', in A. Geddes and J. Tonge (eds), *Labour's Landslide: The British General Election 1997* (Manchester University Press, 1997), table 7.3, p. 112; Butler and Kavanagh, *General Election of 1997*, p. 231.

15 A. Seely, *VAT on Fuel and Power*, House of Commons Briefing Paper 97/87 (9 July 1997); Butler and Kavanagh, *General Election of 1997*, p. 61.

16 Gould, *Unfinished Revolution*, p. 267.

17 For this government as effectively a coalition, see Davis and Rentoul, *Heroes or Villains?*, e.g. pp. 22–3.

18 House of Commons Information Office, *By-Election Results 1992–1997*, Factsheet M14, Members' Series (House of Commons, revised September 2003), tables 1–4, pp. 4–8.

19 P. Ashdown, *A Fortunate Life* (Aurum Press, 2009), p. 276.

20 Ashdown diary, 1 October 1996: P. Ashdown, *The Ashdown Diaries, Vol. 1: 1988–1997* (London: Penguin, 2000), p. 463.

21 P. Joyce, *Realignment of the Left? A History of the Relationship Between the Liberal Democrat and Labour Parties* (Macmillan, 1999), pp. 268–73.

Notes

22 For details, see Ashdown's own diary from the time: Ashdown diary, 18 March 1996 and 14 January 1997: Ashdown, *Diaries, Vol. 1*, pp. 408–16, 504–8.

23 Heath, Cowell and Curtice, *Rise of New Labour*, figures 6.2–6.3, pp. 116–17.

24 G. Evans, J. Curtice and P. Norris, 'New Labour, New Tactical Voting? The Causes and Consequences of Tactical Voting in the 1997 General Election', *British Elections and Parties Review* 8, 1 (1998), p. 69 and table 1, p. 70. 2.2 per cent of respondents told the British Election Study that they switched tactically from the Liberal Democrats to Labour, while 2.5 per cent moved tactically the other way.

25 Butler and Kavanagh, *General Election of 1997*, pp. 311, 313; Ashdown, *Fortunate Life*, e.g. p. 295.

26 See Bartle, 'Why Labour Won', figure 7.1, p. 179.

27 Whiteley et al., 'The Issue Agenda and Voting in 2005', table 2, p. 154, and figure 3, p. 158; T. Quinn, 'Tony Blair's Second Term', in Bartle and King (eds), *Britain at the Polls, 2005*, p. 17.

28 For Blair and Brown's visits to the USA in 1991 and 1993, and the impact President Clinton's election had on the two men, see Seldon, *Blair*, pp. 121–7.

29 ONS, *Average Weekly Earnings in Great Britain, February 2021*, figure 1, annual growth in total pay, www.ons.gov.uk/employmentandlabourmarket/peopleinwork/employmentande mployeetypes/bulletins/averageweeklyearningsingreatbritain/february2021, accessed 28 July 2021.

30 Bartle, 'Why Labour Won', table 7.6, p. 176, table 7.7, p. 177 and table 7.8, p. 183.

31 Ipsos Mori, *Trust in Professions: Long-Term Trends*, 30 November 2017, www.ipsos.com/ en-uk/trust-professions-long-term-trends, accessed 1 April 2025.

32 R. Cracknell, E. Uberoi and M. Burton, *UK Election Statistics: 1918–2019: A Century of Elections*, House of Commons Briefing Paper Number CBP7529 (27 February 2020), table 1c, p. 14.

33 J. Glover, 'From the Economy to Education, Labour is Squeezing Tory Lead', *Guardian*, 6 April 2010; R. Johnston and C. Pattie, 'Where did Labour's Votes Go? Valence Politics and Campaign Effects at the 2010 British General Election', *British Journal of Politics and International Relations* 13, 3 (2011), table 3, p. 290.

34 D. Kavanagh and P. Cowley, *The British General Election of 2010* (Palgrave, 2010), table 16.1, p. 337, and table 12.2, p. 250.

35 Butler and Kavanagh, *General Election of 2001*, tables 12.1–12.2, p. 237, table 12.3, p. 241 and table A1.1, p. 261.

36 D. Kavanagh and D. Butler, *The British General Election of 2005* (Palgrave Macmillan, 2005), table A1.1, p. 204.

37 J. Curtice, 'Turnout: Electors Stay Home – Again', in Norris and Wlezien (eds), *Britain Votes 2005*, tables 3–4, pp. 124–5, and table 2, p. 123.

38 M. Sobolewska and R. Ford, *Brexitland* (Cambridge University Press, 2020), pp. 122–7. Ipsos Mori reported a rather different figure (of 21 per cent) for the 2010 General Election: see Kavanagh and Cowley, *General Election of 2010*, table 11.1, p. 241.

39 D. Mattinson, *Beyond the Red Wall: Why Labour Lost, How the Conservatives Won and What Will Happen Next?* (Biteback, 2020), pp. 9, 91; Bartle, 'Why Labour Won', table 7.3, 'three nations', p. 170.

40 W. Dahlgreen, 'Memories of Iraq: Did We Ever Support the War?', *YouGov*, 3 June 2015, https://yougov.co.uk/topics/politics/articles-reports/2015/06/03/remembering-iraq, accessed 27 July 2021; 'Iraq: Support for the Iraq War', *UK Polling Report*, https://web. archive.org/web/20221030155335/http://ukpollingreport.co.uk/iraq, accessed 27 July 2021.

41 G. Cameron, 'Foreign Policy and the "War on Terror"', in Geddes and Tonge (eds), *Britain Decides*, p. 263; N. Allen, 'A Restless Electorate: Stirrings in the Political System', in Bartle and King (eds), *Britain at the Polls, 2005*, p. 57.

42 G. Evans and R. Andersen, 'The Impact of Party Leaders: How Blair Lost Labour Votes', in Norris and Wlezien (eds), *Britain Votes 2005*, figure 3, p. 169, figures 5–7, pp. 174–5, and p. 176; Mattinson, *Brick Wall*, p. 124.

43 Kavanagh and Butler, *General Election of 2005*, pp. 79, 190–1.

44 A. Russell, 'The Liberal Democrat Campaign', in Norris and Wlezien (eds), *Britain Votes 2005*, tables 3–4, p. 98; L. Chambers, 'British Public: We Will Never Forgive Tony Blair', *YouGov*, 25 May 2016: https://yougov.co.uk/topics/politics/articles-repo rts/2016/05/25/no-public-appetite-forgiving-blair, accessed 27 July 2021.

45 P. Norris and R. Inglehart, *Cultural Backlash: Trump, Brexit, and Authoritarian Populism* (Cambridge University Press, 2019), table 6.1, p. 179.

46 O. Daddow, *New Labour and the European Union: Blair and Brown's Logic of History* (Manchester University Press, 2011), p. 19.

47 S.O. Becker, T. Fetzer and D. Novy, 'Who Voted for Brexit? A Comprehensive District-Level Analysis', *Economic Policy* 32, 92 (2017), table 1, p. 621 and table 6, p. 634.

48 R. Ford and M. Goodwin, *Revolt on the Right: Explaining Support for the Radical Right in Britain* (Routledge, 2014), table 3.2, p. 123 and figure 3.7, p. 133.

49 Sobolewska and Ford, *Brexitland*, table 5.4, p. 133 and figure 6.1, p. 160.

50 Norris and Inglehart, *Cultural Backlash*, pp. 189–92; Sobolewska and Ford, *Brexitland*, figure 5.9, p. 148.

51 J. Gest, *The New Minority: White Working Class Politics in an Age of Immigration and Inequality* (Oxford University Press, 2016), pp. 21–3.

52 Author interview, John Denham, 22 July 2024.

53 Butler and Kavanagh, *General Election of 2001*, p. 245.

54 Kavanagh and Butler, *General Election of 2005*, table 13.1, p. 198.

55 Kavanagh and Cowley, *General Election of 2010*, table 16.3, p. 341.

56 Ford and Goodwin, *Revolt on the Right*, figure I.1, p. 5 and table 2.2, p. 73; Sobolewska and Ford, *Brexitland*, pp. 165, 167.

57 Cracknell, Uberoi and Burton, *Century of Elections*, table 1c, p. 14; Kavanagh and Cowley, *General Election of 2010*, table A1.2, p. 353.

58 M. Hodge, 'The Problem is Alienation, Not Apathy', *Guardian*, 14 March 2002.

59 Mattinson, *Brick Wall*, p. 18.

60 Gest, *New Minority*, pp. 46–7.

61 AMD Digital, G1416's response to 1996 Autumn/Winter directive part 3 & 1997 Spring directive part 2, response reference SxMOA2/1/49/3/2/96, 24 November 1996, 17 March 1997, www.massobservationproject.amdigital.co.uk/, accessed 9 April 2021.

62 C. Seymour-Ure, 'Leaders and Leading Articles: Characterisation of John Major and Tony Blair in the Editorials of the National Daily Press', in I. Crewe, B. Gosschalk and J. Bartle (eds), *Why Labour Won the General Election of 1997* (Routledge, 1998), table 10.2, p. 134; Gould, *Unfinished Revolution*, p. 259.

63 Quinn, 'Second Term', p. 17; A. King, 'Why Labour Won – Yet Again', in Bartle and King (eds), *Britain at the Polls, 2005*, pp. 157–8.

64 Author interviews, Sir Tony Blair, 16 July 2024; Phil Wilson, 17 June 2024.

65 Norris and Inglehart, *Cultural Backlash*, figure 12.9, p. 432 and figure 12.8, p. 430.

Notes

Chapter 9

1 P. Hennessy, *Never Again: Britain 1945–1951* (Jonathan Cape, 1992), p. 454.

2 Ipsos, 'Veracity Index 2023: Trust in Professions Survey', December 2023, www.ipsos.com/sites/default/files/ct/news/documents/2023-12/ipsos-trust-in-professions-veracity-index-2023-charts.pdf, accessed 2 October 2024.

3 Tony Blair, speech on public services, The Grove, Hertfordshire, 29 January 2004: P. Richards (ed.), *Tony Blair in His Own Words* (Politico's, 2004), p. 268.

4 D. Macintyre, *Mandelson and the Making of New Labour* (HarperCollins, 2000), p. 376.

5 Cook, *Point of Departure*, diary entry for 9 August 2001, p. 37.

6 Murphy, *Futures of Socialism*, p. 265.

7 A. Kaletsky, 'Banking Regulation', in C. Clarke (ed.), *The 'Too Difficult' Box: The Big Issues Politicians Can't Crack* (Biteback, 2014), p. 130.

8 M.D. Bordo, A. Redish and Hugh Rockoff, 'Why Didn't Canada Have a Banking Crisis in 2008 (or in 1930, or 1907, or …)?', *Economic History Review* 68, 1 (2015), pp. 218–43; Sveriges Riksbank, *The Riksbank's Measures During the Global Financial Crisis* (Sveriges Riksbank, 2020).

9 A. Darling, *Back from the Brink: 1,000 Days at Number 11* (Atlantic Books, 2011), pp. 9, 19–20.

10 Blair, *Speaking for Myself*, p. 220.

11 Mattinson, *Brick Wall*, p. 142.

12 S. Richards, *Whatever it Takes: The Real Story of Gordon Brown and New Labour* (Fourth Estate, 2010), pp. 99, 102.

13 S. Freedman, *Failed State: Why Nothing Works and How We Fix It* (Macmillan, 2024), p. 47.

14 Author interview, Phil Wilson, 17 June 2024.

15 Author interview, Sir Tony Blair, 16 July 2024.

16 Author interview, Patrick Diamond, 10 July 2024.

17 M. Bevir, *New Labour: A Critique* (Routledge, 2005), p. 128.

18 Sayeed, *Future*, p. 48.

19 King and Crewe, *Blunders*, pp. 196–200.

20 Finlayson, *Making Sense*, p. 107.

21 R. Hattersley, *Choose Freedom: The Future for Democratic Socialism* (Michael Joseph, 1987), p. 142.

22 Sobolewska and Ford, *Brexitland*, figure 5.7, p. 140; Ford and Goodwin, *Revolt on the Right*, p. 130.

23 Ipsos, *How Britain Voted …*, various years from 1997, www.ipsos.com/en-uk/how-britain-voted-1997, accessed 5 October 2024.

24 Cook, *Point of Departure*, diary entry for 8 March 2002, p. 123.

25 Author interview, Phil Wilson, 17 June 2024.

26 T. Horton, 'Solidarity Lost? New Labour and the Politics of the Welfare State', in P. Diamond and M. Kenny (eds), *Reassessing New Labour: Market, State and Society under Blair and Brown* (Wiley-Blackwell, 2011), figure 1, p. S33.

27 Byrne, *Inequality of Wealth*, pp. 167–8.

28 Author interview, Sir Tony Blair, 16 July 2024.

29 Author interview, Patrick Diamond, 10 July 2024.

30 K. Rummery, F. Gains and C. Annesley, 'New Labour: Towards an Engendered Politics and Policy?', in C. Annesley, F. Gains and K. Rummery (eds), *Women and New Labour: Engendering Politics and Policy?* (Policy Press, 2007), pp. 232–7.

Notes

31 Author interview, Patrick Diamond, 10 July 2024; see Giddens, *Third Way*, pp. 18–19.

32 Fielding, *Labour Party*, p. 205.

33 T. Walters and T. Wernham, *The Distributional Impact of Tax and Benefit Reforms since 2010*, IFS Report 319 (IFS, 2024), figure 1, p. 9, and figure 2, p. 11.

34 J. Craig, 'Sustainable Regeneration: Looking Back and Moving Forward', *Power to Change: Backing Community Business*, 13 March 2025, www.powertochange.org.uk/evidence-and-ideas/news-and-events/sustainable-regeneration-looking-back-and-moving-forward/, accessed 26 March 2025.

35 Murphy, *Futures of Socialism*, pp. 9–12, 15.

36 S. Fielding, 'The 1974–79 Labour Governments and "New" Labour', in K. Hickson and A. Seldon (eds), *New Labour, Old Labour: The Wilson and Callaghan Governments 1974–1979* (Routledge, 2004), pp. 291–2.

37 E. Avril, 'What's Left of Blairism? The Labour Party's Changing Conception of the State since the 1980s', in M. Full and M. Lazar (eds), *European Socialists and the State in the Twentieth and Twenty-First Centuries* (Palgrave, 2020), pp. 349–50.

38 Author interview, Patrick Diamond, 10 July 2024.

39 C. Mullin, *A Walk-On Part: Diaries 1994–1999* (Profile, 2011), diary entries for 23 June and 16 November 1994, pp. 10, 38.

40 A. Seldon, 'The Net Blair Effect, 1997–2007', in A. Seldon (ed.), *Blair's Britain*, p. 649.

41 Author interview, Sir Tony Blair, 16 July 2024.

42 T. Blair, *On Leadership: Lessons for the 21st Century* (Hutchinson Heinemann, 2024), p. 33–43.

43 J. Cruddas, *A Century of Labour* (Polity, 2024), pp. 176–81.

44 A.J. Williams, *The Christian Left: An Introduction to Radical and Socialist Christian Thought* (John Wiley and Sons, 2022), p. 43.

45 A. Boulton, *Tony's Ten Years: Memories of the Blair Administration* (Pocket Books, 2009), p. 87; R. Davis, *Tangled Up in Blue: Blue Labour and the Struggle for Labour's Soul* (Ruskin, 2011), pp. 16–17.

46 A. Giddens, *The Consequences of Modernity* (Polity, 1990), p. 156; see P. Kolarz, *Giddens and Politics Beyond the Third Way: Utopian Realism in the Late Modern Age* (Palgrave, 2016), e.g. p. 42.

47 S. Hale, 'Professor Macmurray and Mr Blair: The Strange Case of the Communitarian Guru that Never Was', *Political Quarterly* 73, 2 (2002), pp. 153–5.

48 J. Macmurray, *Conditions of Freedom* (Faber, 1950), pp. 51, 54–6.

49 See D. Sage, 'A Challenge to Liberalism? The Communitarianism of the Big Society and Blue Labour', *Critical Social Policy* 32, 3 (2012), pp. 367–8.

50 Somerville, *Immigration Under New Labour*, pp. 161–3; Consterdine, *Labour's Immigration Policy*, p. 67.

51 TNA PREM 49/3052, Nicola Rossi paper, 'Migration and integration', February 2003.

52 Consterdine, *Labour's Immigration Policy*, p. 78.

53 G. Sturge, *Migration Statistics*, UK Parliament, House of Commons Library, https://commonslibrary.parliament.uk/research-briefings/sn06077/#:~:text=The%20latest%20estimates%20on%20migration,and%20out%20of%20the%20cou, accessed 5 October 2024.

54 A. Asthana, *Taken as Red: How Labour Won Big and the Tories Crashed the Party* (HarperNorth, 2024), pp. 62–3.

55 G. Evans and J. Mellon, 'The Re-shaping of Class Voting', *British Election Study*, 6 March 2020, www.britishelectionstudy.com/bes-findings/the-re-shaping-of-class-voting-in-the-2019-election-by-geoffrey-evans-and-jonathan-mellon/, Ipsos, *How Britain Voted in the*

Notes

2019 Election, www.ipsos.com/en-uk/how-britain-voted-2019-election and *How Britain Voted in the 2024 Election*, www.ipsos.com/en-uk/how-britain-voted-in-the-2024-election, all accessed 5 October 2024.

56 BBC Two TV, *Amol Rajan Interviews … Tony Blair*, 4 September 2024.

57 A. Rawnsley, *Servants of the People: The Inside Story of New Labour* (Hamish Hamilton, 2000), p. 394.

58 Cook, *Point of Departure*, diary entry for 14 January 2002, p. 79.

59 Horton, 'Solidarity Lost?', figure 3, p. S39; L. Goodall, *Left for Dead?: The Strange Death and Rebirth of Labour Britain* (William Collins, 2019), p. 40.

60 Hindmoor, *What's Left Now?*, pp. 220–1.

61 Freedman, *Failed State*, p. 32.

62 Author interview, Sir Tony Blair, 16 July 2024.

63 Mythologising and nostalgia are discussed in P. Allen and N. Matthews, 'New Labour and Political Myth', *Journal of Political Ideologies*, [online early] (2024), pp. 5–11.

64 M. Cates, 'University "Elite Overproduction" has Shifted the UK to the Left', *Telegraph*, 17 July 2023; M. Cates, 'Tony Blair is Still Ruining Britain', *Telegraph*, 22 January 2024.

65 DWP, *Households Below Average Income: An Analysis of the UK Income Distribution, FYE 1995 to FYE 2023*, figure 15, www.gov.uk/government/statistics/households-below-average-income-for-financial-years-ending-1995-to-2023/households-below-average-income-an-analysis-of-the-uk-income-distribution-fye-1995-to-fye-2023, accessed 3 October 2024; A. Henry and T. Wernham, *Child Poverty: Trends and Policy Options*, IFS Report R335 (October 2024), p. 1 and figure 6.1, p. 4.

66 F. Islam, 'Labour's Plan for Benefits Throws Up a Bigger Dilemma', *BBC News Online*, 17 March 2025, www.bbc.co.uk/news/articles/cvgev3dvz3jo, accessed 28 March 2025.

67 Warner and Zaranko, *Past and Future of NHS Waiting Lists*, figures 1–3, pp. 6–7.

68 Office for Students, 'Navigating Financial Challenges in Higher Education', *Insight* 21, (May 2024); B. Laker, 'The Hidden Dangers of Cost-Cutting in UK Universities', *Forbes*, 2 September 2024.

69 DLUHC, *Rough Sleeping Snapshot in England, Autumn 2023*, February 2024, figure 1, www.gov.uk/government/statistics/rough-sleeping-snapshot-in-england-autumn-2023/rough-sleeping-snapshot-in-england-autumn-2023, accessed 4 October 2024.

70 On 'assemblage' see G.C. Savage, 'What is Policy Assemblage?', *Territory, Politics, Governance* 8, 3 (2020), pp. 319–35.

71 Murphy, *Futures of Socialism*, p. 30.

72 See T. Baldwin, *Keir Starmer: The Biography* (William Collins, 2024), pp. 318–19, 354.

Index

EU authorised representative for GPSR:
Easy Access System Europe, Mustamäe tee 50,
10621 Tallinn, Estonia
gpsr.requests@easproject.com

9 781526 146328